IN **PRAISE** OF **HETERONOMY**

INDIANA SERIES IN THE PHILOSOPHY OF RELIGION
Merold Westphal, *editor*

IN **PRAISE OF** HETERONOMY

Making Room for Revelation

MEROLD WESTPHAL

INDIANA UNIVERSITY PRESS

This book is a publication of

Indiana University Press
Office of Scholarly Publishing
Herman B Wells Library 350
1320 East 10th Street
Bloomington, Indiana 47405 USA

iupress.indiana.edu

© 2017 by Merold Westphal

All rights reserved

No part of this book may be reproduced or utilized in any form or by any means, electronic or mechanical, including photocopying and recording, or by any information storage and retrieval system, without permission in writing from the publisher. The Association of American University Presses' Resolution on Permissions constitutes the only exception to this prohibition.

The paper used in this publication meets the minimum
requirements of the American National Standard for Information Sciences—
Permanence of Paper for Printed Library Materials,
ANSI Z39.48-1992.
Manufactured in the United States of America

Cataloging information is available from the Library of Congress.

ISBN 978-0-253-02638-5 (cloth)
ISBN 978-0-253-02652-1 (paperback)
ISBN 978-0-253-02661-3 (ebook)

1 2 3 4 5   22 21 20 19 18 17

In gratitude to

Tom Askew
and
Em Cummins

MENTORS, TEACHERS, FRIENDS

CONTENTS

ix
SIGLA

xiii
PREFACE

1
1. Executive and Legislative Autonomy

23
2. Spinoza's Theology

38
3. Spinoza's Hermeneutics

58
4. Kant's Theology

84
5. Kant's Hermeneutics I

100
6. Kant's Hermeneutics II

124
7. Hegel's Theology I

148
8. Hegel's Theology II

167
9. Hegel's Hermeneutics

189
10. The Inevitability of Heteronomy

211
11. Heteronomy as Freedom

231
INDEX

SIGLA

Unless otherwise noted, quotations from the Bible are from the New Standard Revised Version (NRSV).

HEGEL

DFS *The Difference Between Fichte's and Schelling's System of Philosophy*, trans. H. S. Harris and Walter Cerf (Albany: State University of New York Press, 1977).
EL *The Encyclopedia Logic*, trans. T. F. Geraets, W. A. Suchting, and H. S. Harris (Indianapolis, IN: Hackett, 1991). Cited by page and paragraph number; *Anmerkungen* (remarks) = A and *Zusätze* (additions) = Z. Thus *EL*, nn, ¶nn and possibly An or Zn.
ETW *Early Theological Writings*, trans. T. M. Knox (Philadelphia: University of Pennsylvania Press, 1971).
FK *Faith and Knowledge*, trans. Walter Cerf and H. S. Harris (Albany: State University of New York Press, 1977).
HL *Hegel: The Letters*, trans. Clark Butler and Christiane Seiler (Bloomington: Indiana University Press, 1984).
HP/B *Hegel's Lectures on the History of Philosophy: The Lectures of 1825-1826*, ed. Robert F. Brown (Berkeley: University of California Press, 1990). Based on a more critical edition of the German text than HP/H.
HP/H *Hegel's Lectures on the History of Philosophy*, trans. E. S. Haldane and Frances H. Simson (New York: Humanities Press, 1955/1963).
JR *Jenaer Realphilosophie*, hrsg. Johannes Hoffmeister (Hamburg: Feliz Meiner, 1931).
LJ *The Life of Jesus*, in G. W. F. Hegel, *Three Essays: 1793-1795*, ed. and trans. Peter Fuss and John Dobbins (Notre Dame, IN: University of Notre Dame Press, 1984).
P *Lectures on the Proofs of the Existence of God*, in *Hegel's Lectures on the Philosophy of Religion*, vol. 3, trans. E. B. Spiers and J. Burdon Sanderson (New York: Humanities Press, 1962).

PC   *The Positivity of the Christian Religion*, in *ETW*.
PC 1 dates from 1795–96.
PC 2 is a partial revision from 1800.
PM   *Hegel's Philosophy of Mind*, trans. William Wallace and A. V. Miller (Oxford: Clarendon Press, 1971). The translation of *Geist* as Mind rather than Spirit is dated. I shall use PM but refer to this text as the *Philosophy of Spirit*. Cited by page and paragraph number; *Zusätze* (additions) = Z.
PR   *Hegel's Lectures on the Philosophy of Religion: One Volume Edition, The Lectures of 1827*, ed. Peter C. Hodgson (Berkeley: University of California Press, 1988). Complete three-volume edition published in 1984, 1985, and 1987.
PRi   *Hegel's Philosophy of Right*, trans. T. M. Knox (Oxford: Clarendon Press, 1942). Cited by page and paragraph number; *Anmerkungen* (remarks) = A and *Zusätze* (additions) = Z. Thus PRi, nn, #nn, and possibly An or Zn.
PS   *Hegel's Phenomenology of Spirit*, trans. A. V. Miller (Oxford: Clarendon Press, 1977).
SC   *The Spirit of Christianity and Its Fate*, in *ETW*. Drafts from 1798–1800.
SL   *Hegel's Science of Logic*, trans. A.V. Miller (New York: Humanities Press, 1969).
TE   *The Tübingen Essay on Folk Religion*, in S. Harris, *Hegel's Development: Toward the Sunlight, 1770-1801* (Oxford Clarendon Press, 1972). Also found in *Three Essays*. See LJ above.

KANT

CF   *The Conflict of the Faculties*, trans. Mary J. Gregor and Robert Anchor, in *Religion and Rational Theology*, edited by Allen W. Wood and George di Giovanni. Cambridge Edition of the Works of Immanuel Kant. (New York: Cambridge University Press, 1996).
CPJ   *Critique of the Power of Judgment*, trans. Paul Guyer and Eric Matthews. Cambridge Edition of the Works of Emmanual Kant, edited by Paul Guyer and Allen W. Wood. (New York: Cambridge University Press, 2000).
CPR   *Critique of Pure Reason*, trans. Norman Kemp Smith (New York: Macmillan, 1961).
CPrP *Critique of Practical Reason*, trans. Mary J. Gregor, in *Practical Philosophy*. Cambridge Edition of the Works of Immanuel Kant, general eds. Paul Guyer and Allen W. Wood (New York: Cambridge University Press, 1996).
FJ   Chris L. Firestone and Nathan Jacobs. *In Defense of Kant's* Religion (Bloomington: Indiana University Press, 2008).
GMM   *Groundwork of the Metaphysics of Morals*, trans. Mary J. Gregor, in *Practical Philosophy*.
LPR   *Lectures on the Philosophical Doctrine of Religion*, trans. Allan W. Wood, in *Religion and Rational Theology*.
MM   *The Metaphysics of Morals*, trans. Mary J. Gregor, in *Practical Philosophy*.
R   *Religion within the Boundaries of Mere Reason*, trans. George di Giovanni, in *Religion and Rational Theology*.

SPINOZA

E   *The Ethics and Selected Letters*, trans. Samuel Shirley (Indianapolis, IN: Hackett, 1982). Citations will use arabic numerals for the parts and the following abbreviations:

P	Proposition
Po	Postulate
Pr	Proof
D	Definition
C	Corollary
A	Axiom
S	Scholium
Pref	Preface
App	Appendix
Exp	Explication

Thus $E_2\ P_{16}\ C_2$ = second corollary to proposition 16 in part 2.

TPT *Theological-Political Treatise*, trans. Jonathan Israel (New York: Cambridge University Press, 2007). *TPT* 4, 6 = chapter 4 of *TPT* on page 6.

PREFACE

MARCION WAS A SECOND-CENTURY CHRISTIAN HERETIC. He sharply distinguished Yahweh, the God of the Hebrew scriptures, a vengeful, tribal demiurge, from the loving, universal God of Jesus. Of course, in order to refashion Christianity along these lines he had to either ignore or delete from his canon the judgment parables of Jesus and Paul's teaching about the wrath of God. Pick and choose.

Freud rather tendentiously equates theistic religion with a kind of Marcionite theology. Like dreams, religion is about wish fulfillment. So, "We shall tell ourselves that it would be very nice if there were a God who created the world and was a benevolent Providence, and if there were a moral order in the universe and an after-life but it is a very striking fact that all this is exactly as we are bound to wish it to be."[1]

Not quite. That moral order of the universe might not be too friendly when we are the immoral ones. So we tweak this theology. "Over each one of us there watches a benevolent Providence which is only seemingly stern"—at least so far as we are concerned. So far as our enemies are concerned, or even those who are just different, we are quite happy to see evil punished with rigor. Which leads to a second amendment of the original dream, moving from "me" to "us." In relation to this Father we would like "at least to be his only beloved child, his Chosen People." This takes us to "the historical beginnings of the idea of God." Freud is obviously speaking of his own Jewish people at the source of Abrahamic monotheism. "Very much later, pious America laid claim to being

'God's own Country.'" Here we have "the final form taken by our present-day white Christian civilization."²

What is Marcionite about the Jewish and Christian traditions, as Freud sees them, is their pick and choose character. They attach themselves to the attractive and appealing aspects of the biblical God but find a way to edit out the unpleasant and unpopular characteristics. By creating God in their own, self-flattering image and to serve their own self-interested agenda, they find a way to immunize themselves against those strata of their own scriptures expressed by Amos 3:2

> You only have I known
> of all the families of the earth;
> therefore I will punish you
> for all your iniquities.

and by 1 Peter 4:17

> For the time has come for judgment to begin
> with the household of God.

Rudolf Otto provides a warning and a corrective.³ The Holy in general, and the God of biblical monotheism in particular, is to be understood as the *mysterium tremendum et fascinans*. As *mysterium* God is epistemically Wholly Other, exceeding our language and overwhelming our ability to comprehend; as *tremendum* God is frightening and repelling; as *fascinans* God is reassuring and attractive.

If a dialectical relation is one in which two opposed elements are affirmed at the same time and in balanced tension, then Otto is proposing a dialectical relation between the repellant and attractive aspects of God. We can handle this kind of relation, as when we acknowledge that parents can be loving and caring while *at the same time* demanding and strict. We do not immediately label them schizophrenic, though it may take children a while to learn that the parental *tremendum* and the parental *fascinans* are the flip sides of each other. In good parenting, demands and discipline are rooted in love and caring. I call this Goldilocks parenting: because of the love and caring the demands and discipline are neither too hard nor too soft but "just right."

When it comes to God, it is always tempting to flee this dialectic.⁴ For Marcion and for biblical theism on the Freudian interpretation, justice is tempered with mercy by effectively eliminating the former. God the Father becomes God the doting Grandfather. For our purposes, it is important to note that there can also be an epistemic dimension to the flight from the *tremendum* to the *fascinans*, from the heteronomy of divine revelation to the autonomy of human reason. To praise heteronomy is to keep the door open to divine revelation in the face of philosophies that seek effectively to close it. That is the theme of this book.

No doubt the believing soul is never free from the temptation to flee this dialectic in either the practical (moral, liturgical) or the theoretical (epistemic, theological) dimension by giving hegemony to the *fascinans*, making piety into a marriage of convenience. And no doubt the believing soul never fully succeeds in resisting this temptation. One needn't appeal here to the Screwtapes of the underworld; human nature is sufficiently devious. So every theology and every piety needs to be subjected to a hermeneutics of suspicion.

Paul Moser has recently published a book entitled *The Severity of God*.[5] Put in Otto's language, it is a reminder of the *tremendum* and the need to take it seriously. I speak in praise of heteronomy for the same reason, suggesting that heteronomy in the epistemic sense on which I will focus is a mode of the severity of God (though for biblical faith it is the flip side of God's loving care). I take this heteronomy to be an essential moment in the Abrahamic monotheisms that is unattractive and even repelling to the human self-assertion that modernity shares with many forms of postmodernity.[6]

> For my thoughts are not your thoughts,
> nor are your ways my ways, says the LORD.
> For as the heavens are higher than the earth,
> so are my ways higher than your ways
> and my thoughts than your thoughts. (Isa. 55:8–9)

The biblical name for the requirement to bring our ways into conformity with God's ways is the Law of God. This is moral heteronomy (*heteros nomos*, the law of the other). The biblical name for the requirement to bring our thoughts into conformity with God's thoughts is the Word of God. This is epistemic heteronomy. The theological term is *revelation*, but not the general revelation of God to be found in nature and accessed by human reason.[7] For if human reason is the highest criterion of knowledge, then the truth is already within me and needs but to be "recollected," as Plato would have it. I can claim epistemic autonomy. Any voices other than my own can be at best dispensable reminders of what I already know, like the diagrams Socrates draws for the slave boy in the *Meno*.

What is at issue here is rather the special revelation to be found in divine actions, including speech acts, that occur at particular times and places and bring messages not already buried, however deeply, in human rationality. This heteronomy is the transcendence of God in its epistemic dimension. Events such as the Exodus, the Exile, the Return, the Incarnation, the Atonement, and the Resurrection are taken by Jewish and/or Christian believers to be revelation in this sense, God's self-manifestation. So also is the Word of the LORD as it came to and through Moses and the prophets Jesus, Paul, and Mohammed, along with the written scriptures we know as the Bible or Koran.[8]

Even the concept of special revelation can have a variety of meanings. As I use the term the emphasis falls on Abrahamic monotheists as "people of the book," the idea that the sacred scriptures of Judaism, Christianity, and Islam are the Word of God, a message from God to a human audience. The presupposition is that God is personal and, as such, capable not only of being an agent and not just a cause, but also of performing speech acts, such as making promises and giving commands. It is not just that such events occur whenever "the Word of the Lord came to. . . ." It is the further idea that the holy book in which such events are recorded is itself a complex speech act, a message from on high, or, as preachers like to say, "God's love letter to humankind."[9]

My praise of heteronomy begins with an extended critique of the autonomy project that we associate with modern philosophy. But it goes back at least to Plato's notion of knowledge as recollection and is perhaps best expressed in the twentieth century in Husserl's novella *Philosophy as Rigorous Science*.[10] His claim is that in phenomenology philosophy achieves its goal of being free from contamination and conditioning by particular and contingent psychological or historical influences. This project was especially prominent in the philosophies of religion associated with the Enlightenment. I use the title of Kant's "fourth critique," *Religion within the Limits of Reason Alone*" to designate this broader project. For my money, the most powerful versions in the seventeenth, eighteenth, and nineteenth centuries, respectively, are those of Spinoza, Kant, and Hegel.

Each of these presents a theology that purports to be the voice of pure, universal reason—pure not only in the Kantian sense of a priori but in the Husserlian sense of being unconditioned.[11] Each purports to be neutral, objective, presuppositionless, free from any particular perspective and in that sense universal—the so-called "view from nowhere."¹² *It is precisely this claim to universality that underlies the Enlightenment's autonomy project. For only if my reason is (or with the right method can be made to be) universally (uniformly and univocally) present in human nature can I claim to be autonomous vis-à-vis particular and contingent factors, including divine revelation, on which it would otherwise be dependent.*

But one doesn't need to delve very deeply into Spinoza, Kant, and Hegel to see that such a claim is not just false but plainly false. "Universal Reason" has always already broken up into competing brands or different denominations.¹³ The three theologies are expressions of quite particular worldviews, and each is mutually incompatible with both of the other two. In spite of their claim to be nonsectarian, they are related to one another as are Judaism, Christianity, and Islam or, with a nod to Will Herberg, as Protestant, Catholic, and Jew. There are overlaps, to be sure, but there are also deep divergences that belie the claim to universality and the related claim to autonomy. They are heteronomous in relation to the hermeneutical circle that is their point of departure and the (possibly developing) criterion and warrant for their thought.

One thing these three have in common is the explicit hegemony of philosophical reason over revelational theology for the sake of alleged autonomy. Where the latter does not conform to the former, it is either to be rejected outright or reinterpreted so as to become religion within the limits of reason alone. We can honor one important motive here, horror at religiously legitimated violence and intolerance, without concluding that religion can or should be reduced to some lowest common denominator—especially when that lowest common denominator is not common but conspicuously confessional. The promise is to move beyond the deep disagreements among revelational theologies, but the autonomy project cannot keep that promise. It only relocates the gaps that keep the overlaps from converging into a genuinely universal religion.

I emphasize the close and crucial link between the alleged universality of reason and the desire for human autonomy vis-à-vis divine revelation. But the illusion of reason's universality has another motivation that deserves mention at least in passing. C. S. Lewis describes it this way:

> To be quite frank, we do not at all like the idea of a "chosen people." Democrats by birth and education, we should prefer to think that all nations and individuals start level in the search for God, or even that all religions are equally true. It must be admitted at once that Christianity makes no concessions

to this point of view. It does not tell of a human search for God at all, but of something done by God for, to, and about Man. And the way in which it is done is selective, undemocratic in the highest order.¹⁴

Lewis appropriately notes the beginning of God's dealing with the "chosen people" in the covenant God makes with Abraham. Then he adds:

> For when we look into the Selectiveness which the Christians [and the Jews, he might have added] attribute to God we find in it none of that "favoritism" which we were afraid of. The "chosen" people are chosen not for their own sake (certainly not for their own honour or pleasure) but for the sake of the unchosen. Abraham is told that "in his seed" (the chosen nation) "all nations shall be blest." That nation has been chosen to bear a heavy burden. Their sufferings are great: but, as Isaiah recognised, their sufferings heal others.¹⁵

This kind of universalism is pervasive throughout the Hebrew scriptures.¹⁶

What Lewis calls "selectiveness," theologians often call the "scandal of particularity," the fact that biblically understood, divine revelation comes to particular people at particular times and places and is not, as the autonomy project requires, the standard equipment of human nature. N. T. Wright addresses the issue and makes the same point that Lewis makes: it is *through* God's dealings with Israel, beginning with Abraham, that God offers the divine solution to the universal problem of a humanity united (somehow) in Adam as sinful and estranged from God. The "scandal of particularity"

> comes with the territory of monotheism and election. The [Christian] redrawing of both doctrines around Jesus retains the shocking character of the original [Jewish version], if anything more so . . . [Paul's vision is of] the love that chooses to act in a particular way through a particular people, and ultimately through that people's representative, in order that, through this means, the world as a whole might be rescued. . . . [This] has all the hallmarks of the ancient Israelite sense that the creator God called Abraham and his people in order that through them he might rescue all the tribes of Adam.¹⁷

It is not immediately clear with what right (*quid juris*)¹⁸ or on what grounds philosophers are in a position to insist that God should have done things differently. Is that not to beg the question against the claim

> For my thoughts are not your thoughts,
> nor are your ways my ways, says the Lord.

The Word of the Lord (as understood by the Abrahamic monotheisms) comes to every people in every time and place as an epistemic mixture of *tremendum* and *fascinans*. To pick and choose the attractive parts while neutralizing the unattractive is to make the bold claim to being intellectually and morally superior to that God.

After seeking in chapter 1 to isolate (theoretical) epistemic autonomy from the (practical) autonomy of genuine agency, a different issue, I devote chapters 2 through 9 to exploring how the autonomy project works itself out (and deconstructs itself) in the theologies of Spinoza, Kant, and Hegel. They follow the same basic strategy, giving hegemony to reason/philosophy over revelation/theology; but they begin with very different presuppositions and end up with radically different theologies. They continue to speak of 'God' but their gods are dramatically different from the God of Abrahamic monotheism and more deeply different from one another than the deities of Judaism, Christianity, and Islam.

In chapter 10 I turn to postmodern philosophy.[19] Almost by definition it is the ironic recognition that one universal mark of philosophical reason is its particularity, its de facto heteronomy in relation to the language games, traditions, and social practices that various versions have inherited and by which they are significantly formed. I call this the hermeneutical turn, for these factors define the hermeneutical circle that is the particular perspective, presupposition, or paradigm of any given species of philosophical reason. Although the autonomy project and its allegation of a universal human reason has not disappeared in our day, I find the hermeneutical turn in a wide variety of post-Hegelian and post-Husserlian philosophies.[20] They are postmodern not in the narrow sense of French poststructuralism, but in the broader sense of breaking with modernity's fantasy of philosophical neutrality and objectivity—the view from nowhere.[21]

Stanley Fish expresses this postmodern view of reason when he writes,

> The "I" or subject, rather than being the freestanding originator and master of its own thoughts and perceptions, is a space traversed and constituted—given a transitory, ever shifting shape—by ideas, vocabularies, schemes, models, and distinctions that precede it, fill it, and give it (textual) being.[22]

In spite of acknowledging the finite, conditioned, and thus plural nature of human reason, yea, while insisting on it in a variety of powerful ways, some postmodern philosophers carry on the religion-within-the-limits-of-reason-alone project. Reason may be heteronomous in relation to the human lifeworlds in which it is born, but it can still declare its autonomy vis-à-vis divine revelation understood as a voice independent of and transcendent to any and every version of human reason. Philosophy, as the voice of some such version, retains hegemony over any theological appeals to divine revelation. Thus Heidegger, in some respects the father of the hermeneutical turn, repeatedly insists that it is the task of phenomenology to "correct" theology,[23] and Derrida describes his own postmodern project of "religion without religion"[24] in terms of Kant's description of his own quintessentially modern project.[25]

Secular and atheistic though they may be in various ways, other postmodern thinkers such as Gianni Vattimo, Jean-Luc Nancy, Alain Badiou, and Slavoj Žižek can be read as seeking to retain significance for religion by bringing it within the limits of their own postmodern versions of reason. The same can be said, in the United States, for such thinkers as Mark C. Taylor, John D. (Jack) Caputo, and Richard Kearney.[26]

I welcome and affirm the postmodern critiques of pure reason. But I raise the following question about the theological projects of these secular and atheistic postmodern Kantians.[27] Are not the theologies that accompany their critiques contingently associated with those critiques? For example, I see no conceptual link between Caputo's "weak" theology and his Derridean/deconstructive critique of reason.[28]

Rather than see a choice between faith and reason, I see a choice between two faiths, or perhaps between two generic forms of faith (belief and commitment that are risky because they lack the absolute guarantees promised by modernity). Faith in reason gives hegemony to some version of human reason over any appeal to divine revelation, while faith in revelation gives hegemony to some form of divine revelation. Each genus has numerous species (denominations or sects, if you please).

It is hard to see why there should be any a priori preference for one genus over the other except for the fact that one finds oneself in a lifeworld in which that paradigm prevails. Caputo makes the logic of the hermeneutic situation clear when he writes, "*There are no non-circular arguments against a world outside space and time, no arguments that do not proceed from the assumption that all being must be spatial and temporal* (his italics)."[29] This is why it is not helpful to use the term 'fideism' in a pejorative sense to describe appeals to revelation that do not claim to be backed by some sort of absolute, rational guarantees.

Postmodern thinkers in the other genus have also forsworn such guarantees and operate from within their own non-theistic hermeneutical circles.

We are all in the same boat and can only begin thought where we are, grateful that it is not "nowhere," else we couldn't think at all. The cogency of our theological arguments depends, at least in the first instance, on a sociological "plausibility structure," a contingent community of shared faith.[30] In other words, we are always in some significant measure preaching to the choir. This is not irrational; it is the human condition.

I can make this question sharper by suggesting, positively, that the hermeneutical turn and the postmodern critiques of the "view from nowhere" fit especially well with the "mere Christianity" that is the common core of the revelational faith shared by the Eastern Orthodox, Roman Catholic, and Protestant traditions of Abrahamic monotheism. On the one hand, the doctrine of God as a personal agent who creates everything that is not God implies the finitude of human reason. "My thoughts are not your thoughts" because they are dependent on and are derivative from God's creative act. As Fish has put it, they are conditioned and not originative, or, as Paul puts it, we see "in a mirror, dimly" and "only in part" (1 Cor. 13:12).

From the perspective of "mere Christianity," the postmodern critiques, especially as the hermeneutics of suspicion, also fit well with the notion that human reason is not only finite but also fallen. As Paul puts it, in our sinfulness we "suppress the truth" (Rom. 1:18).[31] What philosophy and psychology call the self-deceptions of "motivated irrationality," theology calls sin, in at least some of its forms.[32] Freud, Marx, and Nietzsche are right to insist that we are not neutral observers but are influenced in our thinking by desires and interests we hide from ourselves (and often for good reason).

But their atheism does not follow from either the finitude or fallenness of human reason. However cogent these critiques may be, they leave undecided what kind of theology should be attached to them. They only constrain the meta-claims we make about whatever we say about God. We are dealing with alternative faiths. As Derrida puts it, "I don't know, one has to believe. . . ."[33]

A biblical faith that affirms the finitude and fallenness of human reason in relation to a personal Creator can and, I believe, should incorporate the hermeneutical turn into its theology. It has at least as good reason to do so as the secular and atheistic postmodern philosophies. The gift of revelation does not cancel our humanity and make our theologies the very voice of God. They can be bold in their proclamation without being arrogant in their meta-claims.

One implication of this kind of analysis is that when modern or postmodern philosophies adopt the religion-within-the-limits-of-reason-alone project, they beg the question against a robustly theistic, revelation based theology.[34] They presuppose a world from which the God of any biblical revelation is missing, and they assume that what purports to be divine revelation is only some human, all too human wisdom. That's not unfair; it's formally unavoidable. We always presuppose something.

Robustly theistic, revelation-based theologies will return the compliment by presupposing a God who could speak words of special revelation to us and a book that records and even contains such revelation. The important thing is not to forget the locus and thus the status of one's discourse. We are always somewhere and never "nowhere."

That does not mean that we should adopt what Peirce calls the "method of tenacity" in upholding our beliefs.[35] Conversation is called for in spite of the fact that it is devilishly difficult (read: impossible) to find some neutral standpoint outside any already prejudiced hermeneutical circle from which to settle these fundamental questions in a neutral and objective manner.

Archimedes famously asked for a *pou sto*, a place to stand from which he could move the earth with a lever. But the Archimedean point cannot be anywhere on earth; it must be somewhere beyond the earth. An epistemic *pou sto*, (over)confidently promised by modernity and realistically forsworn by postmodernity, presupposes some standpoint outside the human condition.[36] To recognize this is not to bring to an end conversation between and among the various alternatives in theology and philosophy of religion; it is only to recognize how difficult it is.

In my final two chapters I turn to the postmodern versions of the Kantian project in the philosophy of religion. I do not devote as much attention to them as to Spinoza, Kant, and Hegel for two reasons. First, I have devoted considerable attention to the issues raised by (some of) them elsewhere. Second, I want to try to establish the necessity of the hermeneutical turn not by appeal to those thinkers who affirm and articulate it but by seeing how it is so dramatically generated in philosophies that expressly deny it by purporting to be the voice of universal reason.

The position of the postmodern versions of the religion-within-the-limits-of-reason-alone project is both curious and delicate. On the one hand, they affirm the heteronomy of human reason in relation to the psychological and historical conditioning that Husserl wanted to exclude; on the other hand, they declare their independence and thus their autonomy in relation to any purported divine revelation. In that independence, philosophy retains hegemony over theology in its postmodern forms as vigorously as in the modern forms we've explored.

So, in chapter 11, I pose the question whether heteronomy vis-à-vis divine revelation is sufficiently different from the heteronomy vis-à-vis human language games, traditions, and social practices to warrant accepting the latter while repudiating the former. In particular, I pose the question whether the heteronomy involved in affirming the divine revelation essential to biblical monotheism compromises human dignity and agency and offer two testimonies suggesting it does not.

I do not pretend to be neutral in discussing these matters. I am a Protestant adherent to what I call "mere Christianity" in the chapters that follow. But I do consider myself to be acting as a philosopher rather than a theologian in doing so. While I discuss divine revelation as a possible basis for religious life, I do not posit it as an actuality nor appeal to it as an authority. I talk about it and about the relation of philosophies and theologies that give hegemony to some form of human reason over any purported divine revelation and those that do the reverse. Without claiming to be the voice of universal reason, I believe that thinkers on both sides of this fence should feel the force of my argument.

What I hope to have shown, at least in some significant degree, is that religion within the limits of reason alone, in either its modern or postmodern versions, is a series of rival faiths to "mere Christianity" and that to assume that it is the task of philosophy to correct theology is to do just that—to make a huge assumption whose a priori privilege is anything but self-evident and whose justification relies on criteria internal to the position to be established.

One can draw skeptical conclusions from such an argument, if one chooses. I prefer Derrida's response: the undecidable calls for decision. I would only add that the hermeneutical turn reminds us that we have always already decided. But in these matters, a motion to reconsider is always in order.

To avoid misunderstanding, I call attention to the weakness of my argument. By that I do not mean that it is a poor one, but rather that it makes limited claims. I do not purport to show that people should opt for "mere Christianity" rather than some modern or postmodern rival. My claim is rather that the religion-within-the-limits-of-reason-alone project, whether in its modern or postmodern versions, provides no compelling reason to reject a revelation-based theism in favor of the hegemony of (some) philosophy over such a putative revelation. At least not in terms of the autonomy argument. Philosophical reason turns out to be just as particular and as conditioned as biblically based faith. Or, to say the same thing differently, reason (in each of its many versions) is itself a form of faith.

NOTES

1. Sigmund Freud, *The Future of an Illusion*, in *The Standard Edition of the Complete Works of Sigmund Freud*, ed. and trans. James Strachey (London: Hogarth, 1953–74), 21:33.

2. *Future of an Illusion*, 21:19–20. This analysis is central to Freud's "theology." See my analysis in *Suspicion and Faith: The Religious Uses of Modern Atheism* (New York: Fordham, 1998), pp. 33–119. There has always been a theological undercurrent to the idea of "American exceptionalism." And we mustn't forget that Freud knew Christian anti-Semitism up close and personal.

3. In *The Idea of the Holy*, trans. John W. Harvey (New York: Oxford University Press, 1958).

4. In his commentary on the most familiar of the "penitential" psalms, Luther writes that it's the same righteousness of God that punishes sin and justifies the sinner. Where either side overbalances the other, the result is not God but an idol. "Psalm 51" in *Luther's Works*, ed. Jaroslav Pelikan and Helmut T. Lehmann (St. Louis, MO, and Philadelphia, PA: Concordia and Muhlenberg, 1955–86), vol. 12, pp. 313–14.

5. Paul Moser, *The Severity of God: Religion and Philosophy Reconceived* (Cambridge: Cambridge University Press, 2013).

6. "Self-assertion" is a term constantly used by Hans Blumenberg to describe modernity in *The Legitimacy of the Modern Age*, trans. Robert M. Wallace (Cambridge, MA: MIT Press, 1983).

7. Kant's famous and eloquent summary of general revelation comes at the conclusion of his Second Critique. "Two things fill the mind with ever new and increasing admiration and reverence, the more often and more steadily one reflects on them: *the starry heavens above me and the moral law within me*. I do not need to search for them and merely conjecture them as though they were veiled in obscurity or in the transcendent region beyond my horizon; I see them before me and connect them immediately with the consciousness of my existence." These are the basis for rational belief in God. CPrR, 269, 5.161–62 (see chap. 1n8)

8. I mention Islam from time to time to remind us that the logic of my argument extends to all of the Abrahamic monotheisms, though my focus will be on biblical religion, which always presupposes special revelation, while acknowledging general revelation as well. See Ps. 19 and Rom. 1–2.

9. Speech acts such as promises or commands can be inscribed as well as uttered, and the inscriber, say a secretary, need not be the speaker. See Nicholas Wolterstorff, *Divine Discourse: Philosophical Reflections on the Claim that God Speaks* (New York: Cambridge University Press, 1995).

10. I call this text a novella because it is short and because it is, in my view, fiction. It is found in Quentin Lauer, trans., *Phenomenology and the Crisis of Philosophy* (New York: Harper & Row, 1965)

and in Peter McCormick and Frederick Elliston, eds., *Husserl: Shorter Works* (Notre Dame, IN: University of Notre Dame Press, 1981).

11. Postmodern philosophies recognize that the categories and principles (paradigms, if you like) that play an a priori role in our thinking are regularly particular and contingent because of the ways in which they are conditioned by psychological and historical factors. See chapter 10.

12. Thomas Nagel coined the phrase in a book entitled, appropriately, *The View from Nowhere*.

13. In the beginning of western philosophy there were Parmenides and Heraclitus, Plato and Aristotle, Stoics and Epicureans, sectarian without any appeal to divine revelation.

14. C. S. Lewis, *Miracles* (New York: Macmillan, 1947), chap. 14, p. 120.

15. Lewis, *Miracles*, p. 122.

16. See chap. 11, note 26.

17. N. T. Wright, *Paul and the Faithfulness of God* (Minneapolis, MN: Fortress, 2013), p. 889. Cf. pp. 447, 1170–71, 1493–95, 1506.

18. Kant uses this legal term to distinguish questions of right from questions of fact. *Critique of Pure Reason*, A 84 = B 116.

19. I distinguish "modern" from "postmodern" philosophies as ideal types rather than as strictly chronological categories. The recognition of reason's particularity is a distinctive mark of the postmodern as I use the term.

20. As I read him, Husserl makes this turn himself, very reluctantly, in *The Crisis of European Sciences and Transcendental Phenomenology* and related writings. I take that to be the meaning of his admission, "Philosophy as science, as serious, rigorous, indeed apodictically rigorous science—the dream is over." Trans. David Carr (Evanston, IL: Northwestern University Press, 1970), p. 389.

21. See note 12 above and the discussion in chapter 10.

22. Stanley Fish, *Think Again* (Princeton, NJ: Princeton University Press, 2015), p. 100. See chapter 10 below.

23. Martin Heidegger, "Phenomenology and Theology," in *Pathmarks*, ed. William McNeill (New York: Cambridge University Press, 1998), pp. 39–62.

24. Jacques Derrida, *The Gift of Death*, trans. David Wills (Chicago: University of Chicago Press, 1995; 2nd ed. 2008), p. 49 in the first edition; p. 50 in the second edition.

25. Jacques Derrida, "Faith and Knowledge: The Two Sources of 'Religion' at the Limits of Reason Alone," in *Acts of Religion*, ed. Gil Anidjar (New York: Routledge, 2002), pp. 42–101. For rather different readings of this text, see John D. Caputo, *The Prayers and Tears of Jacques Derrida: Religion without Religion* (Bloomington: Indiana University Press, 1997), pp. 151–59; and Martin Hägglund, *Radical Atheism: Derrida and the Time of Life* (Stanford, CA: Stanford University Press, 2008), chap. 4.

26. For a three-way comparison of Caputo, Kearney, and my own thought, see Christina M. Gschwandtner, *Postmodern Apologetics?* (New York: Fordham University Press, 2013), chap. 11–13.

27. They are doubly Kantian. First, they see the a priori as human, all too human, but just for this reason (against Kant) as neither universal nor necessary but rather particular and contingent. Second, they carry on the religion within the limits of reason project, giving hegemony to their philosophies over any revelation grounded theism. I am a postmodern (pluralistic) Kantian only in the former sense.

28. See John D. Caputo, *The Weakness of God*, 2006, and *The Insistence of God*, 2013, both from Indiana University Press, Bloomington. Nor do I see any close connection between his version of deconstruction and his politics, though I am far more sympathetic to his politics than to his theology.

29. Caputo, *Insistence*, p. 112.

30. "Plausibility structure" is a notion that comes to us from the sociology of knowledge, an expanded version of Marx's notion of ideology. See Peter L. Berger, *The Sacred Canopy: Elements of a Sociological Theory of Religion* (Garden City, NY: Doubleday, 1967).

31. I have developed this theme in "Taking St. Paul Seriously: Sin as an Epistemological Category," *Christian Philosophy*, ed. Thomas Flint (Notre Dame IN: University of Notre Dame Press,1990), pp. 200–226, and at greater length in *Suspicion and Faith: The Religious Uses of Modern Atheism*.

32. See David Pears, *Motivated Irrationality* (New York: Oxford University Press, 1984).

33. Jacques Derrida, *Memoirs of the Blind*, trans. Pascale-Anne Brault and Michael Nass (Chicago: University of Chicago Press, 1993), p. 129.

34. I believe that at this point there is a significant affinity between my argument and that of Alvin Plantinga in *Warranted Christian Belief* (New York: Oxford University Press, 2000).

35. Charles Sanders Peirce, "The Fixation of Belief," in *Collected Papers of Charles Sanders Peirce* (Cambridge, MA: Harvard University Press, 1960), 5:233–35.

36. Cf. Kierkegaard's claim that reality is a system of the sort Hegel professes, but only for God. *Concluding Unscientific Postscript to Philosophical Fragments*, trans. and ed. Howard V. Hong and Edna H. Hong (Princeton, NJ: Princeton University Press, 1992), 1:118.

IN **PRAISE** OF **HETERONOMY**

1

EXECUTIVE AND LEGISLATIVE AUTONOMY

Abraham Lincoln concluded his famous Cooper Union speech in 1860 with these words: "Let us have faith that right makes might, and in that faith, let us, to the end, dare to do our duty as we understand it."[1] Five years and much tragedy later, he concluded his Second Inaugural Address with similar but importantly different words: "With malice toward none, with charity for all, with firmness in the right as God gives us to see the right, let us strive on to finish the work we are in. . . ."[2] On the "crucial difference" between "our duty as we understand it" and "the right as God gives us to see the right," Ronald White Jr. comments,

> Lincoln answered the question he had been asking himself—how do we know what is right—by changing the grammatical subject of his trajectory. . . . God had not always been the subject in Lincoln's addresses, but in the ethical imperative with which he concluded the Second Inaugural he changed the indicative subject from "we" to "God."[3]

Given his rather privately developed religious faith, one might well have expected the Cooper Union Lincoln to be the one we remember, a fellow son of the Enlightenment, along with Jefferson and other "founding fathers." But "humbled by the intractability of war,"[4] he moved away from human self-confidence, self-sufficiency, and self-assertion toward the heteronomy of "as God gives us to see the right."[5] Our moral knowledge is to come to us from another, more particularly The Other. Heteronomy: *heteros*, the other + *nomos*, law = the law that comes from the other.

I want to side with Lincoln against Enlightenment autonomy, which in various ways is still with us. This means putting in a good word for heteronomy. For in philosophical terms, this move from "we" to "God" as the source and ground of moral and religious knowledge[6] simply is the move from autonomy to heteronomy. Do the norms by which we should live derive from our own cognitive powers (autonomy), or do they come to us from a wisdom and an authority beyond us (heteronomy)? Philosophical modernity, especially in its self-consciousness as the Age of Reason or Enlightenment (*Aufklärung, le Siècle des lumières*), and as the process of secularization,[7] is the move in the opposite direction: from various perceived forms of heteronomy to various projects of autonomy, of which Kant's is the most famous and the most familiar. His (possibly all too) familiar moral philosophy provides the context for our original orientation to the contrast between autonomy and heteronomy.

Without using the term 'autonomy,' Kant introduces this central theme of his moral, political, and religious philosophy in the 1784 essay "What Is Enlightenment?"

> Enlightenment is the human being's emergence from his self-incurred minority [*Unmündigkeit*]. *Minority* is the inability to make use of one's own understanding without direction from another. This minority is *self-incurred* when its cause lies not in lack of understanding but in lack of resolution and courage to use it without direction from another. *Sapere aude!* [dare to be wise, or dare to know, or, in context, dare to think for yourself] Have courage to make use of your *own* understanding! is thus the motto of enlightenment.[8]

But it is only one year later, in *Groundwork of the Metaphysics of Morals*, that Kant develops the concept explicitly in the context of his moral philosophy.[9] For my purposes it is important here to distinguish executive autonomy from legislative autonomy, a distinction Kant makes without naming it.[10] It is the latter that lays the foundation for his philosophy of religion. In a context where Kant equates freedom with autonomy, he writes, "*Will* is a kind of causality of living beings insofar as they are rational, and *freedom* would be that property of such causality that it can be efficient independently of alien causes *determining it*" (*GMM*, 94, 4:446).[11] There is a certain ambiguity in the notion of the will's being determined. In terms of efficient causality, which is the focus here, the will is *determined to act* by the motivation or incentive (*Triebfeder*) that stirs it to act. The heteronomy of being moved to act by "alien causes" means that one is only apparently an agent. By contrast with such heteronomy, the autonomy here required by agency can be called executive autonomy.[12]

But to act is to act in a certain way, and the will is also determined *to act in a certain way* by the cognition that serves as a steering mechanism. The question is, How should I act? or What should I do? rather than What causes me to act?, and autonomy here can be called legislative autonomy on the assumption that there is always some rule or law (Kant speaks of maxims and principles) by which the action is (at least implicitly) guided.[13] I can be reasonably clear about *what* I should do but find myself insufficiently *motivated* to do it; and I can be strongly *motivated* to "do something" without having any idea *what* I should do or without having sufficient confidence that *what* I think I should do is the right thing. In terms of the automotive metaphor, executive autonomy concerns the engine, while legislative autonomy concerns the steering wheel. In both cases, heteronomy means being towed, but for different reasons.

So executive autonomy is different from legislative autonomy, and there are two correspondingly different forms of heteronomy. A strong form of executive heteronomy comes to expression in Freud's famous dictum that "we are 'lived' by unknown and uncontrollable forces."[14] Oedipus gives us another example, one in which ignorance rather than the id is the "unknown and uncontrollable force."

> Or do you dread
> My strength? my actions? I think not, for I
> Suffered those deeds more than I acted them.[15]

At the very least, for Kant autonomy will require libertarian freedom as opposed both to outright determinism and to any sort of compatibilism. But this will be only a necessary condition, and Kant will require that freedom of the will (*Willkür*) be motivated by a distinctive, cognitive directive, the insight of my own reason.

A strong form of legislative heteronomy will be any form of divine command ethics according to which the revealed will of God is the highest norm for human behavior, trumping human reason and making its authority relative and conditional. To call judgments of human insight "reason" is to praise them, but not to justify them. They can be defective in merely human terms, to say nothing about being at odds with divine wisdom and law.

It is this theological form of heteronomy I wish to praise, in large part indirectly by means of a critique of the Enlightenment's autonomy project. The primary home of this heteronomy is biblical religion in both its Jewish and Christian forms. It represents a decisive break with the "first and greatest commandment" of philosophical modernity: in matters of religion and ethics thou shalt exercise legislative autonomy.[16] So it is a biblical, postmodern heteronomy I wish to praise. Obviously, it will be different in important ways from the secular postmodernisms of thinkers such as Nietzsche, Derrida, Foucault, Lyotard, Deleuze, Zizek, and Badiou. But why shouldn't theism have as much right and at least as good reasons as atheism to challenge modernity's self-deification of human reason?[17] Why should Nietzsche have a monopoly on the slogan, "human, all too human?"[18]

The question of executive autonomy belongs to action theory and moral psychology. In the broadest sense the question concerns the necessary and sufficient conditions for me to be an agent, for the motions of my body and the speech acts I utter or inscribe to count as actions, to be in a strong sense mine.[19] In the more specific context of moral philosophy, it is the question of the conditions for an action having moral significance, or, as Kant would have it, moral worth.

Kant's discussion of executive autonomy in this narrower sense comes early and (in)famously in the *Groundwork of the Metaphysics of Morals*. He distinguishes actions done in accord with duty (*pflichtmässig*) from those done *from duty* (*aus Pflicht*) on the grounds that the former may be done from some inclination (*Neigung*) or other. We need to be able to "distinguish whether an action in conformity with duty is done *from duty* or from a self-seeking purpose." This sounds like a simple either/or in which only the former kind of action has moral worth. Sometimes Kant says that where an action is motivated by prudence and personal advantage, as when a shopkeeper does not take advantage of children by shortchanging them, we cannot "believe" or "assume" that the act is done from duty. The moral worth of the action is hidden from us as long as we can see other, prudential motivations at work.[20] At other times he makes a stronger claim that the action was not done from duty "but merely for purposes of self-interest" (*GMM*, 53, 4:397). That is a claim about the action itself, not about our perception of it.

In the suicide example the contrast between duty and inclination is utterly stark. We have a duty to preserve our own lives, but we also have an immediate inclination to do so. So when people care for themselves their action "has no inner worth and their maxim has no moral content. They look after their lives *in conformity with duty* but not *from duty*." Only if one has lost "all taste for life . . . yet preserves his life without loving it, not from inclination or fear but from duty, then his maxim has moral content" (*GMM*, 53, 4:397–98).

When Kant takes this hard line, he rejects sympathy as a morally worthy motivation for benevolence. There are

> many souls so sympathetically attuned that, without any other motive of vanity or self-interest they find an inner satisfaction in spreading joy around them and can take delight in the satisfaction of others so far as it is their own work. But I assert that in such a case an action of this kind, however it may conform with duty and however amiable it may be, has nevertheless no true moral worth but is on the same footing with other inclinations, for example, the inclination to honor. (*GMM*, 53, 4:398)[21]

Where love is an inclination or feeling of benevolence, it, too, is excluded from the realm of morally significant motivations (*GMM*, 54–55, 4:399)

The fairly obvious implication of this is spelled out in the equation of "from duty" with "respect for law": The principle is this: "duty is the necessity of an action from respect for law.... Now, an action from duty is to put aside entirely the influence of inclination and with it every object of the will; hence there is left for the will nothing that could determine it except objectively the *law* and subjectively *pure respect* for this practical law" (*GMM*, 55–56, 4:400).

Passages like these gave rise to Schiller's satire, which is more pointed than poetic in translation.

> Gladly I serve my friends, but alas I do it with pleasure.
> Hence I am plagued with doubt that I am not a virtuous person.

The solution:

> Sure your only recourse is to try to despise them entirely,
> And then with aversion to do what your duty enjoins you.[22]

There has been no shortage of Kant scholars who have tried to rescue Kant from himself (and from Schiller), usually arguing that in the light of everything Kant says about morality in the *Groundwork* and other writings, we should not take him to mean what he quite clearly says in these embarrassing passages. My own conclusion is that Kant says different things in different places and they are not all consistent with each other. He has a deeply Platonic distrust of the "lower parts of the soul," the "pathological," and often this distrust becomes dominant.

Especially in passages like those that provoked Schiller, it would seem that Kant overlooks a possibility that comes nicely to light in a prayer from John Baillie. He cites a number of imperatives from the teachings of Jesus. Each is followed by the same refrain: "O God, incline my heart to follow in this way."[23] He seems to presuppose a second order obligation, not merely to obey Jesus but to be so transformed as to do so out of desire.[24] It is for this second task that he prays for help. I think this is the right direction for a healthy moral psychology.[25] But it strikes me as a very un-Kantian prayer. The task here is not to flee from inclination to duty as motivation; rather our duty is to bring our inclinations so fully into conformity with duty that when we follow our desires we do what is right. This second-order duty seems to me the very definition of moral maturity.

John Hare attributes something like this view to Kant. "What is admirable [in his view], and presumably pleasing to God, is a life in which the inclinations have been so trained that love of the moral law prompts action in accordance with it."[26] But this seems to me to be too charitable a reading, at least for the *Groundwork*. Kant's fivefold formulation of the categorical imperative is fully compatible with speaking about moral motivation as Baillie and Hare do[27]; so I wish we could attribute it to him. But I think we cannot.

My concern, however, is not with this debate, which belongs to the theory of executive autonomy. I mention it only to emphasize that my interest is legislative autonomy, which is a different issue.[28] I think executive autonomy is very important. Both in the narrower, Kantian sense about the nature of the moral life and in the broader political, social, and psychological sense I believe that current debates about the nature of agency and personhood go beyond technical arcana to raise questions of serious existential import.[29]

In the legislative/epistemic sense, I am autonomous if I or some We that is fundamental to my identity as a person is the legitimating source and criterion for my beliefs and / or my knowledge.[30] Since for Kant, as for Lincoln, the knowledge in question is that of norms rather than of facts—how ought we to live our lives?—it makes sense to call this legislative autonomy. What justifies my beliefs about the rules, laws, and ideals by which my behavior is to be guided and to which I am obligated? From whence do my beliefs and the practices growing out of them derive their legitimacy and authority? Or, in short, how do I know what my duty is?

Of course, this epistemic issue can be extended from beliefs and knowledge of norms to facts, physical and metaphysical, natural and supernatural. In the context of religion, it is the question of reason and revelation. It is this autonomy and the contrasting heteronomy with which I am concerned. I plan to speak in praise of heteronomy by showing both (1) how the autonomy project undermines itself and (2) how heteronomy need not be the path to alienation and servility. Just to the degree that we have been shaped by modernity it will be much easier to see heteronomy in a negative rather than in a positive light. We do not automatically find ourselves attuned to the Psalmist, who writes, "Your decrees are my delight, they are my counselors" (Ps. 119:24)[31] In any case, when I speak of autonomy and heteronomy without qualification it will be the legislative/epistemic versions to which I refer.

It is not noticed as frequently as it should be that Kant himself lays the groundwork for distinguishing between these two types of autonomy (and the corresponding modes of heteronomy), precisely by pointing to the distinction while not always observing it. We have already seen him develop what I am calling executive autonomy in the argument that actions of moral worth must be motivated (solely, it would seem) by a sense of duty (*aus Pflicht*). In *Groundwork* Kant also gives us five formulations of the categorical imperative, the highest principle of morality. It is here that we are introduced to legislative autonomy.

The first formula tells us to act only on those maxims we could will to be universal laws. This is followed by a variant version according to which we should act as if our maxims would actually become universal laws of nature through our acting on them.

The third formulation is that we should always treat humanity, whether in ourselves or in another, "*as an end, never merely as a means*" (*GMM*, 80; 4:429). Kant calls this the "principle of humanity" (*GMM*, 80–81; 4:429–30).

The fourth formulation says that the will is to conform to "the idea *of the will of every rational being as a will giving universal law* [*als eines allgemein gesetzgebenden Willens*].... Hence the will is not merely subject to the law but subject to it in such a way that it must be viewed as also giving the law to itself and just because of this as first subject to the law (of which it can regard itself as the author)" (*GMM*, 81; 4:431).[32] Kant calls this "the principle of the **autonomy** of the will in contrast with every other, which I accordingly count as **heteronomy**" (*GMM*, 83; 4:433). The concept of autonomy is linked to that of self-legislation, the authorship and authority of the moral law deriving from myself. Other translators, such as Beck, Abbott, and Ellington, use the language of legislation to render the notion of *Gesetzgebung* that Kant uses here. So this autonomy is appropriately called legislative autonomy.[33] It is quite a different matter from the autonomy of agency, acting *aus Pflicht*.

The principle of autonomy makes reference not merely to me but to "every rational being." Since this raises the question of the relation of this plurality of autonomies, which could entail anarchy, Kant gives his fifth and final formulation in terms of the concept *"of a kingdom of ends."* The language of ends relates it to the principle of humanity (the third of five), but with an emphasis on "*a systematic union* of rational beings through common objective laws, that is, a kingdom of ends . . . because what these laws have as their purpose is just *the relation of these beings to one another* as ends and means" (*GMM*, 83; 4:433; emphasis added). Morality has, we might say, a public, political goal and not just a private, personal purpose.

But Kant links his kingdom of ends formula even more closely to his principle of autonomy. The principle of autonomy leads to the concept of the kingdom of ends, which, in turn, depends on the principle of autonomy (*GMM*, 83, 4:433). Kant makes this linkage precisely in terms of self-legislation.[34] "A rational being belongs as a *member* to the kingdom of ends when he gives universal laws in it but is also himself *subject to these laws*. He belongs to it *as sovereign* when, as lawgiving, he is *not subject to the will of any other*" (*GMM*, 83; 4:433; emphasis added).[35]

N.B. If this self-legislation is to serve peace rather than war, order rather than anarchy, then it cannot be jingoistic or sectarian. Hence the emphasis on universal law that permeates Kant's discussion of the categorical imperative. If human reason is to be the source and criterion of such law, it will have to be universal reason. Conversely, if human reason should turn out to be particular and pluralistic, this project will be in deep trouble.

Kant switches back and forth between his two concepts of autonomy without notice and apparently without noticing that they are different. But we can be clear about the difference. Is the *legitimating norm* of the moral law my own reason or does it come from elsewhere, on the *authority* of the state, the church, or God? This is the question of legislative autonomy. It is epistemic and, eventually metaphysical. Is the *governing motivation* (incentive, *Triebfeder*) for following the moral law, whether its authority is internal or external, duty or inclination? This is a question of moral psychology.

We can put the difference between these questions in Platonic terms: supposing that it is by reason, the highest part of the soul, that I *know* what the moral law requires, is it some desire of the appetitive or spirited part of the soul that *motivates* me to obey that law? The supposition involves legislative autonomy; the question is about executive autonomy.

Kant says that his three presentations of the moral law are "but so many formulae of the very same law" (*GMM*, 85, 4:436). Three? Not five? Yes.[36] He combines the first two as the universal law formula. It expresses the form of the moral law as the product of universal reason.[37] The second (previously third) is the principle of humanity. It expresses the content of the moral law, namely every rational being as an end in itself. The fourth formula, the principle of autonomy, and the fifth, the kingdom of ends formula are combined to signify the harmony of these ends, lest we think the individualism of the first two versions and the fourth expresses some fundamental, pluralistic anarchy. If self-legislation is the product of universal reason, the problem is solved.

We might say that the moral law involves (1) one rule with (2) many beneficiaries in (3) the harmony of a unified community. Thus we have an architectonic of unity, plurality, and totality (or allness).[38] But Kant reminds us that this communal dimension of morality is grounded in the self-legislation of each individual.[39] It signifies "*a complete determination* of all maxims by means of that formula, namely that all *maxims from one's own lawgiving* are to harmonize with a possible kingdom of ends as with a kingdom of nature" (*GMM*, 85–86: 4:436; emphasis added). Here the principle of autonomy is the form (formulas one, two, and four) and the kingdom of ends the content (formulas three and five).

Having introduced the notion of legislative autonomy in terms of self-legislation, Kant proceeds to what strikes me as a glaring non sequitur.

> Now, from this it follows incontestably that every rational being, as an end in itself, must be able to regard himself as also giving universal laws with respect to any law whatsoever to which he may be subject; for, it is just this fitness of his maxims for giving universal law that marks him out as an end in itself; it also follows that this dignity (prerogative) he has over all merely natural beings brings with it that he must always [consider himself] and likewise every other rational being, as lawgiving beings (who for this reason are also called persons). (*GMM*, 87; 4:438)

The claim is that legislative autonomy is a necessary (and apparently sufficient) condition for being an end in itself and never merely a means, a person and not merely an animal, someone of intrinsic worth and dignity. But where is the argument? Suppose we listen to the psalmist's claim[40] that we are heteronomous in relation to God as the supreme lawgiver before whom every version of human reason must bow as merely human. Or to Isaiah:

> For my thoughts are not your thoughts,
> nor are your ways my ways, says the LORD.
> For as the heavens are higher than the earth,
> so are my ways higher than your ways and my thoughts than your thoughts."
> (Isa. 55:8–9).

We don't have to agree with either of them in order to recognize three things. First, that for biblical Judaism and Christianity, God has supreme authority in relation to the right and the good, and that this authority need not conform to what passes as human reason in any particular historical and cultural context. God's thoughts are higher than ours.[41] Second, that in the West either the state or the church (or both) has sometimes been seen to participate in this divine authority in such a way as to render individual judgments about the right and the good heteronomous in relation to them. People were taught that to take issue with either state or church and, a fortiori, to disobey them, was ipso facto to take sides against God. Third, and most important, that whether the legislative heteronomy of the individual is direct in relation to God or indirect via the mediation of church or state, there is no reason why such individuals cannot cogently be considered as ends in themselves, as persons in a strong sense, having a dignity and intrinsic worth that raises them "over all merely natural beings." Even if they are in legislative heteronomy before God, or the state, or the church, they are creatures of God's loving care. A loving God would never and neither the state nor the church should ever or need ever treat them merely as means to their own ends. Just to be clear—my own praise of heteronomy concerns only our relation to God, not to the state or to the church. But it seems to me the logic of the situation extends to possible heteronomy in relation to all three.

A simple analogy can help us to see that, pace Kant, there is no necessary link between legislative autonomy and being an end in itself, a person of intrinsic and not merely instrumental worth. Infants are not capable of legislative autonomy, and children are not allowed to exercise it even when they want to. Even the most permissive parents (and teachers) place constraints on children without their consent, justifying this by the claim that they know better what is best for the child. Nor do we think they shouldn't. But this does not mean that the children are nothing but means to their parents' ends, and in reasonably healthy families they are not treated as such.[42] But even if, as is all too human, the parents are mistaken about what is best for the children, they are not necessarily tyrants. They may well be treating the children to the best of their ability as those whose flourishing is intrinsically and not merely instrumentally valuable. If God is a loving (and *perfectly* wise) parent whose children we remain, the absence of legislative autonomy would not mean alienation and servility.[43] Jesus said, "Truly I tell you, unless you change and become like children, you will never enter the kingdom of heaven" (Matt. 18:3). Or again, "Pray then in this way: Our Father in heaven . . ." (Matt. 6:9).[44] His purpose was to make us more fully human, not less.

No doubt there is something in us that resists childlike trust and obedience to a heavenly parent; a certain conversion would be necessary.[45] But that doesn't entail that heteronomy vis-à-vis divine authority would be a loss of personhood. Excessive claims to authority by state or church may compromise authentic selfhood, for they themselves are human, all too human. But one need not appeal to unqualified legislative autonomy in order to oppose the tyranny of the state or the church. It is enough to argue both (1) that claims to absolute authority on the part of either violate our status as persons who are children of a loving Heavenly Father and (2) that such claims involve confusing the merely human with the divine.[46]

We get a glimpse here of a related non sequitur on which the rise of modernity and especially of its increasing secularism rests to a significant degree. These interlocking historical tendencies have been significantly motivated by the sense, often well justified, that claims by either state or church or both to absolute authority in matters of belief and practice, were excessive and even tyrannical. Since political tyranny and religious inquisition were regularly declared to be the will of God, they made God look bad in a kind of guilt by association. But if the absolutist claims of the King or of the Grand Inquisitor are to be rejected, it will have to be for better reasons than Kant gives us, namely the claim of absolute individual autonomy. For, even if we see church and state as human, all too human institutions, fallible and all too often corrupt, it doesn't follow that the same is true of God. The claim of human institutions to unqualified divine legitimacy can be rejected precisely in order to preserve it for God. In fact, nothing shows the finitude and fallibility of the merely human as much as seeing it in contrast with the God of biblical theism. It simply does not follow that where it is right to reject heteronomy in relation to church and state, it is right to reject it in relation to God.

But Kant does just this. He does so in a section of the *Groundwork* that is confusing and perhaps confused.[47] He first defines autonomy as "the property of the will by which it is a law to itself (independent of any property of the objects of volition)" (*GMM*, 89, 4:440). In other words, so far as morality is concerned, the will should determine itself by and from itself without any reference to anything outside itself. It seems clear that Kant is speaking here of legislative autonomy,[48] since he immediately links this autonomy with the form of the moral law as universal law and as an unconditional, categorical imperative.

Any attempt of the will to "go beyond itself" and determine the content of the moral law by reference to "a property of any of its objects" will result in heteronomy. Instead of being self-legislative, "the object, by means of its relation to the will, gives the law to it. . . . I ought to do something *because I will something else*" (*GMM*, 89, 4:441).[49] In other words, nothing but hypothetical imperatives can result. "If you've made a promise, keep it," is grammatically hypothetical, but it expresses the categorical imperative, "Keep all your promises." The true form of any hypothetical imperative is, "If you *desire* X, you *ought* to do Y." Obligation is dependent on the desire for some "object." This can result only in *"rules* of skill [if you want a delicious cake, follow this recipe], or *counsels* of prudence" [if you want loyal customers, don't short-change their children], but not in *"commands* (laws) of morality," that is, unconditional, categorical imperatives (*GMM*, 69, 4:416).[50] For in the former cases I can always escape the obligation by protesting, "But I don't have that desire, at least not in the present situation."

Ever the architectonic thinker, Kant offers a fourfold classification of moral principles derived heteronomously, that is, when the will is determined by some "property of the objects of volition." On the empirical side is the "principle of *happiness*," while on the rational side is the "principle of *perfection* [*Vollkommenheit*]." The two forms of the former derive from either "physical or moral feeling [*Gefühl*]. The two forms of the latter derive from either the "ontological" or the "theological" concept of perfection (*GMM*, 90–91, 4:441–43).

The concept of physical feelings is too narrow for those feelings, inclinations, or desires which are to be distinguished from moral feelings such as love, sympathy, and gratitude. For in addition to the physical satisfactions that come from food, drink, and sex, there are the non-physical satisfactions that come from getting a degree, getting a job, getting a promotion, having one's proposal accepted, winning a game, spending two hours in a Van Gogh exhibit, and so forth. All of these can contribute toward my happiness; none of them requires moral feelings. So Kant rightly says that "making someone happy is quite different from making him good" (*GMM*, 90, 4:442). Moreover, these satisfactions and the desires from which they arise are contingent on individual character and circumstances and cannot generate categorical obligation. I can always say, "I don't want that (right now)" or "That gives me too little satisfaction to pay that price."

Moral feelings are "closer to morality" insofar as they are other-regarding and not merely self-interested. But they are "superficial" insofar as even moral feelings are as particular and contingent as other feelings and cannot provide a universal and unconditioned criterion for human action (*GMM*, 91, 4:442–43).[51]

Kant considers the ideal of perfection to derive from reason rather than feeling.[52] What he calls the "ontological" version is "empty" and "indeterminate." It can get morally significant content only from "the morality it is supposed to explain," which would be a vicious circle. In other words, perfect being theologies imply no ethics.[53] But it is better than the "theological" version "which derives morality from a divine, all-perfect will [legislative heteronomy]." For either our concept of God will be derived from our concept of morality, resulting in the same circularity just repudiated, or we will have to appeal a concept of God "made up of the attributes of desire for glory and dominion combined with dreadful [*furchtbaren*] representations of power and vengefulness [*Racheifer*]" that would be "directly opposed to morality" (*GMM*, 91, 4:443).

Kant makes it clear that while neither moral sense philosophies nor the perfection traditions are adequate as a grounding of morality, he prefers the latter "since it at least withdraws the decision of the question from sensibility and brings it to the court of pure reason" (*GMM*, 91, 4:443). But it is clear that he wants to protect reason not only from feeling but also from revelation. For however tendentious is the picture of God he links to the theological version of perfection morality, it is clearly drawn from the biblical traditions it caricatures. Wisdom and love do not even appear, and judgment is equated with vengefulness rather than with justice.

Kant makes two critical, interlocking assumptions here. The first is that morality, at least at its highest level, must be grounded on pure practical reason rather than on divine revelation. The second presupposition is that the only God available to be the revealing source and ground of human duty and goodness is one inimical to the moral life. In fact, his portrait of God is quite like the heretical views of Marcion, who repudiated the angry God of the Old Testament in favor of the supposedly kinder and gentler God of the New Testament, especially as portrayed by Jesus and Paul. Of course, Marcion had to ignore the centrality of the wrath of God to the argument of the epistle to the Romans; and he had to ignore the ever-recurring theme of divine judgment in the teaching and parables of Jesus. The gentle Jesus he prefers to the judging Jehovah is a figment of his own imagination.

So far as the "desire for glory and dominion" goes, there are within the Jewish and Christian traditions numerous pictures of God according to which God is not, like Iago or Richard III, filled with envy and a desperate need for power and glory in order to be somebody—like the schoolyard bully who torments others out of a deep inner insecurity. Rather, glory and dominion belong to God by ontological fact and right. God's concern that we humans neither fail to acknowledge this nor try to steal it for ourselves is for *our* good, since we degrade our humanity when we confuse ourselves with divinity. In particular, the glory and dominion of God's kingship are morally necessary lest injustice and oppression prevail. So the Psalmist writes

> But the LORD sits enthroned forever,
> he has established his throne for judgment.
> He judges the world with righteousness;
> he judges the peoples with equity.
> The LORD is a stronghold for the oppressed...
> For he who avenges blood is mindful of them;
> he does not forget the cry of the afflicted...
> For the needy shall not always be forgotten,
> nor the hope of the poor perish forever. (Ps. 9:7–9, 12, 18)

So far as "power and vengefulness" go, the biblical picture[54] is again very different from Kant's portrait. God's power as Creator is, as a simple matter of fact, ultimate, greater than anything within creation or creation as a whole. But it is not "directly opposed to morality," since it is inseparably linked to goodness, love, and mercy.

So far as "vengefulness" goes, we can ask if the term is appropriate. It doubtless occurs in some translations of the Bible.

> O God, to whom vengeance belongeth, shew thyself. (Ps. 94:1, King James Version [KJV])

> Vengeance is mine; I will repay, saith the Lord. (Rom. 12:19, KJV)

The Psalm just quoted speaks of God as the avenger of the afflicted. But (1) given the regular contrast between vengeance and justice in current usage,[55] (2) given the widespread linkage between vengeance and vigilantism, and (3) given that revenge movies are either abhorrent or, at best, a guilty pleasure, such translations may be unfortunate.[56] The language of retribution might be better; for while retributivist theories of punishment are not universally accepted, they do not carry usage-laden associations like (1) and (2) above. I think it is fair to say that biblical writers tend to presuppose, without theorizing about it, retributivist views of punishment. They cannot be translated out of the Bible. Nor need they be, for whatever the English translation, the wrath, judgment, and punishment, or even the vengeance of God are never disassociated from divine justice. Nor is the biblical picture of God like Nietzsche's representation of *"ressentiment"* in *On the Genealogy of Morals*.[57]

Ignoring the biblical link between divine wrath, divine justice, and divine love, Kant arrogates to human reason the unconditional authority to legislate the principles by which we should live; he does so by making sure God appears unworthy of such a role.

It is more than a little ironical that Kant should portray God as a kind of heavenly vigilante. For his view of just punishment is one of the classic expressions of the retributive view. Thus he writes that civil punishment

> can never be inflicted merely as a means to promote some other good for the criminal himself [rehabilitation] or for civil society [deterrence or protection]. It must always be inflicted upon him only *because he has committed a crime*. For a human being can never be treated merely as a means to the purposes of another or be put among the objects of rights to things: his innate personality protects him from this. (*MM*, 473, 6.331)

The retributivist view of just punishment has two distinctive marks. It is (in theory at least) administered only on those who deserve it, and it is that desert that justifies the punishment; so it is intrinsically and not merely instrumentally valuable.[58] Punishment looks back to what a person has done rather than forward to what the punishment might accomplish. Of course, secondly, if such punishment can also produce some good for the individual or society, it should be done in such a way as to maximize these goods. But they can neither be the determining factor in either the decision to punish or the severity of the punishment. For retributivism, the punishment must fit the crime, not the hoped-for consequences of the punishment.

In suggesting that Kant's case for rejecting a theologically grounded ethics is surprisingly weak, I have alluded to a vulnerability that needs to be brought into focus. I have spoken about the "assumptions" and "presuppositions" he makes. Kant purports to be working on the basis of pure practical reason. To speak of reason as pure is to make two claims. First, reason is functioning in an a priori manner. The concepts and principles with which it works are not derived from experience but brought to it as the conditions for its possibility. Second, these concepts and principles are universal, unconditioned or, we might well say, uncontaminated by anything contingent and particular.[59] Equipped with such concepts and principles, thought can be presuppositionless.

Kant assumes that his moral philosophy is pure in this second sense. It takes but little reflection to see that it is not. The assumption that morality must rest on reason rather than revelation and the assumption that the only God available to be the foundation of morality is a God inimical to morality are not the products of pure reason. They are the particular and quite contingent presuppositions of various traditions of which the Enlightenment is, to a considerable degree, the confluence. Calling this particular point of view "reason" doesn't give it the presuppositionless purity and univocal universality that it claims but manifestly does not have.

Calling attention to the Marcionite character of Kant's caricature of God helps to make this clear. To label it heretical is not to declare it false, for the argument I am making here does not appeal to orthodoxy as its criterion. That the Marcionite view is repudiated by many strands of Judaism and of the orthodox Christianity that C. S. Lewis calls "mere" Christianity simply underlines the particularity of the tradition(s) that have shaped Kant's quite particular brand of reason. Kant rejects moral feelings as the ground of morality because they cannot "furnish a uniform standard of good and evil" (*GMM*, 91, 4:442). What he fails to notice is that reason, like feeling, comes in a mutually incompatible variety of versions. Thus, for example, Kant's version of reason says I may not lie to the Gestapo if they ask me if I am hiding Jews in the attic.[60] Most other versions of reason say it is my duty in such circumstances to tell the most convincing lie I can.[61]

Hermeneutical phenomenology might be described as the general theory of the contingency and particularity of what functions as a priori in any thinking.[62] Gadamer calls these assumptions and presuppositions prejudices. He stresses the etymology, prejudice as pre-judgment, so as to deprive the term of its usual pejorative connotations, and he emphasizes traditions as the bearers of these prejudices. Let us use the term 'bias' for those prejudices (presuppositions, a priori anticipations of experience) in which our formation, in particular our preferences, keep us from seeing things as well as we might. This leaves room for good prejudices, like the right pair of eyeglasses that that put us in a position to see more rather than less clearly what is before us.[63]

The hermeneutical situation in which, pace Kant, he is to be found, is what Ricoeur calls "the conflict of interpretations," in this case the interpretations of what 'reason' signifies, what morality requires, and who the God of the Bible is.[64] That Kant's presuppositions are good prejudices and not biases in the pejorative sense requires argument. Where the nature and limits of human reason are themselves in question, it is not enough to announce that one is operating on the basis of pure practical reason. Where the traditions that try to base morality and religion on reason alone are contested by traditions that find human reason to be in need of supplementation and correction by divine revelation, it is not enough to dismiss the latter with a portrait of the biblical God that is clearly a prejudice and arguably a biased one.

Kant develops his account of legislative, epistemic autonomy first in a political plea for freedom of the press and then in his moral philosophy. It becomes central to those philosophies of religion, including Kant's own, that are most distinctively "modern." To explore its fate in the story of modernity, we turn to three powerful but very different versions: Spinoza's, Kant's, and Hegel's.

Notes

1. Quoted in Ronald C. White Jr., *Lincoln's Greatest Speech: The Second Inaugural* (New York: Simon & Schuster, 2002), p. 172.

2. Henry Steele Commager, ed., *Documents of American History*, 6th ed. (New York: Appleton-Century-Crofts), p. 443.

3. White, *Greatest Speech*, pp. 172–73.

4. White, *Greatest Speech*, p. 173.

5. I include "self-assertion" as a descriptor of the *terminus a quo* because it is Hans Blumenberg's favorite terms for the essence of modernity. See *The Legitimacy of the Modern Age*, trans. Robert M. Wallace (Cambridge, MA: MIT Press, 1985).

6. Kierkegaard's pseudonym, Johannes Climacus, calls this the domain of "essential knowing" that relates to the individual's own existence. *Concluding Unscientific Postscript*, trans. Howard V. Hong and Edna H. Hong (Princeton, NJ: Princeton University Press, 1992), I, 197–98. Whether the alternative to God is "I" or "We," we have some version of Protagoras's teaching (as reported by Sextus Empiricus) that "Man is the measure of all things." Joseph Katz and Rudolf H. Weingartner, eds., *Philosophy in the West: Readings in Ancient and Medieval Philosophy* (New York: Harcourt, Brace & World, 1965), p. 29. Cf. Plato's *Theatetus*, especially, 151e–152c and 166c–167d.

7. There is an important and well deserved overlap among the literatures on modernity, secularization, and autonomy.

8. Full title: "An Answer to the Question: What Is Enlightenment?," in *Practical Philosophy*, ed. and trans. Mary J. Gregor, Cambridge Edition of the Works of Immanuel Kant, general eds. Paul Guyer and Allen W. Wood (New York: Cambridge University Press, 1996), p. 17; 8:35. Later Kant writes, "*Thinking for oneself* means seeking the supreme touchstone of truth in oneself (i.e., in one's own reason); and the maxim of always thinking for oneself is **enlightenment**." See "What Does It

Mean to Orient Oneself in Thinking?," in *Religion and Rational Theology*, trans. and ed. Allen W. Wood and George di Giovanni, Cambridge Edition of the Works of Immanuel Kant, general eds. Paul Guyer and Allen W. Wood (New York: Cambridge University Press, 1996), p. 18n; 8:146n. The latter references (8:35 and 8:146n) and similar ones signify the volume and page number in the Academy edition (German). These are useful keys to several other English translations.

9. "What Is Enlightenment?" is a plea for limited freedom of the press, the right of scholars to publish without censorship. As the question of autonomy becomes one of independence from divine revelation and authority, it is hard to see any necessary link between autonomy and freedom of speech and of the press.

10. I owe this distinction to my colleague John Davenport and hope that he will eventually develop it in some detail, especially since the tendency to slide back and forth between the two modes without noticing or announcing it often confuses rather than clarifies the discussion, beginning with Kant.

11. *Groundwork of the Metaphysics of Morals* (*GMM*). On the difference between freedom as autonomy and freedom as spontaneity, see Henry Allison, "Spontaneity and Autonomy in Kant's Conception of the Self," in *The Modern Subject: Conceptions of the Self in Classical German Philosophy*, ed. Karl Ameriks and Dieter Sturma (Albany: State University of New York Press, 1995), pp. 11–29. Both need to be distinguished from autonomy as political liberty. "Respect for another's autonomy thus entails that we may not interfere with another's pursuit of her goals, so long as that pursuit does not... conflict with the possibility of all others' retaining their essential end... their ability to determine their own course in life." Robert Pippin, *Idealism as Modernism* (New York: Cambridge University Press, 1997), pp. 70–71.

12. Kant's discussion of autonomy in *Critique of Practical Reason* (*CPrR*), pp. 173–74, 5:42, concerns executive autonomy. Thus, in expounding the end in itself formula, John E. Hare writes that to treat the others as ends in themselves is to respect their autonomy. "I am constrained, according to this formula, by the consideration that it is wrong, other things being equal, to impede the agency of others. To treat another human being as merely a means is to ignore the other as a centre of agency." *The Moral Gap: Kantian Ethics, Human Limits, and God's Assistance* (Oxford: Clarendon, 1996), pp. 12–13.

13. Habermas's distinction between a motivation crisis and a legitimation crisis has an analogous structure. *Legitimation Crisis*, trans. Thomas McCarthy (Boston: Beacon, 1973). For the question, *What* should I do? is about the legitimation of the action, even if we are dealing with instrumental reason and a fortiori if we are dealing with moral reason.

14. *The Ego and the Id*, in *The Complete Standard Edition of the Complete Works of Sigmund Freud*, trans. James Strachey (London: Hogarth, 1953–74), 19:23. Freud is quoting Groddeck and adds a note: "Groddeck himself no doubt followed the example of Nietzsche, who habitually used this grammatical term [the id, *das es*] for whatever in our nature is impersonal and, so to speak[?], subject to natural law." Nietzsche emphatically denies freedom of the will. See the postcard to Overbeck in which he discovers Spinoza as his precursor. *The Portable Nietzsche*, ed. Walter Kaufmann (New York: Viking Press, 1954), p. 92.

15. Sophocles, *Oedipus at Colonus*, in *Oedipus I*, trans. Robert Fitzgerald (Chicago: University of Chicago Press, 1954), ii, 265–67.

16. Through the analysis of the concepts of morality "we find that its principle must be a categorical imperative, while this commands neither more nor less than just this autonomy" (*GMM*, 89, 4:440). Historical forms of either Judaism or Christianity stray farther and farther from their biblical roots just to the degree that they fall under the influence of this autonomy project. At what point, we might ask, do they lose the right to call themselves by the name of their historical roots?

17. It could be argued that those postmodern philosophies that exclude in one way or another any infinite God continue the self-deification of human reason but do so in terms of a plurality of finite gods (traditions, language games).

18. In a related story, Paul Ricoeur calls Marx, Nietzsche, and Freud the "masters of suspicion." *Freud and Philosophy: An Essay on Interpretation*, trans. Denis Savage (New Haven, CT: Yale University Press, 1970), p. 70. But what about the trio of Augustine, Luther, and Kierkegaard? Do they not critique with equal power the self-deceptions arising from "the usurpation of reason's functions by wishes"? I take this phrase from the back cover of David Pears, *Motivated Irrationality* (Oxford: Clarendon, 1984).

19. This is the philosophical issue underlying the very pressing and practical debate over what constitutes "informed consent."

20. Thus, in discussing Job, Eleanor Stump writes, "When righteousness is joined to superabundant prosperity, the motivation for the uprightness is murky. At best, the source of the uprightness is uncertain." *Wandering in Darkness: Narrative and the Problem of Suffering* (Oxford: Clarendon Press, 2010), p. 207.

21. For Kant's comment on the central role of sympathy in the "moral sense" theory of Hutcheson, see *GMM*, 91, including Kant's note, 4:442–43. On this tradition in British moral philosophy as developed by Hutcheson, Hume, and Adam Smith, see J. B. Schneewind, *The Invention of Autonomy: A History of Modern Moral Philosophy* (New York: Cambridge University Press, 1998), chaps. 16–18.

22. Quoted in H. J. Paton, *The Categorical Imperative: A Study in Kant's Moral Philosophy* (New York: Harper & Row, 1947), p. 48.

23. John Baillie, *A Diary of Private Prayer* (New York: Charles Scribner's Sons, 1949), p. 77.

24. We are reminded of Augustine's adage: Love God and do as you please. But of course, learning to love God in such a way and to such a degree that we can safely do as we please is no simple task.

25. Even a secular one along, say, Aristotelian lines, where the task is to bring both our actions and our emotions into conformity with reason.

26. Hare, *Moral Gap*, p. 30.

27. And Augustine and Aristotle. See notes 24 and 25.

28. One could argue that executive autonomy (my reason as the one proper motivation for the moral life) and legislative autonomy (my reason as the one legitimate source of the moral law) are in some sense mutually implicative. If I understand her, that is what Christine Korsgaard argues in such works as *The Sources of Normativity*, *The Constitution of Agency*, and *Self-Constitution*. Such an argument may well be genuinely Kantian. But it does not abolish the conceptual distinction between the two forms of autonomy. Another study stressing agency is Andrews Reath, *Agency and Autonomy in Kant's Moral Philosophy* (New York: Oxford University Press, 2006), chaps. 7 and 9.

29. See, for example, the extensive discussion in John Davenport, *Will as Commitment and Resolve: An Existential Account of Creativity, Love, Virtue, and Happiness* (New York: Fordham University Press, 2007).

30. This is also a metaphysical issue insofar as the question concerns the ontological ground of those norms. But my focus will be on the epistemic dimension.

31. Psalm 119, by far the longest in the Bible, is a veritable hymn to heteronomy. See the discussion in chapter 11.

32. Reath calls this the "Sovereignty Thesis" in *Agency and Autonomy*, p. 122. There is an echo of Rousseau here. His task is to find a form of association "by means of which each one, while united with all, nevertheless obeys only himself and remains as free as before.... As to the associates, they collectively take the name *people*; individually they are called *citizens*, insofar as participants in the sovereign authority, and *subjects*, insofar as they are subjected to the laws of the state ... and *obedience to the law one has prescribed for oneself is liberty*." *On the Social Contract*, trans. Donald A. Cress, in *Basic Political Writings* (Indianapolis, IN: Hackett, 1987), bk. I, chaps. 6 and 8; emphasis added. Robert Pippin takes Kant's notion to be paradoxical. "The idea of a subject, prior to there being a binding law, authoring one and then subjecting itself to it is extremely hard to imagine. It always seems that such a subject could not be imagined doing so unless he were already subject to some sort

of law, a law that decreed he ought so to subject himself, making the paradox of this notion of 'self-subjection' all the clearer." "Hegel's Practical Philosophy," in *The Cambridge Companion to German Idealism*, ed. Karl Ameriks (New York: Cambridge University Press, 2000), p. 192.

33. Reath offers a nice summary: "We find a set of claims about the moral agent—for instance, that rational agents are in some sense the authors of the moral law, are subject only to laws that they give to themselves, and that such facts are the ground of human dignity. We also find various claims . . . about conditions on the justification of moral principles. . . . Taken together, they constitute Kant's general thesis that autonomy of the will is the foundation of morality. . . . The model for the autonomous agent is the political sovereign not subject to any outside authority." *Agency and Autonomy*, pp. 121–22.

34. See Wood, "Kant's Practical Philosophy," in Ameriks, *Cambridge Companion to German Idealism*, p. 66.

35. See note 25 above. Cf. *GMM*, 88: 4:439–40, where Kant says that "it is easy to explain how it happens that, although in thinking the concept of duty we think of subjection to the law, yet at the same time we thereby represent a certain sublimity and *dignity* in the person who fulfills all his duties. For there is indeed no sublimity in him insofar as he is *subject* to the moral law, but there certainly is insofar as he is at the same time *lawgiving* [*gesetzgebend*, legislating] with respect to it and only for that reason subordinated to it."

36. On the relation of the five to the three, see Wood, "Kant's Practical Philosophy," in Ameriks, *Cambridge Companion to German Idealism*, p. 62.

37. This is why Reath can argue for the equivalence of the formula of Universal Law and the formula of Autonomy. *Agency and Autonomy*, 125, 135–45.

38. In the *Critique of Pure Reason* (*CPR*) this triad represents the categories of quantity. See B 106–14. There will be a similar movement from focus on the individual to concern for the community of morally religious individuals.

39. Unlike Rousseau, Hegel, Habermas, and Gadamer, Kant retains a Cartesian, monological concept of reason.

40. See note 31 above.

41. The first two words of the *Critique of Pure Reason* are "human reason" (three in German: *Die menschliche Vernunft*), and Kant grounds his distinction between appearances and the thing in itself on the difference between human and divine knowledge. See my "In Defense of the Thing in Itself," *Kant-Studien* 59, no. 1 (1968), 118–41. Ironically, he abandons this distinction without notice in his moral and religious philosophy, effectively deifying human reason.

42. For the horrifying possibility of this unnecessary and not inevitable alternative, read Philippa Gregory, *The Other Boleyn Girl* (New York: Scribner, 2001), in which Anne and her sister Mary are shamelessly treated as nothing but means to the ends of their father and, especially, their uncle, Norfolk.

43. In the biblical story the bliss of Eden was not grounded in human self-legislation but on God's command. It was the serpent who suggested the necessity of autonomy ("you will be like God," Gen. 3:5) with disastrous consequences for himself, for Adam, and for Eve.

44. In this context we can see that the "fatherhood" of God is not about gender but about the generation gap, about parental authority and the responsibility of children.

45. The King James Version reads, "Except ye be converted, and become as little children. . . ." This conversion might be defined in terms of the threefold decentering of the self that follows on the address to "Our Father" in the Lord's prayer:

> hallowed be *your* name
> *Your* kingdom come.
> *Your* will be done . . . (emphasis added)

The assumption is that it is as members of God's kingdom that we can most fully be ourselves, just as children can be most fully themselves in a family governed by wise and loving parents.

46. Such claims would be like a babysitter claiming absolute authority over and against the parents. Children ought to mind the babysitter, but only insofar as her rules fall within parameters set by the parents. Parental rules don't have to conform to her ideas in order to have genuine authority. Kant treats church and state as kinds of babysitters, but he gives to the individual a hegemony over the authority of God as the divine parent. This is why self-assertion is a good description of modernity's demand for autonomy. See note 5 above.

47. In "What Is Enlightenment?," pp. 18–22, 8:36–42, Kant had only argued for autonomy vis-à-vis state and church.

48. Highlighting the ambiguity in the notion of the will's determining itself, Allison relates this passage to autonomy/heteronomy in both their executive and legislative forms. Heteronomy doesn't simply mean "that the agent is causally conditioned to act as a result of these needs . . . it is rather that these needs (including psychological or 'ego needs') provide the only available sources of reasons to act." "Spontaneity and Autonomy," in Ameriks and Sturma, *Modern Subject*, p. 18.

49. This may seem to be a repudiation of consequentialism. But in the first place, the examples Kant gives don't all fit into this frame of reference, and in the second place, consequentialism can be given a categorical expression, as in "So act that your action (or the rule of action) will maximize happiness [or pleasure or goodness].

50. Thus John Hare writes that according to the universal law formulation, if my maxim is to be truly moral it must exclude all individual reference, "most importantly, to *me*." *Moral Gap*, p. 10.

51. This is the context for the note repudiating Hutcheson and British moral sense ethics in general. See note 21 above.

52. For a detailed analysis of moral philosophies grounded in the idea of perfection, see Schneewind, *Invention of Autonomy*, chaps. 9–12. Against the background of Stoicism, the discussion concerns Herbert of Cherbury, Descartes, the Cambridge Platonists, Spinoza, Malebranche, and Leibniz.

53. Perfect being theology is a tradition that draws especially on Anselm. For contemporary examples, see Thomas Morris, *Perfect Being Theology*; Hugh J. McCann, *Creation and the Sovereignty of God*; Brian Leftow, *God and Necessity*; and J. P. Moreland and Willliam Lane Craig, *Philosophical Foundations for a Christian Worldview*. While Kant draws on earlier versions of this tradition for his idea of God, he disputes the philosophical claim to knowledge of God by means of the concept of perfection.

54. In a rich variety of Jewish and Christian interpretations.

55. For example, in a flashback Daniel Silva has his hero, Gabriel Allon, recall being recruited in his earlier days for a mission entitled Wrath of God, designed to assassinate the members of the Black September group who had assassinated Israeli athletes at the Munich Olympics. Shamron, then head of "the Office" (the Israeli equivalent of "the Company"), had said, "It's not about justice. It's about vengeance, pure and simple—vengeance for the eleven innocent lives lost at Munich." Daniel Silva, *The English Girl* (New York: HarperCollins, 2013), p. 24. N.B. This quotation is fiction. It usually goes the other way. "This is not about vengeance. What we want is justice." For Nietzsche's comment, see note 57 below.

56. New Revised Standard Version (NRSV), New Jerusalem Bible (NJB), and the New English Bible (NEB), for example, retain "vengeance" in both passages quoted. The New International Version (NIV) uses the language of avenging in both. Luther uses the root word, *Rache*, in both passages. Today it is normally translated as "vengeance" or "revenge."

57. Nietzsche sharply distinguishes revenge (*Rache*) from justice. See *On the Genealogy of Morals*, I, 15, and II, 11. In *Thus Spoke Zarathustra* (II, 5, On the Virtuous) he notes that when people say

"I am just" [*ich bin gerecht*] it sounds just like "I am avenged" [*ich bin gerächt*]. In German the two sentences are virtually indistinguishable to the ear. Cf. II, 7, On the Tarantulas.

58. For discussion of backward-looking, deontological and forward-looking, consequentialist theories of the justification of punishment, see the articles on punishment and legal punishment in the *Stanford Encyclopedia of Philosophy* online. Or *Philosophical Perspectives on Punishment*, ed. Gertrude Ezorsky (Albany: State University of New York Press, 1972); and *Contemporary Punishment*, ed. Rudolph J. Gerber and Patrick D. McAnany (Notre Dame, IN: University of Notre Dame Press, 1972). The defense of the retributive theory in C. S. Lewis's essay "The Humanitarian Theory of Punishment" is found in Gerber and McAnany. It is also found, along with a reply to criticism, in Lewis's *God in the Dock* (Grand Rapids, MI: Eerdmans, 1970), pp. 287–300.

59. On the contamination of "pure" thinking, see my essay "The Prereflective Cogito as Contaminated Opacity," *Southern Journal of Philosophy*, supplement, 45 (2007), 152–77.

60. See "On a Supposed Right to Lie from Philanthropy," in *Practical Philosophy*, pp. 611–15, 8:425–30.

61. Philip Kitcher has argued that along with other texts, Thomas Mann's *Death in Venice* is a literary work with inherent philosophical significance. He "preempts objections that art, because of its appeal to feeling, can't be considered philosophy. He does this by undercutting philosophy's claims to objectivity, showing the extent to which concepts and terminology are subjective and historically contingent rather than instruments of pure reason.... With a figure like Jo the crossing sweeper, Dickens uses sentiment to bring about a 'shift in ethical perspective.'" Leo Carey, "Love in Venice," *New York Review of Books*, January 9, 2014, p. 56. This might well be directed at Kant. As we will see in the next chapter, it could target Spinoza just as well if we substitute 'imagination' for 'feeling.'

62. Pragmatism has its own version of essentially the same thesis—namely, that it is experience, in the broad, pragmatic sense of the term, that gives rise to the a priori. See C. I. Lewis, "The Pragmatic Conception of the *a Priori*," in *Readings in Philosophical Analysis*, ed. Herbert Feigl and Wilfrid Sellars (New York: Appleton-Century-Crofts, 1949), pp. 286–94. Lewis writes, "Our categories and definitions are peculiarly social products" (p. 293).

63. See Hans-Georg Gadamer, *Truth and Method*, 2nd ed., trans. Joel Weinsheimer and Donald G. Marshall (New York: Crossroad, 1989; New York: Continuum, 2004), pp. 265–307 or 268–306. Inexcusably, the 1989 and 2004 versions have different pagination. Gadamer speaks of "true" and "false" prejudices (pp. 298–99, 298). A telescope or microscope would be good metaphors for "good" prejudices relative to what we usually use them for. They are lenses through which we see better.

64. Paul Ricoeur, *The Conflict of Interpretations: Essays in Hermeneutics*, ed. Don Ihde (Evanston, IL: Northwestern University Press, 1974).

2

SPINOZA'S THEOLOGY

Kant first develops his notion of autonomy in a *political sense* as a plea for freedom to publish without censorship.[1] But in "What Is Enlightenment?" there are already overtones of a more far-reaching claim, and, as we have seen, Kant expands his concept of autonomy considerably in the context of his *moral philosophy*. But the most extensive and systematic development of his theory of autonomy occurs in his *philosophy of religion*, most particularly in *Religion Within the Boundaries of Mere Reason* or *Religion Within the Limits of Reason Alone*.[2] This title, however rendered, signifies far more than a book published by Kant. It is a fitting description of the Enlightenment project in the philosophy of religion, a project to which many thinkers contributed.[3] This project aims to extend the ideal of epistemic, legislative autonomy to religion in both its metaphysical and moral dimensions, or, to put it more broadly, to religion in both its theoretical and practical dimensions.[4]

For my money, the most powerful seventeenth-century version of this project is that of Spinoza; the most powerful eighteenth-century version that of Kant himself; and the most powerful nineteenth-century version that of Hegel. The story of the rise and fall of the autonomy project *in its legislative mode* can be told through the analysis and comparison of their philosophies of religion.

What we might call the medieval consensus, going back at least to Augustine, posited the hegemony of revelation over reason, faith over understanding, and thus of theology over philosophy.[5] Whereas patristic thinkers often described their Christian theology as their philosophy,[6] philosophy and theology came to be distinguished in terms of their respective dependence on either unaided human reason or divine revelation, regardless of which was given hegemony.

Luther gives lucid expression to this hegemony while discussing the trichotomist analysis of the human person in terms of spirit, soul, and body. Spirit and soul signify the cognitive and volitional capacities that raise the human self over mere animal existence, but they have different functions. Spirit is "the highest, deepest, and noblest part of man. By it he is enabled to lay hold on things incomprehensible, invisible, and eternal. It is, in brief, the dwelling place of faith and the Word of God." The soul functions by

> giving life to the body and working through the body.... It is its nature to comprehend not incomprehensible things but such things as the reason can know and understand. Indeed, reason is the light in this dwelling; and unless the spirit, which is lighted by the brighter light of faith, controls this light of reason, it cannot but be in error.[7]

In other words, faith (as the reception of the Word, divine revelation)[8] and reason reside in the human spirit and soul, respectively, and spirit is the proper guide of the soul.

The Enlightenment project in the philosophy of religion set out to reverse this relation by developing the hegemony of reason over revelation, understanding over faith, and philosophy over theology.[9] One corollary of this threefold thesis is the elimination of mystery from religion. Faith knows that it does not walk by sight; understanding, in its hegemony, insists that it can and must.[10]

When I speak of religion in terms of revelation, theology, and faith, I have in mind most immediately what I shall call biblical monotheism. It is *biblical* in that it is a view of God widely shared by Jews and Christians over centuries, based on the normative significance of the Bible in their respective versions of it.[11]

It is *mono*theism, for in its Jewish and Christian origins, amid the many gods of the Canaanites, Babylonians, Assyrians, Greeks, and Romans, the claim was that the God of Israel was the only true God, the maker of heaven and earth. In our context, in which polytheism is not, so to speak, on the ballot, the emphasis falls on theism. The God of biblical monotheism is a personal God in at least two senses. This God is an agent and not merely a cause, having purposes and intentions and bringing things to pass in accord with them and not merely in accord with impersonal laws of nature. The laws of nature are themselves the result of divine purpose and choice. This God is also a speaker, one who performs such speech acts as promises and commands.

These "anthropomorphisms" are essential to biblical monotheism. They are not mere metaphors. If the poet writes:

> I must go down to the seas again, for the call of the running tide
> Is a wild call and a clear call that may not be denied;[12]

we think of the trope of personification, but do not think the sea a person capable of speech acts. By contrast, when the Bible speaks of God acting or performing speech acts, theists take God to be a person doing what we do when we act or speak, though not in exactly the same way. God acts and speaks in the truest sense; we do so only by participation or imitation made possible by creation in the image of God. Something like Aquinas's theory of analogy is regularly presupposed, however inarticulately.

N. T. Wright distinguishes three aspects of biblical monotheism: It is *creational* monotheism. This theism is thus distinguished from pantheism, for as Creator, God is an *agent* who *transcends* the world as an entirely separate and independent being. It is *providential* monotheism. It is thus distinguished from deism, for God is an *agent* who is *immanent* within the created world, working out divine purposes in the lives of individuals and nations. Finally, it is *covenantal* monotheism. Here again, God is *immanent* within the world, only now as a *speaker*, entering into ongoing relations with human creatures by means of promises and commands.[13]

Taking C. S. Lewis's title *Mere Christianity* as a model, we could refer to biblical monotheism as mere theism; for it represents a common core of beliefs and related practices such as prayer, sacrifice, thankful praise, and sacred singing across the divides within and between Jewish and Christian piety. Sometimes it is this mere theism that is the target of our trio; but even where it is not, the specifically Jewish or Christian beliefs or practices under fire presuppose mere theism and make no sense without it.[14] If Spinoza, Kant, and Hegel are to contain religion within the bounds of reason alone, they will have to tame this God in some fashion. For the God of mere theism does not purport to fit within the limits of autonomous human speculation.

Enlightenment critique in the service of reason's autonomy takes two forms. The first is outright rejection in the name of reason. Lessing is a good example. He argues that *"accidental truths of history can never become the proof of necessary truths of reason."* To make his point, he makes two concessions.

First, that reports of biblical miracles and prophecies are "as reliable as historical truths ever can be," and second, that "Christ raised to life a dead man" and that "this Christ himself rose from the dead." Then he asks whether on such grounds he should accept that "this risen Christ was the Son of God," in this way altering "all my fundamental ideas of the nature of the Godhead." This would be to ask him to believe "something against which my reason rebels."[15]

It seems not to have occurred to Lessing that his references to "*my* ideas and "*my* reason" (my emphasis) might suggest something rather particular and contingent rather than Reason in a Platonic sense of access to universal, timeless truth by an intellect unconditioned and uncontaminated by any historical, cultural, and linguistic traditions. Lessing's "argument" presupposes, without argument, the identity of "my ideas" and "my reason" with Reason Itself in this Platonic sense. Ironically, the assumption that what "my philosophy" teaches is the voice of Reason is one of the most basic presuppositions of Enlightenment traditions that purport to be presuppositionless, and in that sense neutral and objective.

Although Lessing puts the point in epistemic terms relating to what counts as a valid proof, it is clear that it is his metaphysics that precludes any belief in a divine Christ or a Trinitarian God. It is his "fundamental ideas of the nature of the Godhead" understood as "necessary truths of reason" that make Christian belief impossible for him.[16]

We can call this form of critique the *dogmatic hegemony* of reason over revelation, of autonomous philosophy over heteronomous theology, heteronomous because of its willing dependence on what it takes to be a divine revelation that goes beyond or even against the powers of unaided human intellect.[17]

Spinoza's rejections of miracles take this form. He dismisses them as "completely unreasonable" and a "plain absurdity" (*TPT*, 6, 83, 87). They are incompatible with both his idea of "God" and his idea of how we rightly come to know the truth about "God" (*TPT*, 6, 82–85, 89, 94–95).[18] It is clear that the idea of "God" to which he appeals here is the naturalistic pantheism developed in Part 1 of the *Ethics* and summarized in the formula, *Deus sive natura*, according to which the only reality that deserves the name of deity is the world of nature as explained by the laws of mechanistic physics. Absent any legitimate epistemic base, miracles rely on the ignorance, foolishness, and presumptions of the common people, in whom imagination rules over intellect (*TPT*, 6, 81–84, 91, 93).

The general idea behind this rejection is quite clear.

> If reason must be entirely subject to Scripture despite its protests against it, I ask whether we should do this in accordance with reason or, like blind men, without reason ... who can accept anything with his mind if *his reason* protests against it? For what it is to reject something with your mind but a protest of reason? (*TPT*, 15, 188; emphasis added).

Does this entail that those who deny that the earth is (roughly) round and reject the reality of the Holocaust are heeding the "protest of reason"? Spinoza, who is not reluctant to attribute ignorance and prejudice to the theist, ought to know that to reject a belief is not necessarily to be rational. "His reason" is not automatically identical with Reason when it belongs to those Spinoza calls blind men.

Most of Spinoza's critique of mere theism and mere Christianity, however, has another form.[19] Here autonomy takes the form of what we can call it the *hermeneutical hegemony* of reason over revelation, insight over faith, and philosophy over theology. For instead of dogmatically rejecting various beliefs and practices (in the name of Reason), it reinterprets them, radically changing their meaning (in the name of Reason) while retaining the language of faith. Reason provides the heuristic key to these reinterpretations. "Plain imagination does not of its own nature provide certainty as every clear and distinct idea does. In order that we may be certain of what we imagine, imagination must necessarily be assisted by something, and that something is reason" (*TPT*, 2, 28).[20]

Charles Stevenson's idea of a "persuasive definition" is useful here. It is one that "gives a new conceptual meaning to a familiar word without substantially changing its emotive meaning, and which is used with the conscious or unconscious purpose of changing, by this means, the direction of *people's interests.* ... It [seeks] to place the former qualities in a poor light and the latter in a fine one, and thus to redirect *people's admiration.*"[21] It is not surprising that Stevenson gives Spinoza's persuasive (re)definition of "God" as an example.[22] For, while Part I of his *Ethics* is entitled "Concerning God," it consists of an extended attempt at a persuasive (re)definition of "God" as the world of nature.

Spinoza's hermeneutical theory and practice, or, more specifically, his theory and practice of biblical interpretation is found in his *Theological-Political Treatise* (*TPT*). But it everywhere presupposes the reinterpretation of "God" found in the first book of the posthumously published *Ethics*.[23] So we turn first to the *Ethics*.[24]

As redefined by Spinoza, "God" is an infinite, eternal, substance, indeed, the only reality meriting any of these descriptions. The first thing to notice is that Spinoza uses only abstract, impersonal metaphysical terms to describe "God." "God" is a substance, not a personal being.[25]

Spinoza describes "God" as free, which might seem an exception to this, but he explicitly denies that "God" is free in the sense of having free will; everything happens in accord with the eternal necessity of the laws of nature (as discovered by the physical sciences). "God" is free only in the sense that it is not determined by anything outside of itself, since, as infinite, there is nothing outside of it.[26]

Another way to describe "God's freedom is to say that "God is the immanent, not the transitive, cause of all things" (E1 P18). In other words, "God" is not the creator of a world distinct from God, as understood by mere theism, but something more like the Aristotelian form of the world, the impersonal *power* within the world that makes it what it is and what it "does." In short, "God" is a cause, indeed the ultimate cause, but not an agent. Spinoza consistently rejects as anthropomorphic prejudice that "God" acts for any purpose or end (E1 P36 App, E1 P33 S2, E1 App, E4 Pref) or that "God" has emotions (E1 P8 S2). The most important consequence of this, so far as Spinoza's relation to mere theism is concerned, is this: "He who loves God cannot endeavor that God should love him in return" (E5 P19).[27] Of course, for biblical faith it is the other way around. "We love because he first loved us" (1 John 4:19).[28] But the point is clear. By contrast with the biblical God, Spinoza's is neither an agent nor the kind of being who is capable of love. At no point is the divide between Spinoza and biblical religion deeper and more dramatic.

Stevenson says that a persuasive (re)definition cannot be "merely arbitrary" in the sense of being "suitably decided by the flip of a coin."[29] There has to be some ground on which to make the move from the original to the new meaning. Alasdair MacIntyre suggests such a linkage when he says that for Spinoza "*all* the key predicates by which divinity is ascribed apply to the entire system of things, for it is infinite, at once the uncaused *causa sui* and *causa omnium* (cause of itself and cause of everything) and eternal."[30] But this is manifestly false. To make it true it would be necessary to change "all" to "some" or to insert "legitimately" before "ascribed." For in Spinoza's time and ours personal predicates such as love, mercy, justice, and yes, even anger are ascribed to God, and these are taken to be "key" in the theistic discourses he seeks to replace.

Jonathan Bennett is more careful. "Spinoza's main reason for liking 'God' as a name for the entire natural world is that the world comes closer than anything else to fitting the traditional Judeo-Christian account of God." His "God" is

> infinite, eternal, not acted on by anything else, the ultimate source of the explanation of everything, and not susceptible to criticism by any valid standard.... The most Godlike item he can find is Nature; but it does not completely fit the traditional account of God.... So Spinoza holds that the natural world answers to *many* traditional descriptions of God; *but not to all,* and in particular not to the description 'a person.'"[31]

So Spinoza's (re)definition of "God" is not arbitrary in Stevenson's coin toss sense. But suppose a dog lover, seeking to eliminate the practice of drowning litters of unwanted puppies, were to seek to redefine "person" so as to include "dog" in the service of an animal rights philosophy. Commentators on the writings might point to the linkage of overlapping predicates. Human persons and dogs are animals, they reproduce by means of genital intercourse, and in their infancy they can be and usually are adorably cute. So the redefinition is not arbitrary in the coin toss sense. But, even if we were sympathetic to the notion of animal rights, wouldn't we think there was something arbitrary about selecting these predicates as sufficient warrant for eliding the dramatic differences that separate human persons from dogs? Our dog lover may be, for reasons of experience, more comfortable with one or more pet dogs than with friends or relatives. And we might understand that, just as we understand situations in which a child is more comfortable with their stuffed rabbit than with their siblings or parents. But we would find any attempt to redefine "brother" or "sister" or "parent" as "pet rabbit" to be unpersuasive, to say the least.

I don't profess to offer anything new in this brief sketch about Spinoza's "theology." My point is simply this. Spinoza is caught up in a hermeneutical circle in which his (re)definition of "God" presupposes both the metaphysics of scientific naturalism and the decision to remain in some sense religious in that context. It rests on particular historical traditions and personal preferences that fit badly with his conception of reason as the universal, neutral, natural light. In fact, the very view that human reason is (or can be) such a light is itself the product of a particular (complex) tradition going back at least to Plato. It has been and continues to be highly contested by philosophers. It falls within what Ricoeur calls "the conflict of interpretations."[32]

Before proceeding to Spinoza's own hermeneutical theory, some terminological clarification is in order. Spinoza is often taken to be the paradigmatic pantheist. Is this a good description? Yes, at least in terms of what I take to be the clearest way of distinguishing pantheism from theism.[33] For the theist, there can be God without the world, since the creation of the world is an act of freedom and not any kind of necessity.[34] The whole world and, therefore, everything in it, is contingent. But, of course, there cannot be the world without God, since it depends on God's creative act. For the pantheist, there cannot be the world without "God," *and* there cannot be "God" without the world, for, to use a Neoplatonic term, the world emanates from "God" of necessity. Spinoza puts this in terms of the laws of nature as discovered by modern science. Nothing is contingent, neither "God," who exists of necessity, nor the world, which results of necessity from the eternal nature of "God."

So it is perfectly clear that in the sense just specified Spinoza not only is but wants to be a pantheist. He would resist the term only if it was taken to imply either of two views he wishes to disavow. First, while he insists that there cannot be "God" without the world, he rejects the possible implication that he cannot distinguish "God" from the world. He does this by distinguishing "*natura naturans*" from "*natura naturata*." Nature active as cause and nature passive as effect. The former is "God in so far as he is considered a free cause."[35] The latter is "all that follows from the necessity of God's nature" (E1 P29 S). In terms of contemporary physics, we might see the distinction as that between energy and matter.[36] These are not two different realities but one reality referred to in two different respects, as when we refer to Venus as the morning star and the evening star.

So, when Spinoza summarizes his metaphysics with the formula *Deus sive natura* (E4 Pref), "God" or nature, he is telling us that the proper referent of the former term is the latter. But he is not telling us to think of the totality of finite beings as if they were the deity; rather he is telling us that the power by virtue of which they have their existence and their essence is divine. Moreover, it is wholly immanent within them, impersonal like an Aristotelian form and not personal like a God who in an act of freely chosen love creates a world such that God and the world make two. Spinoza's blessing would be "May the Force be with you."

Whereas, as we shall see, Hegel is eager to deny that he is a pantheist, Spinoza might well let us use the term so long as we remember that he can and does distinguish "God" as cause from the world as effect. He is much more concerned to deny another possible corollary: that he is an atheist. There has been no shortage of major and minor thinkers who have called him an atheist.[37] It wouldn't be until the nineteenth century that Novalis would call him a "God-intoxicated man,"[38] and Heine would claim, "Nothing but sheer unreason and malice could bestow on [his] doctrine the qualification of 'atheism.'"[39]

While the former claim is in some sense true, the latter is false and misleading. There is a perfectly good sense, the standard sense, we might say, in which Spinoza is clearly an atheist. One can only dispute this on semantic grounds. If by an atheist we mean, as we usually do, someone who denies the personal creator, lawgiver, judge, and redeemer of theism, then it is clear that Spinoza is and wants to be an atheist. His decision not to publish the *Ethics* in his lifetime is due to the fact that it is all too clearly an atheist treatise in this sense and therefore politically dangerous.[40] But if by an atheist we mean someone who wants to abandon the word "God" and all forms of "religion within the limits of reason alone," as some atheists do, then Spinoza is not an atheist.[41] He has a very complex theory about "God," and he clearly wants to think of himself as in some sense religious. His ethics culminates in what he calls the "intellectual love of 'God.'"

Since in our time and Spinoza's the former sense in which God is a personal creator is the more common meaning, Spinoza sounds disingenuous when he denies that he is an atheist. But he is not trying to fool us into thinking he is a theist. Since the term "atheist" is highly pejorative in his context, he seeks to redefine it persuasively in a way (the second way above) that allows him honestly to disavow it. He tells us that he wrote the *TPT* to "avert this accusation."[42] But Lambert Van Velthuysen, no doubt thinking of atheism in the first sense above, finds that Spinoza "prompts atheism by stealth . . . teaching sheer atheism with furtive and disguised arguments."[43]

Spinoza replies that Velthuysen would have thought differently if he had known "what manner of life I pursue. . . . For atheists are usually inordinately fond of honours and riches, which I have always despised."[44] To our ears this sounds like sheer sophistry. The syllogism

> All atheists are inordinately fond of honours and riches
> I am not inordinately fond of honours and riches
> Therefore I am not an atheist

seems deliberately to miss the point. It is valid enough. But we are not likely to think it sound since the major premise seems to be manifestly false. But in

Spinoza's context the belief was widespread that moral virtue and rectitude required theistic belief as its proper motivation. So the specification of this general belief in the major premise above would have had more than enough credence for Spinoza to feel the need to disavow atheism. Spinoza might have argued that an atheist in the common sense could be, say, just as honest a merchant as his devoutly Jewish or devoutly Christian competitor. Curiously, he chose rather to retain the necessary linkage between "God" and morality, redefining both in the process.[45]

This involves a thoroughly different concept of love. As in biblical theism, love is the highest virtue,[46] so in the *Ethics* the intellectual love of God is the highest virtue. Since Spinoza belongs to the virtue is happiness tradition and wants to give it a religious twist, this virtue = happiness = salvation. As its name suggests, it is an intellectual virtue. "He who clearly and distinctly understands himself and his emotions [ipso facto] loves God, and the more so the more he understands himself and his emotions" (E_5, P_{15}). This is because "Love is pleasure accompanied by the idea of an external cause" (E_3, Def. of the Emotions 6). But is pleasure the automatic result of understanding that everything is the result of an impersonal necessity entirely oblivious and indifferent to my heart's desires, including my very existence and those I love in a very different sense?

Feuer suggests that this "love" is better described as masochism "translated into metaphysical language."

> The masochist acquiescence in the greatness of nature ... could even give a scientific veneer to Spinoza's views by its arbitrary definition of "right" as "power." ... Is there not a streak of masochism that runs through this doctrine [of the intellectual love of God] which insists that we love God though He never love us? ... Why should men not hate God? ... For God is the cause of sorrow, on Spinoza's ground, and we should hate Him as an idea associated with all our pain. A philosophy similar to Schopenhauer's would then be our conclusion.[47]

This is a harsh judgment, but not without its textual grounds. Cleopatra would have understood it. She says, anticipating the suicide she is about to commit,

> 'Tis paltry to be Caesar:
> Not being Fortune he's but Fortune's knave,
> A minister of her will: and it is great
> To do that thing that ends all other deeds ... [48]

A more charitable reading of Spinoza might be to suggest that what he calls the intellectual love of God would more honestly be called resignation. It is a hyperbolic description of what Kierkegaard calls "infinite resignation," the willingness to surrender the desires of our heart without bitterness, rancor, or resentment.[49] Abigail would have understood this interpretation. Jonathan says to her

> "You seem to believe that our destinies are fixed."
> "At the moment," she murmured, "it would seem so."
> "And are you satisfied with that answer?"
> Abigail dimpled prettily. "Oh, no, Mr. Hilliman. Not at all. I am never satisfied. But I am content. And so must you be."[50]

Content but not satisfied. This is much closer to resignation than to love as a pleasure associated with a cause. Or to masochism, for it accepts but does not require pain.

Whether we speak the language of masochism or resignation, it is clear that Spinoza's redefinition of "God" entails an equally drastic redefinition of "love." Instead of being the paradigm of love, "God" is incapable of love of any sort; and our love for God is more nearly resignation than a desire for personal intimacy.

Speaking of his definitions of the emotions in Part 3 of the *Ethics*, Spinoza writes, "I know that these words are commonly used with a different meaning. But my purpose is to explain not the meaning of words, but the nature of things, and to assign to things terms whose common meaning is not very far from the meaning I decide to give them" (*E*3 D20 {of the Emotions}, Exp).[51] If we were to apply this to his redefinitions of "God" and "love" we would have to say that the claim to be "not very far" from common usage, whether in his day or ours or across the centuries, is too manifestly false to be worthy of debate or discussion.

That, of course, does not settle the substantive question whether his meanings fit the "things" for which he uses them better than the common meanings he seeks to supplant. But we should not let his usage of common terms lull us into thinking that his pantheism is "not very far" from biblical theism. What I've been calling the deep and dramatic difference between Spinoza's religion and mere theism raises the question whether it is intellectually honest for Spinoza to retain the language of "God" and "love." Perhaps Velthuysen was on to something when he accused Spinoza of teaching atheism "by stealth" and with "furtive and disguised arguments." On the one hand he makes quite clear where he parts company with mere theism. But on the other hand he denies that he is an atheist and he insists that the differences between God and "God" is no big deal.

Notes

1. Kant develops this dimension of his thought in more detail in *The Conflict of the Faculties* in *Religion and Rational Theology*, ed. Allen W. Wood and George di Giovanni, Cambridge Edition of the Works of Immanuel Kant (New York: Cambridge University Press, 1996). This text (1798) and "What Is Enlightenment? (1784) can be seen as political bookends on the Kantian shelf labeled "Ethics and Religion."

2. These two translations refer, respectively, to the di Giovanni translation (R) in *Religion and Rational Theology* (1996), from which I shall quote, and the earlier and widely used Greene and Hudson translation (New York: Harper & Brothers, 1960), a reprint of the 1934 edition by Open Court.

3. Since I like the earlier translation of the title better, I shall refer to the multiply authored project as the "Religion within the Limits of Reason Alone project" citing R. It seems to me that 'alone' signifies the autonomy of reason better than 'mere,' though the latter is a perfectly proper translation of '*bloss*.' As in "mere Christianity" and "mere theism" (see chap. 1), "mere reason" suggests something widespread and common to many different contexts, even universal. At the conclusion of the previous chapter, I argued that however widespread Kant's version of reason may or may not be, it is plainly not the universal reason he needs and claims.

4. The project is not exactly new in the seventeenth and subsequent centuries. The ancient philosophical schools, Platonic, Aristotelian, Stoic, and Epicurean, "often criticized [the world of ancient Greco-Roman religion] while claiming to teach the truth to which it pointed." N. T. Wright, *Paul and the Faithfulness of God* (Minneapolis, MN: Fortress Press, 2013), p. 238. Cf. pp. 235 and 255. By contrast, the apocryphal Wisdom of Solomon, a text from the time of Jesus and Paul or perhaps a little before, stands in the Jewish tradition. "Solomon" knows that "I would not possess wisdom unless God gave her to me" (8:21). Wright comments that "the means whereby the writer apparently claims to know what can be said is not simply the combination of accurate sense-impressions and clear reasoning. It is the scriptures of Israel and particularly the narratives of the exodus and the monarchy" (*Paul*, pp. 240 and 243).

5. Though Anselm's notion of faith seeking understanding was widely shared. That Anselm remained within what I'm calling the medieval consensus of reason and philosophy within the limits of faith and theology is argued by Karl Barth in *Anselm: Fides Quaerens Intellectum*, trans. Ian W. Robertson (New York: World Publishing, 1962). For a contemporary statement of this ideal, see Nicholas Wolterstorff, *Reason Within the Bounds of Religion*, 2nd ed. (Grand Rapids, MI: Eerdmans, 1984).

6. In this respect the patristics were closer to biblical than to medieval times. "To the people of his day, [Paul] and his communities would have looked more like a new school of philosophy than a type of religion." Wright, *Paul*, 203.

7. Martin Luther, *The Magnificat*, in *Luther's Works*, vol. 21, ed. Jaroslav Pelikan (St. Louis, MO: Concordia, 1956), pp. 303–304. Luther adds that because "the soul knows and the spirit believes," spirit is "where God dwells in the darkness of faith, where no light is; for [man] believes that which he neither sees nor feels nor comprehends. His soul is the holy place, with . . . all manner of reason, discrimination, knowledge, and understanding of visible and bodily things."

8. Luther defines faith as "the saving and efficacious use of the Word of God." *The Freedom of a Christian* in *Luther's Works*, vol. 31, ed. Harold J. Grimm (Philadelphia: Fortress, 1957), p. 346.

9. While our trio of thinkers can be said to have laid the foundation for fully secular versions of this triple hegemony, as the title I have given to their joint project testifies—religion within the limits of reason alone—they sought to retain some version of religion severely restricted by the limits or bounds of what each of them understood reason to require. Derrida's phrase, "religion without religion," might fit their intentions fairly well. See Jacques Derrida, *The Gift of Death*, 2nd ed., trans. David Wills (1st ed., 1995; Chicago: Chicago University Press, 2008), p. 50 (p. 49 in the 1995 edition).

10. Here the contrast between Julia Ward Howe in her "Battle Hymn of the Republic" and Lincoln in his Second Inaugural Address is of interest. "Lincoln and Howe advanced two very different perspectives on the relationship between the war and God's providential plan. Lincoln assumed a posture of humility, based on the fundamental inscrutability of God's purposes. In contrast, from the first line of her hymn, Howe establishes the transparency of providence. When she writes, 'Mine eyes have seen the glory of the *coming* of the Lord,' she describes a process literally unfolding before her. . . . [Lincoln] recognized that he was offering not a transparent vision like the 'Battle Hymn' but one obscured by human fallibility and partiality." John Stauffer and Benjamin Soskis, *The Battle Hymn of the Republic: A Biography of the Song That Marches On* (New York: Oxford University Press, 2013), pp. 98–99. See note 6 above.

11. This leaves the Muslims out. I shall focus on two-thirds of the Abrahamic monotheisms both because of my very limited knowledge of Islam and, more importantly, because it was Jewish and Christian forms of theism that were the primary target of the Enlightenment critique. Lessing brings Islam into the discussion in *Nathan the Wise*, but that is the exception that proves the rule. For Spinoza, to take our first example, it was Jewish and Christian theologies and practices that were in a very immediate sense the enemy.

12. John Masefield, "Sea Fever."

13. N. T. Wright, *The New Testament and the People of God* (Minneapolis, MN: Fortress, 1992), pp. 248–52. For a brief overview of biblical religion as covenantal, see my *God, Guilt, and Death: An Existential Phenomenology of Religion* (Bloomington, IN: Indiana University Press, 1984), chap. 11. New Testament = New Covenant. For a philosophical analysis of God as a speaker, see Nicholas Wolterstorff, *Divine Discourse: Philosophical Reflections on the Claim That God Speaks* (New York: Cambridge University Press, 1995).

14. Political censorship (of special concern to both Spinoza and Kant) is an exception to that rule, but as indicated in the previous chapter, the heteronomy I seek to praise concerns our relation to God, not to church or state. I share Spinoza's and Kant's concern for free speech and a free press.

15. Gotthold Ephraim Lessing, "On the Proof of the Spirit and of Power," in *Lessing's Theological Writings*, trans. Henry Chadwick (Stanford, CA: Stanford University Press, 1957), pp. 53–54.

16. After Lessing's death, F. H. Jacobi reported that Lessing had been a Spinozist, setting off the so-called "pantheism controversy." This is interesting in the present context, but of no crucial importance. Just what Lessing's ideas of God may have been matters less than what he tells us about them in the passages cited. See Frederick C. Beiser, *The Fate of Reason: German Philosophy from Kant to Fichte* (Cambridge, MA: Harvard University Press, 1987), chap. 2, "Jacobi and the Pantheism Controversy."

17. Thomas Aquinas teaches that faith goes beyond but not against reason (when reason is properly functioning). But Kierkegaard, through his pseudonym Johannes Climacus, claims that faith goes against reason, since in its claims to autonomy human reason is not properly functioning. See Kierkegaard, *Concluding Unscientific Postscript*, trans. Howard V. Hong and Edna H. Hong (Princeton, NJ: Princeton University Press, 1992), 1, 429, 565–66.

18. I shall put Spinoza's "God" in quotation marks (unless it is part of a larger quotation) as a reminder of its diametrical difference from the God of theism and most ordinary usage. Similarly, I

shall use the impersonal pronoun 'it.' (See note 26 below.) Following standard usage (Chicago has four million people, but 'Chicago' has seven letters), I shall use scare quotes when mentioning the word 'God' rather than using it to refer either to the God of theism or the "God" of Spinoza.

19. We shall see that this is true of Kant and Hegel as well.

20. Spinoza regularly insists that biblical religion rests on imagination. But the intellect to which he appeals as superior to imagination is limited to abstract, impersonal concepts. This involves the huge assumption that we can understand God and ourselves best within these limits.

21. Charles Stevenson, *Facts and Values: Studies in Ethical Analysis* (New Haven, CT: Yale University Press, 1963), pp. 32, 34 (emphasis added).

22. Stevenson, *Facts and Values*, pp. 41–42.

23. In 1675 Spinoza wrote to Oldenberg that he was ready to publish the book we know as the *Ethics*, but "a rumour became widespread that a certain book of mine about God was in the press, and in it I endeavour to show that there is no God. This rumour found credence with many." Some theologians complained about him to the Magistrates and the Cartesians began to denounce him. *Spinoza: The Letters*, trans. Samuel Shirley (Indianapolis, IN: Hackett, 1995), letter 68, p. 321. As a result, the work was only published after Spinoza's death.

24. Yirmiyahu Yovel tells us that the first part of the *Ethics* was already drafted by 1660. *Spinoza and Other Heretics: The Marrano of Reason* (Princeton, NJ: Princeton University Press, 1989), p. 5. Speaking of the entire *Ethics*, Steven Nadler says that he had "a fairly substantial draft in hand" by 1665. *A Book Forged in Hell: Spinoza's Scandalous Treatise and the Birth of the Secular Age* (Princeton, NJ: Princeton University Press, 2011), p. 16. This means it was possible for Spinoza to draw on it in writing *TPT* (1670).

25. An important element in what Heidegger calls onto-theology is that it describes God only in such abstract, impersonal terms as *causa prima, ultima ratio, and causa sui*. See my analysis in the title chapter of my *Overcoming Onto-theology* (New York: Fordham University Press, 2001), pp. 1–28, and "Onto-Theology" in *Dictionary for Theological Interpretation of the Bible*, ed. Kevin J. Vanhoozer (Grand Rapids, MI: Baker Academic, 2005), pp. 546–49. Spinoza is a prime example.

26. Jonathan Bennett writes, "We can use 'he' for God, thinking of God as a person; if we came to think of God as impersonal, we should switch to 'it.'" *A Study of Spinoza's Ethics* (Indianapolis, IN: Hackett, 1984), p. 34. But Bennett thinks 'it' is as misleading as 'he' since that would imply that "Spinoza kept reminding his readers that the item in question is not a person," which he did not. I think it is less misleading to say 'it' so as regularly to remind ourselves of the impersonal nature of his "God."

27. Henry Hatfield suggests that Goethe gives us a "secularized" version of this asymmetry. "The actress Philina, an attractive if somewhat promiscuous little thing, remarks to the hero: 'If I love you, what business is it of yours?'" *Goethe: A Critical Introduction* (New York: New Directions, 1963), p. 66. See Goethe, *Wilhelm Meister's Apprenticeship*, trans. Eric A. Blackall and Victor Lange (Princeton, NJ: Princeton University Press, 1995), p. 139, where the translation reads "if I love you, what's that to you?"

28. Some ancient manuscripts read "We love him" or "We love God."

29. Stevenson, *Facts and Values*, p. 35.

30. Alasdair MacIntyre, "Pantheism," in *The Encyclopedia of Philosophy*, ed. Paul Edwards (New York: Macmillan, 1967), 6, 33b (emphasis added).

31. Jonathan Bennett, *A Study of Spinoza's* Ethics, pp. 33–34 (emphasis added). Bennett sees a second linkage in Spinoza's "view of Nature as a fit object for reverence, awe, and humble love," p. 34.

32. Paul Ricoeur, *The Conflict of Interpretations: Essays in Hermeneutics*, trans. Don Ihde (Evanston, IL: Northwestern University Press, 1974).

33. Paul Tillich says that 'pantheism' "should be defined before it is used aggressively." *Systematic Theology* (Chicago: University of Chicago Press, 1999c), 1, 233. I agree that the term, like others,

should be defined. So I state as clearly as I can the meaning of the term as I use it. I think my usage is descriptive rather than "aggressive," unless insisting that it be distinguished from biblical theism is considered aggressive. But why?

34. The Bible concludes with a reminder of God's freedom in creation.
You are worthy, our Lord and God,
to receive glory and honor and power,
for you created all things,
and by your will they existed and were created. (Rev. 4:11)

35. Remembering that "God" is a free cause not by virtue of free will but by being infinite, conditioned by nothing outside of it.

36. Edwin Curley suggests that *natura naturans* ('God') is the laws of nature and *natura naturata* (world) is all the realities (things, events, facts) that occur in accordance with those laws. *Behind the Geometrical Method: A Reading of Spinoza's* Ethics (Princeton, NJ: Princeton University Press, 1988), pp, 36–50, and *Spinoza's Metaphysics: An Essay in Interpretation* (Cambridge, MA: Harvard University Press, 1969), chaps. 1–2. If the laws of nature were understood merely as descriptions of natural regularities, this would leave out the element or energy, power, or force. Spinoza's "God" is a cause and not merely a pattern. But Curley is surely on target in suggesting that Spinoza's metaphysics is a scientific naturalism. The world is "governed" by nothing but the laws of nature as discovered by the natural sciences.

37. Including Bayle, Leibniz, Priestley, Jacobi, and Coleridge. See my *Transcendence and Self-Transcendence* (Bloomington: Indiana University Press, 2004), pp. 41–42.

38. *Novalis: Werke, Tagebücher und Briefe Friedrich von Hardenbergs*, ed. Hans-Joachim Mähl and Richard Samuel (Darmstadt: Wissenschaftiche Buchgesellschaft, 1978), II, p. 812, fragment 346.

39 Heinrich Heine, *Religion and Philosophy in Germany*, trans. John Snodgrass (Boston: Beacon, 1959), p. 72.

40. See letter 68 to Oldenburg. *Spinoza: The Letters*, trans. Samuel Shirley (Indianapolis, IN: Hackett, 1995), p. 321.

41. Those who today say "I consider myself to be spiritual but not religious" may be first cousins of Spinoza, atheists in one sense but not in the other.

42. Letter 30, p. 186. Cf. *TPT*, 2, 27 and 6, 87.

43. Letter 42, p. 236. What Velthausen rightly perceives is that Spinoza's naturalistic *Deus sive natura* metaphysics is constantly presupposed in *TPT*.

44. Letter 43, p. 237.

45. For a more detailed discussion of Spinoza's atheism and his formula, *Deus sive natura*, see *Transcendence and Self-Transcendence*, pp. 41–52.

46. See the Shema in Deut. 6:4–5, Jesus's summary of the law in Matt. 22:34–40, Mark 12:28–34, and Luke 10:25–28 and Paul's praise of love in 1 Cor. 13, concluding in "the greatest of these is love."

47. Lewis Samuel Feuer, *Spinoza and the Rise of Liberalism* (Boston: Beacon, 1958), pp. 85, 111, 216. Cf. pp. 217–18, 239, 241.

48. William Shakespeare, *Antony and Cleopatra*, 5.1.2–5.

49. Søren Kierkegaard, *Fear and Trembling/Repetition*, trans. Howard V. Hong and Edna H. Hong (Princeton, NJ: Princeton University Press, 1983), pp. 27–53, "Preliminary Expectoration."

50. Stephen L. Carter, *The Impeachment of Abraham Lincoln* (A. A. Knopf: New York: 2012), last page—a final word on the civil war, Lincoln's presidency, his (fictitious) impeachment, and its personal and national implications, all seen under the aspect of the necessity called destiny.

51. To speak of "the meaning I decide to give them" is to betray the particularity and contingency of the perspective from which Spinoza speaks.

3

SPINOZA'S HERMENEUTICS

When we turn to the *Theological-Political Treatise* we find the theological part, primarily the theory and practice of interpreting the Bible, sandwiched between political bookends. At the heart of the theological argument is a plea for the autonomy of philosophy from theology, and, indeed, the hegemony of the former over the latter, relocating religion within the limits of reason alone. At the heart of the political part is a plea for the autonomy of the state from religion (religious authorities), and, indeed, the hegemony over the former over the latter. For Spinoza felt unjustly oppressed by the theocratic form of both the Jewish and the Calvinist communities in which he found himself.[1] Together these two autonomies underlie his primary political concern, freedom of speech and freedom of the press. The subtitle makes this clear:

> Containing several discourses which demonstrate that freedom to philosophize may not only be allowed without danger to piety and the stability of the republic but cannot be refused without destroying the peace of the republic and piety itself. (*TPT*, 1)

Spinoza's concern was well grounded. He was in Holland because his parents had fled the inquisition in Portugal. He had been excommunicated from the Jewish community in Amsterdam.[2] The publication data for *TPT* are given as Hamburg, Heinrich Kuhnraht, and 1670. Only the date is correct; for the work was published in Amsterdam by Jan Rieuwertsz. The double fiction of place and publisher were deemed necessary because of the censorship laws in the Dutch Republic. Moreover, as already noted, the *Ethics* was only published posthumously because it was deemed too dangerous to publish it in Spinoza's lifetime. We might say that he was ecumenically anti-clerical, opposing theocracy in the Catholic, Jewish, and Protestant versions with which he was all too intimately acquainted.

Like Bonhoeffer (see note 1 above), we can appreciate Spinoza's case for religious liberty, including the right to be a heretic, without buying into his subordination of theology to philosophy. The one does not in any way require the other. Theology need not be theocratic, and philosophy can be oppressive, as we learned all too well in the twentieth century.

After occasional references to this political or human rights issue throughout the *Treatise*, Spinoza's coda or peroration in chapter 20 returns to this theme as the second bookend. The final chapter is entitled "Where it is shown that in a free state everyone is allowed to think what they wish and to say what they think" (*TPT*, 20, 250), where "to say" clearly includes "to publish." The best states allow the freedom to philosophize (*TPT*, 20, 254). He allows the state to prohibit or punish subversive speech, but he defines subversion not in terms of opposition to the current political or religious powers that be but as threat to the social contract from which any regime derives its legitimacy.

In other words, his plea for freedom to philosophize is placed in the context of his larger political philosophy. It has been described as "the first statement in history of the standpoint of a democratic liberalism. It was written during the high tide of Republican rule."[3] These three terms, democracy, liberalism, and republicanism are all freely used in discussing Spinoza's politics. They are not synonymous, and if I were concerned with his political theory in general I would need to sort them out. But the fascinating stories of his relation to the political events, personalities, and theories of his time, including Hobbes's have been well told elsewhere[4] and concern my project only in so far as (1) politics and religion, both in theory and in practice, are inextricably linked for Spinoza, as his title suggests, and (2) more specifically, his account of the hegemony of philosophy over theology is for him not only of intrinsic importance but is also in the service of freedom of speech and of the press.

Living and working in a Dutch Republic where Calvinism was both religiously and politically powerful, Spinoza adopted, or sounded as if he adopted, three principles fundamental to the Protestant Reformation. One is the priesthood of the believer. Spinoza doesn't use this language, but he affirms its central idea, namely that the interpretation of Scripture is not the monopoly of the clergy (supported by the political authorities in a de facto theocracy) but the privilege and responsibility of each individual. "I conclude that everyone should be allowed the liberty of their own judgment and authority to interpret the fundamentals of faith according to their own minds" (*TPT*, Pref., 10).

A second Reformation theme is the inner witness of the Holy Spirit. In answer to the double question, How can I know that the Bible is the divinely inspired Word of God? and How can I know what it means?, the Catholic answer was the magisterium of the Church. It is on the authority of the church hierarchy that I am to believe the Bible to be an authoritative divine revelation; and it is on the same authority that I am to believe what the church tells me the Bible teaches.

The reformers insist that the church is human, all too human. It is as much subject to (and therefore not lord of) Scripture as is the individual. It is up to God to persuade us of the divine authority of the Bible and to teach us what it means. This is accomplished by the inner witness or testimony of the Holy Spirit.

Calvin focuses on the first of the two questions above. "Scripture Must Be Confirmed by the Witness of the Spirit. Thus May Its Authority Be Established as Certain; and It Is a Wicked Falsehood that Its Credibility Depends on the Judgment of the Church."[5] Later he adds, "For, that the Word may not beat your ears in vain, and that the sacraments may not strike your eyes in vain, the Spirit shows us that in them it is God speaking to us, softening the stubbornness of our heart, and composing it to that obedience that it owes the Word of the Lord."[6]

More the existential theologian than the system builder, Luther focuses on the second question, How can I know what the Bible teaches? He writes, "No one can correctly understand God or His Word unless he has received such understanding *immediately* from the Holy Spirit . . . the Holy Spirit instructs us as in His own school, outside of which nothing is learned but empty words and prattle."[7]

Spinoza may have first encountered a hint of the Reformation slogan, Word and Spirit, in the Hebrew Bible. In Isaiah 59:21 we read, "my spirit that is among you, and my words that I have put in your mouth, shall not depart out of your mouth . . . says the Lord, from now on and forever." So on his title page, after the subtitle cited above, Spinoza cites 1 John 4:13, "*By this we know that we remain in God, and God remains in us, because he has given us of his spirit.*" In the following text it becomes clear that this spirit is what he calls natural reason or the natural light of reason and that "we" to whom the spirit has been given are those who restrict their religion within the limits of that reason, not those who believe, with John, that God loves and that God forgives (*TPT*, 1, 13–14; 4 61; 7 104 and 111; 15, 188). When Paul speaks of the spirit of God "he means his own mind" (*TPT*, 11, 159)! Those who appeal to the testimony of the Holy Spirit

> assert this from passion or vanity.... But no spirit other than reason gives testimony about the truth and certainty of things that are purely matters for philosophy [such as God], and reason, as we have already shown, claims the realm of truth for itself. If therefore they pretend to have any other spirit that makes them certain of the truth, they are making a false claim ... [and committing] treason against the majesty of reason." (*TPT*, 15, 193–94)

The third Reformation theme is *sola scriptura* (scripture alone). For Luther and Calvin, it means first of all that the Bible is the highest norm, the supreme court, as it were, for the beliefs and practices of the Christian community and its members. Nothing that comes from human tradition, even church tradition, or the unaided use of human reason can stand as unconditionally authoritative without the imprimatur of scripture. Scripture trumps any other card. Second, it means that scripture interprets itself; one need not go outside the text itself to such sources as church tradition or autonomous reason to discover the true meaning of the Bible (to whose divine origin and authority the Holy Spirit bears witness in our hearts).

The first part of the *sola scripture* doctrine is not a hermeneutical principle. It does not tell us how to interpret the Bible—only that such interpretation is of utmost importance and, accordingly, that learning how rightly to interpret the Bible is a crucial and not a casual task. But the second part is a hermeneutical principle, and it is this part with which Spinoza gleefully associates himself: to find the meaning of biblical texts do not appeal to any principles or ideas outside the text but only to the text itself. He promises to "demonstrate how Scripture should be interpreted, proving that we must derive all our knowledge of it and of spiritual matters from Scripture alone and not from what we discover by means of the natural light of reason" (*TPT*, Pref., 10).[8] We must not "attribute anything to the prophets,[9] which they have not clearly stated themselves" (*TPT*, 1, 15). For the purpose is to discover "the thinking of the Bible's authors" and in doing so to

> admit no other criteria or data for interpreting Scripture and discussing its contents than what is drawn from Scripture itself and its history ... knowledge of all these things, that is, of almost everything in Scripture must be sought from the Bible itself, just as knowledge of nature has to be sought from

nature itself.... All of our knowledge of the Bible, hence, must be derived only from the Bible itself." (*TPT*, 7, 98–99)

But what of those words "and its history" and "almost"? We are not to take Spinoza's *sola scriptura* in too rigid a sense. He is defending what Nicholas Wolterstorff calls authorial discourse hermeneutics, seeking to discover what speech acts the author performed by inscribing his text. These speech acts are public and not to be confused with some inner psychic event that the interpreter is somehow supposed to re-enact.

> The myth dies hard that to read a text for authorial discourse is to enter the dark world of the author's psyche It is nothing of the sort. It is to read to discover what assertings, what promisings, what requestings, what commandings, are rightly to be ascribed to the author on the ground of her having set down the words that she did in the situation in which she set them down. Whatever be the dark demons and bright angels of the author's inner self that led her to take up this stance in public, it is that stance itself that we hope by reading to recover, not the dark demons and bright angels."[10]

Spinoza understands that in order to discover and recover the author's meaning in this sense we need to look at more than the text itself, though not to some inner psychic events in the mind of the author. In the first place, we will have to understand the language(s) in which the Bible is written, and this will obviously involve the study of other texts. Second, we will have to investigate the history of the texts. In other words, we will have to engage in biblical criticism, both the "lower" criticism that seeks to establish the most reliable text and the "higher" criticism that asks questions about the history of the text itself, its date, authorship, collating, editing, and so forth. Finally, it will be necessary to understand the historical context in which the text was written and first received. To grasp what the author was saying and how it would have been understood by the first readers, we need to know as much as we can about the original setting, including the beliefs and practices that were most likely shared by author and readers (*TPT*, 7, 98–103, 109).

All of this involves the study and knowledge of materials other than the Bible itself; but they are all in the service of understanding what the author was trying to communicate to the original audience. Today this would be called the grammatico-historical hermeneutic. "The grammatico-historical method... refers to studying the biblical text, or any other text, in its original historical context, and seeking the meaning its author(s) most likely intended for its original audience(s) or addressees based on the grammar and syntax."[11]

So Spinoza is not the precursor of the new criticism, which seeks quite strictly to interpret poems exclusively in terms of the text itself (excluding even other poems by the same author).[12] What Spinoza's *sola scriptura* is meant to exclude is, however, quite clear. The extra-biblical material that we must not draw on is our own beliefs about the truth. He forbids us from using them in determining what the Bible teaches. That privilege belongs to the authors (including redactors) whose world and worldview are not ours, and we must not force their square pegs into our round holes.

His primary target here is Maimonides, who holds that "Scripture must be adapted to reason" (*TPT*, 15, 186). Scripture is only allowed to teach what reason confirms. "For if it was clear to him on the basis of reason that the world was eternal, he would not hesitate to bend Scripture to devise an interpretation that would ultimately render it saying apparently the same thing. In fact, he would be immediately convinced that Scripture intended to teach the eternity of the world, despite the fact that it everywhere says the opposite" (*TPT*, 7, 113).[13]

In 1666 Ludwig Meyer (Lodewijk Meijer), a student and friend of Spinoza, adopted Maimonides's strategy for reconciling faith and reason in a book entitled *Philosophy, Interpreter of Scripture*. "Philosophy, according to Meijer, was not the handmaiden of religion . . . on the contrary, Scripture had to answer to philosophy. Indeed, the exact truths proclaimed by Scripture were accessible to human reason alone, without the need of any special acts of divine revelation."[14]

By contrast, Spinoza insists, "In order to know whether or not Moses believed that God is fire, we certainly must not argue on the basis of whether this statement agrees or conflicts with *reason* but only from other statements made by Moses himself . . . we are not permitted to adjust the meaning of Scripture to the dictates of *our reason or our preconceived opinions*; all explanation of the Bible must be sought from the Bible alone" (*TPT*, 7, 101).[15]

It might seem, then, that Spinoza is not engaged in the hermeneutical version of the Enlightenment project of religion within the limits of reason alone, that he is not offering "persuasive (re)definitions" of biblical texts in support of the hegemony of philosophy over theology and of reason over revelation. But this would be to ignore his repeated and sharp distinction between questions of meaning and questions of truth. Unlike theology, philosophy does not assume that when we have discovered the genuine meaning of the biblical writers we have discovered the truth. "It is one thing to understand Scripture and the minds of the prophets and quite another to understand the mind of God which is the very truth of a thing" (*TPT*, 12, 168).

Spinoza is quite emphatic about this, insisting that

> we are concerned here only with [the scriptures'] meaning, not with their truth. Moreover, in seeking the sense of Scripture we must take care especially not to be blinded by our own reasoning, in so far as it is founded on the principles of natural knowledge (not to mention our preconceptions). In order not to confuse the genuine sense of a passage with the truth of things, we must investigate a passage's sense only from its use of the language or from the reasoning which accepts no other foundation than Scripture itself. (*TPT*, 7, 100)[16]

Within the presupposed framework of Spinoza's naturalistic metaphysics, there could be no such thing as the divine inspiration of any texts. There could be classics, such as Homer, or Shakespeare, or Dostoyevsky, but none of these comes to us with divine authority.[17] This means that scriptural status is no guarantee of truth.

Spinoza has two reasons for this sharp separation of meaning from truth. The two defects of the biblical writers with respect to truth are tradition and imagination. Their writings "have varied not only in accordance with the imagination and temperament of each individual prophet, but also according to the beliefs in which he was brought up . . . [they have] depended upon the disposition of his bodily temperament, his imagination, and the beliefs he has previously adopted" (*TPT*, 2, 28 and 30). Their writings were "built upon the basic principles that were most familiar and acceptable at the time" (*TPT*, 11, 162).

In the first place, the biblical writers reflect the particular traditions of their times. Spinoza doubles up on this particularity by referring to individual temperament. The result is clear. Absent a God who can speak and who can speak through the speech of inspired individuals,[18] biblical texts are of merely biographical and historical significance, telling us about individuals and cultures from long ago and far away. In them we hear voices that are human, all too human. They articulate human traditions, not divine truth.

The second limitation of the prophets is that they "think" in the language of the imagination. Spinoza is emphatic in his claim that their only superiority is in the domain of imagination, putting them on a par (at best) with writers like Homer, Shakespeare, and Dostoyevsky.[19] Or, to put it a bit differently, this makes them (at best) geniuses as that notion is developed by Kant and the romantics. Spinoza does not rate such genius very highly. "We have proved in chapter 2 of this treatise that the prophets possessed extraordinary powers of imagination but not of understanding, and that it was not the deeper points of philosophy that God revealed to them but only some very simple matters, adapting Himself to their preconceived beliefs" (*TPT*, 13, 172).

To call a writer a great imaginative thinker is, for Spinoza, to damn with faint praise, most especially when the contrast is with philosophy. In Part II of his *Ethics*, which was in process and everywhere presupposed throughout the writing of *TPT*, he distinguishes three levels of knowing. Since there are two levels that make up the first kind of knowledge, this scheme maps rather nicely onto Plato's four stages of the divided line and the allegory of the cave as a commentary on them.

Spinoza calls his first level "opinion" or "imagination." It arises from sense experience or language that evokes such images. The second level is called reason. It rests on "common notions and adequate ideas of things." Euclidian geometry is given as an example. This means that the *Ethics* would be an example of reason, for it is given in the form of geometrical proofs; but *TPT* also falls into this category, it would seem, for while not in geometrical form, Spinoza regularly claims to have proven or demonstrated the claims he makes.[20]

The highest level is called intuition. It presupposes adequate ideas of both God and finite things. The example is solving the equation $1:2 = 3:x$. We don't need to give any proof or follow any rule. Without discursive thought, we just see that it is 6 (*E2 P40 S2*). If the second kind of knowledge is philosophy, the third kind is Spinoza's version of the beatific vision, a richly mediated vision that has surpassed its mediation and become an immediate intuition.[21] The platonic analogue would come from the *Symposium*. In Diotima's speech, one ever mounts the "heavenly ladder" from lower to higher forms of beauty "until at last he comes to know what beauty is." At this moment of "final revelation... there bursts upon him that wondrous vision which is the very soul of beauty... beauty's very self... heavenly beauty face to face."[22] Spinoza seems to have in mind an almost mystical intuition, tutored, to be sure, by philosophical reflection, of *natura naturans* and *natura naturata* in their interrelation and in their infinite and absolute self-containedness.

Why the differences among these kinds of knowing are important is clear from *E2* P41: "Knowledge of the first kind is the only cause of falsity; knowledge of the second and third kind is necessarily true." N.B. Spinoza does not say that the first kind of knowledge is necessarily false, only that it alone is the home of falsehood. For statements like 'snow is white (at first)' and 'the Cubs finally won the World Series in 2016' it does fine. But it is inherently unreliable, especially when it comes to questions about God, who we are, and how we should live; for such matters we must turn to philosophy.

In his argument against Maimonides, Spinoza suggests that to make philosophy the criterion of scriptural meaning would make philosophers into a new magisterium. "This would surely produce a new ecclesiastical authority and a novel species of priest or pontiff, which would more likely be mocked than venerated by the common people" (*TPT*, 7, 114). He fails to see the irony of protesting against this at the level of meaning, while doing exactly the same thing with respect to truth.

In any case, the truth that comes from reflective reason as it culminates in immediate intuition is the truth that sets us "free" in Spinoza's view. It culminates in that tranquility of mind that the ancients called *ataraxia* and *apatheia* and that Spinoza calls the intellectual love of God.[23] It is love because it is about desire and its fulfillment; and it is intellectual because it is about the desire for understanding, knowledge, and truth.

I have previously raised the question whether resignation would not be a better term, given the iron necessity and total indifference of nature to human concerns. But Spinoza seems to be working with something like the French adage, "To understand all is to forgive all." It would read "To understand the necessity of things, not just in discursive proofs but in an immediate vision, is to love "God" = Nature (*Deus sive Natura*).[24]

But again, wouldn't 'resignation,' even 'infinite resignation' be a better term? A person sentenced to life in prison without the possibility of parole may at some point give up all hope of getting out and simply see the inevitability of permanent incarceration. It may be that resignation will prevail over resentment and despair, though this is by no means guaranteed. But would it not be an abuse of language to say that the prisoner loves the system in any sense of 'love'? Or to call this "freedom," as Spinoza does in concluding his *Ethics*?[25] And then to go on and say, "A freeman thinks of death least of all things, and his wisdom is a meditation of life, not of death" (*E4* P67)? It strikes me that our prisoner will think of death quite a bit, both as the only possible release from this bondage and in the depressing thought, "this is where I am going to die." Like all analogies this one is imperfect. But it seems to me more compelling than what Spinoza says about our existence in what Weber calls the "iron cage."[26]

At this point we need to remind ourselves that we are here concerned with Spinoza's "divided line" not for its own sake but for its role in the sharp dichotomy he makes between meaning and truth in biblical texts. By making the prophets (at best) geniuses of imagination, he locates them at the lowest level(s) of knowing. With careful scholarly work we can discover (uncover, recover) their original meaning, but we should not turn to them in our search for truth about God, the world, and ourselves. They have been excluded from the double domain in which we find nothing but such truth and restricted to the cognitive spheres where error is prevalent.

The extent of this prevalence comes to light in Spinoza's sustained denigration of the "common people," Plato's hoi polloi, the many. The prophets "accommodate" themselves to the thought world of the common people unavoidably, given their own limitations (*TPT*, 1, 23; 2, 35; 3, 43; 4, 64). It is a world of ignorance, superstition, foolishness, mere opinion, and delusion (*TPT*, Pref., 3, 4, 7, 12; 6, 81–82; 7, 97–98), of childish, infantile, womanish, fickle, and capricious thinking (*TPT*, Pref. 4; 3, 44; 12, 163; 14, 178). Because of their intellectual limits, the common people speak of God anthropomorphically (*TPT*, 13, 177; 1, 23). Their thinking arises out of passions such as hope and fear rather than reason; indeed, it is a "treason against the majesty of reason" (*TPT*, 7, 98; 15, 193–94). Because they are "not competent" to think philosophically, they think that historical narratives and, more particularly, miracle stories can tell us who God is and how we should live in relation to God (piety) (*TPT*, 5, 76–78; 6, 81–82, 91).

In his litany of accusations against the common people, Spinoza includes the two intellectual defects that he regularly attributes specifically to the prophets: dependence on imagination (*TPT*, 6, 93; 13, 172), which includes both sense experience and narrative form, and prejudice, which may be personal, but is usually carried by socially transmitted traditions (Pref., 5–7; 15, 186). In short, "They are merely speaking from their emotional prejudices." In passages like these 'prejudice' probably has its pejorative sense of an irrational bias. But even in the neutral, Gadamerian sense of any a priori assumptions that are tradition borne, it would signify for Spinoza a deviation from rationality. For it would signify limitation to some historically specific culture or society rather than reliance on the "natural light of reason," which is assumed to be universal and univocal.

Spinoza's intellectual elitism represents a sustained bias against anything historically particular, sense experience, emotions in the ancient sense of passions of the soul, narrative discourse, and literature as a discourse that combines all of these lapses from pure, uncontaminated reason. Probably the best example of the claim that something historically particular is of universal significance is the Bible with reference to God's election of Israel to be a light to the nations and the fulfillment of the covenant promises in Jesus of Nazareth in whom God loves the whole world. From Aristotle on there has been a variety of empiricisms claiming that we delude ourselves when we seek to separate human thought from sense experience. Spinoza acknowledges that there are good emotions as well as bad ones; but the idea of emotional intelligence is foreign to his way of thinking,[27] along with the notion that emotions may not only be brought into harmony with reason but that they have an intelligence of their own.[28] The philosophical and theological significance of narrative as a form of discourse has been analyzed and often affirmed in contemporary theory.[29] Finally, the philosophical significance of literature has been defended and developed not only by literary critics but by philosophers as well.[30]

I do not mention these modes of thought that contest Spinoza's account of where the truth is to be found with the assumption that they got it right where he got it wrong. The point, which hardly seems in need of argument, is rather to emphasize the historical and cultural particularity of his thought in spite of the claim, all too obvious to many thinkers of his time, that philosophical reason rises to an ethereal realm of nature uncontaminated by anything smacking of nurture. He is as much a child of his time as the prophets were of theirs. The assumption that his ideas are the voice of Reason and that all these conflicting views are due to the ignorance of the common people is a thinly disguised form of complacent self-congratulation, widely enough shared over centuries since Plato to be called a tradition. This means that he got it wrong wholesale, even if here and there he got it right retail. For the wholesale claim that fares poorly in relation to the alternatives cited above is precisely the claim that human reason can be autonomous, self-sufficient and unconditioned by factors that come to it from without.

Of course, it does not follow that there is divine revelation in the sense claimed by the Abrahamic monotheisms or that human thought is better off when dependent on it. But just to the degree that human thought is de facto conditioned in ways suggested by the traditions mentioned above, this double claim of mere monotheism is scarcely refuted by the claim to be the voice of Reason as such, superior by virtue of its universality. Such thinking rather tends to refute itself (in its various versions, as we shall see) by attributing to itself an ahistorical purity we can see it does not possess.

The traditions that appeal to a divine revelation that comes *to* human reason as a gift rather than arising *from* it as an accomplishment and the traditions that equate revelation with unaided human reason (if they even use the language of revelation at all), will have to fight it out on a level playing field. Within the conflict of interpretations, each side is an interpretation guided by a confluence of human traditions whose claims either to be the voice of God or to be the voice of Reason are anything but self-evident in any sense beyond being axiomatic for a particular group of believers.[31] In the present case, Spinoza's scientific naturalism is anything but a neutral, objective criterion by which to settle such a debate. It is one of the faiths in dispute.

In other words, the metaphysical criteria that guide the hermeneutical practices of mere monotheism and religion within the limits of reason alone are themselves not only in dispute but at the very heart of the dispute. What we might call the Primal Presuppositions of the two broad traditions of biblical interpretation do not cease to be just that, presuppositions embedded in historical traditions, simply by taking on a foundational role for the practices that presuppose them. The presupposed criteria are themselves in need of justification, and it is anything but clear that any justifications offered by either side will be unconditioned by tradition borne presuppositions themselves.[32] So it is a bit misleading to speak of the conflict between faith and reason; it is rather the conflict between two faiths, faith in some particular revelation and faith in some particular version of reason.

J. Samuel Preuss nicely summarizes the thrust of Spinoza's book in his own title *Spinoza and the Irrelevance of Biblical Authority*. Spinoza does not think the bible is without interest; if we happen to be interested, we learn a lot about the ancient Hebrews and the early Christians and meet some very interesting characters in the process, perhaps as interesting as Achilles, Lear, and Raskolnikov. What the Bible lacks is authority.

We must distinguish questions of meaning and truth here. When it comes to meaning, the biblical text is the final authority, as we have seen above in relation to Spinoza's version of the *sola scriptura* principle. We might say that he is a moderate hermeneutical textualist. It is at the level of truth, or theoretical and practical normativity, that the Bible is irrelevant as an authority. This is because it is simply the product of those who operate at the level of the common people in a cognitive domain shot through with error. In other words, the Bible may be of literary and historical interest, but when it comes to truth about God, the world, and ourselves, it needs to be corrected by outright denial and especially by systematic reinterpretation.[33] Such views, with or usually without reference to Spinoza, are widespread in biblical scholarship and theology today, which is why Spinoza's book is not merely of historical interest.

Spinoza softens this hard judgment somewhat by acknowledging that the Bible contains some good practical instruction. In this respect, it can be useful to the common people who are only able to operate at its level. But he makes this claim in two puzzling ways. First, he repeatedly says that the Bible teaches nothing about God but only about morality in the broad sense of piety and obedience (*TPT*, Pref., 9–10; 2, 38; 7, 102; 11, 160; 14, 179–83; 15, 186 and 190–91). According to his own hermeneutics this cannot refer to the true sense or meaning of the biblical writers; for they clearly have a lot to say about the nature of God as a personal agent and speaker and thus about God as just and loving, about God's actions in human history, and about divine speech acts including covenantal promises and commands. It is precisely because Spinoza recognizes such teaching in the Bible that he appeals to reason as a criterion by which to reject or reinterpret them.

So perhaps he means that it is (only) with regard to morality in the sense of piety and obedience (what we might call the realm of practical unreason) that we (even the intellectual elite?) might find benefit in the Bible. Spinoza has not argued that the lowest level(s) of knowing produce nothing but error, only that they are highly prone to error in multiple ways (as sketched above). So it might be that in keeping with the adage that a broken watch tells the right time twice a day, he is pointing to the region where biblical meaning conveys genuine truth (along with plenty of superstition and delusion that needs to be purged). He concludes "that the authority of the prophets carries weight only in moral questions and with regard to true virtue, and that for the rest their opinions matter very little to us" (*TPT*, Pref., 9).

But here we come to a second puzzlement. Spinoza regularly summarizes biblical moral teaching in terms of justice and charity (*TPT*, Pref., 10; 7, 111; 13, 174–77; 14, 178, and 182–85; 15, 192; 19, 239). That would be hard to contest. But his own philosophical ethics barely mentions these.[34] Its focus is rather on the Hellenistic theme of mental tranquility, the *ataraxia* and *apatheia* of the Stoics, Epicureans, and Skeptics. It is far more concerned with my relation to nature and its necessity than to my neighbor.

So we don't have a significant overlap between biblical and philosophical virtue in spite of initial impressions. If Kant's moral philosophy reverberates with Jewish/Christian overtones,[35] the same cannot be said of Spinoza's. Biblical morality is not to be equated with superstition and delusion. It is the point at which the common people are helped more than harmed by their reliance on biblical authority. But their morality and philosophical virtue remain poles apart. The common people and the philosophical elite are like east and west: never the twain shall meet.

Perhaps this should not puzzle us after all. In biblical contexts there is a tight relation between theology as the metaphysics of God and ethics as the norms for human behavior. The same is true for Spinoza.[36] And since his theology is radically different from that of mere monotheism, it should not surprise us that it should issue in a very different ideal for human life.[37]

Spinoza is arguing for the political right to make biblical authority irrelevant by rejecting some of its teachings and reinterpreting others. In many parts of the world today such freedom to speak and to publish according to one's own beliefs is taken for granted. So we look to Spinoza with gratitude for being a founding father of a freedom we highly prize. More specifically, in the field of biblical interpretation, there are many, across the theological spectrum, who are grateful for his insistence on a grammatico-historical hermeneutic: find the original meaning of Scripture solely from the text and its linguistic and historical context.

Of course, both at the level of meaning and of truth his specific conclusions will be debatable and debated, like those of any other scholar. But there is one fundamental thesis that runs through both the *Ethics* and the *Treatise* that should be rejected both by those who are in general sympathetic with his readings and by those who are not. It is the claim that his work is the product of autonomous reason. This would mean that his natural powers, unaided and unconditioned by anything that comes to them from outside of those powers, is the sole source of his ideas. Since the natural light of reason is alleged to be universal, contamination by particular presuppositions would put paid to the assertion of autonomy. Autonomous thinking is not, to quote Hegel from another context, "its own time apprehended in thoughts."[38] It is ahistorically presuppositionless, without prejudice in either the pejorative sense or the neutral, hermeneutical sense of a prejudgment or paradigm that functions as the a priori condition of a particular theory or practice.[39]

Spinoza tells us, in effect, "They have prejudices; I do not." "They" are both the common people and the prophets who do not rise above them for two reasons: their distinctive genius is that of imagination rather than intellect, and they accommodate themselves to the common people in order to be taken seriously (*TPT*, Pref. 5–6; 2, 30 and 33; 6, 91; 11, 162). This means that the biblical texts are children of their time, dependent on whatever opinions and traditions prevailed at the time of their writing and redacting.

But religion within the limits of reason alone will have to be presuppositionless both at the level of meaning and at the level of truth. Regarding the former, Spinoza writes, "I resolved in all seriousness to make a fresh examination of Scripture with a free and unprejudiced mind, and to assert nothing about it, and to accept nothing as its teaching, which I did not quite clearly derive from it" (*TPT*, Pref., 9). As we have seen, this is his version of *sola scriptura*. Neither the appeal to reason (as with Maimonides and Meyer) nor the appeal to theological tradition (whether explicit or implicit) should control one's exegesis. As stated here, this rule is an ideal, a norm to which he commits himself. Of course, like any other scholar, he subsequently writes as if he has lived up to its requirements.

More problematic is the claim that his writings are neutral and objective in the sense of presuppositionless when it comes to truth, which he has sharply separated from biblical meaning or sense. We have seen that his scientific naturalism, that he elevates into a metaphysics, is constantly presupposed whenever questions of truth arise. Although he fails to follow Spinoza in sharply distinguishing questions of authorial meaning and philosophical/theological truth, Jonathan Israel, our translator and editor, makes the point.

> While his emphatic rejection of all *a priori* assumptions about its revealed status and his rigorous linguistic and historical empiricism are undoubtedly key features of Spinoza's Bible criticism, it is nevertheless incorrect to infer from this that his method was, as has been claimed, basically a "bottom-up, inductive approach . . ." or maintain that "Spinoza wants to start not with general presuppositions, whether theological or philosophical dogma, but with particulars and facts—with history—and then work his way up to broader generalizations. . . ." In other words, he begins with lots of prejudgments about the real meaning of texts.[40]

As a critique of Spinoza's theory and practice of biblical meaning, this critique strikes me as missing its target. The grammatico-historical hermeneutic he practices (however well) is neutral with regard to the metaphysical opposition of scientific naturalism and mere monotheism. Scholars on both sides of that fence can practice such exegesis in good conscience. The place where

Spinoza's scientific naturalism provides him with "lots of prejudgments" is with questions of truth.

Israel makes this point, but confuses things in doing so. He speaks misleadingly when he links his critique to "the real meaning of texts." His real target is not texts as bearers of authorial meaning but texts as bearers of authoritative truth. This becomes clear when he argues that if Spinoza's thought was as presuppositionless as he claims,

> the result would certainly have been a complete inability... to envisage and treat history as a purely natural process devoid of supernatural forces.... Far from strictly eschewing 'general presuppositions,' Spinoza's text criticism, then, was firmly anchored in his post-Cartesian metaphysics without which his novel conception of history as something shaped exclusively by natural forces would certainly have been inconceivable. Spinoza's philosophical system and his austerely empirical conception of text criticism and experimental science are, in fact, wholly inseparable.[41]

Given Spinoza's emphatic distinction between questions of meaning and truth, I think Israel's last sentence is just plain wrong. I see no reason why grammatico-historical exegesis cannot be practiced within the framework of biblical monotheism. Moreover, I think the world of scientific naturalism can be "envisaged" and "conceived" by those who do not espouse it. But it is surely true that Spinoza's "post-Cartesian metaphysics" is the presupposition of his view of "history as something shaped exclusively natural forces." When it comes to questions of truth, the exclusiveness of natural forces precludes the reality of a personal God, so Spinoza dramatically reinterprets this notion; it precludes the possibility of miracles, so Spinoza flatly rejects them; and it precludes the possibility of revelation in the sense of God speaking words of promise and command to particular people at particular times, so Spinoza reinterprets revelation (prophecy) by denying it to the biblical prophets. It is philosophers and not prophets who speak divine truth.

Nietzsche loved Spinoza and delighted in discovering him.[42] Among the reasons he might have included in his list is the way Spinoza's illustrates his perspectivism. So far from occupying the "view from nowhere," Spinoza speaks from a very particular perspective. Conditioned by the personal and historical factors that constituted that perspective, Spinoza's thought illustrates the impossibility of the autonomy project. The word we might speak here in praise of heteronomy is simply this: it is inevitable.

Notes

1. Dietrich Bonhoeffer would be sympathetic to the political point, but not the theological point. As Kevin Hart puts it, where theological claims become "mistakenly embedded in social structures, generating unfair privileges, Christian ethics needs the correction associated with the Enlightenment insistence 'on the equal dignity of all people as ethical beings' (*E*, 374), while remaining wary of the Enlightenment's tendency to figure human reason as an abstract principle that 'dissolves and undermines all particular content' (*E*, 374)." *Kingdoms of God* (Bloomington: Indiana University Press, 2014), pp. 109–110. The interior quotations from Bonhoeffer are from *Ethics* (vol. 6 in *Dietrich Bonhoeffer's Works*), ed. Clifford Green (Minneapolis, MN: Fortress Press, 2005).

2. For the document in which "we ban, cut off, curse and anathemize Baruch de Espinoza . . . with all the curses written in the Torah," see Yirmiyahu Yovel, *Spinoza and Other Heretics: The Marrano of Reason* (Princeton, NJ: Princeton University Press, 1989), p. 3.

3. Feuer, *Spinoza and the Rise of Liberalism*, p. 65. Cf. pp. 80–81, 101, 104; and *Spinoza's Theological Treatise*, trans. with an interpretive essay by Martin D. Yaffe (Newburyport, MA: Focus Publishing, 2004), p. 267: "Spinoza's *Theologico-Political Treatise* (1670) is the philosophical founding document of both modern liberal democracy and modern biblical criticism." Other helpful treatments of Spinoza's politics include Steven B. Smith, *Spinoza, Liberalism, and the Question of Jewish Identity* (New Haven, CT: Yale University Press, 1997); and Yovel, *Spinoza and Other Heretics*.

4. See previous note.

5. John Calvin, *Institutes of the Christian Religion*, ed. John T. McNeill (Philadelphia: Westminster Press, 1960), 1.7.Title. Cf. 1.7.4, 2.5.5, and 3.1.1.

6. Calvin, *Institutes*, 4.14.10. The *Westminster Confession*, I, 5, summarizes the Calvinist teaching. "We may be moved and induced by the testimony of the Church to an high and reverent esteem of the Holy Scripture . . . yet, notwithstanding, our full persuasion and assurance of the infallible truth, and divine authority thereof, is from the inward work of the Holy Spirit, bearing witness by and with the Word in our hearts."

7. Martin Luther, *The Magnificat*, in *Luther's Works*, vol. 21, ed. Jaroslav Pelikan (St. Louis, MO: Concordia, 1956), p. 299; emphasis added. This is the same spirit who illumined the prophets of old. Thus "David shows an art and a wisdom that is above the wisdom of the Decalog, a truly heavenly wisdom, which is neither taught by the Law nor imagined or understood by reason without the Holy Spirit. . . . This is the general practice of reason that has been deprived of the Word and the Spirit. It wants to flee from God." *Psalm 51*, ed. Jaroslav Pelikan, in *Luther's Works*, vol. 12 (St. Louis, MO: Concordia, 1955), pp. 314, 404. Luther's sustained polemic against human reason unillumined by biblical faith is especially strong in his *Lectures on Galatians: 1535*, in *Luther's Works*, vols. 26–27, ed. Jaroslav Pelikan (St. Louis, MO: Concordia, 1963–1964).

8. It will become clear that so far from believing that we gain "all our knowledge . . . of spiritual matters from Scripture alone," he explicitly denies it. We have just seen him claim that reason is the only source of truth about the kinds of things Paul and subsequent theologians discuss. Spinoza speaks carelessly here.

9. Spinoza uses 'prophets' not in the narrow sense in which the Hebrew Bible is divided into three parts: the law, the prophets, and the writings. He uses it to signify the biblical authors of both the Old and New Testament and, presumably, those whose teachings were written up by others as authoritative.

10. Nicholas Wolterstorff, *Divine Discourse: Philosophical Reflections on the Claim that God Speaks* (New York: Cambridge University Press, 1995), p. 93. On the psychologism that seeks the meaning of texts in those inner demons and angels, as espoused by Schleiermacher and Dilthey, see my discussion in *Whose Community? Which Interpretation?* (Grand Rapids, MI: Baker Academic, 2009), chap. 2.

11. Craig L. Blomberg, "The Historical-Critical/Grammatical View," in *Biblical Hermeneutics: Five Views*, ed. Stanley E. Porter and Beth M. Stovell (Downers Grove, IL: IVP Academic, 2012), p. 27.

12. See, for example, the classic essay "The Intentional Fallacy" by William K. Wimsatt and Monroe C. Beardsley, in *The Verbal Icon: Studies in the Meaning of Poetry* (Lexington: University of Kentucky Press, 1954), pp. 3–18.

13. Maimonides's hermeneutic might bring to mind the Alexandrian tradition (Clement and Origin in the context of Philo) of allegorical or "spiritual" interpretation of the Bible. According to it at least some, and often the most important meanings of the biblical text do not arise from the author's intention but from what is already known from elsewhere. The difference is that this elsewhere is some other portion of Scripture (for example, interpreting the Old Testament in terms of the New). For a helpful discussion see Sandra M. Schneiders, "Scripture and Spirituality" in *Christian Spirituality: Origins to the Twelfth Century*, ed. Bernard McGinn, John Meyendorff, and Jean Leclercq (New York: Crossroad, 1988), pp. 1–20.

14. Steven Nadler, *A Book Forged in Hell: Spinoza's Scandalous Treatise and the Birth of the Secular Age* (Princeton, NJ: Princeton University Press, 2011), p. 123. Nadler, whose title comes from an early critique of *TPT*, discusses Meyer throughout his book, especially in chap. 6. J. Samuel Press devotes the second chapter of his *Spinoza and the Irrelevance of Biblical Authority* (New York: Cambridge University Press, 2001) to Meyer's "new hermeneutic." See *TPT*, p. 271n40.

15. Emphasis added. Note the slippage from "reason" to "our reason or our preconceived opinions," which urgently poses the question, Who are we? Spinoza insists that the minds of the prophets are not the mind of God (*TPT*, 12, 168). The underlying assumption here is that "we" somehow have a higher standing, an assumption made explicit elsewhere. Cf. 15, 191.

16. Cf. *TPT*, 15, 187–88; emphasis added. "It is indeed true that Scripture must be explained by Scripture, so long as we are only deriving the sense of the passages and the meaning of the prophets, but after we have arrived at the true sense, we must necessarily use *our* judgment and reason before giving assent to it." Where Israel says "preconceptions," the translations of Elwes, Curley, and Yaffe say "prejudices." This need not have the sense of an irrational bias; it can have the Gadamerian sense of an a priori assumption that shapes thought, for better or for worse, without critical scrutiny. Thus traditions are prejudices, pre-judgments we bring with us to experience more than we derive them from experience. See chap. 1 at note 56.

17. David Tracy writes, "On historical grounds, classics are simply those texts that have helped found or form a particular culture. On more explicitly hermeneutical grounds, classics are those texts that bear an excess and permanence of meaning, yet always resist definitive interpretation." *Plurality and Ambiguity: Hermeneutics, Religion, Hope* (San Francisco: Harper & Row, 1987), p. 12. Cf. Gadamer's discussion of the classical in *Truth and Method*, 2nd rev. ed., trans. Joel Weinsheimer and Donald G. Marshall (New York: Crossroad, 1989; New York: Continuum, 2004), pp. 285–90 and 286–91, respectively.

18. For a philosophical analysis of this double presupposition, common to all forms of what I've been calling mere theism, see Wolterstorff, *Divine Discourse*.

19. See, for example, Harold Bloom's treatment of the Yahwist portions of the Pentateuch. *The Book of J: Translated from the Hebrew by David Rosenberg; Interpreted by Harold Bloom* (New York: Grove Press, 1990). Bloom puts this writer, whom he takes to be a woman, on a par with Homer, Shakespeare, and Tolstoy.

20. See the typical quotation in the previous paragraph.

21. For Spinoza's dependence upon and revision of scholastic thought, see Harry Austryn Wolfson, *The Philosophy of Spinoza* (New York: Meridan Books, 1958). See II, 155–158, on the difference between the second and third kinds of knowledge.

22. Plato, *Symposium* 210e–211e.

23. So it is entirely appropriate that Jonathan Bennett's discussion of the third kind of knowing immediately leads into his discussion of the intellectual love of God. *A Study of Spinoza's Ethics* (Indianapolis, IN: Hackett, 1984), pp. 364–72.

24. "From the third kind of knowledge there necessarily arises the intellectual love of God" ($E5$ P32 C).

25. Part V is entitled, "Of the Power of the Intellect, or of Human Freedom."

26. Max Weber writes, "The puritan wanted to work in a calling; we are forced to do so." The "tremendous cosmos of the modern economic order" is an "iron cage" in which "material goods have gained an increasing and finally an inexorable power over the lives of men as at no previous period in history." It is a "mechanized petrifaction" of which it can be said, "this nullity imagines that it has attained a level of civilization never before achieved." Here it is society rather than nature that issues in the blind necessity that governs our lives. We would be shocked and Weber would be ridiculed if he were to speak of an intellectual love of capitalism born of sociological knowledge. *The Protestant Ethic and the Spirit of Capitalism*, trans. Talcott Parsons (New York: Charles Scribner's Sons, 1958), pp. 181–82. Once again, the analogy is imperfect, but, I think, illuminating.

27. Daniel Goleman, *Emotional Intelligence: Why It Can Matter More Than IQ* (New York: Bantam Books, 1995).

28. See, especially, the work of Martha Nussbaum in *Upheavals of Thought: The Intelligence of Emotions* (New York: Cambridge University Press, 2001), against the background of *The Fragility of Goodness: Luck and Ethics in Greek Tragedy and Philosophy* (New York: Cambridge University Press, 1986) and *The Therapy of Desire: Theory and Practice in Hellenistic Ethics* (Princeton, NJ: Princeton University Press, 1994). The subtitle of the first of these suggests that especially for the Stoics, with whom we might confuse Spinoza, the path between reason and emotion is not a one-way street.

29. See Alasdair MacIntyre, *After Virtue* (Notre Dame, IN: University of Notre Dame Press, 1981) A second edition, published in 1985, is also vailable from Notre Dame Press; John J. Davenport, *Narrative Identity, Autonomy, and Mortality* (New York: Routledge, 2012); Stanley Hauerwas and L. Gregory Jones, eds., *Why Narrative? Readings in Narrative Theology* (Grand Rapids, MI: Eerdmans, 1989); and Eleonore Stump, *Wandering in Darkness: Narrative and the Problem of Suffering* (New York: Oxford University Press, 2012).

30. See, for example, Nussbaum, *Upheavals of Thought*; Stanley Cavell, *Disowning Knowledge: In Seven Plays of Shakespeare*, updated ed. (New York: Cambridge University Press, 2007), including essays from *Must We Mean What We Say* (1969 and 1976) and *The Claim of Reason* (1979). For the very philosophically astute literary critic Gerald Bruns, "In modern writing, philosophy and poetry fold into one another." From the back cover of *On the Anarchy of Poetry and Philosophy: A Guide for the Unruly* (New York: Fordham University Press, 2006).

31. Any claim can become subjectively self-evident to an individual or group for whom it needs no proof and is beyond dispute. But this kind of we-hold-these-truths-to-be-self-evident status is relative to particular individuals or groups and is no certain sign of truth. Jefferson's self-evidence did not extend to slaves, and for Nazis it was self-evident that it was Jews who did not have the right to life, liberty, and the pursuit of happiness.

32. John D. Caputo makes this typically postmodern point about the dependence of philosophical argument on presuppositions when he writes, "*There are no non-circular arguments against a world outside space and time, no arguments that do not proceed from the assumption that all being must be spatial and temporal* (emphasis in original)." *The Insistence of God* (Bloomington: Indiana University Press, 2013), p. 112.

33. For a shameless claim that it is the task of philosophy to "correct" theology by being the keeper of the categories used by the latter, see Martin Heidegger, "Phenomenology and Theology," in William McNeill, ed., *Pathmarks* (New York: Cambridge University Press, 1998), pp. 39–62.

34. See $E4$, appendixes 11 and 15.

35. John E. Hare writes that Kant "is still close enough to the Christian tradition to make use of its resources when he thinks he can." He speaks of "the Christian seriousness of Kant" in *The Moral Gap: Kantian Ethics, Human Limits, and God's Assistance* (Oxford: Clarendon, 1996), pp. 1 and 34.

36. In this respect, Karl Barth's *Church Dogmatics* is formally akin to the *Ethics*. He writes, "Ethics, so called, I regard as the doctrine of God's command and do not consider it right to treat it otherwise than as an integral part of dogmatics, or to produce a dogmatics which does not include it." *Church Dogmatics: The Doctrine of the Word of God*, trans. G. T. Thomson (Edinburgh: T & T Clark, 1936), I, 1, p. xiv.

37. Some of the virtues of Jewish and Christian thought, such as pity or compassion and repentance become vices for Spinoza. See *E4* P50 and P54.

38. Hegel, *Philosophy of Right*, trans. T. M. Knox (Oxford: Clarendon, 1942), Pref., p. 11.

39. The concept of a paradigm as an a priori frame of reference presupposed by rather than arising out of some form of inquiry has passed into general usage from Thomas Kuhn, *The Structure of Scientific Revolutions*, 2nd ed. (Chicago: University of Chicago Press, 1970). A paradigm shift is like a gestalt switch in which one's entire point of view is changed.

40. Jonathan Israel, introduction to *TPT*, pp. xiv–xv. Israel argues that Spinoza is far more Cartesian than Baconian. The interior quotations are from Preuss, *Spinoza and the Irrelevance of Biblical Authority*, pp. 160–61.

41. Israel, introduction to *TPT*, p. xv.

42. Friedrich Nietzsche, letter to Overbeck of July 30, 1881, in *The Portable Nietzsche*, ed. Walter Kaufmann (New York: Viking, 1954), p. 92.

4

KANT'S THEOLOGY

Kant developed his concept of autonomy first in a political context, as a plea for freedom of the press; then in the context of his moral philosophy, in both its executive and legislative dimensions; and finally, in his philosophy of religion, his contribution to the Enlightenment project in philosophy of religion that I call "religion within the limits of reason alone,"[1] borrowing the title of his "fourth Critique."

He makes a double claim about the relation of religion to morality. First, a moral agent "is in need neither of the idea of another being above him in order that he *recognize his duty* [legislative autonomy], nor, that he observe it, of an *incentive other than the law itself* [executive autonomy] . . . [morality] in no way needs religion . . . but is rather self-sufficient by virtue of pure practical reason." Just so we don't miss that he is affirming both legislative and executive autonomy, he repeats that "morality needs absolutely no material determining ground of the free power of choice, that is no end, either in order *to recognize what duty is or to impel its performance*" (R, 57, 6.3–4; emphasis added).[2]

Then, referring to his "moral argument' for the postulates of God and immortality in his second Critique, he makes a second claim. "Morality thus inevitably leads to religion, and through religion it extends itself to the idea of a mighty lawgiver outside the human being in whose will the final end (of the creation of the world) is what can and at the same [time, *zugleich*] ought to be the final human end" (R, 59–60, 6.6).[3] This end, of course, is the highest good, happiness in proportion to virtue, an idea that "rises out of morality and is not its foundation" (*R*, 58, 6.5).

Thus, when Kant says, "*Religion* is (subjectively considered) the recognition [*Erkentniss*] of all our duties as divine commands" (*R*, 177, 6.153–54)[4] and calls this a definition, he is not really defining religion as he understands it. For it is more than this, and essentially so. This notion corresponds to the idea of God as a moral lawgiver, but leaves out the part about hope and the highest good, precisely the point at which religion "extends" morality. Kant does not have a finite or perverse God who wills such a good, but either cannot or will not bring it about. According to the postulate, God is the moral governor of the world and, with the help of immortality, will bring it about that happiness will be proportionate to virtue.[5] "If morality recognizes in the holiness of its law an object worthy of the highest respect, at the level of religion it represents an object of *worship* in the highest cause that brings this law to fruition, and thus morality [not God?] appears in its majesty" (*R*, 60, 6.6–7).[6]

It is the idea of God as moral governor even more than the idea of God as moral lawgiver that takes us to the heart of Kant's religion.[7] Kant clearly thinks that this "extension" of morality into religion signifies something new and important. In a famous letter to Stäudlin written within weeks of the publication of *Religion*, he distinguishes the three basic philosophical questions: "(1) What can I know? (metaphysics). (2) What ought I to do? (moral philosophy). (3) What may I hope? (philosophy of religion)." He then adds a fourth question, "What is man?" and explains, "With the enclosed work, *Religion within the Limits* [*of Reason Alone*], I have tried to complete the third part of my plan."[8]

Morality concerns duty, while religion is about hope, and taken together, *Practical Reason* and *Religion*[9] extend morality into a transcendental philosophy of hope.[10] The moral life requires hope if it is not to collapse into Sisyphean futility. What are the conditions for the possibility of rational hope? That is already the question of "The Dialectic of Pure Practical Reason" (*CPrR*, bk. II). With the introduction of radical evil in *Religion*, the question of hope becomes even more central, more complex, and more urgent as well.

We can make the fourth question, What is man?, gender inclusive (Kant says *Mensch* and not *Mann*) and at the same time give it its existential thrust if we render it, Who am I? In that case Jean Valjean in the musical *Les Misérables* proves to be an interesting Kantian. Having served a long prison term and been released on parole, he has established a new identity as a factory owner and mayor of the town. In doing so, however, he has broken his parole.

His nemesis, Javert, is about to imprison another man whom he mistakes for Valjean. Letting that happen would, of course, leave Valjean free and clear. In the song "Who am I?" he struggles with this temptation. But in good Kantian fashion he cannot treat this innocent man as a means to his own freedom, so he gives himself up to Javert and ends his song

> Who am I?
> Who am I?
> I am Jean Valjean.[11]

He is the one who sees his duty and does it in spite of powerful inclination to the contrary.

Somehow, however, Valjean remains out of Javert's clutches long enough to visit Fantine on her death bed. A former worker in his factory who has been unjustly fired by his foreman and forced into prostitution, she is concerned for her young daughter Cosette. Out of a sense of responsibility and compassion, Valjean promises to care for her.

> But Fantine, I swear this on my life...
> [Cosette] shall live in my protection...
> Your child will want for nothing...
> And none will ever harm Cosette
> As long as I am living.

But the problem is obvious. Valjean is in no position to make such a promise. As soon as Javert catches up with him, he will be returned to prison and unable to care for Cosette. But his promise is more than the wish-fulfilling dream of the better life of which the young Cosette so hauntingly sings ("Castle on a Cloud"). It is an expression of hope.

Valjean has learned something about hope and in a Kantian sense: it is at once religious and integral to his moral life. Just before he fesses up to being Jean Valjean in "Who am I?," he sings

> My soul belongs to God, I know
> I made that bargain long ago
> He gave me hope, when hope was gone
> He gave me strength to journey on!

It is in this strength that he acknowledges, "I am Jean Valjean," and it is in this hope that he promises to care for Cosette.

We see something of Kant's primacy of practical reason at work in Valjean. His double answer to the question, Who am I? does not focus on theoretical, metaphysical knowledge but on the two questions that belong to practical reason, the moral and religious questions of duty and of hope. I am, he tells us in effect, the one who does my duty in the face of powerful inclination to the contrary; and on the basis of my faith in God I live in hope that happiness will somehow come to those who deserve it. To be sure, the question of immortality does not arise, for Valjean's hope is focused on this life. But his moral and religious life have an interestingly Kantian form.

For me the most interesting and important questions about Kant's religion begin with the question What religion does he present to us in his major texts? But before turning to that question, something must be said, briefly, in reply to two objections to speaking about Kant's religion at all.

The first is that however much Kant may want to speak of God as moral legislator and governor, he has himself cut himself off from such discourse. Such an argument would gain no credence if based solely on Kant's repudiation of the traditional proofs for the existence of God. For there is a great deal of religion, even theistic religion, that does not rely on such proofs. More serious is the claim that Kant's narrowly empiricist, virtually positivist account of knowledge renders meaningful God-talk impossible.[12] But such an argument overlooks the fact that Kant regularly insists that we can think what we cannot know. For example, "But though I cannot *know*, I can yet *think* freedom" (*CPR*, B xxviii; cf. B xxvi).

Moreover, with special reference to God, freedom, and immortality, he writes, "I have therefore found it necessary to deny *knowledge* in order to make room for *faith*" (*CPR*, B xxx). Because the critical philosophy undermines the kind of speculative dogmatism that gives rise to skepticism as the other side of the same coin, it is able to resist the kind of thinking that will "threaten to make the bounds of sensibility [and thus of knowledge as defined by the critical philosophy] coextensive with the real" (*CPR*, xxiv–xxv). Kant thinks that we can think meaningfully and, as we shall see, believe reasonably, beyond the limits of knowledge. By refusing to "make the bounds of sensibility coextensive with the real," Kant refuses to limit meaning and truth to the realm of "knowledge" as defined by the first Critique.

Second, there is the question whether Kant reduces religion to morality. Thus Denis Savage claims that

> it must be said that Kant's theory of radical evil presented in *Religion* contains nothing basically new as compared with his theory of moral good and evil presented in his ethical works, the *Foundations of the Metaphysics of Morals*,

the *Critique of Practical Reason,* and the *Metaphysics of Morals.* And this is as it should be, for the whole idea of the work *Religion within the Limits of Reason Alone* is to show that all statements of revealed religion, if they have any objective validity at all, are completely translatable—without remainder—into the concepts and expressions of rational ethics.[13]

But already in the second *Critique,* with the postulates of God and immortality we are beyond "rational ethics." It is as if Kant has been meditating on Psalm 49.

> We can never ransom ourselves,
> or deliver to God the price of our life ...
> In order to live for ever and ever
> and never see the grave.
> For we see that the wise die also ...
> Their graves shall be their homes for ever ...
> they are like the beasts that perish.
> Such is the way of those who foolishly trust in themselves,
> and the end of those who delight in their own words ...
> But God will ransom my life;
> he will snatch me from the grasp of death.[14]

Kant is closer to Aristotle than to Heidegger, so he speaks of happiness rather than being-toward-death. But in recognizing death and life after death as ontological limits to human happiness in this life, he moves beyond morality to a religion that affirms both the necessity and the actuality of divine help.[15]

Beyond this, with the introduction of radical evil in *Religion,* new "postulates" (rationally justified beliefs that do not qualify as knowledge) emerge.[16] It becomes possible to speak of Kant's religion as one of freedom and grace[17] and to say that "Kant is reflecting religiously on possible solutions to the problem of sin and the question of hope" (FJ, 65). It is as if Kant has been anticipating Vigilius Haufniensis's verdict on the limitation of ethics. "Ethics points to ideality as a task and assumes that everyman possesses the requisite conditions." It rests on "the presupposition that virtue can be realized [by unaided human effort]." "Sin, then, belongs to ethics only insofar as upon this concept it is shipwrecked with the aid of repentance."[18] Accordingly, Kant will reflect on the need for and nature of repentance. So, instead of speaking of Kant's reduction of religion to morality we might "instead read *Religion* as *raising* morality to the level of religion."[19]

Actually, we might better stick with Kant's own language of "extending" morality to religion rather than "raising," since he retains a powerful hegemony for morality over religion, a limiting authority that expresses whatever truth there is in the reduction thesis. He thus keeps morality above religion in two ways.

First, in the area of practice, there is the reduction of God-pleasing behavior to obeying the moral law. "*Apart from a good life-conduct, anything which the human being supposes that he can do to become well-pleasing to God is mere religious delusion and counterfeit service of God*" (R, 190, 6.170; cf. CF, 263, 7.37). This is a decisive departure from mere Christianity (with which Kant is engaging here), so it is both surprising and disappointing that Kant treats this principle as an axiom, "a principle requiring no proof." It is anything but the self-evident product of an allegedly universal reason.

Later, he repeats this principle and gets more specific. "The true (moral) service of God [*Dienst Gottes*] . . . can consist only in the disposition of obedience to all true duties as divine commands, not in actions determined exclusively for God." But "through a *delusion* which creeps upon us, [such actions are] easily taken for the *service of God* [*Gottesdienst*] itself and is also commonly given this name" (R, 208, 6.192).[20]

In the following pages, which bring *Religion* to a close, he specifies four examples of such ecclesial or private piety: private prayer, church-going, baptism, and communion (R, 208–15, 6.192–202). Kant refers to these four activities as "*means of grace*." But when he gets specific about what this means, he cheats. Such activity, "when not undertaken in a purely moral spirit but as a means *in itself* capable of propitiation God and thus, through him, of satisfying all our wishes, is a *fetish-faith*" (R, 209, 6.193). I call this cheating because the idea of actions "well-pleasing to God" or "determined exclusively for God" (such as prayers of praise and thanksgiving) need not have any propitiating (atoning) value, much less the wish fulfilling power to which Kant alludes.[21] In the absence of a good argument, Kant gives us a very bad, "straw man" argument. Kant regularly takes advantage of his (largely) Lutheran audience by asserting that no form of love for or duty to God could be thought of as intrinsically pleasing to God unless it (ironically) were conceived as a means of earning our salvation by good works.

The good Lutheran (among others) knows that such "good works" as the four "means of grace" just mentioned do not earn or merit divine forgiveness, justification, reconciliation, and so forth, and certainly do not guarantee that I will soon be able to afford that Jaguar or get *her* to fall in love with me. But that does not keep them from being "well-pleasing to God" and thus, quite possibly, among the "good works" that God commands. After all, Jesus found the law to be summarized in two commands, not just one: love God and love your neighbor.[22] Nor did he reduce the former to the latter by denying to the love of God independent and intrinsic value, making it merely instrumental, either a mere means to the latter or a delusional fetish.

The *sursum corda* has been part of the eucharistic liturgy of Christian churches since at least the third century and is widely used today throughout what I've been calling "mere Christianity," Orthodox, Roman Catholic, and Protestant. It states, "It is right to give [God] thanks and praise," and then expands this thought, "It is a right, and a good and joyful thing, always and everywhere to give thanks to you, Father Almighty, Creator of heaven and earth."[23] Kant tells us that this is a "delusional fetish" unless we see the value of thankful praise to God as merely of instrumental and not intrinsic value, as a means to the end of better obeying the categorical imperative so long as we are not yet fully rational. Kant is entitled to this view, but not to the claim that his religion is compatible with Christianity. 'Delusion' is a strong word, but it seems to me that Kant is self-deceived in making such a claim.

Second, in the theoretical realm (not What can I know? but What may I rationally believe?), there is the reduction of rational belief (Kantian faith) to what can be justified in terms of moral philosophy, to which Kant gives complete hermeneutical hegemony. As we will see in some detail, theology is the handmaid of moral philosophy both as natural (the postulates of the second Critique) and as revealed (the "postulates" that emerge from biblical contexts in *Religion*).[24] Biblical theologians may ask the question, What does the Bible teach? and the pastors they train may preach and teach the answers to this question in the churches. But this is only a concession to human weakness. This form of revealed religion is in principle both necessary insofar as we are less than fully rational and unnecessary insofar as we grow up into rational adulthood. So it is in principle dispensable. Just to the degree that we have emerged from our pre-enlightened, "self-incurred minority,"[25] we will reinterpret the Bible in persuasive redefinitions so that it only either teaches rational morality itself or serves as a "vehicle" thereto, a means to that end.

Treating Kant as an evidentialist in the tradition of classical foundationalism,[26] Wolterstorff puts it this way:

> Kant was convinced that *morality* is the only area of human existence in which there is any hope of finding the adequate evidence [for religious belief]. Adequate reasons for religious beliefs will always prove to be moral principles.

> It would be a serious mistake to say of Kant that he tried to *reduce* religion to morality. What he tried to do, rather, was show that [only] morality provides us with *reasons* for holding certain central religious beliefs, thus making us *justified* in holding them.²⁷

I am not sure Kant's transcendental form of argument (What are the necessary conditions for the possibility of hope?) fits very well into what Wolterstorff calls the evidentialist/classical foundationalist model, but the key point is clear enough. Without entirely reducing religion to morality, Kant makes moral philosophy the ultimate criterion of religious belief. In a strange irony, Kant replaces political censorship with philosophical censorship. Philosophy becomes the *magisterium*, the final authority, not over what may be printed, but over what we should believe. This presupposes not only the primacy of reason over faith, but also that philosophy is the voice of Reason.

But whose philosophy? Which Reason? As we are in the process of seeing, Spinoza, Kant, and Hegel (among many others) present their philosophies as the voice of universal Reason. But they are mutually incompatible, and their claims look more like those of, say, Judaism, Christianity, and Islam to be the true religion. When Kant says that religion within the limits of reason alone will never be sectarian (*CF*, 273, 7:49–50) he betrays a serious blind spot to the variety of quite particular versions of that project, each claiming a grounding free of particular presuppositions.

Clearer vision shows that we are in what Ricoeur calls "the conflict of interpretations" where interpretation always takes place within a hermeneutical circle defined by presuppositions that can be located historically and culturally.²⁸ We are in Gadamer's world in which thought is always relative to prejudices (pre-judgements, presuppositions, a priori anticipations) that are borne by specific traditions that are both particular and contingent rather than universal and necessary.²⁹ In relation to such traditions, "Reason" itself is heteronomous.

Despland finds Kant's "praise of Enlightenment, making of an admittedly admirable but local and dated movement among a small elite, the sole bearer of a universal moral imperative," to be "ridiculous" and is "tempted to meet [it] only with laughter and not bother with refutation."³⁰ With particular reference to Kant, Horkheimer and Adorno write, "The difficulties in the concept of reason caused by the fact that its subjects, the possessors of that very reason, contradict one another, are concealed by the apparent clarity of the judgments of the Western Enlightenment."³¹

Given these caveats, I find it hard to see why anyone would want to deny that in Kant we find "some form of theological affirmation."[32] But that is not a very bold claim. We want to know more specifically what form of religion goes beyond and thus "extends" morality while staying "within the limits of [Kantian] reason alone."

In giving their detailed response to this exegetical question, Firestone and Jacobs focus on two subsidiary, evaluative questions: Is Kant's religion internally coherent and is it compatible with the critical philosophy as a whole but especially as developed in the first Critique?[33] They claim he has good replies to those who find "conundrums" (Wolterstorff) or "wobbles" (Michalson) in his theology. In answering the exegetical question, What kind of religion does Kant affirm? I shall seek to answer two quite different evaluative questions. They remain even if, as I am inclined to doubt, Firestone and Jacobs should prevail over Wolterstorff and Michalson: What is the nature of the reason within whose limits Kant seeks to keep religion, and what is the significance of those limits?

I have just indicated briefly my answer to these two questions. On these points Kant makes two claims he cannot sustain. The reason to which he appeals is quite particular and not universal[34], and the religion that stays within the bounds of this reason is not compatible with the Christian faith but an alternative and a rival to it (as well as to the philosophical theologies of Spinoza and Hegel).[35] For better or for worse, Christianity is a religion of heteronomy rather than autonomy. In putting in a good word for heteronomy I do not claim to validate the theoretical and practical claims of Christianity (or other forms of Abrahamic monotheism, equally heteronomous). I only hope to keep open the space within which Christianity can make its claims without a priori assumptions that beg the question against it, namely that it cannot make universal claims because it does not rest on universal reason.

My short answer to the exegetical question is that Kant is a deist. Charles Taylor describes him as "on the verge of deism."[36] So perhaps I should hedge my bets a bit and say he is a certain kind of deist, which inevitably poses the question, What kind? 'Deism,' like 'romanticism,' 'liberalism,' and 'baroque,' signifies a "family resemblance" among various modes of thought and/or action rather than a single, univocal essence. There is a debate over whether Kant should be numbered among the deists.[37] I am less interested in taking sides than in using various meanings of the term heuristically to see to what degree they do or do not illuminate Kant's thought. Byrne seems to me fully justified in saying that Kant is "closer to eighteenth century deism than he is to orthodox Christianity."³⁸ I would go farther and say that it is illuminating to call Kant a deist (with qualifications) but misleading to call him a Christian thinker, in spite of his use of Christian language. We have already seen that Spinoza is in a very standard sense an atheist in spite of his profuse use of God talk. Everything depends on how the terms are persuasively redefined.

Ironically, the sense of 'deism' that doesn't fit Kant at all is the sense he gives to the term. It is a subdivision of *theologia rationalis*, for which knowledge of God is derived solely from reason and not from revelation. So far so good. But it further limits itself to "transcendental concepts (*ens originarium*, [*ens*] *realissimum, ens entium*)."³⁹ In other words it uses only abstract, impersonal, metaphysical language for speaking about God and thus God is "a being which possesses all reality, but which we are unable to determine in any more specific fashion" (*CPR*, A 631 = B 659). By contrast, those Kant calls theists employ concepts taken from the nature of the soul and affirm "a concept of the original being as a supreme intelligence" and thus one with "understanding and freedom." For the deist God is a *"cause of the world,"* while for the theist God is "the *Author of the world*" (*CPR*, A631–32 = B659–60). The "theistic" concept of God that Kant works with in the first Critique is that of a highest, purposive intelligence (A 583n, 670, 672–73, 685–87 = B 611n., 698, 700–701, 713–15; cf. FJ, 3). Taken together, the abstract and concrete, impersonal and personal concepts of God represent "a mere *ideal*, [but] it is yet *an ideal without a flaw*, a concept which completes and crowns the whole of human knowledge. Its objective reality cannot indeed be proved, but also cannot be disproved, by merely speculative reason." This leaves Kant free to hope for "a moral theology that can make good this deficiency" (*CPR*, 641 = B 669).⁴⁰

Kant's deist sounds a lot like Spinoza, and it is perhaps with him in mind that Kant writes:

> Since we are wont to understand by the concept of God not merely an eternal nature that works blindly, as the root-source of all things, but a supreme being who through understanding and freedom is the Author of all things; and since it is in this sense only that the concept interests us, we could strictly speaking, deny to the *deist* any belief in God.... However... it is less harsh and more just to say that the *deist* believes in a *God*, the *theist* in a *living God*. (*CPR*, A 632–33 = B 660–61; cf. A625 = B653 and *LPR* 386, 28:1047)

It is clear that Kant is not a deist in his own sense, which in any event is closer to what we would call pantheism or scientific naturalism, nor do contemporary scholars who call Kant a deist have this meaning in mind. As an "Author" who unites intelligence with freedom, Kant's God is an agent and not merely a cause.[41] So he might have said "personal God" rather than "living God"; for agency in the sense of intentional, voluntary causation is a decisive mark of personhood.[42] The other key marker, it seems to me, is a special case of agency, the ability to perform speech acts.

There is another sense of 'deism' that makes it precisely a theory about the scope of divine agency. God is the Creator of the world, the giver of the moral law (through reason),[43] and the judge who upholds that law in the life to come. Thinking in terms of ideal types, we can say that a deist is one who sees God as an intelligent, purposive agent but limits that agency to the beginning and end of all things. God does not "interfere" as an agent or speaker within our experience of either nature or history. For the creation of the world is not an event within either nature or history but the presupposition of both; the giving of the moral law through reason is, so to speak, simultaneous with creation (no need for Moses, or Jesus, or Mohammed, since the natural law is eternal and given through reason at creation); and the last judgment at which happiness and virtue are made to coincide is once again not an event within either nature or history.[44]

This exclusion of divine agency from the time between the Garden of Eden and the New Jerusalem, to use biblical imagery, is what distinguishes the deist from the theist as I will be using the terms. We can speak of the deism of restricted divine agency. For the deist that agency is wholly transcendent to the worlds of our experience here and now, while for the theist that agency is both transcendent and immanent. As transcendent it is not reducible to the ordinary, everyday causation we experience in nature and history[45]; but as immanent it occurs from time to time within those realms and is a sign that God's presence is not restricted to either once upon a time or the sweet bye and bye.

Another difference is the desire of deists to forget their dependence on a particular tradition of special revelation. As N. T. Wright writes, "the idea of the one God as 'judge' grows directly out of the ancient Israelite perception of this God as 'creator.' This particular God has a *responsibility* to sort out the mess in his creation, to call it to account, to set everything right. He also has the *power* and authority to do so in a way that no other being has."[46] The deist strategy is to assimilate the biblical doctrine of God as creator and judge to the diagrams Socrates draws for the slave boy in Plato's *Meno*. In both cases, they are but occasions or triggers that help us to "remember" what we already know without their help. This epistemic theme of knowledge as recollection in the deism I'm sketching will be central in our next chapter, where I will suggest a third definition of deism for use in analyzing Kant's religion, one we can call epistemic deism.

This restriction of divine agency can be expressed in terms of the watchmaker God. In 1802 William Paley, drawing on Joseph Butler, presented a form of the teleological or design argument for the existence of God using the analogy of a watchmaker.[47] Just as one seeing the intricate structure of a watch infers a watchmaker as its intelligent designer, so one infers God as the creator of the amazingly complex world. My typical deist is deeply impressed by this argument and can put the restriction of divine agency this way: a finite and imperfect watch maker might have to repair or merely rewind the watch from time to time, but an infinite and perfect creator of the world would not have to "interfere" in nature (miracles) or history (revelation) to fix it up or to keep it going.

Two comments. First, the inherent pluralism of reason is knocking at the door once again. For the Humean, Kantian, and Darwinian versions of reason, the design argument isn't the sound, theoretical proof of God's reality it was taken to be. The handwriting on the wall for the Enlightenment project in the philosophy of religion is even shorter than that for Belshazzar.[48] It consists of only two words: whose "reason"?

Second, Hume famously questions whether, even if some sort of design argument were legitimate, it is strong enough to warrant belief in an infinite and perfect God. Here it looks as if the deist who draws on Paley's argument, both to ground God's reality and the restriction of divine agency on the basis of universal reason, is in bad faith, managing not to notice a dependence on biblical revelation and theological tradition that is not too hard to see. These two comments have a bearing on Kant; but it is only indirect, since he does not ground his theology on a watchmaker argument for God.

Although he is tremendously impressed with the teleological argument for God's reality, Kant is not a watchmaker deist. That line of thinking is for him at best a hypothesis of theoretical reason that (1) cannot be proved, (2) cannot be disproved, and (3) can be given a regulative use that guides inquiry but does not provide warrant for theoretical belief.[49] He is also sensitive to Hume's point that the designer God is not yet the *"living"* God that is religiously significant.

But in the second Critique Kant finds another basis for affirming a God who is an agent and not merely a cause, and he is the kind of deist who places that agency (largely, if not entirely) outside of human experience and history. So for him the idea of an absentee landlord is perhaps a better metaphor than that of a watchmaker. In the famous postulates of immortality and God the focus is on God as Judge and therefore on the life to come, but they include God as Creator as well, if in a muted fashion.

The argument is familiar. The highest good is the combination of virtue (as the worthiness to be happy) with happiness in proportion to virtue (justice). Since our will is not holy, we are never perfectly virtuous, but since ought implies can, we can be (as reason requires).[50] This means that the life of moral virtue must be seen as an endless progress that approaches moral perfection asymptotically. But this requires two things that are not in our power: immortality as the unending time in which the make endless progress, and a God who is a cause distinct from nature as the "supreme cause of nature," with understanding and will (CPrR, 241–41, 5.125). This God is an agent who sees, in an intellectual intuition outside of time, the endless series as a whole and in accordance with divine holiness and justice gives to each "the share he determines for each in the highest good" (CPrR, 239, 5.123). We might call this Kant's doctrine of justification, for it involves attributing to the individual a righteousness that at no point in this life or the life to come is ever actual.[51] (It also seems to imply a doctrine of divine judgment about which Kant remains largely silent.)[52]

But this is not just a verdict. God actually rewards virtue with happiness, and this has important consequences for our concept of God as more than the abstract *ens realissimum* or even the wise designer of the world. Because, according to the postulates of the second Critique, "the completion of the *summum bonum* can be achieved only through divine agency, we are entitled to hope for happiness through the agency of a God whose will, as a holy will, desires that His creatures should be worthy of happiness, while, as an omnipotent will, it can confer this happiness on them."[53] Kant gets expansive:

> I find that the moral principle admits [the highest good] as possible only on the presupposition of an author of the world possessed of the *highest perfection*. He must be *omniscient* in order to cognize my conduct even to my inmost disposition in all possible cases and throughout the future, *omnipotent* in order to bestow results appropriate to it, and so too *omnipresent, eternal*, and so forth. (CPrR, 252, 5.140)

The religion of the second critique is therefore about hope for the highest good on the basis of divine agency in the life to come. But the postulates on which this hope rests also have a cognitive significance that Kant stresses. Presumably because the deduction of freedom as a necessary presupposition of practical reason was already established in the *Groundwork*, he adds it to his list of postulates. He thereby reminds us of the second edition Preface to the first Critique. There he tells us that their triple affirmation "is not permissible unless at the same time speculative reason be deprived of its pretensions to transcendent insight" as when principles of knowledge "threaten to make the bounds of sensibility coextensive with the real" (*CPR*, B xxx and xxiv–xxv). Accordingly, the affirmation of the postulates is in effect a rejection of the Epicurean rejection of "everything that cannot accredit its objective reality by manifest examples to be shown in experience" (*CPrR*, 237, 5.120).

Again, in that second edition Preface, Kant famously says he has "found it necessary to deny *knowledge* [of God, freedom, and immortality], in order to make room for *faith* [*Glaube*]" (*CPR*, B xxx). Now, in the second Critique, he describes his postulates as expressing "rational belief" (*Vernunftglaube*, *CPrR*, 255, 5.144). Because they are grounded in reason, Kant's claims for these beliefs are surprisingly strong. The beliefs on which hope rests are given "objective reality" and as such are "justified." They represent an "extension" or an "increment" to "knowledge," to theoretical reason (*CPrR*, 236–58, 5.119–48). In accord with the principle of the primacy of practical reason, speculative, theoretical reason "must accept these proposition and, although they are transcendent for it, try to unite them as a foreign possession handed over to it, with its own concepts."[54] Because they "belong inseparably to the practical interest of pure reason it must accept them—indeed as something offered to it from another source, which has not grown on its own land but yet is sufficiently authenticated (*CPrR*, 236–77, 5.119–21). The relation of practical to theoretical reason here is analogous to the relation between divine revelation and human reason in the Abrahamic monotheisms. But it does not compromise epistemic autonomy, for it is human reason in one mode giving something to human reason in another.

If we speak of a certain type of deism as the deism of restricted divine agency, we can call the Kant of the second Critique an epistemic deist on the basis of practical reason. In this way he is both united with and distinguished from quite a few other deists.

But when we turn from the second Critique to *Religion*, matters get more complex. With a glance in the rear-view mirror in the doctrine of original sin, Kant affirms radical evil in human beings. There is, to be sure, an original predisposition (*Anlage*) to good in human nature (*R*, 74, 6.26). But there is also a propensity (*Hang*) to evil in human nature, according to which we are "by nature evil" (*R*, 76, 79, 6.28, 32).[55] It looks as if the optimism expressed in the "ought implies can" principle may need qualification.

We are still in the framework of the *Groundwork* and the second Critique when Kant writes

> reason does not leave us altogether without comfort with respect to the lack of a righteousness of our own (which is valid before God). Reason says that whoever does, in a disposition of true devotion to duty, as much [as] lies within his power to satisfy his obligation (at least in a steady approximation toward complete conformity to the law), can legitimately hope that what lies outside his power will be supplemented by the supreme wisdom *in some way or other*. (*R*, 191, 6:171)

Here the supplement is presumably the divine grace that rewards our virtue (at least in the life to come) with proportionate happiness, what Byrne calls "distributive grace."[56] But given our propensity to evil in virtue of which we are by nature evil, can we blithely assume "a disposition of true devotion to duty"?

In the *Groundwork* and in his second Critique presentation of the immortality of the soul, it seems that there is no qualification to our ability to do what we ought to do.[57] Our moral failures, in theological terms our fallenness, have not damaged our ability to will and to do the good. This is why Kant's "ought implies can" principle is often labeled Pelagian. But here, in *Religion*, it sounds as if we need some help in becoming truly good.[58] Human depravity or the corruption of the human heart "is the propensity of the power of choice to [adopt] maxims that subordinate the incentives of the moral law to others (not moral ones)." In this condition of "*perversity* . . . there can still be legally good (*legale*) actions, yet the mind's attitude is thereby corrupted at its root (so far as the moral disposition is concerned), and therefore is designated as evil" (*R*, 78, 6.30; cf. 91–92, 6.47).

What is needed is a radical change in which one freely adopts as one's supreme maxim the rule never to subordinate moral maxims to non-moral maxims, that is, never to subordinate duty to inclination or virtue to happiness. In theological language we can speak of conversion or regeneration. Kant speaks of the "restoration of the original predisposition to good," of a "*change of heart*," a "*revolution*," a "new man," a "rebirth," and a "new creation" (*R*, 91–92, 6.46–47). Such a conversion would not guarantee moral perfection, since one can fail to live up to one's own ideals; but in its absence one would not even be on "the road of endless progress toward holiness" presupposed by Kant's religion of hope (*R*, 91, 6.47). One's virtues would be, as Kierkegaard is fond of saying, "splendid" or "glittering vices."[59] "For how can an evil tree bear good fruit?" (*R*, 90, 6.45). As with Augustine, Luther, and Kierkegaard, the problem is not sins but sin; or as Kant puts it, it is a mistake "to fight vices individually, while leaving their universal root undisturbed" since then "the foundation of the maxims of the human being remains impure" (*R*, 92, 6.47–48).

But can we convert ourselves? Or is the Lutheran liturgy right when it says, "We confess that we are captive to sin and cannot free ourselves."[60] Here Kant's Lutheran background comes to the surface.

> This evil is *radical*, since it corrupts the ground of all maxims; as natural propensity, it is also not to be *extirpated* through human forces, for this could only happen through good maxims—something that cannot take place if the subjective supreme ground of all maxims is presupposed to be corrupted. Yet it must equally be possible to *overcome* this evil, for it is found in the human being as acting freely." (*R*, 83, 6.37)

The change in wording from 'extirpated' (*vertilgen*) to 'overcome' (*überwiegen*) cannot disguise the paradox or antinomy that comes to light here. We cannot, but we must be able to. A corollary of the Pelagian version of the "ought implies can" principle is what Wolterstorff calls the Stoic maxim. "The human person must make or have made *himself* into whatever he is or should become in a moral sense, good or evil. These two [characters] must be an effect of his free power of choice, for otherwise they could not be imputed to him" (*R*, 89, 6.44). In relation to this "Stoic" principle, Wolterstorff sees a "conundrum" in the Kantian versions of anything that implies that our moral status is improved by divine agency,[61] and he calls attention to Kant's own awareness of the problem.

> The concept of a supernatural intervention into our moral though deficient faculty, and even into our not totally purified or at least weak disposition, to satisfy our duty in full—this is a transcendent concept, merely in the idea of whose reality no experience can assure us.—But even to accept it as an idea for a purely practical intent[62] is very risky[63] and hard to reconcile with reason; for what is to be accredited to us as morally good conduct must take place not through foreign influence but through the use of our own powers. (*R*, 207, 6.191)

Here the Stoic principle seems to preclude divine help in the matter of conversion. But Kant immediately continues

> Yet its impossibility (that the two may not occur side by side) cannot be proven either, since freedom itself, though not containing anything supernatural in its concept, remains just as incomprehensible to us according to its possibility as the supernatural [something] we might want to assume as surrogate [*Ersatz*] for the independent yet deficient determination of freedom.[64]

If the first Kantian supplement of divine grace involved justification and happiness, this second supplement involves conversion and worthiness to be happy. It is a threat to Kant's Pelagian optimism about our moral powers. When Kant speaks in this manner about supernatural cooperation, Michalson finds him to be "deeply ambivalent,"[65] and no doubt he is. But more to the point, there is a paradox or an antinomy in his argument, and he knows it.

It seems to me that his solution, stated simply, is to modify the "ought implies can" principle from its Pelagian to a semi-Pelagian form. He signals this right after affirming the Stoic principle. That we are created good means that we are created for the good, that we have a predisposition to the good and then by choice become either good or evil.

> Granted that some supernatural cooperation is also needed to his becoming good or better, whether this cooperation only consist in the diminution of obstacles or be also a positive assistance, the human being must nonetheless make himself antecedently worthy of receiving it; and he must accept this help (which is no small matter), i.e. he must incorporate this positive increase of force into his maxim: in this way alone it is possible that the good be imputed to him, and that he be acknowledged a good human being. (*R*, 90, 6.44)[66]

In other words, the "justification" mentioned above presupposes this "conversion."

We can understand Kant's position here in terms of that Aristotelian hole into which I am able to fall but out of which I am unable to climb (without help). It might be that the ladder I need is available, but not unconditionally. I might have to ask for it, say "pretty please," promise to be more careful, tell five dirty jokes, or sing "Dixie." It doesn't matter what the condition is, so long as I am able to meet it. Now I am both unable and able to get out of the hole. I am unable to do so without help, but I am able to do what needs to be done to get that help. Whether I get out is up to me. Of course, as the second Critique has argued, I need help if happiness is eventually to be proportioned to virtue. But here we are talking about virtue and goodness itself, the worthiness to be happy. Applied to being "able" in terms of the power of free choice,

I am unable to change my moral status (justification) or my moral character (conversion, regeneration) by myself; I need divine aid. In passages already cited, Kant speaks of a "supplement" or a "surrogate" to our own efforts, of "help," "supernatural cooperation," "positive assistance," "aid," "supernatural intervention." But that aid is available if I meet the preconditions, and I am able to do that. This is the amended ought-implies-can principle and the modified Stoic principle.

In the passage just cited, Kant seems to specify two such conditions: being worthy and being willing to accept help.[67] It is hard to see just how, on Kantian terms, we can be worthy of grace insofar as the will is "corrupted at its root (so far as the moral disposition is concerned), and therefore is designated as evil" and our virtues are "glittering vices" (Kierkegaard). Perhaps we become worthy by acting virtuously in the merely legal sense (doing the right thing but from the wrong supreme maxim). Or perhaps acknowledging that we need help and being willing to accept that help is sufficient prior worthiness. Kant speaks of doing what lies within our (limited) power, and perhaps these actions are the extent of that power prior to conversion.

I call this a semi-Pelagian modification of the "ought-implies-can" principle.[68] That doctrine affirmed that we need divine grace, but not for "the beginnings of faith." Our wills are not so damaged by our fallenness that we cannot, as it were, take the first step toward God, in response to which God will give us the help we need to go further.[69] Whether or not this is internally consistent as Kant presents it, his view seems clear enough; and it allows him to speak of divine agency not only in rewarding our virtue (the first supplement) but in forming it as well (the second supplement).[70]

Kant's primary discussion of the moral "revolution" I've been calling conversion or regeneration comes in the General Remark that concludes Part One of *Religion: Concerning the restoration to its power of the original predisposition to the good* (R, 89–97, 6.44–53). A linear sketch of the argument, some of which has already been cited, may be useful here.

1) The "Stoic" principle is stated (89, 6.44).

2) Reference is made to supernatural cooperation and the need for prior worthiness and acceptance (89–90, 6.44).

3) The question is posed whether we, being evil, can make ourselves good (90, 6.44–45).

4) The possibility of such a restoration cannot be denied because a) such a return is no more incomprehensible that the prior fall into evil and b) we ought to do this so, in accord with the semi-Pelagian "ought-implies-can" principle, we must be able to do so, though we may need assistance (90, 6.45).

5) Any such assistance will be and remain "inscrutable" to us (90, 6.45).

6) Our hope for this needed change rests on the hope that there is a germ of goodness in us that "cannot be extirpated or corrupted" (90, 6.45; cf. 93–94, 6.49–50). Apparently, at this stage, this goodness consists in our being able to make ourselves worthy of help and being willing to accept it. Or perhaps in our ability to be virtuous in the merely legal sense (action in conformity with duty but from a faulty maxim).

7) The restoration in question is a radical change of heart, a revolution or rebirth that takes us from merely legal virtue to genuine moral virtue and sets us on "the road of endless progress toward holiness" (91–92, 6.46–47).

8) The "innate corruption of the human being" denies us insight into the possibility of this change; but it must be in fact possible. "For if the moral law commands that we *ought* to be better human beings now, it inescapably follows that we must be *capable* of being better human beings" (94, 6.50). Although stated without qualification here, in context we must take this to be the revised "ought-implies-can" principle.

9) Given that the propensity to evil is "inextirpable," moral goodness can only consist in "a progression from bad to better extending to infinity," grounded in a transformation of one's supreme maxim that is "unchangeable" (94–95, 6.51).

10) A person cannot have assurance that such a transformation has occurred, but may "*hope* that, by the exertion of *his own* power he will attain to the road that leads in that direction [infinite moral progress]." This sounds like the unrevised Pelagian view, especially since it is immediately followed by a restatement of the "Stoic" principle. A person "cannot be judged *morally* good except on the basis of what can be imputed to him as done by him" (95, 6.51).

11) Although Kant's rhetoric in (8) and (10) seems to lapse into a Pelagian view of the human will, he calls himself and his readers back to the revised, "semi-Pelagian" view. He takes Christianity to be on his side in holding that "to become a better human being, everyone must do as much as it is in his powers to do and only then . . . if he has made use of the original predisposition to the good in order to become a better human being, can he hope that what does not lie in his power will be made good by cooperation from above" (95, 6.52).

12) Kant reminds us that we are dealing with "inscrutable" matters of hope rather than knowledge. For he continues the previous quotation, "Nor is it absolutely necessary that the human being know in what this cooperation consists.... For here too the principle holds, 'It is not essential, and hence not necessary, that every human being know what God does, or has done, for his salvation': but it is essential to know *what a human being has to do himself* in order to become worthy of this assistance" (95–96, 6.52).[71]

We might expect Kant to say three things about the relation of divine agency in relation to moral conversion, what Byrne calls "transforming grace."[72]

1) This agency falls outside the realm of human knowledge and experience.[73] It is a noumenal matter, not phenomenal. As cited above, it is "unknown," "mysterious," "incomprehensible," and "inscrutable."

2) The hope for this divine assistance is grounded in a need of practical reason, in keeping with the (modified) "ought-implies-can" principle in relation to radical evil in human nature.

3) As such, this hope rests upon a belief that is rationally justified. Once again, "I have found it necessary to deny *knowledge*, in order to make room for *faith*" (CPR, B xxx), and, given the primacy of practical reason, this belief must be integrated into the theoretical knowledge to which it comes from outside. It can be added to God, freedom, and immortality as a fourth postulate of practical reason.[74]

What we find instead, is a rather clear affirmation of the first two conclusions, but not the third. He says that we may hope for this assistance, but not that we are justified in believing in it. This is surprising, since, it seems to me, Kant has given sufficient grounds, in his own terms, for drawing the latter conclusion. Perhaps he is such a good deist that he is deeply uncomfortable with the notion of any divine agency beyond that implied in the postulates of God and immortality.[75] This would explain his later comments on grace (1798).

> If by nature we mean the principle that impels us to promote our *happiness*, and by grace the incomprehensible moral disposition in us—that is, the principle of *pure morality*—then nature and grace not only differ from each other but often come into conflict. But if by nature (in the practical sense) we mean our ability to achieve certain ends by our own powers in general, then grace is none other than the nature of the human being insofar as he is determined to actions by a principle which is intrinsic to his own being, but supersensible (the thought to duty). Since we want to explain this principle, although we

know no further ground for it, we represent it as a stimulus to good produced in us by God. (*CF*, 268, 7.43)

Here Kant seems to have abandoned his semi-Pelagian version of "ought implies can" and returned to the original, Pelagian version. Rather than affirm the objective reality of divine assistance in our moral development, he gives an essentially Feuerbachian interpretation of a "transforming grace" that might occur in our present lifetimes. Perhaps Michalson had Feuerbach in mind when, in thinking about Kant's impact on subsequent religious thought, he places Kant "in the West's search for a 'substitute for supernaturalism' in the account of transcendence and divine action."[76]

Of course, Kant is not a Feuerbachian who systematically reduces theology to anthropology, making anything we say about God *really* about ourselves. In the postulates of the second Critique he unabashedly affirms the objective reality of a God who is an agent. But when it comes to the idea of divine assistance in our moral life itself, as distinct from the consequences of that life, he gets very skittish. In *Religion* he doesn't fully draw the conclusion of his own argument; and in *Conflict* he sounds indeed like Feuerbach.

Hare argues that while Kant believes in moral progress, "he thinks of this progress as dependent upon divine assistance," and he rejects the suggestion that "Kant is not being sincere in these passages, that he is putting in God in order to avoid problems with the censor or the pietists he grew up with."[77] But the question that concerns us is not the sincerity of Kant's motives; it is rather the teaching of his text. Perhaps the best summary would be that he unambiguously affirms divine agency in the beginning and at the end of all things, and ambiguously affirms it in between in relation to the conversion that sets us on "the road of endless progress toward holiness." Do we have a third postulate of practical reason here, affirming divine aid and thus divine agency in the conversion that sets us on this road? Almost, perhaps, not quite. Kant clearly thinks it not irrational to hope for divine assistance here, but doesn't affirm its necessity to the moral life with the same categorical manner in which he gives that status to God and immortality.

The question of divine agency will occupy us again in the next chapter in a different context, a third definition of deism. But so far we can conclude that Kant is not a deist in his own, onto-theological sense of the term. On the other hand, he does seem to be a deist of restricted divine agency. His God is indeed an agent, but only within the limits of his version of reason. This God is deeply different from the "Gods" of Spinoza and Hegel, who are not agents, precisely because his version of reason is different from theirs. What we might call the polytheism of modernity expresses the conspicuous plurivocity of a reason that claims to be univocal.

Notes

1. I prefer this translation of his title because "alone" makes clearer than "mere" that the rational religion Kant seeks to develop excludes any historically particular revelation as its foundation.

2. For citations of this sort, see *sigla* and chapter 1, note 8.

3. Kant uses this language of "extension" when introducing the postulates of God and immortality in the second Critique (*CPrR*, 237, 5.121). Religion is "added" to morality (*CPrR*, 244, 5.130).

4. In the second Critique religion is defined as "*the recognition of all duties as divine commands, not as sanctions—that is, chosen and in themselves contingent ordinances of another's will*—but as essential *laws* of every free will in itself, which must nevertheless be regarded as commands of the supreme being because only from a will that is morally perfect (holy and beneficent) and at the same time all powerful . . . can we hope to attain the highest good" (*CPrR*, 244, 5.129). In other words, the link posited in religion between God and the moral law has nothing to do with either our knowledge of the moral law or its authority but only with the hope that it has a just, cosmic enforcer.

5. John E. Hare distinguishes two versions of the highest good in Kantian texts. The "less ambitious" one suggests that each of us can hope that eventually we will be happy in accord with our virtue. See *CPrR*, 231, 5:113, and CPR, 640, A 812 = B840. The "more ambitious" one consists in "the combination of universal happiness with the most lawful morality" (*CPJ*, 318, 5.453). Hare thinks these dominate, respectively, in the first and second Critiques. For the question I shall be posing about God as moral governor of the world, the difference is not important. *The Moral Gap* (Oxford: Clarendon, 1996), pp. 72–73.

6. One of Scott Turow's characters says of his wife, "But she come to lose her faith, Maria did. Not her values, mind you." *Identical* (New York: Central Grand, 2013), p. 40. As we shall see, with appropriate qualifications this is not a bad description of the moral values Kant retained from the pietistic Lutheranism of his upbringing.

7. In speaking of Kant's religion, I mean the religion presented in his texts not the view of the "historical Kant" to be inferred behind the text. I am not inclined to see them as different at the time of writing, though his personal views were certainly different in his youth under the influence of pietism and possibly different by the time of the *Opus Postumum*. See Peter Byrne, *Kant on God* (Aldershot, England: Ashgate, 2007, pp. 125–26, and Chris L. Firestone and Nathan Jacobs, *In Defense of Kant's* Religion (Bloomington: Indiana University Press, 2008—henceforth "FJ," p. 22).) In his letter to Stäudlin he insists that in *Religion* he has "proceeded conscientiously . . . with a befitting candor. . . . " *Kant: Philosophical Correspondence, 1759-99*, ed. Arnulf Zweig (Chicago: University of Chicago Press, 1967), p. 205; and in the letter to Friedrich William II (included in the preface to *The Conflict of the Faculties*), he insists that he presents "this account of my teachings . . . with the utmost *conscientiousness*" since in his seventy-first year "I may well have to answer for this very soon to a judge of the world who scrutinizes men's hearts" (*CF*, 242, 7.9–10). I see no reason to question his sincerity. Furthermore, what Kant's religion may be is to be determined by the text, not by any interpreter's judgment of the success or failure of his account.

8. Zweig, *Correspondence*, p. 205. On the three questions, see *CPR*, A 804–5 = B 832–33. On the fourth question, see Kant's *Logic*, 9.25, and Martin Heidegger, *Kant and the Problem of Metaphysics*, 5th ed., enlarged, trans. Richard Taft (Bloomington: Indiana University Press, 1997), p. 145.

9. There are important contributions to Kant's religion in both the first and third Critiques, as well as other writings. To keep things manageable, I will focus on the second Critique and, especially, *Religion*.

10. "Kant sought from beginning to end to include a critical account of religious experience at the transcendental boundaries of reason." (FJ, 22).

11. Lyrics available at numerous places on the internet.

12. See Byrne, *Kant on God*.

13. Denis Savage, "Kant's Rejection of Divine Revelation and His Theory of Radical Evil," in *Kant's Philosophy of Religion Reconsidered*, ed. Philip J. Rossi and Michael Wreen (Bloomington: Indiana University Press, 1991), pp. 73–74.

14. Psalm 49:6–15, as found in *The Book of Common Prayer*.

15. The phrase "delight in their own words" suggests an epistemic dimension to the psalmist's heteronomy that would not have been part of Kant's meditation.

16. This is a soft definition of 'postulate.' In the strict sense a postulate must be a conceptually necessary condition for the moral life to make sense.

17. Gordon E. Michalson Jr., *Fallen Freedom: Kant on Radical Evil and Moral Regeneration* (New York: Cambridge University Press, 1990), p. ix.

18. Søren Kierkegaard, *The Concept of Anxiety*, trans. Reidar Thomte (Princeton, NJ: Princeton University Press, 1980), pp. 16–19. The third cited phrase comes between the first two.

19. Stephen R. Palmquist, "Cross-Examination of *in Defense of Kant's* Religion," *Faith and Philosophy* 29, no 2. (April 2012), p. 172.

20. '*Gottesdienst*' is the standard name for the Sunday-morning worship service as given, for example, on church bulletin boards.

21. If Kant were proceeding syllogistically he would be committing the fallacy of four terms, changing the meaning of a key premise in the middle of an argument.

22. Matt. 22:34–40, Mk. 12:28–34, and Lk.10:25–28, quoting Deut. 6:4–5 (the great *Shema*) and Lev. 19:18.

23. I've taken this English translation from *The Book of Common Prayer*.

24. On the distinction between natural and revealed, see *R*, 177–79, 6.154–57.

25. See the discussion of "What Is Enlightenment?" at the outset of chapter 1 above.

26. For an illuminating account of these two key terms in "Reformed epistemology," see the essays by the editors in Alvin Plantinga and Nicholas Wolterstorff, eds., *Faith and Rationality: Reason and Belief in God* (Notre Dame, IN: University of Notre Dame Press, 1983), pp. 1–15, 16–93, and 135–86.

27. Nicholas P. Wolterstorff, "Conundrums in Kant's Rational Religion," in Rossi and Wreen, *Reconsidered*, pp. 40–41.

28. Paul Ricoeur, *The Conflict of Interpretations: Essays in Hermeneutics*, ed. Don Ihde (Evanston, IL: Northwestern University Press, 1974).

29. Hans-Georg Gadamer, *Truth and Method*, 2nd rev. ed., trans. Joel Weinsheimer and Donald G. Marshall (New York: Crossroad, 1989; New York: Continuum, 2004).

30. Michael Despland, foreword in *Kant and the New Philosophy of Religion*, ed. Chris L. Firestone and Stephen R. Palmquist (Bloomington: Indiana University Press, 2006), p. xi.

31. Max Horkheimer and Theodor W. Adorno, *Dialectic of Enlightenment*, trans. John Cumming (New York: Continuum, 1982), p. 83.

32. Nathan A. Jacobs, "A Reply to Critics of *In Defense of Kant's* Religion," *Faith and Philosophy* 29, no. 5 (April 2012), p. 211.

33. Their task is to defend *Religion* from negative answers to both of these questions. See note 7 above.

34. See, for example, *R*, 146, 6.115.

35. In the letter to Stäudlin (see note 6 above), Kant says that *Religion* presents "openly the way in which I believe that a possible union of Christianity with the purest practical reason is possible." *Philosophical Correspondence*, p. 205.

36. Charles Taylor, *A Secular Age* (Cambridge, MA: Harvard University Press, 2007), p. 311.

37. This can be seen briefly by looking at Ernest Campbell Mossner, "Deism," in *The Encyclopedia of Philosophy*, ed. Paul Edwards (New York: Macmillan and the Free Press, 1967), 2:326–36, with its overview of deism in Britain, France, Germany, and the United States.

38. Byrne, *Kant on God*, p. 153.

39. In this respect it looks like what Heidegger calls onto-theology, which speaks of God as *causa prima*, *ultima ratio*, and *causa sui*. Martin Heidegger, *Identity and Difference*, trans. Joan Stambaugh (New York: Harper & Row, 1969), p. 60. Kant uses the term 'onto-theology' in a quite different, more specific sense for those "deists" who espouse the ontological argument, the belief that we "can know the existence of [God] through mere concepts, without the help of any experience whatsoever" (*CPR*, A 632 = B 660).

40. The phrase, "a concept which completes and crowns the whole of human knowledge," nicely introduces the positive theological reflections that follow the negative conclusions of the dialectical portions of both the first and the third Critiques. On the relation between the two types of predicates, see *CPrR*, 245n, 5.131.

41. In a different context David Burrell writes, "What is at issue [between the theist and pantheist] is a clean discrimination of creation from emanation, of intentional activity from necessary bringing forth." For Aquinas, the theist in question here, it is necessary to preserve "the gratuity and intentionality of the very activity which denominates God not as prime mover or first being, but creator." *Knowing the Unknowable God: Ibn-Sina, Maimonides, Aquinas* (Notre Dame, IN: University of Notre Dame Press, 1986), p. 15.

42. Kant is not usually accused of being a Thomist, but in speaking of God in this way he notes that he is speaking "in accordance with the principles of analogy," which he sharply distinguishes from anthropomorphism, which treats human and divine predicates as univocal (*CPR*, A 626, 641 = B 654, 669). For his sustained defense of analogical predication see *LPR*, 365–67, 28:1021–23, and 385–87, 28:1046–48. These lectures are largely an exposition of Baumgarten's *Metaphysica*, but since they come after the first Critique, where Kant appeals to analogy, and often echo its metaphysical skepticism, we cannot simply consider it pre-critical.

43. Our third definition of deism will come in the next chapter and will concern the relation of reason to revelation as a special case of divine agency within history. The first two are Kant's own "pantheistic" definition and the present one, which we can call the deism of restricted agency.

44. I once described the deist God as the "author and enforcer of the moral law, not only in this life but in the life to come." That would fit Lord Herbert of Cherbury, the "father of English deism," (see Mossner, "Deism," pp. 327b–328a). But the idea of a divine agency upholding the moral law "in this life" would sound to my typical deist too much like an "interference" in a well-designed universe, too much like a miracle, to which deists tend to be allergic. See my "The Emergence of Modern Philosophy of Religion," in *A Companion to Philosophy of Religion*, 2nd ed., ed. Charles Taliaferro, Paul Draper, and Philip L. Quinn (Oxford: Wiley-Blackwell, 2010), p. 134.

45. As such it falls outside the authority of the natural and human sciences (*Natur-und-Geisteswissenschaften*), which, in turn, operate without appeals to or subjection to its authority. So understood, we might speak of their methodological atheism. Kant emphatically denounces as dogmatism any attempt to convert this immediately into an ontological atheism.

46. N. T. Wright, *Paul and the Faithfulness of God* (Minneapolis, MN: Fortress, 2013), p. 934.

47. In *Natural Theology, or Evidences of the Existence and Attributes of the Deity Collected from the Appearances of Nature*.

48. In Daniel 5 the words MENE, MENE, TEKEL, PARSIN, as interpreted by Daniel, announce God's judgment on Belshazzar and the end of his rule.

49. On the difference between a hypothesis and a postulate or rational faith, see *CPrR*, 241, 5.126 and 254, 5.142.

50. The "ought-implies-can" principle is not qualified here, which is why Kant is sometimes called a Pelagian, one who acknowledges moral fault but does not see it as impairing our ability to do right.

51. The forensic, judicial character of God's verdict is total for Kant. There is no hint of forgiveness or reconciliation. Here Kant would seem closer to the elder brother than to the father in the parable of the prodigal son.

52. But see *R*, 110n, 6.69. Romans 2:7–8 tells us that "to those who by patiently doing good seek for glory and honor and immortality, [God] will give eternal life; while for those who are self-seeking and who obey not the truth but wickedness, there will be wrath and fury." Kant focuses on the hopeful side of this and ends up having less to say about divine judgment than Jesus does.

53. Frederick Copleston, S. J., *A History of Philosophy*, vol. 6 (London: Burns and Oates, 1996¹), p. 343.

54. The relation of practical to theoretical reason here is analogous to the relation between divine revelation and human reason in the Abrahamic monotheisms.

55. Kant doesn't have any more luck than those theologians who have tried to reconcile the universality of radical evil with its origin in human freedom. The interpretation of Firestone and Jacobs is no help. They say that for Kant, humanity is an Aristotelian secondary substance and that its choice of the wrong supreme maxim is thus universal. But what it can mean to attribute choice (*Willkür*) to a secondary substance such as humanity escapes me entirely. See FJ, pp. 134–49.

56. Distributive grace is "the divine willingness to award human beings happiness or blessedness despite the fact that they never attain moral perfection." Byrne, *Kant on God*, p. 140. This might better have been called justifying grace, but Byrne uses that as a synonym for atoning grace, unfortunately, since justification and atonement are two quite distinct concepts.

57. But in a footnote, Kant anticipates the move he will make decisively in *Religion*. He attributes to Christian ethics, in distinction from the Greek schools, the hope that "if we act as well as is within our *power*, then what is not within our power will come to our aid from another source, whether or not we know in what way" (*CPrR*, 243n, 5.127n). In context this seems to apply to virtue itself rather than happiness in proportion to virtue.

58. In letters to Lavater from 1775, Kant writes, "On the contrary, nothing is needed for my union with this divine force except my using my natural God-given powers in such a way as not to be unworthy of His aid or, if you prefer, unfit for it ... the consoling hope is offered us that, if we do as much good as is in our power, trusting in the unknown and mysterious help of God, we shall (without meritorious 'works' of any sort [*sic*—we are to be worthy!]) partake of this divine supplement ... we ought to seek [righteousness] with all our might, having faith (that is, an unconditional trust) that God will then supplement our efforts and supply the good that is not in our power" (Zweig, *Correspondence*, pp. 81–83).

59. Drawing on Lactantius and Augustine, Kierkegaard often describes the virtues of the "pagans" in this way. See, for example, *Works of Love*, trans. Howard V. Hong and Edna H. Hong (Princeton, NJ: Princeton University Press, 1995), pp. 53, 196, and 269. What he calls "pagan" often turns out to be Christendom.

60. *Evangelical Lutheran Worship* (Minneapolis, MN; Augsburg Fortress, 2006), p. 94.

61. Wolterstorff, "Conundrums," pp. 48–52.

62. That is to say, as a postulate of practical reason.

63. The idea of effects of grace is "risky" because it so easily leads, on Kant's view, to enthusiasm, superstition, illumination, and thaumaturgy. See *R*, 96–97, 6.53, where Kant says the idea of effects of grace cannot be put to either theoretical or practical use.

64. Where di Giovanni translates *Ersatz* as 'surrogate,' Greene and Hudson say 'supplement.' The latter seems to fit Kant;'s larger argument better.

65. Michalson, *Fallen Freedom*, p. 5. Cf. p.9.

66. Cf. the letter to Lavater in note 58 above, where the condition for the "divine supplement" of "aid" or "help" is that I be "not unworthy."

67. Rufus Jones expresses this latter condition quite vividly. "As ocean floods the inlets, as sunlight environs the plant, so God enfolds and enwreathes the finite spirit. There is this difference, however, inlet and plant are penetrated whether they will or not. . . . Not so with God. He can be received only through appreciation and conscious appropriation. He comes only through doors that are *purposely* opened to him." *The Double Search* (Philadelphia: John C. Winston Company, 1906), p. 44.

68. I think it is a mistake to make Kant into an Augustinian just because in *Religion* he is not simply a Pelagian. See Philip J. Rossi's discussion of Jacqueline Mariña's argument in "Reading Kant Through Theological Spectacles," in *Kant and the New Philosophy of Religion*, ed. Chris L. Firestone and Stephen R. Palmquist (Bloomington: Indiana University Press, 2006), pp. 107–23.

69. Semi-Pelagianism was condemned at the Council of Orange in 529. But on this point Kant is not making a break with "mere Christianity." For some Christian traditions seem to teach that grace is necessary and is available to those who, by doing what they can, are worthy of it.

70. On the paradox or antinomy that Kant is dealing with here and his vacillation between Pelagian and semi-Pelagian positions, see FJ 17, 44–45, 49, 55, 57, 72–74, 79, 94.

71. The General Remark ends here in the first edition (1793). The second edition (1794) adds the warning against belief in "effects of grace" cited above, note 61.

72. Byrne, *Kant on God*, p. 140. Or "sanctifying grace," since in Christian theology not only conversion but subsequent progress and growth require divine assistance. As *The Book of Common Prayer* puts it in the collect for the Sunday closest to September 14, "O God, because without you we are not able to please you, mercifully grant that your Holy Spirit may in all things direct and rule our hearts."

73. In the first Critique, Kant tends to identify knowledge with experience.

74. With reference to Kant's discussion of divine assistance in relation to moral conversion, Christopher McCammon writes, "Kant's procedure here is analogous to what we find in the famous 'moral proof' of God's existence in the *Critique of Practical Reason*. . . . Kant has shown us the need for God's existence as a necessary postulate for any who desire moral progress in themselves in the world." "Overcoming Deism: Hope Incarnate in Kant's Rational Religion," in Firestone and Palmquist, *New Philosophy*, p. 82.

75. Michalson suggests that Kant's "talk about grace and supernatural action would be alarming to a certain sort of deist"—maybe even to the sort Kant himself is—in *Fallen Freedom*, p. 91.

76. Gordon E. Michalson Jr., "In Defense of Not Defending Kant's *Religion*," in *Faith and Philosophy* 29, no. 2 (April 1999), p. 189.

77. John E. Hare, "Kant on the Rational Instability of Atheism," in Firestone and Palmquist, *New Philosophy*, p. 74.

5
KANT'S HERMENEUTICS I

It was suggested in the last chapter that two decisive marks of a personal God are agency and speech. Both are affirmed by mere Christianity; neither by Spinoza. So far we have seen Kant to be a deist of restricted divine agency, thereby separating himself from Spinoza and (as we shall see) from Hegel by affirming God as an agent and not merely a cause, and also separating himself from Abrahamic monotheism (Jewish, Christian, or Muslim) by virtue of the restrictions. In this chapter, we look further into his account of divine agency, but in the context of his ideas about divine speech acts, typically referred to as revelation, as in the claim that the God of the Bible (or Koran) can perform such speech acts as promises and commands and that the Bible (or Koran) is the written word of God, a record of divine speech acts that is itself a complex speech act.

We can approach these issues with the help of a third definition of deism. Wood introduces his version of this one by citing three earlier ones. For Stillingfleet, a deist affirmed "the Being and Providence of God, but expressed mean esteem of the Scripture and the Christian religion." For Dryden, deism is "the opinion of those that acknowledge one God without the reception of any revealed religion." And for Samuel Johnson, deism is "Belief in a God, but rejection of all other articles of religious faith." From these, Wood extracts the following: "a deist is a believer in a natural religion, a religion founded on unaided reason, but not in a revealed religion."[1]

Wood's version has the advantage over the other definitions of focusing on the issue of epistemic autonomy. Deism in our third sense is about the relation of reason and revelation in religion. As the project of "reason within the limits of reason alone," it is the claim that the natural and allegedly universal powers of human reason are the sole foundation of true religion. So Byrne's definition is also helpful, according to which the essential claim of deism is that "natural religion is sufficient."[2] We can call this the deism of natural religion, the deism of the sufficiency of reason, or the deism of epistemic autonomy.

That leaves open two questions, about which those typically considered to be deists have a variety of views. What religious beliefs can be warranted by "mere reason" (*blosse Vernunft*)?[3] and What, precisely, is to be said about revelation? Since the typical deist affirms God as Creator and Judge at the last judgment, we can say at least that the typical deist takes God to be an agent. But is God a speaker as well? What is to be said about revelation?[4] Wood's "not in a revealed religion" can be nuanced in different ways of which outright denial is only one.

We need to be clear what is meant by revelation. The basic idea is that of communication that comes from God as its ultimate source. Theologians sometimes distinguish general from special revelation. General revelation is essentially identical with reason, at least in its highest and proper function. Typical deists, including Kant, have no problems with revelation in this sense. As Byrne puts it, "since the human faculties are created and designed by God, then the discoveries of reason can be regarded as God speaking to us."[5] Thus Kant writes, "The God who speaks through our own (morally practical) reason is an infallible interpreter of His words in the Scriptures" (*CF*, 286, 7.67).[6]

Special revelation involves divine discourse distinct from (though not necessarily different from)[7] the proper functioning of created, human reason, unaided by such revelation. It occurs at a particular time and place when God speaks to a particular individual or people. It can be taken to be a species of miracle, for it involves divine action (speech acts) between the Alpha of Creation and the Omega of the Last Judgment whose ultimate cause is God as distinct from nature or human agency. When Kant and other deists distinguish natural or rational from revealed religion it is revelation in this sense that they have in mind. Unless otherwise indicated 'revelation' will signify special revelation from here on. Kant will refer to it as "supernatural divine revelation" (*R*, 178, 6.154).

Kant opens Part IV of *Religion* with a discussion of natural and revealed religion. Since it contains important theses about revelation and since his hermeneutics presupposes his view of revelation, it is worth summarizing.

1) "*Religion* is (subjectively considered) the recognition (*Erkenntniss*) of all our duties as divine commands" (*R*, 177, 6.153). We have seen that this is an essential but incomplete definition of Kantian religion.[8] It also involves, at the very least, belief in God and immortality.

2) This does not require "assertoric knowledge" of God's reality, but only "*assertoric* faith" (*R*, 177n, 6.153–54n). Does this mean that there will be any new postulates of practical reason, beliefs that are undecidable by theoretical reason but warranted by practical reason as necessary to the moral life?

3) This definition precludes "the erroneous representation of religion as an aggregate of *particular* duties immediately related to God.... There are no particular duties to God in a universal religion for God cannot receive anything from us" (*R*, 177n, 6.154n.)[9] The crucial premise here seems to be, not the prior definition but that "God cannot receive anything from us." This seems to function as an axiom (basic presupposition), for Kant offers no argument to support it. By contrast, Paul thinks that even apart from special revelation God is clear enough through "the things he has made" that we should "honor him as God [and] give thanks to him" (Romans 1:19–21). These surely sound like duties to God not covered by Kant's moral philosophy. In other words, that it is erroneous to think of religion as including particular duties to God is relative to the quite particular presupposition that God cannot receive anything from us. A different axiom would undermine Kant's conclusion as erroneous. His claim that his axiom is the product of "reason alone" shows that his version of "pure" reason is particular and contingent rather than universal and necessary, since the axiom on which it rests is neither self-evident, needing no argument, nor the product of a compelling rational argument.

Runzo makes this point at a very general level when he says, "[W]e have good reason neither to suppose that there is a universally valid pure concept of God nor for supposing that, even if there were such a concept, all rational people would apply it . . . in the same way." That human understanding is relative "to one's own historical place and cultural context affects both the concepts which one will form *via rational theology* and the sorts of judgments which one will make as to what those conceptual-schema-relative concepts tell one about revealed theology." The fact that institutional religion is context relative "undermines the notion that where religion fails [to rest on universal grounds], human reason succeeds."[10]

4) For revealed religion "I must first know that something is a divine command in order that I recognize it as my duty," while for natural religion "I must first know that something is duty before I can acknowledge it as a divine command" (R, 177, 6.154). Clearly what is at issue here is legislative autonomy as described in the previous chapters.

5) Four stances toward natural and revealed religion can be distinguished. (a) The *rationalist* takes "natural religion as alone morally necessary, i.e., a duty." (b) The *naturalist* "denies the reality of any supernatural divine revelation." (c) The *pure rationalist* "allow[s] this revelation, yet claim[s] that to take cognizance of it and accept it as actual is not necessarily required for religion." Finally, (d) the *supernaturalist* "holds that faith in divine revelation is necessary to universal religion (R, 1177–78, 6.154–55).

6) Since the rationalist must

> hold himself within the limits of human insight . . . he will never deny in the manner of a naturalist, nor will he ever contest either the intrinsic *possibility* of a revelation in general or the *necessity* of a revelation as divine means for the introduction of true religion; for no human being can determine anything through reason regarding these matters. (R,178, 6.155; emphasis added)

Whereas Spinoza is a rationalist and a naturalist, Kant is (so far) only a rationalist.

7) Whereas "every human being can be convinced through his [own] reason" of natural religion, revealed religion is "*learned religion*," which means that some "have to be guided" (*geleitet werden müssen*) by others. 'Guided' is not quite the right word here. The slave boy in Plato's *Meno* is guided by Socrates, who draws various figures to help him see whether his answers are good ones or not. But, far from depending on Meno's authority, he can see for himself whether he has or has not got it right; he is "convinced through his [own] reason"—once he has Socrates' diagrams before him. So his is a "natural" not a "learned" geometry, in spite of the fact that he "learned" it, let us say, shortly before his fourteenth birthday.

The issue is the authority of the one who guides, and the boy does not depend on the authority of Socrates. But if he is learning about the Persian wars, he will be dependent on the authority of Herodotus (whose reliability has been a matter of debate from ancient to modern times).[11] It is this difference, based on the alleged universality of reason (as if theology and geometry were the same kinds of discipline), that gives to natural religion "the essential characteristic of the religion which ought to bind every human being" (R, 178, 6.155). Here again the basic issue is epistemic (legislative) autonomy. Only the products of self-legislation are binding. I have no obligations to another that are not first obligations to myself. See (4) above.

8) Religion can thus be both natural and revealed if it is so constituted that human beings *could and ought to have* arrived at it on their own through the mere use of their reason, even though they *would* not have come to it as early or as extensively as is required, hence a revelation of it as a given time and a given place might be wise and very advantageous to the human race, for then . . . everyone can henceforth convince himself of its truth by himself and his own reason (R, 178, 6.155–56).

Here again autonomy is the key. Commenting on this passage, Firestone and Jacobs call attention to Kant's use of Platonic recollection theory, his "transcendental Platonism" (FJ, 157–58).[12] Not only is revelation possible, it "could present itself as a catalyst for awakening truths already embedded in reason. . . . Kant is not adverse to the idea that an insight (a rational insight) may be awoken by engagement with a purported revelation" (FJ, 118).

9) This has two interesting consequences, but Kant fails to notice the significance of the latter. First, "such a supernatural revelation might well subsequently be entirely *forgotten* without the religion in question losing the least thereby, either in comprehensibility or certainty, or in its power over minds." Second, if a revealed religion "were not preserved in a totally secure tradition or in holy books as records, it would *disappear* from the world" (R, 178, 6.156; emphasis added).[13] What Kant fails to notice (or does he just fail to mention it?) is that he is talking about a religion that can be "considered" (*angesehen werden kann*, R, 178, 6.156) to be revealed. All that is needed for "revealed" religion is the combination of scripture and tradition that individuals or communities *take to be* of divine origin, whether it is or not, whose content overlaps significantly with the contents of rational religion.[14] This can be the Socratic, not necessarily divine "means" for introducing true religion. To invoke a distinction from Kierkegaard, what is needed is religious genius, not necessarily anyone with apostolic authority, the bearer of genuinely divine speech acts.[15]

10) Kant's exploration of religion that is at once natural and revealed and thus learned will be in terms of a particular, historical example, a holy book that is "considered" to be a revelation from God. "In our case this book can be

the New Testament, as the source of the Christian doctrine of faith," a good choice since it is "a book inextricably interwoven with teachings that are ethical and hence related to reason." In doing so Kant is not "wanting to intrude into the business of those to whom is entrusted the interpretation of this very book as an aggregate of positive doctrines of revelation, or to challenge their exegesis based on scholarship." There is no threat here, since he does not plan to tell Christian theologians what they should teach for the purposes of public worship.[16] Moreover, theological scholarship "proceeds toward one and the same end as the philosophers, namely the moral good" (R, 179, 6.156–57; cf. 61, 6.9). Kant appears to foresee some kind of harmony between philosophy and theology, reason and revelation.

But he may be proceeding a bit too quickly. It is true that the theologians are, or at least should be, concerned with the moral good. But they may have goals that go beyond Kant's. Ethical teachings are "inextricably interwoven" throughout the New Testament, but that implies that they are not its sole content, even if we add God and immortality. It is not self-evident that what the (Kantian) philosopher says about other teachings in the New Testament will be in harmony with what Christian theologians of various sorts say about them. What he says about private prayer, church going, baptism, and communion is not promising for any harmony thesis (R, 208–15, 6.192–202; see the brief discussion in chapter 4).

So what is the Kantian stance in relation to the four attitudes distinguished in (5) above? It seems as if we could eliminate naturalism and supernaturalism right off the bat, leaving rationalism and pure rationalism as the alternatives. But perhaps it is not quite that simple. Rationalism and pure rationalism aren't the same logical "size," and already in their names as well as in their content look more like a genus and a species. In fact, it has been helpfully suggested that rationalism is the genus and the other three options are all species that define various forms of rationalism (FJ, 211–19). By itself, rationalism might well be called "soft deism."[17] But Kant asks for a more specific definition with regard to revelation.

The naturalist denies its possibility. This is clearly not Kant's position, as he makes clear in (6). The theologian may not be glad to hear that "if God should really speak to a human being, the latter could still never *know* that it was God speaking. It is quite impossible for a human being to apprehend the infinite by his senses . . . and *be acquainted with* [*kennen*] it as such" (CF, 283, 7.63; cf. LPR 444, 28.1118). But the theological agnosticism of the first Critique cuts both ways. We cannot *know*, in the narrow critical sense of knowledge, either the reality or the unreality of God or revelation.[18]

Kant is equally explicit about the undeniable possibility of revelation in the *Lectures*, where he insists that

> no human being can hold it impossible that in order to bring the human species to a highest stage of perfection in its vocation, God might have given to it, in a higher revelation, certain truths necessary to happiness into which reason, through its own cultivation, can perhaps never come to have insight. For who dares to specify the plan or the means by which God might help human beings. (*LPR*, 445, 28.1119–20)

He immediately adds, "The precise cognition of and adherence to the path reason prescribes is all that God himself teaches to make us worthy of any higher insight which might be provided to supplement reason's deficiencies." This sounds familiar, except that in this case the possible supplement is epistemic rather than moral.

Surprisingly, Savage takes Kant to be a naturalist, arguing that while he holds revelation to be logically possible, he takes it to be "objectively, materially impossible." But the reasons he gives don't support this conclusion. Any divine revelation could only be "at best, either a repetition or a symbolic expression of the moral laws of our rational nature . . . all duties alleged to be of special divine revelation are to be rejected if taken for anything more than a restatement or imaginative representation of the ethical duties of reason."[19]

There are three problems here. First, this presupposes a reduction of religion to morality that doesn't fit Kant, as we have seen. Second, Savage presupposes that Kant precludes the possibility that God might give and humans might benefit from a religion that does not get beyond "repetition" or "restatement" in a "symbolic" or "imaginative" mode. But that's a pretty good statement of the position Kant affirms, or at least holds open.

Third, Savage argues that for Kant there can be no "evidence" in favor of revelation. In support of this he quotes the passage cited above from *Conflict* to the effect that if God did speak to us we could not know that it was God.[20] Given Kant's virtually positivist definition of knowledge, this is almost trivially true, but it overlooks the fact that Kant takes us to have rational grounds for beliefs in what we cannot "know." Whether or not Kant affirms the reality of revelation, I take him to have denied knowledge on this matter in order at least to "make room" for faith. So far as "knowledge" is concerned, Kant is a naturalist, but he regularly refuses to make "the bounds of sensibility coextensive with the real" (*CPR*, B xxiv–xxv).²¹

Is Kant, then, the kind of rationalist who can be called a pure rationalist? Wood thinks not. This position

> apparently takes the position that God has given us certain commands supernaturally while denying that we are morally bound to carry them out. This surely cannot be a position Kant intends to embrace. Kant's only purpose in mentioning pure rationalism at all seems to be the theoretical one of cushioning his evident denial of pure supernaturalism.²²

This is careless reading. The issue is not whether we should obey God's commands, which we can know without the benefit of revelation, but whether it is a duty to affirm the reality of revelation. Kant's point is that it is permissible (rather than obligatory); his purpose is to point out that the rationalist need not be a naturalist, the latter espousing a negative dogmatism incompatible with the critical philosophy.

Furthermore, there is an ambiguity in Wood's definition of the position, which may be different from Kant's. For him pure rationalism is "the view that recognizes the *reality* of supernatural revelation but nevertheless denies that belief in it is morally necessary." But the verb Kant uses in relation to revelation is *zulassen*. Di Giovanni renders it "allows," while, following Greene and Hudson, Wood has "recognizes." It can also mean both 'concede' or 'permit.' 'Concede' and 'recognize' are rather stronger than 'permit' and 'allow.' So it is not entirely clear whether the pure rationalist affirms the reality or only the possibility of revelation (in either case differing from the naturalist). Since Kant clearly affirms the possibility and may affirm the actuality,²³ I think it is safe to call him a pure rationalist.

One cannot preclude the stronger of these two senses, as Wood does, on the grounds that Kant "is simply an agnostic about supernatural revelation" according to *CF*, 283, 7.63. This agnosticism does not justify Kant's "refusal to admit the possibility that anyone might have adequate grounds for claiming the authenticity of any particular putative revelation. To repeat, Kant's conception of rational faith means that we sometimes have good grounds to affirm what we cannot know in his restrictive sense of knowledge.

But surely we can at least quickly and confidently eliminate the possibility that Kant is a supernaturalist rationalist. Well, yes and no. For rationalism, as defined above, natural religion alone is "morally necessary, i.e. a duty." So when Kant says that for the pure rationalist taking revelation to be actual "is not necessarily required for religion," and that the supernaturalist takes it to be "necessary to universal religion," we are likely to assume that he means "morally necessary, i.e. a duty."

But there are two other senses of necessity that are relevant in this context, and we should be as clear as we can which is in play. It is possible that Kant slides from one to another without noticing or making us notice. There is conceptual necessity, according to which a certain belief, say in revelation, or practice, say the Eucharist, is essential rather than accidental to a given religion. In this sense revelation and the Eucharist are necessary to mere Christianity but neither is necessary to natural or rational religion. If this is what the supernaturalist is affirming, then Kant is right to say, "The point of dispute can therefore concern only the reciprocal claims of the pure rationalist and the supernaturalist ... or what either accepts as necessary and sufficient, or only as accidental, to the one and only true religion" (R, 178, 6.155). Of course, the rationalist philosopher and the supernaturalist theologian have different views about what "the one and only true religion" is. So "the point of dispute" arises because the two parties have two different religions in mind. In this sense Kant cannot be a supernaturalist.

But there is also historical or developmental necessity. Just as the slave boy needed Socrates developmentally but not epistemically, so human beings, both as a species and as individuals, may need a revelation that contains the pure religion of reason (but in a different form) before they can discover it to be a ladder that can be thrown away or a snake skin that can be shucked off. Developmentally speaking, it may be that "I must first know that something is a divine command in order that I recognize it as my duty," before I come to understand that "I must first know that something is duty before I can acknowledge it as a divine command" (R, 177, 6.154), just as children may learn that enough sleep and a balanced diet are necessary to good health on parental authority before they acknowledge this on the basis of their own insight.

At the very least, Kant denies knowledge in order to "make room" for this possibility. In (6) above, Kant holds that by virtue of the limits of the critical philosophy, the rationalist will neither deny the possibility of revelation nor its necessity in this third, developmental sense. It may be necessary "as divine means for the introduction of true religion." In (8) above he reaffirms this possibility: "hence a revelation of [true religion] at a given time and a given place might be wise and very advantageous to the human race, for then ... everyone can henceforth convince himself of its truth by himself and his own reason." Finally, in (9) above, Kant indicates that the instrumental character of this possible revelation renders it in principle temporary. For "such a supernatural revelation might well subsequently be entirely *forgotten* without the religion in question losing the least thereby, either in comprehensibility or certainty, or in its power over minds."[24]

Three things to notice. First, this dispensability thesis is the Achilles heel to any claim that Kant's religion within the limits of reason alone is compatible with mere Christianity rather than a rival to it. Mere Christianity is not reducible to whatever overlap with natural religion it may contain, and the claim that only the content of this overlap is true religion belongs to a rival religion.

Second, even if Kant goes so far as to hold that this possibility of divine revelation is actualized in the New Testament (the example he chooses, R, 179, 6.157), his argument for the developmental necessity of Christianity as a revealed religion requires only that its sacred books be "considered" to be divine discourse. Prophets and apostles need to be religious geniuses, not necessarily bearers of divine discourse.

Third, there is a sense in which Kant can be both a pure rationalist and a supernaturalist. On his own definition, the supernaturalist "holds that faith in divine revelation is necessary to *universal religion*" (R, 178, 6.155; emphasis added). By universal religion Kant understands religion within the limits of reason alone, and divine revelation is certainly neither morally nor conceptually necessary to it. Nor is it easy to think of anyone who says it is. So why does Kant define the supernaturalist position as a possible stance toward *universal* religion? Presumably because he has shifted the meaning of necessity to developmental necessity. For the rationalist, even the pure rationalist, can also be a supernaturalist in this sense, holding that divine revelation is historically or developmentally necessary to universal, rational religion.

So, in sum, I find Kant to be a rationalist or "soft deist," who holds that natural religion is sufficient and that it alone is morally necessary; a pure rationalist, who holds that divine revelation is at least possible but neither morally nor conceptually necessary to true religion; and a supernaturalist, who holds that revelation or at least belief in revelation is historically and developmentally necessary to religion within the limits of reason alone. His treatment of the Christian religion and its New Testament presuppose an education of the human race thesis[25] that makes him at first friendly but eventually hostile to their teachings.

Does the idea of divine agency in the form of speech acts, that is, revelation, give rise to a new postulate of practical reason? Clearly no. Hare is right to remind us that for Kant, we can legitimately believe what we cannot know "in his narrow sense of 'know,'" and that "[i]t no more follows that we should not *believe* in supernatural revelation than that we should not *believe* in God. He thinks there are good moral grounds for theistic belief."[26] So there is an analogy between the epistemic status of belief in God and belief in divine revelation. But it is not strong enough to make the latter belief a postulate of practical reason. While Kant surely holds divine revelation to be possible and maybe holds that it is actual, he takes it to be neither morally nor conceptually necessary to true religion, the religion that is itself at least conceptually necessary to the moral life.[27] While it is developmentally necessary, this is temporary as we have seen;[28] supernatural revelation could be entirely forgotten without any loss to the "comprehensibility," "certainty," or "power" of natural religion.[29] This is not the case with God and immortality.

It appears that the Enlightenment imperative to emerge from our self-incurred childhood[30] becomes, in *Religion*, the exhortation to become increasingly rational by freeing ourselves as much as possible from putative revelation, even Christianity, which Kant takes to be the highest form of revealed religion. It may well be that religiously speaking, ontogeny recapitulates phylogeny, and the individual's development must pass, like that of the species, through a childhood of dependence (heteronomy) on revealed religion as such. But the time has come at both the individual and the institutional levels to grow out of this immaturity and graduate to a religion within the limits of reason alone. "The leading string of holy tradition, with its appendages, its statutes and observances, which in its time did good service, become bit by bit dispensable, yea, finally, when a human being enters upon his adolescence, turn into a fetter" (*R*, 151, 6.121). Already in our teens we are to shake off the shackles of biblical religion.[31] As Firestone puts it, theology, based on revelation, "must be upheld, not because it promises theological data that cannot be gleaned from the inner recesses of reason, but because theology as a distinct discipline promises to hasten the day that rational religion will become complete and be the religion of the land."[32]

Here Kant draws a rather clear implication of much of what he says. But rather than suggest that we simply drop the religion of our personal and historical childhood so as to enter the age of reason, he often guides us in an apparently different direction. Keep the words and images of revealed religion (at least temporarily), but interpret them differently. In that way incorporate them into religion within the limits of reason alone. Here Kant's deism becomes a hermeneutical project and principle.

Kant finds three kinds of content in the New Testament. There are the teachings that essentially duplicate those of natural religion. Thus the section in Part IV entitled "The Christian Religion as Natural Religion."[33] Second, there are those parts that, at least as all too often interpreted, produce delusion, counterfeit service of God, idolatry, superstition, priestcraft, servile worship of God, and fetishism.[34] The central thesis here is: "*Apart from a good life-conduct, anything which the human supposes that he can do to become well-pleasing to God is mere religious delusion and counterfeit service of God*" (R, 190, 6.170). Or as he might put it, Christianity can be and all too often is a "terrible, horrible, no good, very bad" religion.[35] We are not far from Voltaire's "*écrasez l'infâme*."[36] Insofar as the negative side of deism is the critique of Christian beliefs and practices, Kant is clearly a deist.

Finally, there are those beliefs and practices that, taken at face value do not overlap with rational religion and all too easily result in some form of delusion and superstition; but properly (re)interpreted they can play a role in the developmental necessity of true religion. They can become means to the end of religion within the limits of reason alone, or, to use Kant's favorite term, they can become its "vehicle." Wherever mere Christianity is not the "republication of the religion of nature,"[37] it is to be reinterpreted with natural religion as the criterion so as to be suitable as such a vehicle. Thus, for example, prayer and praise are of no intrinsic value as appropriate ways in which individuals and communities of faith relate to God; but they can be of instrumental value so long as they are understood solely as aids in obeying the moral law.

The result is that the relation between the believer and God is as impersonal as that between the Internal Revenue Service and the taxpayer. One side makes the rules and enforces them;[38] the other side either obeys or disobeys them. Or, to put it another way, Kant is at home in the impersonal law court world of the Pauline doctrine of justification, where what matters is the happiness made possible by a verdict of "not guilty." But ironically, given his praise of Jesus, he is a stranger to the world of the prodigal son, where happiness rests on the more intimate, interpersonal foundations of forgiveness and reconciliation grounded in love.[39] If there is a hymnbook for religion within the limits of reason alone, it does not contain the hymn by Charles Wesley that concludes its reflection on the death of Jesus with these words:

> My God is reconciled;
> His pardoning voice I hear;
> He owns me for his child;
> I can no longer fear:
> With confidence I now draw nigh,
> And "father, Abba, Father," cry.⁴⁰

There can be significant overlap between the second and third groups. The same ideas can propagate either delusional devotion or the pure piety of reason, depending on how they are interpreted. As suggested above, the idea that Christianity is either a "repetition" or "restatement" of natural religion or its representation in a "symbolic" or "imaginative" mode begins to look like Kant's own position, not one he would reject. The resistance of Reardon and Hare against interpreting *Religion* as a *translation* of revealed religion into a vehicle for rational religion,⁴¹ and of Ward and Palmquist against saying that Kant takes biblical material as *symbolic* of something other than its meaning in its original context and for subsequent Christian tradition seems to me misguided (see FJ, 69, 78–81, 153–54, and 209).⁴²

In this way, Kant's theory of revelation gives rise to his hermeneutics. We can anticipate that this will involve the use of persuasive (re)definitions.⁴³ Just as Spinoza takes the concept of God from its biblical, personalist context and redefines it as nature under mechanistic necessity (*Deus sive Natura*), so Kant will make *his version* of reason the hermeneutical key to interpreting the Bible so as to make it a useful vehicle for religion within the limits of reason alone. As it turns out, we have already encountered the basic principles of his hermeneutics and need but to formulate them to see that.

Notes

1. Allen W. Wood, "Kant's Deism," in Philip J. Rossi and Michael Wreen, *Kant's Philosophy of Religion Reconsidered* (Bloomington; Indiana University Press, 1991), p. 2.

2. Peter Byrne, *Kant on God* (Burlington, VT: Aldersgate, 2007), p. 169. Byrne adds that for the typical deist "revelation is out" in the sense that "there is no need of revelation." Then he adds a second point: "the idea of revelation can only serve to cloak the introduction of superstition into the world." Kant will make both of these claims, but without the crucial "only." For him, as we shall see, there is more to the story.

3. In an unsurprising passage, Kant writes, "Natural religion, as morality ... combined with the concept of that which can actualize its ultimate end (the concept of *God* as moral originator of the world), and referred to a duration of the human being proportionate to the entirety of this end (immortality) is a pure practical concept of reason" (R 179, 6.157). In chapter 4, we saw that transforming

grace in conversion almost got added to God and immortality and a postulate of practical reason, but not quite.

4. For the link between revelation and speech, see Nicholas Wolterstorff, *Divine Discourse: Philosophical Reflections on the Claim that God Speaks* (New York: Cambridge University Press, 1995). He argues that in a biblical context, revelation consists in God's performing such speech acts as promises and commands. That God typically speaks indirectly through prophets and apostles and in the writings that make up Scripture does not change the fact that when revelation is claimed such promises and commands are said to come from God.

5. Byrne, *Kant on God*, p. 165. Cf. p. 157. See the argument by Denis Savage that Kant and Aquinas agree on this point. "Kant's Rejection of Divine Revelation and His Theory of Radical Evil," in Rossi and Wreen, *Reconsidered*, p. 56.

6. In Romans 1 and 2, Paul speaks of both metaphysical and moral knowledge of this sort, though he finds it to be dramatically distorted by sinfulness.

7. Augustine, Aquinas, and Calvin, for example, think there is a significant (but not total) overlap between what reason and revelation teach us about God.

8. See, for example, note 3 above.

9. See the discussion of four "means of grace" in previous chapter 4.

10. Joseph Runzo, "Kant on Reason and Justified Belief in God," in Rossi and Wreen, *Reconsidered*, pp. 34–35.

11. Assuming, as is quite reasonable, that the *Histories* are in print at the time of the dramatic date of the encounter with Socrates.

12. Perhaps more precisely, his "transcendentally chastened form of Platonic idealism" (FJ, 155).

13. Cf. *R*, 151, 6.121, where "religion will gradually be freed ... of all statutes that rest on history and unite human beings provisionally ... through the intermediary of an ecclesiastical faith." We are reminded of Wittgenstein's ladder, that can be safely thrown away once it has been used. Ludwig Wittgenstein, *Tractatus Logico-Philosophicus*, 6.54.

14. Thus the appropriate reference to "purported revelation" in FJ, 118.

15. Søren Kierkegaard, "The Difference between a Genius and an Apostle," in *Without Authority*, trans. Howard V. Hong and Edna H. Hong (Princeton, NJ: Princeton University Press, 1997), pp. 91–108, and in *The Book on Adler*, trans. Howard V. Hong and Edna H. Hong (Princeton, NJ: Princeton University Press, 1998), pp. 173–88. In a classic of liberal Protestantism, Adolf Deissmann writes, "Paul must be classed with the few people regarding whom that much misused phrase 'religious genius' can rightly and fittingly be used." *Paul: A Study in Social and Religious History* (New York: Harper & Brothers, 1957). It will be recalled that this is how Spinoza treats the Hebrew prophets.

16. What Kant refers to, condescendingly, as "popular faith" (*Volksglaube*; *R*, 144, 6.112).

17. Ernest Campbell Mossner uses this term in relation to Rousseau, in "Deism," in *The Encyclopedia of Philosophy*, ed. Paul Edwards (New York: Macmillan and the Free Press, 1967), 2:332b.

18. Showing his consistency on this point, Kant says the same about miracles in general, where nature miracles rather than divine speech acts are front and center. See the General Remark that concludes Part Two (REL 122–26, 6.84–89).

19. Savage, "Rejection," pp. 57–58. Byrne also takes Kant to be a naturalist. See *Kant on God*, pp. 159–66.

20. Savage, "Rejection," pp. 60–62. For a similar claim, see Joseph Runzo, "Justified Belief," in Rossi and Wreen, *Reconsidered*, p. 25; and Byrne, *Kant on God*, pp. 163–67.

21. Kemp Smith's "coextensive with the real" is a rather free but helpful rendering of Kant's claim that dogmatic, speculative metaphysics threatens "to extend the boundaries of sensibility ... beyond everything" (Guyer and Wood's rendering of *über alles zu erweitern*).

22. Wood, "Kant's Deism," p. 11. For Hare's response and a threefold defense of Kant as a pure rationalist, see John E. Hare, *The Moral Gap: Kantian Ethics, Human Limits, and God's Assistance* (Oxford: Clarendon, 1996), pp. 42–44, including note 10.

23. Hare is one who thinks Kant does affirm this actuality. See *Moral Gap*, p. 38. I think (a) the text is ambiguous, and (b) all Kant's argument requires is that certain texts are taken to be divine revelation.

24. Thus Runzo writes that ecclesial religion based on belief in divine revelation "may be socially and historically necessary, because of our human weaknesses, to have institutional religion convey rational religion, but it is imperative ultimately to break out of the debilitating restraints which those very institutions impose on the human will and understanding. Runzo, "Justified Belief," p. 24).

25. I am thinking here of Schiller's *On the Aesthetic Education of Man* and Lessing's *The Education of the Human Race* as a kind of genre. J. B. Bury's brief discussion of the theme of progress in Kant focuses on his ethical writings, *Idea of a Universal History on a Cosmopolitan Point of View* (1784), and *Perpetual Peace* (1795), but not on *Religion*. See *The Idea of Progress: An Inquiry into its Growth and Origin* (New York: Dover, 1955), pp. 243–50.

26. Hare, *Moral Gap*, p. 47. Hare does not claim postulate status for belief in revelation.

27. Kant claims that we have a need but not a duty to believe in God, and by extension, immortality (*CPrR*, 241, 5.125). But such belief remains morally necessary in the sense that the moral life is incoherent without it.

28. In note 9 above.

29. See *CF*, 241–42, 7.8–9, where the revealed teachings of Christianity are, from the standpoint of reason, "superfluous" and "nonessential" though possibly "useful."

30. See the discussion of *What Is Enlightenment?* in chapter 1 above.

31. In his letter to Lavater in April of 1775, Kant says that once rational religion is sufficiently established, then "the scaffolding must be taken down," referring to the dogmas of the New Testament, those "confessions and ceremonies" that depend on "historical reports." *Philosophical Correspondence, 1759–99*, ed. Arnulf Zweig (Chicago: University of Chicago Press, 1967), pp. 80–81.

32. Chris L. Firestone, "Making Sense Out of Tradition: Theology and Conflict in Kant's Philosophy of Religion," in *Kant and the New Philosophy of Religion*, ed. Chris L. Firestone and Stephen R. Palmquist (Bloomington: Indiana University Press, 2006), p. 145.

33. This is an important theme of English deism. See John Toland (1696), *Christianity not Mysterious: Or a treatise Shewing That there is nothing in the Gospel Contrary to Reason, Nor above it: And that no Christian Doctrine can be properly call'd a Mystery*, and Matthew Tindal (1730), *Christianity as Old as the Creation: Or, The Gospel a Republication of the Religion of Nature*.

34. These are the themes of Part IV of *Religion*.

35. Taken from the title of a children's book by Judy Viorst in which a young boy has an unusually bad day. It is not about religion.

36. "Crush the infamous thing," referring to religious superstition in general and the Catholic church in particular. In a letter to d'Alembert, Nov. 28, 1762.

37. See note 33 above.

38. Within the limits set by the other side! Democracy is the political form of autonomy, as Rousseau understood clearly. But when applied to religion, this model makes God into a President or Prime Minister who can be voted out of office or neutralized by a recalcitrant legislature. See my essay "On Thinking of God as King," *Christian Scholar's Review* 1 (Fall, 1970), pp. 27–34.

39. On the utter centrality of reconciliation in Pauline theology, see N. T. Wright, *Paul and the Faithfulness of God* (Minneapolis. MN: Fortress Press, 2013), pp. 879–91 and 1197–98, with reference to 2 Cor. 5:11–21, Rom. 5:6–11, Rom. 11:13–15, along with pp. 1487–1516.

40. The hymn goes by its opening words, "Arise, My Soul, Arise."

41. At FJ 48, we read, "*Religion*-as-Translation presents the text not as an extension of Kant's arguments in the critical philosophy but as a translation of the Christian faith." But these are not mutually exclusive. On the interchangeability of translation and interpretation in the philosophical hermeneutics of Gadamer, see my *Whose Community? Which Interpretation?* (Grand Rapids, MI: Baker Academic, 2009), pp. 98–99, 105–7.

42. Palmquist is quoted as saying, "Kant's purpose in devoting a whole section to [the gospel narrative] is not to ridicule those who believe it is true. . . . Rather, it is to confirm its *suitability* to serve as a symbolic vehicle for true religion" (FJ, 154) This is a good, general statement about Kant's positive use of biblical materials. Cf. the quotation from Ward on p. 153.

43. See the discussion in chapter 2 above.

6

KANT'S HERMENEUTICS II

Kant's hermeneutics can be summarized in terms of five theses: hegemony, means/end, dispensability, recollection, and harmony. Utterly fundamental is the *hegemony thesis*, the claim that the pure, that is the a priori and presuppositionless religion of practical reason is the norm or criterion for interpreting biblical texts and ecclesiastical traditions governing both beliefs and practices, doctrine and devotion—the whole of "revealed" or "learned" religion. Thus "ECCLESIASTICAL FAITH HAS THE PURE FAITH OF RELIGION FOR ITS SUPREME INTERPRETER" (R, 142, 6.109).[1] Scripture is the norm for ecclesiastical faith, but Scripture itself, in turn, has "no other expositor . . . except the *religion of reason* and *scholarship* (which deals with the historical element of Scripture). And of these two, the first alone is *authentic* and valid for the whole world, whereas the second is merely *doctrinal*," that is, the system of "ecclesiastical faith for a given people at a given time" (R, 145, 6.114).[2] The moral predisposition in us is "the foundation and at the same time the interpreter of all religion" (R, 151, 6.121). This clearly presupposes Kant's view of reason as universal and historically unconditioned.

In carrying out such interpretation the philosopher "*borrows*" from the biblical theologian scriptural and traditional material "to use for his own purpose," and "he employs them "in not quite the same sense" (R, 62, 6.9–10).[3] Such interpretation "may often appear to us as forced, in view of the text (of the revelation), and be often forced in fact; yet if the text can at all bear it, it must be preferred to a literal interpretation that either contains absolutely nothing for morality, or even works counter to its incentives" (R, 142, 6.110).⁴

Reason has a right to this hegemony, on Kant's view, because it is the realm of universality. Whereas ecclesiastical faith rests on some particular historical revelation embodied in a holy scripture,

> [t]he only faith that can found a universal church is *pure religious faith*, for it is a plain rational faith which can be convincingly communicated to everyone, whereas a historical faith, merely based on facts, can extend its influence no further than the tidings relevant to a judgment on its credibility can reach. Yet due to a peculiar weakness of human nature, pure faith can never be relied on as much as it deserves, that is, [enough] to found a Church on it alone. (R, 136–37, 6.102–3)⁵

As usual with Kant, universality is linked to necessity. Tenets of faith conceived as divine commands

> are either merely *statutory*, which are contingent for us and [must be] revealed [if we are to know them], or *moral* doctrines, which involve consciousness of their necessity and can be recognized a priori—that is, *rational doctrines*. . . . To claim *universal validity* for a dogma . . . involves a contradiction: for unconditioned universality presupposes necessity, and since this occurs only where reason itself provides sufficient grounds for the tenets of faith, no mere statute can be universally valid. (CF, 273, 7.49)⁶

The contrast between *statutory* and *moral* teachings is not that between religious beliefs and religious practices but between beliefs and practices grounded in a revelation that is historically particular and contingent and those grounded in a reason whose insights are (allegedly) universal and necessary.

The utterly crucial conclusion, on which Kant's entire religion within the limits of reason alone rests, is that "a division into sects can never occur in matters of pure religious belief." Sectarianism arises only from "substituting empiricism in matters of faith for rationalism and *passing off what is merely contingent as necessary in itself*" (CF, 273, 7.50; emphasis added).

Mere Christianity makes a universal claim: all people should respond in faith and obedience to the good news about Jesus as Lord and Savior.⁷ But it does not do so on the grounds that its beliefs and practices arise out of necessary truths of reason. It is rather Kant who presents his religion as having that form, and, as we have been seeing, it is he who is "passing off what is merely contingent as necessary in itself." For the claim that religion must be grounded in necessary truths of reason is anything but a necessary truth. It belongs to a particular cultural moment, shared by Spinoza, Kant, and Hegel, who can't agree on what those necessary truths of reason are.

The result is, pace Kant, the profusion of philosophical sects. These three philosophies of religion are mutually incompatible, each with the other two, though each is presented as the voice of universal reason, free from sectarian presuppositions. We don't have to look too hard to see the particularity and contingency of the axioms on which each of these theologies rests. In Kant's case these include such claims as that we can have no particular duties to God and that the only way we can please God is by obeying the moral law.

American pragmatism has helped us to see that beliefs can have an a priori function while being contingent and corrigible rather than universal and necessary truths of reason.[8] Thomas Kuhn's *The Structure of Scientific Revolutions* and Hans-Georg Gadamer's *Truth and Method* develop the same insight in terms, respectively, of "paradigms" and "prejudices." In Kantian language, "pure" reason is contaminated with contingent commitments. His religion is different from but no less particular than that of Jesus, who treats love of God and love as neighbor as two domains of duty, not just one. If the dialectic of enlightenment means that "enlightenment reverts to mythology,"[9] one of its central myths is the self-congratulatory mythos-to-logos story according to which objective, neutral, universal reason replaces contingent, sectarian narratives as the foundation of culture and society.

If the *hegemony thesis* is the first principle of Kant's hermeneutics, the second principle, the *means/end thesis,* is a kind of corollary to the first. Revealed religion is not an end in itself but a means toward and in the service of the pure religion of reason that is its proper criterion. The former is the "vehicle" of the latter.[10] The passage cited at (6) in chapter 5 focuses on this role of revealed religion in the "introduction" of true religion.

Michalson calls this hermeneutic "highly reductionistic," and in a very specific sense, for

> human consciousness (represented in this case by Kantian morality) controls the text, dictating what it can or should mean.... The text is there to serve morality, not the other way around. Consequently, human subjectivity as the locus of moral awareness in the world takes command over the text. The implicit assumption here is that biblical materials are under a kind of conceptual control.... Scripture makes manifest a moral consciousness that derives its validity from the universal structure of reason, and not from what scripture itself offers us.[11]

The philosopher's autonomy trumps the autonomy of the text. Insofar as the text is not allowed to speak to us on its own terms, we have, ironically, a kind of philosophical censorship.[12] The text is reduced to what the philosopher will allow it to say. It is in the sense of this hegemony that religion is "reduced" to morality, insofar as scriptural texts must either be themselves teachers of pure, rational morality or instrumentally in the service of that morality. They have no other legitimate purpose.

By contrast with Michalson, Palmquist praises Kant for his "realistic, pragmatic" approach to the human weakness that makes revealed religion developmentally necessary. "Ideal" religion would dispense "with all the historical trappings involved in defending specific religious dogmas and/or requiring members to participate in certain religious rituals." But Kant "readily admits" that this is more a hope than a reality and that "most people will settle for something less than ideal religion," and he "allows for many forms of belief and practice that fall short of the ideal, provided they prompt people to move in the right direction."[13]

Di Giovanni says much the same, although he does not praise Kant for it, when he says that Kant converts Christian dogmas into "rational myths."[14] Real religion relies on myths, whereas ideal religion does not. The contrast here is not between myth and history; the point is rather that narratives of either kind arise at particular times and places within a particular culture. Lacking the (alleged) universality of reason, they are not essential to true religion. But they can be pragmatically rational if they are put to a use endorsed by reason, namely as the "vehicle" that "introduces" religion within the limits of reason alone and sustains it among those not yet fully rational—Palmquist's (and Kant's) "most people."

Third, as developmentally necessary to both the individual and the species, divine revelation belongs to the childhood immaturity from which enlightenment is to free us. Thus, the *dispensability thesis*. "THE GRADUAL TRANSITION OF ECCLESIASTICAL FAITH TOWARD THE EXCLUSIVE DOMINION OF PURE RELIGIOUS FAITH IS THE COMING OF THE KINGDOM OF GOD" (R, 146, 6.115). This would surely have come as a surprise to John the Baptist, to Jesus, and to many of those who heard them proclaim the nearness of the kingdom of God. Although they didn't all have the same expectations, they shared with Mary, the mother of Jesus, the belief that in their time God was fulfilling long-standing covenant promises and

> has helped his servant Israel,
> in remembrance of his mercy,
> according to the promise he made to our ancestors,
> to Abraham and his descendants forever.[15]

Similarly, Zechariah, the father of John the Baptist, believes that God

> has shown the mercy promised to our ancestors,
> and has remembered his holy covenant,
> the oath that he swore to our ancestor Abraham...[16]

One of the irreconcilable differences between Kant's religion and biblical religion is that in his theology of hope there is no room for the promises of God as the basis of that hope. Whereas the New Testament consistently interprets Jesus and the community of faith in him as the fulfillment of the ancient promises to Israel, Kant sees Christianity as "a total abandonment of the Judaism in which it originated" (R, 156, 6.127). Thus Hare writes that "the Abrahamic, Mosaic, and Davidic covenants are not the acts of the God of Christianity, to the extent that we understand [reinterpret] his acts within what Kant calls 'the pure religion of reason.' If I am right about the core of traditional Christianity, the new covenant [new testament] is also unintelligible for Kant within these limits."[17]

In any case, we have already encountered this dispensability thesis at (9) in chapter 5 with the citation from 6.156 and subsequently from 6.121, where "holy tradition" has already become in adolescence a "disposable ... fetter."[18] In other words, developmental necessity is temporary. It signifies "the reliance of man upon revealed religion *up until* the time he is of sufficient intellectual maturity to appreciate a religion of pure reason."[19]

Fourth, the encounter between Socrates and the slave boy in Plato's *Meno* is a helpful model for this kind of accidental and therefore eliminable necessity of a certain means to a certain end. Thus, another corollary: the *recollection thesis*. On the Platonic model, knowledge that is fully autonomous and thus already in the mind but "forgotten" (not consciously present), can be "recollected" with the help of some empirical stimulus. Thus, the dialectic of developmental dependence and epistemic independence.[20] This enables Kant to draw profusely on biblical materials, without which his philosophy of religion is quite unimaginable, without compromising his commitment to legislative, epistemic autonomy. The New Testament is the source of his religion, but not its norm or authority. "Thus, while Kant may utilize biblical language and even quote Scripture, his arguments are not necessarily dependent upon such language and content *or automatically outside the limits of reason alone*" (FJ, 118; emphasis added).[21]

In this Platonic context, (putative) revelation can "present itself as a catalyst for awakening truths already embedded in reason" (FJ, 118, referring to 6.155, as cited in (8) chapter 5). In the *Lectures* Kant combines the *hegemony thesis* with this *recollection thesis*.

> Thus we can have no correct insight into the external revelation of God, and we can make no right use of it, until we have made an entirely rational theology our property. But on the other side an external divine revelation can be an *occasion* for the human being to come for the first time to pure concepts of God which are pure concepts of the understanding... the religion of reason... must precede every other revelation and serve as a gauge (*LPR*, 444, 28.118–19; emphasis added).[22]

It is important not to get carried away here by suggesting that in being the occasion that awakens what reason could and ought to discover on its own, revelation can "correct" (FJ, 203) "add" to and "deepen" reason.[23] The passages in which the language of occasionalism is used make it clear that nothing more is involved than the awakening of reason to its own content. Firestone properly reminds us, "This does not mean, however, that theology provides an independent source of information about God that threatens to undo reason and the vocation of philosophy... everything *believed in rationally* must be rooted in the moral and cognized for the sake of hope according to strict critical guidelines."[24] This is a restatement of the hegemony thesis.

Fifth and finally, we come to the *harmony thesis*. *Religion* is not exactly a paean to revealed (learned, ecclesiastical, statutory) religion. Even when it is not morally and intellectually corrupting, it is subject to the hermeneutical hegemony of ahistorical reason; it is but a means (vehicle) to the end of religion grounded in such reason; and it serves this role temporarily because it is only accidentally related to that religion as the occasion for its recollection. But precisely because of this positive role it plays we should see a fundamental harmony between revealed religion, at least in its sectarian, Christian form, and rational religion as the truly universal religion. "[Christianity's] best and most lasting eulogy is its harmony, which I demonstrated in [*Religion*], with the purest moral belief of religion" (*CF*, 242, 7.9).

In a section devoted to the *hegemony thesis*, Kant says that in relation to "some historical ecclesiastical faith or other... an empirical faith which, to all appearances, chance has dealt to us, we require an interpretation of the revelation we happen to have, i.e. a thoroughgoing understanding of it in a sense that harmonizes with the universal practical rules of a pure religion of reason" (R, 142, 6.109–10).[25] It is to be noticed that this harmony is something that is required rather than something that is discovered. This is why Kant immediately goes on to the passage cited above in which "forced" interpretations are nevertheless acceptable in the service of this hegemony and this harmony.

In the Preface to the second edition of *Religion*, Kant speaks of two experiments. The first is to represent the relation between "the pure *religion of reason*" and "what is historical in revelation" as two concentric circles, since the latter can contain the former,[26] while the reverse is not true (R, 64, 6.12).[27] The philosopher, presumably the voice of pure practical reason, restricts himself to the former, though this would seem to include the task of providing an interpretation of the latter that meets the harmony requirement. Here we get a more concrete image of both the means/end thesis and the dispensability thesis. The inner circle relates to the outer as kernel to husk as in the case of the of pea and its pod, the maple seed and its helicopter, or the diaspores that are transported by various types of tumbleweed as their vehicle.

For the second experiment Kant plans

> to start from some alleged revelation or other and, abstracting from the pure religion of reason . . . to hold fragments of this revelation, as a *historical system*, up to moral concepts, and see whether it does not lead back to the same pure *rational system* of religion. . . . If this is the case, then we shall be able to say that between reason and Scripture there is, not only compatibility but also unity. (R, 64, 6.12–13)[28]

Were this not the case there would be a conflict between the religion of "reason" and the religion of "revelation."[29] The *harmony thesis* of Kant's hermeneutics requires that this not be allowed to emerge.

There would seem to be two problems with this detente. In the first place, since for this experiment the philosopher is to make pure practical reason the criterion of biblical interpretation and is under direction to develop meanings that harmonize with rational religion, the process would seem to exhibit a "vicious circularity." "The result of such an experiment is a foregone conclusion."[30]

With less drama but with equal force, Byrne puts it this way.

> The goal of *Religion* is to show how the possible unity of the Christian religion with the purest practical reason is to be understood. This is an easy goal to

accomplish *if* the principle for interpreting Christian scriptures adopted is that of seeking for their moral meaning alone. And this is Kant's hermeneutic. The supreme norm for interpreting Scripture is the religion of reason (*Religion* 6:114 [cited above]) and thus the moral philosopher must take priority over the scriptural scholar in determining the authentic meaning of Biblical texts.[31]

When one applies the "appropriate constraints,"[32] it is just too easy to show the harmony between the inner and outer circle.

A second problem is Kant's image of concentric circles, meant to express the overlap between rational and revealed religion. There is a more accurate image for this relation, a Venn diagram with two overlapping circles neither eccentric nor concentric. Let the left-hand circle be B for biblical religion (since it is historically first) and let the right-hand circle be K for Kant's religion of reason. There will be three areas: BK for the area of overlap, B* (left of the overlap) for those elements of biblical religion not contained in Kant's religion, and K* (right of the overlap) for those elements of Kant's religion not contained in biblical religion. For present purposes, we can let B contain the beliefs and practices of mere Christianity, leaving aside those about which Christian's disagree.[33]

The harmony required by Kant's project (shared in various ways by many thinkers from the seventeenth century to the present) evaporates when we look at K*. Kant's theology includes the five hermeneutical principles just spelled out, none of which is compatible with *biblical religion*. What Kant says about historical revelation in general and the Bible in particular makes his religion a rival to *mere Christianity*. What Kant says about the contents of B (both in terms of outright rejection and systematic reinterpretation) rests on particular presuppositions dramatically different from those at work in B.

We have seen this difference emerge at various points along the way, most fundamentally in Kant's flight from the scandal of particularity in religion, unaware as he is of his own historical particularity vis-à-vis other philosophers and other religious traditions. Only someone caught up in a particular language game that we might call the Autonomy Project can deny, as he does with his Platonic rationalism, that he is in a hermeneutical circle that gives him a specific location within particular traditions (Platonic, Stoic, Newtonian, Deist, and so forth). Just as Kant's semantic and epistemic space (read: hermeneutical circle) is an intersection of such individual thinkers and traditions of thought, so Jesus and Paul have their roots in Abraham, Moses, David, and Isaiah, and mere Christians have their roots in the particular revelations and traditions associated with all of these. By calling his presuppositions Reason, Kant does not make them any less particular than they actually are. Surely there are religious delusions; but there are philosophical delusions as well.

In chapter 4 we have seen Kant's reinterpretation of the biblical notions of *justification* and *conversion*; and in chapter 5 we have seen his reinterpretation of the biblical notion of *revelation*. Each of these is an illustration of Kant's hermeneutics at work, offering persuasive redefinitions designed to bring these concepts within the limits of reason alone. But the focus has been on the questions of divine agency and divine speech. Now that we have the principles of Kant's hermeneutics before us, it may be useful to look at two other translations from the language of revelation to the language of reason, namely, Kant's account of atonement and his "Christology" as presented in Part II of *Religion*. Here we see a harmony indeed, but it is the harmony between Kant's theology and his hermeneutical principles.

For Kant as for mere Christianity, justification involves the conferring of a not-guilty status before the law, the imputation of a righteousness that at no point in time has actually been achieved; and for both it is intimately tied to the hope of eternal life. We might think of atonement and conversion as the proper grounds that justify justification. It is surely to be hoped that conferring a not-guilty verdict on the manifestly guilty is not the product of judicial indifference or corruption on God's part. As Paul puts it, God "must be just and the justifier" of those who believe in Jesus (Rom. 3:26 KJV).

We may see conversion as the subjective ground, the change of posture in the individual (coming to faith in mere Christianity, adopting a new highest maxim in Kant) that justifies God in imputing innocence to the guilty. Atonement, then, would be the objective ground. As radically evil we are guilty before the law and have incurred a debt that must be paid. In the context of a retributivist standpoint, sin must be punished before justification (to say nothing of forgiveness and reconciliation) can be anything but "cheap grace." Mercy must not make a mockery of justice.

Having presented his Christology (to which I shall turn in due course), Kant lists three problems. It is the third, which he takes to be the "greatest," that introduces the theme of atonement (*R*, 112, 6.71). Our life after conversion as the adoption of the good principle as our highest maxim is not perfectly in tune with the holy law. But God, who sees our steady, unending progress in that direction grounded in a new disposition (*Gesinnung*) of the heart and sees this in an intellectual intuition as a completed whole, is justified by that progress in declaring us justified, in good standing before the law (*R*, 108–9, 6.66–67).

But that leaves standing the guilt incurred before conversion.³⁴ In spite of the good disposition and "however steadfastly a human being may have persevered in such a disposition ... *he nevertheless started from evil*, and this is a debt which is impossible for him to wipe out [by post-conversion moral progress]" (*R*, 112, 6.72).³⁵ This debt represents an infinite guilt

> not so much because of the *infinity* of the highest lawgiver whose authority is thereby offended ... but because the evil is in the *disposition* and the maxims in general (in the manner of *universal principles* as contrasted with individual transgressions): consequently every human being has to expect *infinite* punishment and exclusion from the Kingdom of God. (*R*, 113, 6.72)

This punishment is payment for a debt³⁶ that is "not a *transmissible* liability which can be made over to somebody else, in the manner of a financial debt." But this punishment does not make moral sense either before conversion (since at any time further guilt may be incurred) or after conversion (since endless progress makes me innocent, in God's eyes, before the law).

> Yet satisfaction must be rendered to Supreme Justice, in whose sight no one deserving of punishment can go unpunished. But since neither *before* nor *after* conversion is the punishment in accordance with divine wisdom but is nevertheless necessary, the punishment must be thought as adequately executed in the conversion itself. (*R*, 113–14, 6.72–73)

For mere Christianity, atonement as the objective ground of justification, forgiveness, and reconciliation is expressed in a variety of ways, including sacrifice, redemption, ransom, expiation, and so forth. But all atonement metaphors are interpretations of the death of Jesus and its import for the salvation of sinners.³⁷

For Kant, by contrast, conversion itself is the punishment that atones for past guilt without any reference to Jesus. The objective ground is reduced to the subjective ground; we atone for our own sins, and the question of divine agency does not arise beyond what it does in the case of conversion. Although this is a very different way of speaking about atonement from that of the Bible, Kant does not hesitate to use the language of the Bible and Christian theology, including such key terms as satisfaction, sacrifice, substitution, and savior.³⁸

Thus conversion itself as "the putting off of the old man and the putting on of the new" (Col. 3:9–10) in which "the subject dies unto sin" (Rom. 6:11) is the "punishment" that renders "*satisfaction*" to "Supreme Justice, in whose sight no one deserving of punishment can go unpunished."[39] The abandonment of evil and the adoption of the good principle involves pain and thus "is in itself already *sacrifice* (as 'the death of the old man,' [Rom. 6:6] 'the crucifying of the flesh' [Gal. 5:24]." The new, good "disposition which [the human person] has incorporated in all its purity, like unto the purity of the Son of God—or (if we personify this idea) this very **Son of God**—bears as *vicarious substitute*[40] the debt of sin for him, and also for all who believe (practically) in him: as *savior*, he *satisfies* the highest justice through suffering and death" (R, 113–15, 6.73–74; emphasis on 'satisfaction' and 'sacrifice' added).[41] Kant reminds us that this biblical and theological language is that of the imagination in which the suffering of the new human being "is depicted [*vorgestellt wird*] in the representative of the human kind as a death suffered once and for all" (R, 115, 6.74–75).

In Kant's theory of atonement, the Son of God appears, not as Jesus of Nazareth but as an imaginative personification of the good disposition which one adopts in conversion. Only afterward does he bring Jesus into the discussion, though not by name, and he says three things about him. First, he reminds us that the good principle, which he has identified as the Son of God and savior, "did not descend among humans from heaven at one particular time but from the very beginning of the human race" (R, 121, 6.82). This is an example of Kant's view of (putatively universal) reason as (general) revelation in its Platonic form. Second, he says that what appeared in this actual human being is the good principle. Jesus is the incarnation, not of the maker of heaven and earth, but of the moral law as always, already embedded in human reason, and "by exemplifying this principle" he becomes "an example for everyone to follow" (R, 121, 6.82). These two comments make it clear that this Son of God is not the Jesus of the New Testament.

Third,

> [i]t is easy to see, once we divest of its mystical cover [*Hülle*] this vivid mode of representing things, apparently also the only one at the time *suited to the common people* [*populäre Vorstellungsart*], why it (its spirit and rational meaning) has been valid and binding practically, for the whole world and at all times.... Its meaning is that there is absolutely no salvation for human beings except in the innermost adoption of genuine moral principles in their disposition. (R, 121, 6.83)

Mere Christians will readily agree that Jesus is "an example for everyone to follow." But they will be puzzled and offended by the idea that the story of

Jesus as the one who atones for our sins and not we ourselves is the husk, "*suited to the common people,*" that must be removed to get to the rational kernel hidden within.⁴² They will hear a new elitism, the *Pfaffentum* of the philosophers, an academic "PRIESTCRAFT AS A REGIME IN THE COUNTERFEIT SERVICE" of God (*R*, 194, 6.175). They will not recognize this as a higher form of their childhood faith into which they should grow up. Kant, however, reminds us that he is committed to such a demythologizing or antinarrative procedure by his hermeneutical principles. "Finally, any attempt like the present to find a meaning in Scriptures in harmony with the *most holy* teachings of reason must be held not only as permissible but as a duty" (*R*, 122, 6.83–84).

In talking about atonement, Kant has invoked his "Christology," and we now turn to it as another example of his hermeneutic principles at work. He introduces it under the heading, THE PERSONIFIED IDEA OF THE GOOD PRINCIPLE (*R*, 103, 6.60). This idea (*Idee*) signifies "*Humanity . . . in its ful moral perfection*" personified, that is, as an individual not as a species. We have just seen the good disposition identified as the Son of God. Here it is the idea of an individual perfectly in conformity with that disposition and thus with the moral law. The idea of this ideal human "is in [God] from all eternity," "proceeds from God's being," is "God's only-begotten Son" (John 3:16); is "the *Word* (the *Fiat!* [*das Werde*])⁴³ through which all other things are, and without whom nothing that is made would exist" (John 1:3); is "the reflection of [God's] glory" (Heb. 1:3); is the one in whom "God loved the world" (John 3:16). This "*prototype* [*Urbilde*] has *come down* to us from heaven" (John 3:13) to take on "all sufferings up to the most ignominious death [Phil. 2:8], for the good of the world and even for his enemies [Rom. 5:10]" (*R*, 104, 6.60–61).

This Son of God is not Jesus of Nazareth. As Jacobs puts it, "Kant is clear that rational faith in the prototype is distinct from historical faith in a particular historical figure. In this light, any reading that conflates his discussion of the prototype in Books 2 and 3 with a discussion of Jesus is misguided."⁴⁴ First, the biblical language Kant uses is justified as a subjective necessity, a manner in which we *might* represent (*kann angesehen werden*) the idea of a morally perfect individual and because we "*cannot* form for [ourselves] any concept of the degree and the strength of a force like that of a moral disposition except by representing it surrounded by obstacles and yet—in the midst of the greatest possible temptations—victorious" (*R*, 104, 6.61; emphasis added).⁴⁵ Accordingly, "this narrative is a type of symbolic theology meant to help us grasp the nature of the prototypical disposition we ought to appropriate" (FJ, 168).

To reinforce the difference between Jesus and this *Idee*, this *Urbilde*, we are repeatedly told that it comes to us through reason, not experience and history. Any historical human individual could be at best an example of this prototype (*R*, 105–7, 662–64; and 121, 6.82–83). In other words, Kant's "Christology" is another expression of his Platonism. Jesus is to reason's eternal Idea of a perfect individual as the diagrams Socrates draws for the slave boy are to the Pythagorean theorem. He is dispensable. "There is no need, therefore, of any example from experience to make the idea of a human being morally pleasing to God a model to us; the Idea is present as model already in our reason."[46] Moreover, any actual person is an inadequate approximation for "the required prototype always resides only in reason, since outer experience yields no example adequate to the Idea." Since this Idea belongs to the very being of God, Kant emphasizes "THE OBJECTIVE REALITY OF THIS IDEA" (*R*, 104–6, 6.61–64).[47] It is the ahistorical objectivity of a Platonic idea rather than the historical objectivity of the New Testament.

But we have also seen Kant identify as the Son of God the new disposition that emerges in us from our adoption of the good principle. This is something more subjective; this Son of God does not sound like an eternal aspect of the being of God. We may have what Wolterstorff calls a "conundrum" and Michalson calls a "wobble" in Kant's theory.

Something similar happens with the Holy Spirit. Kant calls attention to the worry that conversion may not be the permanent commitment to the good principle presupposed by his notion of a "continuous advance *in infinitum*." At first he suggests referring the anxious individual to the assurance that "His (God's) Spirit gives witness to our spirit" that we are children of God (Rom. 8:16). But this suggests a feeling of supposedly supernatural origin, about which we are easily deceived; so instead he advises us to "work out [our] salvation with *fear* and *trembling*" (Phil. 2:12; *R*, 109, 6.67–68). We may hope, but without certainty. This, however, doesn't quite seem enough to Kant, so he adds, "The good and pure disposition of which we are conscious (and which we might call [*nennen kann*][48] a good spirit that presides over us) thus carries confidence in its own perseverance and stability, though indirectly, and this is our Comforter (Paraclete)[49] whenever our lapses make us anxious about its perseverance" (*R*, 111–12, 6.70–71).

By identifying the new, good disposition that results from moral regeneration first with the Son of God then here with the Holy Spirit, Kant seems to be working toward a doctrine of the Trinity "within the bounds of reason alone."⁵⁰ It sounds a lot like Feuerbach's claim that what divine names or predicates *really* refer to is something human—ideal, to be sure, but that which is praiseworthy within the limits of humanity alone. This aura is not diminished when we are told that to believe in the Son of God as the objective prototype is to "self-assuredly trust that [the human being], under similar temptations and afflictions (so far as they are made the touchstone of that idea), would steadfastly cling to the prototype of humanity and follow this prototype's example in loyal emulation" (R, 104–5, 6.62). Faith in the Son of God is confidence in my own moral strength. Perhaps what we end up with in Kant's *Religion* is an unstable blend of Platonic objectivism and Feuerbachian subjectivism.

Kant does not share Feuerbach's atheism, but the logic of his project keeps pushing him in that direction. This is what justifies the context in which Michalson places Kant's *Religion*.

> Think of the history of religious thought in the West since about 1750 as an ongoing referendum on the idea of 'otherworldliness.' . . . A vote in the referendum over other-worldliness is ultimately a vote concerning the relevance or importance to human life of a transcendent power or a hidden, saving action. . . . God's central position and commanding role are gradually displaced by an increasing preoccupation with human subjectivity, crystallized in the Cartesian *cogito* in ways that we now associate with an emergent modernity . . . the divine will is set in competition with—if not eclipsed altogether by—an autonomous human subject.⁵¹

Firestone and Jacobs place heavy, and in my judgment, warranted stress on the Platonism of Kant's "Christology" in Part II (FJ, 155–58, 164–65, 178). In that context they speak of the "pure cognition" of the prototype, the Idea of a morally perfect human individual eternally present in God and present in every time, place, and culture in human reason (R, 105, 6. 62–63; 108, 6.66). Of course, 'pure' signifies the a priori and universal as distinct from the empirical. But what about 'cognition'? Does it suggest a kind of speculative metaphysical knowledge that violates the constraints of the first Critique? Pamela Sue Anderson argues vigorously to this effect.⁵²

It seems to me that the objection is unfounded. A lot depends on how one reads 'cognition.' Jacobs writes,

> Cognition is clearly more than mere opinion (*Meinung*) but interpreters of Kant dispute whether cognition (*Erkenntnis*) is closer to knowledge (*Wissen*) or rational belief (*Glaube*). . . . Kant makes an important distinction between empirical cognition and pure cognition, or the cognition of reason. The latter is where matters of God, freedom, and immortality fall. Therefore, I will be

using the term 'cognition'... in this latter sense, as a process that grounds rational belief, not full-fledged knowledge."[53]

In addition to God, freedom, and immortality, we can add the Ideas of reason in the Dialectic of the first Critique—God, soul, and world, for what is at issue in the prototype is just that, a Platonic Idea of reason. Each one represents "something which does not allow of being confined within experience, since it concerns a knowledge (*Erkenntnis*)[54] of which any empirical knowledge ... is only a part. No actual experience has ever been completely adequate to it, yet to it every actual experience belongs" (*CPR*, A 310–11 = B 367, A 334–35 = B 391–92).[55]

Kant seems to be appealing to the notion that we can think beyond the limits of what we can know. Andrew Chignell suggests that the dispute is "largely a terminological issue.... If Firestone and Jacobs had spoken instead about pure 'thinking' (*Denken*), I think they could have had some of what they wanted by way of theological/moral content without raising these hackles."[56] In fact they do just that. In developing the concept of pure cognition, they cite the passage from *CPR*, xxvi, about the right to think beyond the limits of knowledge and say, "For Kant, we can think and talk about matters that have no direct empirical evidence" (FJ, 112).

Chignell makes a second suggestion. "If what they wanted from 'pure cognition' however, was supposed to be *synthetic* judgments, then they might have avoided controversy by making use of one of the notions of justified belief (*Glaube*) in Kant."[57] Again, they do just that. There is the suggestion by Jacobs, cited above, that in some contexts, *Erkenntnis* is closer to *Glaube* than to *Wissen*. With Firestone, he writes, "Yet, there are also objects of cognition that are possible objects of faith and, as such, these cognitions rise above the status of mere opinion.... While certain non-empirical cognitions cannot have objective sufficiency, Kant does maintain that if reasons exist for deeming these cognitions subjectively sufficient, they can have objective validity" (FJ, 112).

Firestone and Jacobs are especially concerned with the consistency between *Religion* and the critical philosophy of the first Critique. They can rightly claim, I believe, that neither as thought that goes beyond experience nor as justified belief that strays beyond the limits of mere knowledge does Kant's account of our "pure cognition" of the prototype violate the constraints of the first Critique.

The second way of distinguishing the pure cognition of the prototype from both legitimate empirical knowledge and illegitimate speculative metaphysics, namely as belief that is justified by its role in our moral life, raises the question: Is the prototype a postulate of pure practical reason, a transcendental condition for the possibility of the moral life making sense? Firestone and Jacobs make just such a suggestion (FJ, 117). While the appearance of an historical individual who is a striking example of the prototype may be useful, it is not necessary, as we have seen. However,

> [e]ven if not practically necessary, the appearance is a necessary possibility... We find then, a careful balance in Kant's thinking on this point. The *required* prototype is a universally valid pure cognition, but an empirical cognition of this ideal must be possible to whatever extent outward deeds provide evidence of an inward disposition. (FJ, 169–70).

In chapter 5 we raised the question whether belief in divine revelation, which Kant refuses to rule out, has the status of a postulate. The answer was negative because such a belief was only developmentally necessary and therefore dispensable. Here, however, we might say that Kant's "Christology" of the prototype that is not Jesus has the status of a postulate of pure practical reason, a belief about the nature of God that is morally and conceptually necessary to the moral life even if not metaphysically justified as rational. We might say the same about Kant's theory of atonement, although it does not involve any belief about God, since we atone for our own pre-conversion sins. Neither theme in his theology involves any appeal to divine agency, but both seem to have a necessity to the moral life more than developmental necessity.

I am not aware of Kant's calling these "doctrines" of his rational theology postulates. Perhaps as a generic deist, he is content to give that status only to God and immortality. But as a distinctively Kantian deist, he at least comes very close to adding a couple of more specific postulates. We might call them quasi-postulates. In chapters 4 and 5, respectively, we saw that belief in divine agency in conversion and in special revelation almost rose to this level, but not quite.

In all these cases, conversion, revelation, atonement, and "Christology,"[58] Kant is working out implications of his three most fundamental theological themes, God, immortality, and radical evil, each of which is grounded in his moral philosophy. In each case, he identifies beliefs that go beyond both knowledge, as he defines it, and moral philosophy, as he develops it.[59] He argues that these beliefs are either permitted[60] or required (possible or necessary) for the moral life. In doing so he is not a Christian theologian offering interpretations (translations) of Scripture and tradition; he is trying to think through the meaning of God and immortality in the light of radical evil.

But in doing so he helps himself generously to the language and imagery of the Bible and Christian tradition. In order to stay strictly within the limits of reason alone, he offers a series of persuasive redefinitions or what we might call "polemical redefinitions."[61] So what shall we say about the relation of Kant's religion to mere Christianity?

Palmquist defends the notion that Kant's "approach was designed to defend and promote the Christian religion."[62] Michalson sees in his account of moral regeneration a "virtually confessional appeal to scripture."[63] Jacobs acknowledges that Kant's account of the prototype "bears an uncanny resemblance to the Christ of Christianity (apparent from the number of Kant interpreters that assume the prototype *is* Jesus of Nazareth)."[64] However, he also reminds us that various elements of Kant's theology "*look* very Christian. But looks can be deceiving."[65]

I have been emphasizing the incompatibility of Kant's religion with mere Christianity. I agree with Firestone and Jacobs on this point,[66] and with di Giovanni, who writes, "Kant presents his religion as the *true* religion, opposing it to historical Christianity (unless the latter, of course, is re-interpreted according to his own precepts)."[67] The compatibility expressed in parentheses is both question-begging and too cheaply achieved. So in order to make my position on the substantive question as precise as possible, I want to distinguish three senses in which Kant can be said to oppose his own religion to the Christian religion.

First, especially in Part IV of *Religion* Kant identifies beliefs and practices at least sometimes presented as Christian that he considers superstitious and/or morally corrupting. So there is some truth in Hare's claim that "Kant's polemic is against what he sees as a corruption of Christianity, rather than against Christianity itself.... We have to avoid hearing Nietzsche in his work louder than Luther."[68] Palmquist also presents Kant as a reformer.[69] Mere Christians will be sympathetic to some of Kant's prophetic protests against what he, and sometimes they consider degenerate forms of Christianity. But sometimes they will not, for there is Nietzsche as well as Luther in Kant. From the perspective of enlightened autonomy, much of Christianity must be rejected as slave religion.

Second, we can refer back to our Venn diagram in which BK represents the overlap between biblical religion and Kant's religion, B* represents the other aspects of biblical religion, and K* represents the other aspects of Kant's religion. In making the claim that K, including BK, is the true religion of reason, he also makes the claim that BK is the essence of all religion (at least as far it is not delusional or morally corrupting). It is the kernel, the core of Christianity; the rest, B* insofar as it has not been excluded above on Nietzschean/Lutheran grounds, is the shell or the husk, possibly useful but dispensable. To mere Christians this will seem like saying that the essence of marriage is the raising of children and faithfulness to one's spouse is optional and temporary, of value only insofar as it supports parenting. Or like saying that the Russian and Chinese governments are like western democracies because they have elections and allow women to vote. Yes, something like Kant's ethic is fundamental to the Christian faith, but so is a great deal more. Both in his kernel and husk imagery and in the principle of hermeneutical hegemony, Kant dispenses with this "more" wholesale, and thereby places his religion in stark opposition to mere Christianity.

Third, he also replaces the Christian faith retail. The actual polemical reinterpretations of biblical and theological themes that Kant presents are dramatically different from and incompatible with their verbal analogs. When Kant has finished reshaping the square pegs of the Jewish rooted and historically particular worldview of Christianity so they will fit into the round holes of (his version of) reason, they are no longer recognizable as square pegs, nor are they intended to be.

I want to be as clear as possible about what I take to be the significance of the systematic opposition Kant places between his rational religion and the revealed religion he respects (in a measure) and whose language he is not loath to borrow. I am a mere Christian, and I assume that where Kant deviates from the historic Christian faith he is mistaken and misguided. But that is not what I am trying to show here. That Christianity is the true religion is not the premise or the conclusion of my argument. I am trying to describe the relation between two mutually incompatible religions (but with some overlap) that any careful observer ought to be able to recognize, whatever their religious or non-religious identity. One might develop a similar comparison of Judaism and Islam or Christianity and Buddhism regardless of whether one belongs to either or neither. My claim is simply that Christianity and Kant's religion are, to repeat, deeply divergent.

So what? Well, at least with regard to the harmony thesis, I hope to have shown that Kant is simply wrong. There is harmony insofar as there is overlap; and there is the essentially tautological harmony between the religion of pure reason and the historical materials Kant uses after reinterpreting them precisely in order to exhibit this harmony. But both formally (wholesale) and materially (retail) there is a deep chasm between the two, since those reinterpretations do violence their texts, as Kant, to his credit, acknowledges. To paraphrase Kierkegaard's Johannes Climacus, "Christianity may be wrong, but this much is certain; Kant is wrong, for he claims a harmony between Christianity and religion within the limits of reason alone that the evidence undermines."[70]

The presence of various overlaps does not keep Judaism, Christianity, Islam, Hinduism, and Buddhism from being rival religions, incompatible with one another at crucial points. Add Kant's religion to that list. The fact that it appeals to an allegedly universal reason and has no texts with the normative function of a scriptural revelation should not hide from us the historically particular presuppositions of his religious theory and practice. In the specificity of their semantic and epistemic space, they are irreconcilable not only with Spinoza and Hegel, but also with mere Christianity.

After reducing Christ to the example of a Platonic idea, invoking the kernel and husk imagery, and insisting on a hermeneutical hegemony in the service of "harmony with the *most holy* teachings of reason," Kant tries to sustain his harmony thesis by quoting Jesus: "he who is not against us is for us" (Mark 9:40). But his text is against the Christian faith at so many places and in so many ways that his ability to quote the Bible supports neither his harmony thesis nor his claim to be the voice of a universal reason.

Notes

1. Kant describes religions that rest on some particular, historical scripture as "revealed," "learned," "statutory," and "ecclesiastical." While not synonymous in terms of their connotations, they refer to the same phenomena. The opposite, of course, is rational or natural religion.

2. Outer revelation comes either through works or words. "*Inner* divine revelation is God's revelation to us through our own reason; this latter must *precede all other* revelation and serve for the estimation of outer revelation. It has to be the touchstone by which I recognize *whether an outer revelation is really from God*, and it must furnish me with proper concepts of him" (*CF*, 443, 28.1117). In other words, a biblical text can teach me about God only insofar as it is brought into conformity with a reason that purports to be universal.

3. The latter phrase is borrowed from an analogy between the natural law theorist and the Codex of Roman Law, where the same terms in different contexts have different meanings.

4. I assume that by 'literal' here Kant does not mean interpretations that ignore the rhetorical force of such figures of speech as metaphors, metonymies, ironies, and so forth, but rather those interpretations that stick as much as possible to the meanings the text would have had for its author(s) and intended readers, whatever rhetorical resources it employs. 'Literal' often, but not always, has this sense in discussions of biblical interpretation.

5. Cf. *R*, 142, 6.109—"We have noted that, although a church sacrifices the most important mark of its truth, namely the legitimate claim to universality, whenever it bases itself upon a faith of revelation which, as historical faith . . . is incapable of transmission that commands conviction universally, yet, because of the natural need of all human beings to demand something that *the senses can hold on to* . . . (a need which must also be seriously taken into account when the intention is *to introduce* a faith universally) some historical ecclesiastical faith or other, usually already at hand, must be used."

6. Kant treats these necessary truths as self-evident. They are "indubitable" because "these alone are teachings that *carry their own proof* and on which, therefore, the accreditation of any other must principally rest" (*R*, 181, 6.159; emphasis added). This necessity seems different from and stronger than the necessity of the postulates, which are not necessary truths in themselves but beliefs that are necessary if the moral life is to make sense.

7. Hence the global missionary movement began with the apostle Paul and continues to this day.

8. See C. I. Lewis, "The Pragmatic Conception of the a Priori," in *Readings in Philosophical Analysis*, ed. Herbert Feigl and Wilfrid Sellars (New York: Appleton-Century Crofts, 1949), pp. 286–94. C. G. Hempel makes point when he acknowledges that the verification criterion of cognitive meaning is not an insight into some truth but a "proposal" adopted for some particular purpose. "Empiricist Criteria of Cognitive Significance: Problems and Changes," in *Aspects of Scientific Explanation*, (New York: Free Press, 1965), pp. 101–19.

9. Max Horkheimer and Theodor W. Adorno, *Dialectic of Enlightenment*, trans. John Cumming (New York: Continuum, 1982), p. xvi.

10. Especially in Part III of *Religion*. See pp. 140, 146–47, 149, and 152n; 6.106, 115–16, 118, and 123n, and cf. 64, 6.13.

11. Gordon E. Michalson Jr., *Fallen Freedom: Kant on Radical Evil and Moral Regeneration* (Cambridge: Cambridge University Press, 1990), pp. 80–81.

12. But not, in should be noted in fairness, one he envisages as enforced by the state. As we saw in chapter one, Kant's autonomy project begins with politics, moves to ethics, and eventually to religion.

13. Stephen R. Palmquist, "Philosophers in the Public Square," in *Kant and the New Philosophy of Religion*, ed. Chris L. Firestone and Stephen R. Palmquist (Bloomington: Indiana University Press, 2006), p. 243.

14. George di Giovanni, "On Chris L. Firestone and Nathan Jacob's *In Defense of Kant's Religion*: A Comment," *Faith and Philosophy* 29, no. 2 (April 2012): 164.

15. Mary's *Magnificat* is found in Luke 1:46–55.

16. The *Benedictus*, Luke 1:72–73. In the remainder of his hymn, Zechariah interprets the hoped for victory over "our enemies" as the forgiveness of sins and light to those who sit "in the shadow of death."

17. John E. Hare, *The Moral Gap: Kantian Ethics, Human Limits, and God's Assistance* (Oxford: Clarendon Press, 1996), p. 33. On biblical religion as covenantal religion, see my *God, Guilt, and Death: An Existential Phenomenology of Religion* (Bloomington: Indiana University Press, 1984), chap. 11. Cf. Matt. 26:28, where Jesus, sharing the cup of wine with his disciples, says, "for this is my

blood of the covenant, which is poured out for many for the forgiveness of sins." Some manuscripts have "new covenant," linking Jesus's words to Jeremiah 31:31–34.

18. Ernst Cassirer suggests that even in his youth Kant distinguished the admirable pietism of his parents from the rigid and mechanized form he already found enslaving, presumably as experienced at his school. *Kant's Life and Thought*, trans. James Haven (New Haven, CT: Yale University Press, 1981), pp. 15–18.

19. Quoted in FJ, p. 100, from Gordon E. Michalson Jr., *The Historical Dimensions of a Rational Faith: The Role of History in Kant's Religious Thought* (Washington, DC: University Press of America, 1979), p. 116. FJ then summarizes, "Kant's vision, under this interpretative option, is one of a purely moralistic society in which all formal or ecclesiastical religion is disbanded; however, Kant is sober enough to understand that a historical, intermediate period is inevitable."

20. See (7) and (8) in chapter 5, along with the subsequent discussion of developmental necessity.

21. It might be more precise to substitute 'normatively' and 'epistemically' for 'necessarily' and 'automatically,' respectively. With reference to Kant's account of moral regeneration, Michalson says that "the scriptural account is called upon because the [philosophical] conceptuality has exhausted itself." *Fallen Freedom*, p. 81. The defense of Kant against this kind of objection that runs throughout FJ appeals regularly to Kant's Platonic account of reason and its independence of the empirical and historical.

22. This epistemic occasionalism echoes the causal occasionalism of Malebranche.

23. Chris L. Firestone, "Making Sense out of Tradition: Theology and Conflict in Kant's Philosophy of Religion," in Firestone and Palmquist, *New Philosophy*, p. 150. The same is true of Firestone's claim that Kant seeks a "dialectical" relation between theology and philosophy. "Response to Critics of *In Defense of Kant's Religion*," in *Faith and Philosophy* 29, no 2 (April 2012): 196–97.

24. Firestone, "Making Sense," p. 145.

25. See *Metaphysics of Morals*, 599, 6.488: "We can indeed speak of a 'Religion *within the Boundaries* of Mere Reason' which is not, however, derived *from* reason alone but is also based on the teachings of history and revelation, and considers only the *harmony* of pure practical reason with these (shows that there is no conflict between them)."

26. So far that includes a theory of duties as God's commands, belief in God and immortality, and at least hope for help in giving permanent priority to the good principle over the evil principle, that is, conversion or moral regeneration.

27. Speaking of *Religion*, Kant writes, "The title indicates that I intended, rather, to set forth as a coherent whole everything in the Bible—the text of the religion believed to be revealed—that can *also* be recognized *by mere reason*" (CF, 239, 6n).

28. It has been argued that the second experiment occurs only in Part IV of *Religion* (FJ, 114–19). But translations or interpretations of Christian themes designed to make them harmonious with rational religion are found throughout the text.

29. The quotation marks signify respective claims that are anything but self-evident, namely, that reason is ahistorically universal and that Scripture is of divine and not merely human origin.

30. Quoted at FJ, 98, from Michalson, *Historical Dimensions*, pp. 90–91. The phrase "vicious circularity" is FJ's summary of this objection.

31. Peter Byrne, *Kant on God* (Burlington, VT: Ashgate, 2007), p. 158. The historical dimension that makes this harmony problematic is filtered out as "quite indifferent" as per *Religion* 143, 6.111. Unlike Spinoza, Kant does not seem to distinguish questions of meaning from questions of truth.

32. The phrase is Hare's in *Moral Gap*, pp. 40–41.

33. For example, baptism is conceptually necessary to mere Christianity, though there is a difference over whether it is infants or confessing adults who should be baptized.

34. Byrne suggests the term "justifying grace" for "whatever divine mechanism" is required to expunge that guilt. *Kant on God*, p. 140. But this is doubling misleading. It conflates justification with atonement, which happens in neither Kant nor mere Christianity; and it overlooks the fact that no "divine mechanism" is called for in Kant's theory of atonement.

35. Nicholas Wolterstorff finds a "conundrum" in Kant's theory of atonement, since he first says we cannot wipe out this guilt and then says we can. "Conundrums in Kant's Rational Religion," in *Kant's Philosophy of Religion Reconsidered*, ed. Philip J. Rossi and Michael Wreen (Bloomington: Indiana University Press, 1991), pp. 42–45.

36. In German *Schuld* means both guilt and debt. Cf. the alternative renderings of the Lord's Prayer as either "forgive us our trespasses" or "forgive us our debts."

37. Not all theological interpretations of the death of Jesus involve atonement. There is another strand of thought in the New Testament that focuses on the victory won over sin, death, the devil, the principalities and powers and so forth. Gustaf Aulén insists, mistakenly in my view, on the inseparability of the victory and deliverance motif from the atonement and reconciliation motif. *Christus Victor: An Historical Study of the Three Main Types of the Idea of Atonement*, trans. A. G. Hebert (Eugene, OR: Wipf & Stock, 2003), p. 71. They belong together as interpretations of the death of Jesus, but one concerns the power of evil forces over us, the other the guilt we have incurred. Augustus Toplady has a better theology in the hymn, "Rock of Ages": "Be of sin the double cure, Cleanse me from its guilt and pow'r."

38. Given the radical reinterpretations Kant gives to these terms from the Bible and Christian tradition, it is clear that his use of them does not mean he "has suddenly had a fit of orthodoxy," as Michalson reminds us. *Fallen Freedom*, p. 108).

39. The satisfaction theory of the Atonement has Anselm's *Cur Deus Homo?* as its classic statement. Unfortunately, there it is God's honor that must be satisfied. Kant is at least in tune with the better versions in which it is God's justice and the punishment it requires that is at issue. Thus Paul concludes his summary of justification on the basis of the expiating death of Jesus, "God meant by this to demonstrate his justice ... showing that he is himself just and also justifies anyone who puts his faith in Jesus. (Rom. 3:21–26, Revised English Bible).

40. The substitution motif has its roots in the sacrificial system laid out in Leviticus; in Isaiah 53:6, "and the Lord has laid on him the iniquity of us all"; John 1:29, "Here is the Lamb of God who takes away the sin of the world"; and 1 Peter 2:24 with 3:18," He himself bore our sins in his body on the cross. ... For Christ also suffered for sins once for all, the righteous for the unrighteous." Bach expresses the shared understanding of mere Christianity in *St. Matthew Passion*.

How amazing is this punishment!	*Wie wunderbarlich ist doch diese Strafe!*
The good shepherd suffers for the sheep;	*Der gute Hirte leidet für die Schafe;*
The righteous master pays the debt his servants owe.	*Die Schuld bezahlt der Herre, der Gerechte, für seine Knechte.*

41. N.B. The subject of the verb 'bears' is 'disposition.'

42. This is another dimension of what we might call Kant's Platonic pietism. His "common people" are Plato's hoi polloi, the many who remain unenlightened, in the cave. See Kant's reference to "popular faith" (*Volksglaube, R*, 144, 6.112).

43. In Luther's translation of Genesis 1:3, "Let there be light" is "*Es werde Licht*." Haydn quotes this line in *Die Schöpfung* ("The Creation"), though the choral explosion comes on the next line, *Und es ward Licht* ("And there was light").

44. Nathan A. Jacobs, "A Reply to Critics of *In Defense of Kant's* Religion," in *Faith and Philosophy* 29, no. 2 (April 2012), p. 219. "In Books 2 and 3, Kant consistently refers to *the prototype*, while in Book 4 he refers to Jesus [but not by name] as *the Teacher of the Gospel*" (pp. 218–19). Cf. FJ, 116–17. In Book 2, Jesus [but not by name] is an example of the prototype.

45. I render Kant's *kann* as 'might' rather than 'may,' as in both English translations, because it is immediately followed by an 'if" (*wenn*), suggesting possibility rather than permission.

46. With regard to the holy books of Judaism, Christianity, Islam, and Hinduism, Kant says that "their historical element ... is something in itself quite indifferent, and one can do with it what one wills" (*R*, 143, 6.111).

47. I switch to the upper case for Idea to emphasize the now explicit Platonism of Kant's account. This Idea is an objective, eternal aspect of the being of God, accessible to us through reason. Plato speaks of the imitation (a moral concept) and participation (an ontological concept) of earthly individuals in the transcendent Ideas. Kant has only the former of these available to him.

48. See note 45 above.

49. "But the Comforter, which is the Holy Ghost, whom the Father will send in my name, he shall teach you all things, and bring all things to your remembrance, whatsoever I have said unto you" (John 14:26, KJV; cf. 14:16 and 15:26). NRSV has Advocate for Comforter. Kant uses *Tröster*, the term Luther uses in his translation of the Bible. 'Paraclete' is a reference to the Greek term translated in these ways.

50. At *R*, 143–44, 6.112, it is the religion that follows the hegemony principle in hermeneutics that is "the Spirit of God, who guides us into all truth" (John 16:13).

51. Michalson, *Fallen Freedom*, pp. 1–2.

52. Pamela Sue Anderson, "The Philosophical Significance of Kant's *Religion*: 'Pure Cognition of' or 'Belief in' God," in *Faith and Philosophy* 29, no. 2 (April 2012): 151–62.

53. Nathan Jacobs, "Kant's Prototypical Theology: Transcendental Incarnation as a Rational Foundation for God-Talk," in Firestone and Palmquist, *New Philosophy*, p. 131. Cf. FJ, 109, 112–13.

54. In their Cambridge translation, Guyer and Wood render *Erkenntnis* as 'cognition.'

55. Cf. B 395n, where Kant links the two trios of rational concepts or ideas: God, freedom, and immortality, and God, soul, and world. Throughout the Dialectic of the first Critique he repeatedly reaffirms that inadequacy of anything empirical to these a priori concepts.

56. Andrew Chignell, "Introduction: Defending Kant at the AAR," in *Faith and Philosophy* 29, no. 2 (April 2012): 148n.

57. Chignell, "Introduction," p. 148n.

58. This is not a commentary on *Religion*, and my treatment has been selective rather than comprehensive. The most important omission is Kant's account of the church and the Kingdom of God in Part III. Unsurprisingly, the same hermeneutic is at work there, with similar results.

59. Thus, no reduction of religion to morality, but only the hegemony of morality over religion.

60. Since it would be dogmatic to rule them out and they may be useful to the moral life.

61. Following N. T. Wright in *Paul and the Faithfulness of God* (Minneapolis, MN: Fortress Press, 2013), pp. 1242. Wright is not speaking about Kant but about Paul in relation to second temple Judaism.

62. Palmquist, "Public Square," p. 233 and 233n5. But the evidence he cites does not support this claim. "The title [of *Religion*] indicates that I intended, rather to set forth as a coherent whole everything in the Bible—the text of the religion believed to be revealed—that can *also* be recognized *by mere reason*" (*CF*, 239, 7.6n).

63. Michalson, *Fallen Freedom*, p. 81.

64. Jacobs, "Prototypical Theology," p. 137.

65. Jacobs, "Reply to Critics," p. 225.

66. See Firestone, "Response to Critics," pp. 195–96; and Jacobs, "Reply to Critics," p. 225.

67. di Giovanni, "Comment," p. 163. Cf. p. 164.

68. Hare, *Moral Gap*, p. 50. Hare recognizes that this is not the whole story.

69. Stephen R. Palmquist, "Cross-Examination of *In Defense of Kant's* Religion," in *Faith and Philosophy* 29, no. 2 (April 2012): 179.

70. Climacus writes, "But if Christianity is perhaps in the wrong, this much is certain: speculative thought [Hegel and the Hegelians] is definitely in the wrong, because the only consistency outside of Christianity is that of pantheism, the taking of oneself out of existence back into the eternal through recollection." *Concluding Unscientific Postscript*, trans. Howard V. Hong and Edna H. Hong (Princeton, NJ: Princeton University Press, 1992), I, 226. The epistemic Platonism here attributed to Hegel is shared by Spinoza and Kant. My argument is that their common claim to be the voice of a universal reason is refuted by the mutual incompatibility of their three systems.

7

HEGEL'S THEOLOGY I

Hegel's theology begins its development in a series of drafts and fragments from his student and tutor years at Tübingen, Berne, and Frankfurt. They are dated from 1793 to 1800 and thus precede his philosophical appointment at Jena in 1801. Many of these were first published in 1907 by Nohl in *Hegel's theologische Jugendschriften*. Most of them are translated by T. M. Knox in G. W. F. Hegel, *Early Theological Writings*, bearing the titles given them by Nohl.[1] They lay the theological foundations for Hegel's mature thought that is at once a philosophical and a political theology.

It has been objected that the titles of Nohl and Knox are misleading, that the early writings are "antitheological."[2] There is a point to this, but ultimately it is misleading. If we distinguish philosophical theology (a largely metaphysical theorizing about God) from philosophy of religion (a largely sociological theorizing about the cultural significance of religious beliefs and practices, when the term is not used as a synonym for philosophical theology), this early Hegel is far more the sociologist than the metaphysician of the religious life. It is at Jena that he becomes the philosopher we know as Hegel; it is there that metaphysics will begin its rise to hegemony over sociology while incorporating social history into metaphysics. Ultimate reality is human history.

What the "antitheological" Hegel vigorously opposes is biblical religion in both its Jewish and Christian forms, which he compares unfavorably with Greek religion.[3] So he opposes Christian theology, as he understands it, because of the kind of religious life in which it is embedded; and he praises the "folk religion" of the Greeks in part because theology as theory plays such a minimal part in it. Orthodoxy is not a primary religious value. These writings are nevertheless Hegel's early theology in the sense of presenting the norms he thinks should govern religious life in its cognitive, active, and affective dimensions. What they have to say about God is often only implicit. They set the stage for his mature pantheism of spirit.

In the 1793 essay on folk religion, now known as the "Tübingen Essay," the contrast between alienating (Christian) and liberating (Greek) religion is presented as the difference between objective and subjective religion.[4] Objective religion is the primacy of theoretical reason, equating religion with the science of God. In focusing on argument and evidence, understanding and memory, it abstracts religion from life, especially the life of morality and beauty.[5] It becomes an arid rationalism.[6] Grounded in mere Understanding it gives rise to "the self-conceit of a sect" and becomes ideological. "The understanding is a courtier who adapts himself complaisantly to the caprices of his lord. It knows how to scare up justifying arguments for every passion. . . . It is especially a servant to self-love" (*TE*, 488–89). If we ask whether Hegel means personal or communal self-love, the answer, undoubtedly, is both.

Hegel links the Enlightenment with Christian orthodoxy in this respect (*TE*, 490, 492, 494).[7] It is in this context that Hegel develops a polemic against the Understanding (*Verstand*) as a defective mode of cognition (*TE*, 484–90). All the "theology" that the common people need is moral belief in God and immortality. The rest can be left to the theologians (*TE*, 482–86).[8]

There are three essential marks to such a popular religion that Hegel calls subjective, folk religion. First,

> [i]ts doctrines must be grounded on *universal Reason*. . . . Even if their authority rests on a divine revelation the doctrines must necessarily be so constituted that they are authorized really by the universal Reason of mankind, so that *every man* sees and feels their obligatory force when it is [they are?] drawn to his attention.

Otherwise they become they become "precise—intolerant—symbols" (*TE*, 499; emphasis added).[9]

But Hegel's concept of "universal Reason" is not quite the same as that of Spinoza and Kant. "In good men subjective religion is very nearly the same, while their objective religion may be of almost any stripe—'What makes me to you a Christian, makes you to me a Jew' says Nathan [act IV, scene 7]" (*TE*, 487).[10] Very nearly the same? It turns out that "a universal Church of the spirit [grounded in universal Reason] is only an ideal of reason." Reality is something else (Cf. *PC* 2, 169–70, 172). The doctrines of folk religion are not only to be simple but also "humane in the sense that they are appropriate to the spiritual culture and stage of morality that a people has reached" since "doctrines founded on universal Reason are compatible with every level of folk-culture, and the culture will gradually modify the doctrines in accord with its changes" (*TE*, 495, 500, 502). Therefore, folk religion can rightly express itself in the ceremonies, myths, and folk festivals of a quite particular culture.

This can include sacrifices so long as they involve thanksgiving but not atonement, an "irrational absurdity" (*TE*, 503–4). Given the importance of atoning sacrifice in both the Jewish and Christian scriptures, this is the claim that biblical religion is an "irrational absurdity"; and since "universal" Reason comes in culturally relative forms, the question arises: whose reason makes this claim; what are its credentials; in what sense, if any, is it universal? Surely it is not the case that *"every man* sees and feels the obligatory force" of the claim that atoning sacrifice is an "irrational absurdity."

Hegel is working here with what we might call historical holism. "The spirit of a people, its history, its religion, the level of its political freedom cannot be treated separately either with respect to their mutual influence, or in characterizing them [each by itself]—they are woven together in a single bond" (*TE*, 506; translation modified]. This seems to be a bi-modal claim, indicative and imperative, an is-and-ought-to-be proposition. Here Hegel introduces us to his conception of universal Reason as embedded in particular histories, but he does not tell us how this contingent concreteness does not compromise and contaminate the universality. There is unfinished business here.

The second essential mark of folk religion is this: "Fancy [*Phanatasie*, imagination], heart, and sensibility must not thereby [that is, in relation to universal Reason] go empty away" (*TE*, 499). This is the reason why Reason requires embodiment in culturally contingent ceremonies, myths, and festivals. The Reason of folk religion cannot be an intellect in opposition to other "parts of the soul." Platonic, Gnostic, and Cartesian dualisms are anathema. Thus folk religion must be rich in sensibility, images, feelings, and beauty; it must embody practical reason and thus the will, motives, action, and morality; in short, it must be a religion of the heart (*TE*, 482–88, 491). Thus the earliest Hegel belongs to what Henrich identifies as one of the major strands of post-Kantian critique of Kant, namely, "the criticism of Kant's ethical writings, in terms of the [anti-Kantian] postulate of the ultimate unity of man (i.e. one cannot divide humans into a merely rational and a merely sensual part)."[11]

Finally, folk religion "must be so constituted that all the needs of life—the public affairs of the State are tied in with it" (TE, 499). It will be a public, civil religion both ideologically and institutionally. In this way, given the Greek model Hegel is working with, folk religion "goes hand in hand with freedom" (TE, 505). It must exclude every form of "ecclesiastical and political slavery" (TE, 497).[12] We might call it a religion of autonomy, not the autonomy of the individual but of each culture.

There is virtually nothing about God or the gods in the Tübingen Essay. But it is easy to suspect, given his enthusiasm for Greek religion and the antipathy for biblical religion,[13] that Hegel feels more at home with the gods of Olympus than with the God of Sinai, Zion, and Calvary, at least in terms of their cultural spirit as distinct from their metaphysical letter. Given his praise for the "spirit of innocence" in which the Greek sacrifices took place (TE, 504), he might have sympathized with Nietzsche's suggestion that before Zeus, the Greeks interpreted themselves in terms of "foolishness, *not* sin! . . . In this way, the gods served in those days to justify man to a certain extent even in his wickedness, they served as the originators of evil—in those days they took upon themselves, not the punishment but, what is *nobler*, the guilt."[14]

As we will see, Hegel's early theological writings anticipate Nietzsche's genealogy of biblical religion from a spirit of slavery (heteronomy). But he is not headed for Nietzsche's will to power philosophy; nor is he advocating a return to Greek polytheism. As he makes his theology more explicit, it can be described as what I call a pantheism of spirit and which Henrich calls a "Spinozism of freedom."

> The post-Kantian intellectual movement begins with a revival of Spinozism.... So they thought that if there is a God—and Spinoza, of course, taught that there is one—it is not outside us, addressing us through demands and acts of revelation, but *inside* us . . . if we are free, it must be possible to think that our freedom is not simply in contradiction with, but something that is already essentially a part of the life of God. This is what the rallying cry of the 'Spinozism of freedom' meant to the generation of Hegel, Hölderlin, Fichte, and Schelling.[15]

N.B. If human freedom is *essentially* part of the life of God, its employment cannot estrange us from God. The biblical narrative of sin and exile, redemption and reconciliation becomes quite unnecessary. On this point Hegel and

Spinoza are at one in implying that even Kant's narrative of radical evil and semi-Pelagian salvation, including its reinterpretation of atonement in accord with "mere reason" is at worst "irrational absurdity" and at best an unnecessary and dangerous concession to those not yet ready for philosophical prime time.

Just about the time Hegel began work on the essay now known as "The Positivity of the Christian Religion," his correspondence with Schelling, his friend from days at the Tübingen seminary, shows a decisive departure from a theistic conception of a personal God. In January, 1795, Schelling writes that "Kant has swept *everything* away," but alas, the "crowd" doesn't notice.

> I am convinced that the old superstition of so-called natural religion [deism] as well as of positive religion [orthodox Christianity] has in the minds of most already once more been combined with the Kantian letter.[16] It is fun to see how quickly they can get to the moral proof. Before you can turn around the *deus ex machina* springs forth, the personal individual Being who sits in Heaven above!

But Fichte will correct this. He "will raise philosophy to a height at which even most of the hitherto Kantians will become giddy.... Now I am working on an ethic *à la* Spinoza" (*HL*, 29). Fichte leads us back to Spinoza!

Hegel replies in the same month. He would like "to disturb as much as possible the theologians who in their antlike zeal procure *critical* building materials for the strengthening of their Gothic temple." In other words, both oppose the attempt to support Christian orthodoxy with Kantian arguments. But Hegel suggests, contra Schelling, that Fichte himself is largely to blame.[17] At the same time, he seems reluctant to abandon entirely the theology of the Kantian postulates of the second Critique.[18] He concludes with a question about Schelling's reference to the moral proof "'which they know how to manipulate so that out springs the individual, personal Being.' Do you really believe we fail to get so far? Farewell. Reason and Freedom remain our password, and the Invisible Church our rallying point" (*HL*, 31–32).[19]

In February, Schelling replies, with reference to the moral proof and a personal God,

> I confess [your] question has surprised me. I would not have expected it from an intimate of Lessing's. Yet you no doubt asked it only to learn whether the question has been entirely decided *in my own mind*. For you the question has surely long since been decided. For us as well [as for Lessing] the orthodox concepts of God are no more.[20] My reply is that we get even *further* than a personal Being. I have in the interim become a Spinozist. (*HL*, 32)[21]

Schelling goes on to explain in Fichtean terms that God is the Absolute Self, that personal consciousness requires a subject and an object, and that the Absolute Self could not have an object on pain of not being absolute. "Consequently there is no personal God" (HL, 33).[22]

Hegel's reply does not come until April. He comes down on the side of Schelling and Fichte rather than Kant and Storr.[23] He expects all knowledge to be revolutionized by the Kantian system. It will include

> the idea of God as the Absolute Self.... After a more recent study of the postulates of practical reason I had a presentiment of what you clearly laid out for me in your last letter, of what I found in your writing, and of what Fichte's *Foundation of the Science of Knowledge* will disclose to me completely. The consequences that will result from it will astonish many a gentleman. Heads will be reeling at this summit of all philosophy by which man is being so greatly exalted.

But, as if recollecting the *Pantheismusstreit* that erupted over Jacobi's claim that Lessing had been a Spinozist[24] and anticipating the *Atheismusstreit* in which Fichte would be judged to be an atheist and lose his professorship at Jena, Hegel notes that this will have to be an "esoteric philosophy" (HL, 35).[25]

Later in this year (1795) Hegel begins work on the essay we know as "The Positivity of the Christian Religion." 'Positivity' is an epistemic category. A religion is positive rather than natural or rational when it is grounded in any authority, human or divine, that relativizes the autonomy of reason (PC 1, 71, 74, 100–101, 143–44; PC 2, 174). A couple years later Hegel will define positive religion in terms of the objective/subjective dichotomy from Tübingen. It is one "in which the practical is present [only] theoretically—what was originally subjective is only something objective; a religion whose representation of something objective cannot become subjective, established as a principle of life and action."[26] Since a lifeworld grounded in an orthodoxy of human or divine authority [objectivity] can become a way of life [subjectivity], even if only for slaves, as Hegel will have it, this exclusion of subjectivity from objectivity that constitutes positivity must concern some specific form of subjectivity. In context, the opposition must be between some external authority and an internal autonomy. Here again, autonomous reason is not abstractly universal but embedded and expressed in diverse cultures (PC 1, 145–52). It is "we" not "I" as such who must be free of any external authority. That's what folk religion was all about.

The Jews are paradigms of positivity. But both 'positivity' and 'objectivity' are too abstract to capture the lifeworld of the Jews among whom Jesus appeared. Only the language of slavery will do. The Jews prided themselves in their "slavish obedience" and "mechanical slavery," becoming "lifeless machines . . . in a monkish preoccupation with petty, mechanical, spiritless, and trivial usages" (PC 1, 69, cf. PC 1, 139–40, 158–59; and PC 2, 178–81).

Jesus himself "was free from the contagious sickness of his age. . . . He undertook to raise religion and virtue to morality and to restore to morality the freedom which is its essence" (PC 1, 69, cf. 75). But his essentially Kantian spirit[27] was up against insuperable obstacles in the Jewish culture to which he had to accommodate his teaching. In a religion dominated by priests and in a culture that "confined virtue to a blind obedience to these authoritarian commands," any appeal "to reason alone [Vernunft allein] would have meant the same thing as preaching to fish." Accordingly, Jesus could only appeal to "an equal authority, a divine one." (PC 1, 70, 76, cf. PC 1, 73, 98–101, 139–40, 158; PC 2, 178, 180–81).[28] Such an appeal could only mean that reason would be seen as receptive rather than legislative (PC 1, 85). Accordingly, it became necessary to appeal to himself as Messiah and to support such a claim with an appeal to miracles (PC 1, 77–79). This, again, means that reason can only be a servant and not "free as a master" (PC 1, 80).

This positivity gives to Jewish religion a sectarian character that excludes other sects. This is especially true in view of the union of "church" and "state" in ancient Israel—a sectarian state. With Lessing's *Nathan* in the background, this signifies religious intolerance, inquisitions, and holy wars (PC 1, 93). So, in spite of his folk religion ideal, Hegel puts in a sustained, classically liberal plea for the separation of church and state, apparently not noticing the irony involved (PC 1, 93–97, 104–7, 112, 114, 119–20, 123, 127–28, 139–40).[29] Of course, he is not worried about ancient Israel and there is as yet no modern Jewish state. His target is Christendom as the sectarian (Constantinian) union of church and state that separates not only Christians from Jews and Muslims but also Catholics from Protestants—not only in terms of religious beliefs and practices but in terms of civil and political rights as well. He does not seem to notice the irony involved in supporting his argument for the overcoming of oppositions within a culture with an argument for the separation of church and state as private and public institutions.

Hegel seeks to explain why Christianity became positive (heteronomous) in spite of Jesus, by referring to its Jewish origins. But he also asks another question: why was it so successful in the ancient world that it became Christendom? In a section entitled in Hegel's manuscript "Difference between the Greek Imaginative Religion [*Phantasie-Religion*] and the Christian Positive Religion" Hegel asks,

> How could a [pagan] religion have been supplanted after it had been established in states for centuries and intimately connected with their constitutions? What can have caused the cessation of a belief in gods to whom cities and empires ascribed their origin, to whom the people made daily offerings.... How could the faith in the gods have been reft from the web of human life with which it had been interwoven by a thousand threads? (*PC 1*, 152)[30]

Hegel gives a transcendental/sociological answer to this sociological question. It is not so much about the difference between folk religion and positive religion as between the life worlds that were the conditions of the possibility of each. Working with the contrast between democratic Athens and republican Rome on the one hand and imperial Rome on the other, Hegel attributes the triumph of Christianity to the loss of political freedom in the latter. Instead of seeing one's homeland as one's end (for which one would be willing to die),[31] the state becomes a despotic machine and is viewed as a means to the ends of the individual. The integrated political-cultural-religious community is dissolved into the individualism of *homo economicus* (*PC 1*, 154–65).

In short, "God's objectivity is a counterpart to [*ist in gleichen Schritte gegangen*] the corruption and slavery of man, and it is strictly only a revelation [*Offenbarung*], only a manifestation [*Erscheinung*] of the spirit of the age" (*PC 1*, 163). This sounds a lot like Feuerbach's atheism in which God is the projected image of ideal human life. Hegel's own conversion of theology into anthropology here is especially clear in the double "only" [*nur*].[32]

But we should not be surprised. Hegel had already written, "Apart from some earlier attempts, it has been reserved in the main for our epoch to vindicate at least in theory the human ownership of the treasures formerly squandered on heaven; but what age will have the strength to validate this right in practice and make itself its possessors?" (*PC 1*, 159).[33] In about half a century, Feuerbach, one of the "young Hegelians,"[34] will write,

> The divine being is nothing else than the human being, or, rather, the human nature purified, freed from the limits of the individual man, made objective—i.e., contemplated and revered as another, a distinct being.... Man—this is the mystery of religion—projects his being into objectivity, and then again makes himself an object of this projected image of himself thus converted into a subject.[35]

Up to this point, Hegel has seemed to be engaged more with Kant and Lessing on the autonomy of reason in religion than with Spinoza, Fichte, and Schelling on a pantheistic rather than a deistic grounding for this hegemony. Thus he writes,

> One leading trait in the church's moral system is its erection on religion and our dependence on the deity. Its foundation is not a datum of our own minds, a proposition which could be developed out of our own consciousness ... morality is not a self-subsistent science or one with independent principles; neither is the essence of morality grounded on freedom, i.e. it is not the autonomy of the will. (PC 1, 135)

But in the Feuerbachian sounding passages he seems to be moving toward a kind of sociological pantheism that might well be called a "Spinozism of freedom." Thus he writes, "But the view becomes glaringly positive if human nature is absolutely severed from the divine, if no mediation between the two is conceded except in one isolated individual, if all man's consciousness of the good and the divine is degraded to the dull and killing belief in a superior Being altogether alien to man." What is needed for a more satisfactory theology is "a metaphysical treatment of the relation between the finite and the infinite" (PC 1, 176).[36]

When we turn to the drafts now known as "The Spirit of Christianity and Its Fate" (1798–1800), we find the polemic against the Jewish religion renewed at a fully Nietzschean level (SC, 182–205). It involves an unambiguous rejection of Abrahamic monotheism.

> "There is one God" is an assertion which stands on the summit of the [Jewish] state's laws[37]... one might say: What deeper truth is there for slaves than that they have a master?... the existence of God appears to the Jews not as a truth but as a command. On God the Jews are dependent throughout, and that on which a man depends cannot have the form of a truth. (SC, 196)

This is an especially vivid statement of epistemic autonomy in the form of some version of knowledge as recollection.

Hegel interprets this fundamental Jewish experience as a tragedy, but one different from the Greek type.

> The great tragedy of the Jewish people is no Greek tragedy; it can rouse neither terror [*Furcht*] nor pity, for both of these arise only out of the fate which follows from the inevitable slip of a beautiful character; it can arouse horror [*Abscheu*] alone. The fate of the Jewish people is the fate of Macbeth who stepped out of nature itself, clung to alien Beings, and so in their service

had to trample and slay everything holy in human nature, had at last to be forsaken by his gods (since these were objects and he their slave) and be dashed to pieces on his faith itself. (*SC*, 205)[38]

Hegel cannot be accused of anti-Semitism here, and for two reasons. First, he is not talking about the Jews of his contemporary Europe but about the people of the Old Testament and their religion. I give the Christian name for the Jewish scriptures (*Tanakh, Miqra*) because, in the second place, Hegel's clear target is not ancient Judaism but contemporary Christianity, Abrahamic/Mosaic monotheism as interpreted in the gospels and epistles of the New Testament. Like Nietzsche, he tickles the fancy of Christian anti-Semites only long enough to prepare for the reversal in which Christianity is revealed as the true villain, the heir of Jewish slavery.

Here as in the previous essay Jesus is free from the slavish spirit of his contemporaries, preaching a religion of love, beauty, and reconciliation rather than one of rights and (especially) duties.[39] The Greek ideal has won out over the Kantian rigorism (*SC*, 197–98). But if this Jesus represents the spirit of Christianity, its fate is to succumb to the Jewish lifeworld in which it appeared and to remain a religion of slavery. Thus Hegel gives his distinctive take on the idea that Jesus wasn't a Christian. He was better than that. Much better.

As an alternative to Christian heteronomy Hegel projects onto Jesus his own emerging pantheism. It is the metaphysical presupposition underlying his categorical rejection, as we have just seen, of the idea that mediation between God and human beings is the work of "one isolated individual," implying "the dull and killing belief in a superior Being altogether alien to man" (*PC 1*, 176). For mere Christianity

> there is one God;
> there is also one mediator
> between God and humankind
> Christ Jesus, himself human
> who gave himself a ransom for all. (1 Tim. 2:5)

There are two very basic presuppositions to this mediation. The first is that God is not "altogether alien to man." There is, to be sure, a double opposition or separation between God and human beings. But to this there corresponds to a double unification. This double double is the story of creation, fall, and redemption. Creation represents an opposition insofar as ontologically speaking there is an "infinite qualitative difference" (Kierkegaard, Barth), a relation of transcendence between the Creator and any particular creature or even the whole of creation; at the same time, there is a unification insofar as human beings are created in the image and likeness of God and are meant to enjoy fellowship with God. The Garden of Eden is the biblical symbol for the originally intended harmonious presence of God as Creator with all of the created order.

But a more radical opposition emerges in the fall, when humans disrupt their Edenic harmony with God through a disobedient and rebellious declaration of independence.[40] This, in turn, leads to the possibility of a more radical unification, as God takes the initiative to provide a path of forgiveness and reconciliation by means of atonement, repentance and faith.

Attempts to "rescue" Jesus from the Judaism that preceded him and the Christianity that followed him[41] often make Paul the villain, the "inventor" of a Christianity thoroughly discontinuous with Jesus. Hegel's Jesus is a teacher of reconciliation; but Paul is also the teacher of a second unification. For those in Christ there is a new creation.

> All this is from God, who reconciled us to himself through Christ, and has given us the ministry of reconciliation; that is, in Christ God was reconciling the world to himself... we entreat you on behalf of Christ, be reconciled to God For our sake he made him to be sin who knew no sin, so that in him we might be come the righteousness of God. (2 Cor. 5:18–21)

N. T. Wright cites this passage when he seeks to summarize his magisterial interpretation of the writings of St. Paul. "My proposal is that Paul's aims and intentions can be summarized under the word *kattallag*, 'reconciliation.' . . . There are many passages in Paul that stake a claim to sum up what he thought he was doing, but this one trumps most of them."[42]

The idea of reconciliation as a more radical unification than creation in the image of God has traditionally been expressed in the paradoxical theme of a *felix culpa*, "O happy fault that earned for us so great, so glorious a Redeemer.[43] Thus the hymn by Johnson Oatman Jr.

> Holy, holy, is what the angelvs sing,
> And I expect to help them make the courts of heaven ring;
> But when I sing redemption's story, they will fold their wings,
> For angels never felt the joys that our salvation brings.
> So, although I'm not an angel, yet I know that over there
> I will join a blessèd chorus that the angels cannot share;
> I will sing about my Savior, who upon dark Calvary
> Freely pardoned my transgressions, died to set a sinner free.

Hegel will not like the references here to a sacrifice of atonement although its stated purpose is reconciliation.[44] But, given the mega-narrative of creation, fall, and redemption, it is hard to see how he could justify the claim that for biblical religion "human nature is absolutely severed from the divine" and God is "a superior Being altogether alien to man" (*PC 1*, 176). Within a pantheistic framework the biblical story will have to be completely abandoned or at least radically rewritten, but that is no excuse for not recognizing the biblical story for what it is. In both the Jewish and Christian scriptures it is the story of humankind as the prodigal son, the memory of a deep estrangement and the promise of glorious reunion.

The second presupposition of mediation through an individual is that this narrative of reunion through redemption, repentance, and reconciliation takes the form of covenant making, breaking, and renewal. In response to human self-alienation from God that is sin, God expresses the desire to overcome the opposition by making promises of restored fellowship, sometimes unconditional and sometimes conditional. The oft-repeated phrase that defines covenantal unification is "I will be your God, and you will be my people."[45] The Christian Bible concludes with the vision of a new heaven, a new earth, and a new Jerusalem "coming down out of heaven from God."

> See, the home of God is among mortals.
> He will dwell with them as their God;
> they will be his peoples,
> and God himself will be with them;
> he will wipe every tear from their eyes.
> Death will be no more;
> mourning and crying and pain will be no more,
> for the first things have passed away. (Rev. 21:1–4)

This is the ultimate fulfillment of the renewed covenant promised in Deuteronomy 30 and reiterated by the prophets. But it reaches back beyond the hope of a renewed and restored Israel (as in Deuteronomy) to the original covenant with Abraham and its promise that "in you all the families of the earth shall be blessed" (Gen. 12:3). The particular has become the universal.

Since promises are relations of persons to persons and not the kind of thing available to knowledge as recollection (there being no promises in mathematics, the paradigm of recollection), the biblical covenants of reconciliation are mediated through individuals to whom and through whom the promises are made.[46] Thus there are the Abrahamic, Mosaic, and Davidic covenants; there are the promises of a new covenant given through Deutero-Isaiah, Jeremiah, and Ezekiel; and eventually there is the claim that Jesus is "the mediator of a better covenant, which has been enacted through better promises. For if that first covenant had been faultless, there would have been no need to look for a second one" (Heb. 8:6–7).[47] At the last supper, which Christians understand to be the institution of the Eucharist or Holy Communion, Jesus himself affirms this prophetic theme. He shares the cup of wine with his disciples, saying, "this is my blood of the [new] covenant, which is poured out for many for the forgiveness of sins" (Matt. 26:28; cf. Mark 14:24; Luke 22:20).[48]

In order to extract Jesus from the covenantal framework and the double opposition and unification it presupposes, Hegel seeks to attribute to him a religion that is all unification (*Vereinigung*) without opposition (*nichts Entgegengesetztes*) (*SC*, 255). To this end he presents Jesus as a teacher of love but not obedience (*SC*, 223, 241) and of God as Father but not as Lord (*SC*, 244, 253). This is easily accomplished. Whenever the gospel texts present Jesus as teaching obedience, as in the commands to love God and neighbor, or teaching God as Lord (Sovereign), as in the parables of judgment, one avers that this is not the true religion of Jesus but the unfortunate, even tragic concessions he had to make to his Jewish lifeworld. The danger, of course, is that the result is likely to be a Jesus who is the projected image of one's own preferences. If those preferences are the necessary truths of a truly universal Reason, that would be one thing. But if they are the opinions of a particular individual or the presuppositions of a contingent cultural tradition, caught up in one hermeneutical circle among many, the task of justifying them becomes extremely difficult. One is reminded of George Tyrell's description of Adolf Harnack's *What Is Christianity?* as "only the reflection of a Liberal Protestant face [Harnack's own], seen at the bottom of a deep well."[49] Hegel's Jesus, in both its Kantian and post-Kantian versions, looks like portraits of Hegel at two different stages of his theological development.

Starting from the premise that Jesus presents God as Father (which is undeniable) but not as Lord (which is more than a little tendentious), Hegel in effect attributes to Jesus a radically rewritten Nicene Creed. This is the most ecumenical or universal creed of the Christian churches, stemming from the first ecumenical council, the Council of Nicea in 325. It is used by the Eastern Orthodox churches,[50] the Roman Catholic church, and the Anglican and Protestant churches. The relevant portion of that creed reads as follows:

> We believe in one Lord, Jesus Christ
> the only Son of God,
> eternally begotten of the Father,
> God from God, Light from Light,
> true God from true God,
> begotten not made,
> of one Being (*homoousious*) with the Father.

The key term, *homoousious*, can be rendered consubstantial, of one substance, of one being, of one nature, or of one essence. There is a double claim here. Ontologically speaking, the Son is the same kind of being as the Father, and there is a uniqueness about this relation. Jesus is the "only Son of God" in this sense, and to make this point he is said to be "begotten not made." Created persons can become children of God—"But to all who received him, who believed in his name, he gave power to become children of God" (John 1:12)—but not in this sense, for they are made and not begotten. That is why Paul speaks of believers as children of God by adoption[51]; and that is why John of the Cross, when speaking of a union with God that could be called divinization, regularly insists that "souls possess the same goods by participation that the Son possesses by nature."[52]

Commenting on John 1:12, Hegel at first seems to follow this dimension of mere Christianity. "They do not become other than they were, but they know God and recognize themselves as children of God, as weaker than he, yet of a like nature in so far as they have become conscious of that spiritual relation suggested by his name." But perhaps he is moving in a different direction when he continues, "They find their essence in no stranger, but in God" (SC, 259).[53] Does he mean that as children of God believers are consubstantial with the Father?

This begins to be confirmed when he continues further: "Up to this point we have heard only of the truth itself and of man in general terms. In verse 14 ["And the Word became flesh and lived among us, and we have seen his glory, the glory as of a father's only son"] the Logos appears modified as an individual." In this Hegel finds "the Jewish principle of opposing thought to reality, reason to sense; this principle involves the rending of life and a lifeless connection between God and the world" (SC, 259). Jesus is free from this in so far as he teaches that the ontological oneness of father and son is a general truth about human nature. He teaches his followers to think of God as their father. But that relation "is a living relation of living beings, a likeness of life. Father and son are simply modifications of the same life, not opposite essences, not a plurality of absolute substantialities Thus the son of God is the same essence as the father" (SC, 260).

Hegel here appeals to the Arab understanding of the life of a clan. The individual member "is not simply a part of the whole; the whole does not lie outside him; he himself is just the whole which the entire clan is.... It is true only of objects, of things lifeless, that the whole is other than the parts; in the living thing, on the other hand, the part of the whole is one and the same as the whole" (SC, 260). Hegel uses a similar organic metaphor when he writes, "A tree which has three branches makes up with them one tree: but every 'son' of the tree, every branch ... is itself a tree. The fibers bringing sap to the branch from the stem are of the same nature as the roots" (SC, 261).

The quarrel between Hegel's theology and mere Nicene Christianity is not over the theological usefulness of such ethnic and organic metaphors. It is over their proper place. Are they possibly helpful in articulating the Nicene Creed's claim that Jesus is "the only Son of God" in the sense that Jesus and the Father are "modifications of the same life"; or are they helpful in replacing that Christology with an anthropology in which all human persons are part of the one divine life in the way in which each Arab is part of the life of the clan? As Hegel sees it, the former view was a Jewish misunderstanding of what Jesus was trying to teach, namely, the latter view (SC, 259, 261). They attributed to him the former view, which we might call Nicene in order to remind us that in Hegel's view it was and is the fate of Christianity to side with the Jews rather than with Jesus.

Hegel clearly wishes to side with (his) Jesus. When he taught that "the son of God is the same essence as the father" (*homoousious*), this was not a unique truth about Jesus of Nazareth as the incarnate Son of God, but a general truth about the relation of human persons to the one divine life. "All thought of a difference in essence between Jesus and those in whom faith in him has become life, in whom the divine is present, must be eliminated" (SC, 268) In other words, human persons are "begotten not made." The difference signified by creation and a fortiori the difference signified by sin are not in play. There is unification without opposition. This means that Jesus declared himself "against the thought of a personal God" (SC, 271).

This way of speaking about the relation of part to whole echoes Spinoza's way of relating the many finite modes with the one infinite substance, the immanent power of nature of which each is an expression. We are well on our way to a "Spinozism of freedom" or what could also be called a pantheism of spirit. All that is needed is to replace the category of life with that of spirit as the proper name for the substance, the whole.

Hegel begins this move when he writes that the Jews could not recognize divinity in a man because

> of the depth of their servitude, of their opposition to the divine, of an impassible gulf between the being of God and the being of men.... Spirit alone recognizes spirit.... The hill and the eye which sees it are object and subject, but between man and God, between spirit and spirit, there is no such cleft of objectivity and subjectivity; one is to the other another only in that one recognizes the other; both are one." (*SC*, 265)

For Hegel the Kingdom of God is "a living bond which unites the believers." This friendship, "described in the language of reflection [*Reflexion*] as an essence [*Wesen*],⁵⁴ as spirit, is the divine spirit, is God who rules the communion. Is there an idea more beautiful than that of a nation of men related to one another by love?" (*SC*, 278). Whether we call this a social humanism or a pantheism of Spirit, it is clearly not the monotheism of the Abrahamic traditions. "The objective aspect of God, his configuration (*Gestalt*), is objective only in so far as it is simply the presentation [*Darstellung*] of the love uniting the group" (*SC*, 292–93). The objective reality of God is nothing more than the sentiment that unites a people.⁵⁵

There are two things of importance here. First, the emphasis falls on the human community. The idea of God as a ruler of the communion [*Gemeine*], as if the Kingdom needed a King, is due to reflection. As we will see, this becomes Hegel's name for a defective mode of thinking, and it already is. "Reflective thinking, which partitions life, can distinguish it into infinite and finite, and then it is only the restriction, the finite regarded by itself, which affords the concept of man as opposed [*entgegengesetzt*] to the divine. But outside reflective thinking, and in truth, there is no such restriction" (*SC*, 262).⁵⁶ In other words, reflective thinking does not have the ability to think spirit as spirit, to think the human self as divine.

Second, Hegel moves beyond Spinoza by subsuming the categories of infinite/finite and life under the category of love. Henrich writes, "Out of the concept of love and through the concept of life, the concept of spirit arises continuously."⁵⁷ I have argued that love is more basic than life for Hegel.⁵⁸ Hegel probably didn't get the chance to read Anne Perry's crime fiction, set in Victorian London. Her hero is William Monk. He has become the head of the

Thames River Police and is married to Hester, a nurse who served nobly with Florence Nightingale in the Crimean War. Together they have all but officially adopted a street urchin named Scuff. At age sixteen, he is, by fits and starts, becoming a thoughtful and responsible young man. In a moment when circumstance brings forcefully to mind the depth of the love that has developed in both directions between Scuff and his "parents," she asks herself, "Could the connection of love be as powerful as that of blood?"[59]

Hegel would be among the first to say yes. Blood (birth and ethnicity) is a category of nature. Love is a category of spirit, and nature can be and should be *aufgehoben*, relativized in spirit.[60] Nature is the stage on which the plays of spirit are enacted, and the mise-en-scène can and should be governed as much as possible by the content of the play.[61] The racism and nationalism of the Nazi ideology of blood and soil, would be a terrible inversion of the relation of nature to spirit in Hegel's view. For political as well as for religious reasons, Spinoza's nature pantheism needs to be transformed into a pantheism of spirit, a "Spinozism of freedom."

It is true that in the *Philosophy of Right* love is only the principle of the family, while law is the principle of the state. But law is as much an expression of spirit as love,[62] and the same principle of the teleological supremacy of spirit over nature is at work as in the notion of "a nation of men related to one another by love." The identity of a nation (*Volk*) resides less in its blood and soil than in its culture and values, legal, moral, and religious, and even its manners, including its ideas of acceptable language (political correctness).

I've been calling Hegel's theology pantheistic. In his 1827 philosophy of religion lectures he argues that Spinoza is not a pantheist in several senses of the term, and in any case, he, Hegel, is not a Spinozist. In reply to a critique by a certain Tholuck, Hegel offers a fourfold disavowal.[63] He begins with a threefold defense of Spinoza.

First, if by pantheism one means that all finite things taken, as it were, in a heap, are God, either individually or collectively, that is not only not Spinoza but "No one has ever held that" (PR, 123).

Second, against the suggestion that pantheism is atheism and thus a threat to religion, Hegel suggests that it should rather be seen as acosmism for "it is precisely the aggregate of finitudes (the world) that has [in God] disappeared." In and as itself, apart from the immanent, divine power of being, such an all "simply *is not*" (PR, 125).

Third, against the suggestion that pantheism erases the distinction between good and evil and is thus a threat to morality, Hegel replies that for Spinoza, "This distinction is not [applicable] within God as such, within God under this definition as substance. But for human beings there is this distinction" (*PR*, 127). Spinoza does indeed say that we call things good or evil relative to our desires and aversions, and we call things right or wrong according to the social standards we accept. In other words, moral values have human desires and decisions as their foundation, and it can make no sense to call Spinoza's God (*Deus sive Natura*) good.

On these three points Hegel simply asserts that neither he nor Spinoza is a pantheist in any of these senses. On a fourth point he finds it necessary to disavow Spinoza and his version of pantheism. We have already encountered his fundamental critique, namely, that the category of substance needs to be *aufgehoben* in the category of spirit.

> God is the absolute substance. If we cling to this declaration in its abstract form, then it is certainly Spinozism or pantheism. But the fact that God is *substance* does not exclude *subjectivity*. . . . That God is substance is part of the presupposition we have made that God is *spirit*, being essentially present to itself.

This movement from substance to spirit is the movement from abstract to concrete (*PR*, 118–19).

There is surely a point to each of these disavowals. But they should not blind us to the fact that there is a clear sense in which, vis-à-vis the theism of the Abrahamic traditions, Hegel's view is best seen as a form of pantheism. While for theism there is an asymmetry in which there can be God without the world but not the world without God, for pantheism there cannot be God without the world any more than the world without God. Thus, in the 1824 version of these lectures, he favorably cites Meister Eckhart, "The eye with which God sees me is the eye with which I see him; my eye and his eye are one and the same. . . . If God did not exist nor would I; if I did not exist nor would he."[64]

Moreover, there is a clear sense in which Hegel's pantheism is atheism. The alpha privative in Greek (and English) signifies a negation that is not necessarily an active opposition; absence is sufficient. Thus an amoral person is one in whose life moral norms play no part, and atonal music is music that lacks a tonal center or key. In this sense an atheist is one for whom the God of theism, an agent and speaker distinct from the worlds of nature and history, is absent. It seems to me that Spinoza and Hegel are both atheists in this sense. Of course, if by atheist one means someone who thinks nothing deserves to be called God, then neither is an atheist. Hegel uses 'atheist' in this latter sense; I am using it in the former. That someone is correctly described as an atheist in this sense is, in itself, neither to praise nor to blame. One would need one or more normative presuppositions to convert the description into an evaluation.

It may seem problematic to devote so much attention to Hegel's early theological writings. After all, he didn't publish them. But they do represent a decisive break with orthodox Christianity, with Spinoza, and with Kant. I believe that as such they express the permanent, inner core of Hegel's theology. In the chapter after next I will try to explain why his mature philosophy of religion has a far less Nietzschean tone even while it continues to be a pantheism of Spirit.[65]

Notes

1. A detailed list and dating of early drafts and fragments is given in H. S. Harris, *Hegel's Development: Toward the Sunlight, 1770-1801* (Oxford: Clarendon Press, 1972), pp. 517–27.

2. Walter Kaufmann, *From Shakespeare to Existentialism* (Garden City, NY: Doubleday, 1960), p. 130. Kaufmann adds, "A new reading of these antitheological essays furnishes the best introduction to Hegel's later works."

3. Hegel's idealization of Greek culture and religion is a late moment in the story told by E. M. Butler in *The Tyranny of Greece over Germany* and Henry Hatfield in *Aesthetic Paganism in German Literature*. In the background are Winckelmann, Goethe, and Schiller. Given Hegel's love of Sophocles, it is not surprising that Peter Wake can write a book entitled *Tragedy in Hegel's Early Theological Writings* (Bloomington: Indiana University Press, 2014).

4. The paradigm of objective religion is Christian orthodoxy, especially as presented by Hegel's theology professor Gottlob Christian Storr. For his importance as a foil for Hegel's thinking, see the many references in Harris, *Toward the Sunlight*.

5. For Hegel 'abstraction' always means distorting something by extracting it from the context in which it has its meaning and function. The Lockean sense of abstracting universal ideas from particular things or images is only a special case, and seldom what Hegel has in mind. To make language usable, in Locke's view, "the mind makes the particular ideas received from particular objects to become general; which is done by considering them as . . . separate from all other existences, and circumstances of real existence, as time, place, or any other concomitant ideas. This is called ABSTRACTION, whereby ideas taken from particular beings become general representatives of all of the same kind." *An Essay Concerning Human Understanding*, II, XI, 9. Cf. III; III, 6–7; and IV; VII, 9.

6. Thus objective religion is "divorced from experience and anesthetized by dogmatism." Wake, *Tragedy*, p. 31.

7. He treats the quarrel between the two as a Democrat would view an internal debate within the Republican Party. A plague on both their houses. From his point of view the debate between the Enlightenment and Christian orthodoxy is ironic, given the assumptions they share. See *PS*, 328–55.

8. Here Hegel sounds first like the Lutheran pietists and then a lot like a kind of Kantian deist, especially in *The Conflict of the Faculties*. In his 1795 essay, "The Life of Jesus" (*LJ*), he presents Jesus as a teacher of a very Kantian morality. But throughout these essays he will separate himself further and further from Kant. On the relation of this Kantian moment to his Greek ideal, see Harris, "Toward the Sunlight," p. 194, and Fuss and Dobbins in *Three Essays* (see *LJ* in sigla), p. 13.

9. Given his polemic against Understanding (*Verstand*), we are already getting Hegel's reinterpretation of the Kantian distinction between it and Reason (*Vernunft*).

10. Cf. Hegel's later reference to Lessing's *Nathan the Wise* and the immediately following contrast between rational and fetish faith (*TE*, 495). Hegel will cite this passage from *Nathan* again at *PC* 1, 92.

11. Dieter Henrich, *Between Kant and Hegel: Lectures on German Idealism*, ed. David Pacini (Cambridge, MA: Harvard University Press, 2003), p, 83.

12. Cf. *TE*,502, where the anti-clerical theme is repeated in the claim that "the thirst for power of the priests in a religion of this sort is limited."

13. Sacrifice as atonement is fundamental in both the Hebrew Bible and the New Testament. Hegel's repudiation is categorical.

14. Friedrich Nietzsche, *The Genealogy of Morals*, II, 23. Cf. *Ecce Homo*, "Why I Am So Wise," 5: "A god who would come to earth must not *do* anything except wrong: not to take the punishment upon oneself but the *guilt* would be divine." Cf. Hegel, *PC*, 1, 164: "Piety and sin are two concepts which in our sense of the words the Greeks [to their credit] lacked; for us the former is a disposition which acts from respect for God as lawgiver, and the latter is an action in contravention of a divine command." This occurs in a context in which Greek religion is praised over against Judaism and Christianity. Hence the insertion.

15. Henrich, *Between Kant and Hegel*, pp. 91–95. In a 1796 draft now known as the "The Earliest System-Program of German Idealism" (translated in Harris, *Toward the Sunlight*) Hegel writes, "Absolute freedom of all spirits who bear the intellectual world in themselves, and cannot seek either God or immortality outside themselves (p. 511). See Harris's analysis in *Toward the Sunlight*, pp. 249–57, and mine in "*Von Hegel bis Hegel*: Reflections on 'The Earliest System-Program of German Idealism,'" in *The Emergence of German Idealism*, ed. Michael Baur and Daniel O. Dahlstrom (Washington, DC: Catholic University of America Press, 1999), pp. 269–87.

16. Doubtless Schelling has especially in mind their theology professor, Storr. See note 4 above.

17. Hegel is referring to Fichte's *Attempt at a Critique of All Revelation* (1792), while Schelling is drawing on the 1794 *Wissenschaftslehre* (Science of Knowledge), which Hegel has not yet read.

18. See his reference to "God and immortality" above.

19. Butler comments that Hegel's "puzzlement at Schelling's rejection of the personal individual God of classical theism shows that he himself still holds to the orthodox concept of God" (*HL*, 30). The God in question is indeed a personal Being, but not that of orthodox theism. It is rather the deistic God of the Kantian postulates, and Hegel is more curious and questioning than firmly committed to such a belief.

20. According to Jacobi, Lessing had told him, "The orthodox concepts of the Divinity are no longer for me; I cannot stomach them. *Hen kai pan!*" I know of nothing else." See *Concerning the Doctrine of Spinoza in Letters to Herr Moses Mendelssohn*, in Friedrich Heinrich Jacobi, *The Main Philosophical Writings and the Novel* Allwill, trans. George di Giovanni (Montreal: McGill-Queens University Press, 1994), p. 187. On *Hen kai pan* (One and All), see Henrich, *Between Kant and Hegel*, pp. 88–99. It functions here as a summary of Spinoza's pantheism.

21. Writing in 1833, Heine speaks of Spinoza's "intellectual supremacy" in "our day." ... Germany is now the fertile soil of pantheism. This is the religion of our greatest thinkers, of our best artists ... pantheism is the open secret of Germany." Heinrich Heine, *Religion and Philosophy in Germany*, trans. John Snodgrass (Boston: Beacon Press, 1959), pp. 69, 79.

22. For a similar argument, see Hölderlin's letter to Hegel just before Schelling's letter (*HL*, 33).

23. On Storr, see notes 4 and 16 above.

24. See Jacobi, *Doctrine of Spinoza*, pp. 173–251; and "Jacobi and the Pantheism Controversy," in Frederick C. Beiser, *The Fate of Reason: German Philosophy from Kant to Fichte* (Cambridge, MA: Harvard University Press, 1987), pp. 44–49. On the atheism controversy, see *Fichte: Early Philosophical Writings*, trans. Daniel Breazeale (Ithaca, NY: Cornell University Press, 1988), pp. 40–45.

25. In a letter to Schelling from December of 1794, Hegel had written, "The time has come, I believe, for us to become generally freer to speak out" (*HL*, 28), probably referring to constraints they felt at the Tübingen seminary. Now he senses that it would not be a good idea to speak more freely about the theory of God as the Absolute Self even away from the seminary.

26. Hegel, *Werke in zwanzig Bände* (Frankfurt am Main: Suhrkamp, 1971), I, 239.

27. Hegel had just finished his essay, "The Life of Jesus" (*LJ*), in which he portrays Jesus as a Kantian moralist when he began work on the positivity essay. See note 8 above.

28. Like many Enlightenment thinkers, Hegel is protesting against any priesthood that confuses its authority with God's. But, ironically (especially in a Lutheran context), he accepts the equation of the two modes of authority and proceeds on the assumption that the only way to overcome the clerical hegemony Kant calls *Pfaffentum* is to dispense with divine authority as well.

29. In his mature thought there will be an ongoing tension between his communitarian and liberal instincts, which he works hard to reconcile. See the discussions in Stephen B. Smith, *Hegel's Critique of Liberalism*; Robert R. Williams, ed. *Beyond Liberalism and Communitarianism*; Frederick Neuhouser, *Foundations of Hegel's Social Theory*; Michael O. Hardimon, *Hegel's Social Philosophy*; and several essays in Z. A. Pelczynski, ed., *The State and Civil Society: Studies in Hegel's Political Philosophy*, including my own "Hegel Radical Idealism: Family and State as Ethical Communities." On the relation of church and state, see the long addition to ¶270 in the *Philosophy of Right*.

30. Hegel does not seem to notice that this could be a description of ancient Israel.

31. Hegel may be thinking of Horace, as he tries to keep the spirit of republican Rome alive in the imperial age. *Dulce et decorum est pro patria mori* (Sweet and honorable it is to die for one's country). *Odes*, III, ii, 13.

32. In *History and Truth in Hegel's Phenomenology*, 3rd ed. (Bloomington: Indiana University Press, 1998), pp. 196–98, I have argued for a deep similarity between Hegel's theology of 1807 and that of Emile Durkheim, who writes, "Behind these [religious] figures and metaphors, be they gross or refined, there is a concrete and living reality. Thus religion . . . is a system of ideas with which the individuals represent to themselves the society of which they are members, and the obscure but intimate relations which they have with it." *The Elementary Forms of the Religious Life*, trans. Joseph Ward Swain (New York: Free Press, 1965), p. 257. Hegel seems already to be anticipating Durkheim's version of Feuerbach.

33. For the Hegelian, Marxian, and Freudian dimensions of Feuerbach's atheism, see my *Suspicion and Faith: The Religious Uses of Modern Atheism* (New York: Fordham University Press, 1998), chaps. 20–21. Here Hegel anticipates the Marxian dimension.

34. See Lawrence S. Stepelevich, ed., *The Young Hegelians: An Anthology* (New York: Cambridge University Press, 1983).

35. Ludwig Feuerbach, *The Essence of Christianity*, trans. George Eliot (New York: Harper and Brothers, 1957), pp. 14, 29–30.

36. Hegel clearly has Christianity in mind. Only a pantheist could say that the God of biblical theism is "absolutely severed" and "altogether alien" from man. As we will see, the important theme of reconciliation in his later work will be conceived in abstract, metaphysical terms as the reconciliation of the finite and the infinite.

37. The *Shema* is indeed central to the religion of biblical Israel. "Hearken O Israel: YHWH our God, YHWH (is) One! Now you are to love YHWH your God with all your heart, with all your

being, with all your substance!" (Deut. 6:4–5, as found in *The Five Books of Moses*, trans. Everett Fox (New York: Schocken, 1995). The *Shema* is echoed in the opening of the Decalogue, "I am YHWH your God, who brought you out from the land of Egypt, from a house of serfs. You are not to have any other gods before my presence . . . you are not to bow down to them you are not to serve them" (Ex. 20:2–3, 5); and Jesus alludes to it when he gives as the greatest commandment, "You shall love the Lord your God with all your heart, with all your soul, and with all your mind" (Matt. 22:334–40; cf. Mark 12:28–34; and Luke 10:25–28). It ranks first even before the commandment to love one's neighbor as oneself. N. T. Wright sees 1 Cor. 8:6 as "an explosive redefinition of the Shema," *Paul: In Fresh Perspective* (Minneapolis: Fortress, 2005), p. 93, and finds it reverberating throughout Paul's theology in *Paul and the Faithfulness of God* (Minneapolis, MN: Fortress, 2013). Hegel is surely right in seeing a deep connection between Jewish and Christian monotheism.

38. Discussing this passage, Wake asks if there is a different form of catharsis that corresponds to this different kind of tragedy. *Tragedy*, pp. 126–27. Fair enough, but for Hegel the question is not about our (aesthetic) experience as observers of ancient Israel but about our own direct (religious) experience of the sacred. If we are to be purged of anything, it is biblical faith.

39. Shortly before beginning *SC*, Hegel wrote a short draft on love (*ETW*, 302–8). Dieter Henrich writes, "Hegel's system arises without a break from his assumption of love as a foundational concept [*Grundwort*]." *Hegel im Context* (Frankfurt am Main: Suhrkamp, 1967), p. 27. See note 55 below. Curiously and ironically, in his mature political philosophy, Hegel stresses the correlation of rights and duties in Ethical Life (*Sittlichkeit*), especially in the family and the state. *Philosophy of Right*, ¶¶153–56. But these are not relations to a transcendent God.

40. "But if the god is to be absolutely different from a human being, this can have its basis not in that which man owes to the god (for to that extent they are akin) but in that which he owes to himself or in that which he himself has committed. What, then, is the difference? Indeed, what else but sin." Søren Kierkegaard, *Philosophical Fragments/Johannes Climacus*, trans. Howard V. Hong and Edna H. Hong (Princeton, NJ: Princeton University Press, 1985), pp. 46–47.

41. Thinkers as diverse as Wrede, F. C. Baur, Nietzsche, and Tolstoy are examples.

42. N. T. Wright, *Paul and the Faithfulness of God*, pp. 1487–89. The following, taken from the liturgy for Holy Communion in the *Book of Common Prayer*, could be used by any Christian congregation: "Holy and gracious Father: In your infinite love you made us for yourself; and when we had fallen into sin and become subject to evil and death, you, in your mercy, sent Jesus Christ, your only and eternal Son, to share our human nature, to live and die as one of us, to reconcile us to you, the God and Father of all."

43. With roots in Ambrose, Augustine, and Aquinas, this is sometimes sung at the Easter Vigil.

44. We saw above that Hegel considers this idea an "irrational absurdity" (*TE*, 503).

45 For example, Ex. 6:6–7, 29:45; Lev. 26:11–12; Deut. 27:9, 29:13; Jer. 24:7, 31:31–34; Ezek. 11:20; 14:11; 34:24, 30; 36:28; 37:23, 27; Zech. 13:9; 2 Cor. 6:16–18. On the structure of covenantal religion, see my *God, Guilt, and Death: An Existential Phenomenology of Religion* (Bloomington: Indiana University Press, 1984), chap. 11; and Martin Buber, *Moses: The Revelation and the Covenant* (New York: Harper & Row, 1958), pp. 101–9, and *The Prophetic Faith* (New York: Harper & Row, 1960), pp. 8–18.

46. Mediation through an individual is not incompatible with a universal significance. Thus God says to Abram, who only becomes Abraham in Genesis 17, "in you all the families of the earth shall be blessed" (Gen. 12:3).

47. Hebrews 9:15 and 12:24 present Jesus as the mediator of a "new covenant."

48. Some, but not all, of the ancient manuscripts have "new covenant." Whether or not the word 'new' was in the original manuscripts, it is clear that from early on Christians have understood Jesus to be referring to the new covenant promised in Deuteronomy and by Deutero-Isaiah, Jeremiah, and Ezekiel. In context, this is the most natural interpretation. See the previous note. The covenant with Abraham was instituted with a ritual act that involved the shedding of blood. See Gen. 15:7–11.

49. C. George Tyrell, *Christianity at the Crossroads* (New York: Longmans, Green and Co., 1909), p. 44.

50. The dispute over the *filioque* clause, which they reject, is not relevant to the present discussion.

51. See Rom. 8:15, 23; 9:4; Gal. 4:5, and Eph. 1:5.

52. *The Collected Works of St. John of the Cross*, trans. Kieran Kavanaugh, O. C. D. and Otilio Rodriguez, O. C. D. (Washington, DC: ICS Publications, 1991), p. 624. Cf. pp. 93, 164–65, 560–61, 595, 623, 671, 677, 706. The concept of participation clearly has a Platonic sense here, signifying an ontological gap between an eternal archetype and its temporal ectype. This same idea of becoming by grace what God (or Christ) is by nature is also found in Tauler and in the *Theologia Germanica*. See Johannes Tauler, *Sermons*, trans. Maria Shrady (Mahwah, NJ: Paulist Press, 1985), p. 103; and *The Theologia Germanica of Martin Luther*, trans. Bengt Hoffman (Mahweh, NJ: Paulist Press, 1980), p. 79.

53. For Spinoza individual persons as modes of the one substance are weaker than it (= nature as the infinite power or energy), but they are *homoousious* with it. They are parts of the same whole, not as one stamp is part of the entire collection, but as one part of an organism is a partial expression of its entire life. Thus a human hand is fully human.

54. *Wesen* can mean essence, but also substance, being, creature, living thing. Here it seems to me a better rendering would be "as a being."

55. The quotation continues: "simply the pure counterpart of that love, and it contains nothing not already in love itself (though here it appears as love's counterpart), contains nothing which is not at the same time feeling [*Empfindung*]."

56. Hegel is also developing the notion of representative thinking as conceptually inadequate. "Intuition, representative thinking [*das Anschauende, Vorstellende*], is something restrictive, something receptive only of something restricted. . . . The infinite cannot be carried in this vessel" (*SC*, 253).

57. Henrich, *Hegel im Context*, p. 67. See note 39 above.

58. In *History and Truth*, pp. 130–38.

59. Anne Perry, *Blood in the Water* (New York: Thorndike Press, 2014), p. 43.

60. Hegel recognizes the natural basis of love, most particularly in sex. But as the principle of the family, sex needs to be elevated to a spiritual and not merely a natural relation. See my analysis in "Hegel's Radical Idealism: Family and State as Ethical Communities," in Pelczynski, *State and Civil Society*, pp. 84–88.

61. Of course, the stage can present limitations to a production. I once saw Mozart's *Don Giovanni* performed (magnificently) in a college dining room. Not quite the stage of the Met or Covent Garden.

62. If it is fair to say that Hobbes's theory of natural law is based on nature rather than spirit, then Hegel's concept of *Naturrecht* can be described as anti–Hobbesean. "It was Hobbes who first studied the 'laws of civil life' with the explicit purpose of placing political action from now on on the incomparably more certain basis of that scientifically controlled technics which he had come to know in the mechanics of his time." Jürgen Habermas, "The Classical Doctrine of Politics in Relation to Social Philosophy," in *Theory and Practice*, trans. John Viertel (Boston: Beacon Press, 1973), p. 63. When Marx tells us in the preface to the first edition of *Capital* that he is expounding the "natural laws of capitalist production . . . working with iron necessity" and that his standpoint is that of "natural history," he is closer to Hobbes and Darwin than to Aristotle and Hegel. *Capital: A Critique of Political Economy*, trans. Samuel Moore and Edward Aveling (New York: International Publishers, 1967), I, 8 and 10.

63. See my discussion in "Hegel," in *The Blackwell Companion to Modern Theology*, ed. Gareth Jones (Oxford: Blackwell Publishing, 2004), pp. 298–300.

64. *Hegel's Lectures on the Philosophy of Religion*, vol. I, ed. Peter C. Hodgson (Berkeley: University of California Press, 1984), pp. 347–48.

65. On the ambiguities of tone, see Jacques Derrida, "Of an Apocalyptic Tone Newly Adopted in Philosophy," in *Derrida and Negative Theology*, ed. Harold Coward and Toby Foshay, (Albany, NY: State University of New York Press, 1992), pp. 25–71; and the commentary by John D. Caputo in *The Prayers and Tears of Jacques Derrida* (Bloomington: Indiana University Press, 1997), pp. 88–101.

8

HEGEL'S THEOLOGY II

The usual story is that Hegel is the culmination of German Idealism, drawing on and revising the work of Kant, Fichte, Schelling, and a few others. There is much truth in this approach.[1] But it is also true that Hegel tells us "thought must *begin* by placing itself at the standpoint of Spinozism; to be a follower of Spinoza is the essential *commencement* of all Philosophy . . . when a man *begins* to philosophize, the soul must *commence* by bathing in this ether of the One Substance" (*HP/S*, III, 257; emphasis added).

One doesn't have to know a lot about Hegel to know that this emphasis on beginning and commencement makes for a backhanded compliment. True reality and genuine knowledge are present at the beginning only in an abstract and undeveloped form (*an sich*); only at the end is it concretely present in its fullness (*für sich*). So "substance with Spinoza is not yet determined as in itself concrete" (*HP/S*, III, 258). "There is an absolute substance, and it is what is true. But it is not yet the whole truth, for substance must also be thought of as inwardly active and alive, and in that way must determine itself as spirit. . . . If thinking stops with this substance, there is then no development, no life, no spirituality or activity" (*HP/B*, 154–55).[2]

We have seen Hegel, in his early theological writings, begin with Spinoza and move beyond him toward a "Spinozism of freedom" or a pantheism of spirit.[3] In the *Phenomenology* Hegel puts it this way:

> That the True is actual only as system or that Substance is essentially Subject, is expressed in the representation of the Absolute as *Spirit*—the most sublime

Concept and the one which belongs to the modern age and its religion.... But this being-in-and-for-itself [the True, the Absolute, both abstractly and concretely considered] is at first only for us, or *In itself*, it is spiritual Substance. It must also be this *for itself* it must be the knowledge of the spiritual, and the knowledge of itself as Spirit. (*PS*, 14)⁴

No one has ever accused Hegel's prose of the sin of lucidity. But several things are clear enough. First, Hegel distances himself from Spinoza. His metaphysics of nature (*Deus sive natura*) must be *aufgehoben*, reduced to a subordinate part of a metaphysics of Spirit.⁵ Nature will be the stage on which the play of Spirit is acted out. The play's the thing that concerns us most.

Second, as with Spinoza, metaphysics is of religious significance. For both thinkers, religion is ineluctably metaphysical and vice versa, where 'metaphysics' signifies theoretical or speculative knowledge of reality that exceeds the realm of knowledge=experience as defined in Kant's first Critique.⁶ On the question of metaphysics Hegel distances himself from Spinoza by having a different metaphysics and from Kant by grounding religion in metaphysical knowledge.

Third, the movement from Substance (Nature) to Spirit (History) is most essentially a matter of knowledge. There is a gnostic element in Hegel,⁷ and there is no primacy of practical reason nor any postulates of pure practical reason. Once again Hegel distances himself from Kant. Tucker writes,

> By Hegel's definition, God is not fully God until he *knows* himself to be God; self-knowledge or self-consciousness in this specific sense belongs to the nature, essence, or 'concept' of God. At the outset, of creation [*sic*], moreover, he lacks the requisite self-consciousness: God is God, but is not yet conscious of himself as such. Hence, the historical process of God's self-realization is essentially a knowing process."⁸

This process takes place at the level of Absolute Spirit, that is, in Art, Religion, and Philosophy. The difference between the latter two stages is that what has the form of consciousness in Religion is recognized as self-consciousness in Philosophy. Thus Tucker can write, "The movement of thought from Kant to Hegel revolved in a fundamental sense around the idea of man's self-realization as a godlike being, or alternatively, as God."⁹

Finally, like Spinoza's Substance, Spirit is the One that includes many multiplicities within itself, "moments" in Hegel's lingo.¹⁰ Some of these can be seen as structural and thus co-temporal; but others are developmentally temporal. So Spirit, the True and the Absolute, turns out to be historical. It is not only the pinnacle of a structural hierarchy but also, as it becomes absolute in self-knowledge, the completion of an historical development. Both philosophy and theology are historical for Hegel in a way that neither Spinoza's nor Kant's can be, for Reason itself turns out to be, like the Spirit to which it belongs, essentially historical.

We see the difference between structural hierarchy and historical development in the *Phenomenology*. In the Introduction Hegel describes the moments of the whole as shapes or *"patterns of consciousness"* (*Gestalten des Bewusstseins*) and describes his treatise as "the Science of the *experience of consciousness*" (*PS*, 56). These form a structural but not an historical hierarchy. But when he gets to chapter 6, entitled "Spirit," he writes, "These shapes [*Gestalten*) however, are distinguished from the previous ones by the fact that they are real Spirits, actualities in the strict meaning of the word and instead of being shapes merely of consciousness, are shapes of a world" (*PS*, 265). What follows in chapters 6 through 8 are discussions of political-social life, art, religion, and philosophy that have a distinctly historical and developmental character (anticipating Hegel's subsequent writings and lectures on politics/society, art, religion, and philosophy).

Michael N. Forster argues, in part on the basis of this distinction and the fact that the original title for the book was "The Science of the Experience of Consciousness," that Hegel's original intention extended only through the first five chapters and that the addition of the historically oriented "shapes of a world" was an "afterthought."[11] H. S. Harris perceptively adds,

> Hegel was able to make history subordinate in his speculative *Logic* precisely because he allowed it [history] to be predominant in the lengthy formation of subjective consciousness for truly logical "objectivity," which is the theme of the *Phenomenology*. In the *Phenomenology*, it is the "historical proof" that matters most; that is what is signalized by Hegel's decision (reached quite late in the process of composition) to change the subtitle of his "first part" from "Science of the Experience of Consciousness" to "The Phenomenology of Spirit."[12]

This "historical proof" turns out to be a kind of proof of the existence of Hegel's God. At any rate, it is the turn to Spirit in its historical concreteness that gives a theological significance to the *Phenomenology*. Harris writes, "The 'experience of consciousness' *must* happen in a single lifetime; the 'phenomenology of Spirit' *cannot* happen so ... Hegel is proclaiming that it is not the comprehension of 'self' but the comprehension of the whole social history of selfhood that is the topic of *The System of Science: First Part*."¹³ But at the same time he says, "'The experience of consciousness' is necessarily a psychological experience of the singular subject, since only singular subjects are 'conscious,' but the 'phenomenology of Spirit' is the biography of God, the metaphysical substance who becomes 'as much subject as substance' when He [*sic*] is comprehended as 'Spirit.'"¹⁴

What have here is an historicized version of Spinoza, a pantheism of history. So the use of 'He' here, as in discussions of Spinoza, is misleading, if all but inevitable, since this 'God' is not an actual, conscious personal agent but is more like an Aristotelian form of the world, the indwelling life of the cosmic acorn that becomes the world-historical oak tree in the self-consciousness of the human spirit in art, religion, and philosophy (Absolute Spirit in the System). Each of these is itself an historical development from less adequate to more adequate. It is only in this Aristotelian sense that this 'God' is the "maker" of heaven and earth, and "He" is surely not capable of entering into covenantal relations with human individuals or communities.¹⁵ The emphasis on the unity of the whole to which nothing is transcendent and the impersonal character of the whole that contains finite persons as parts combine to warrant using the term pantheism to describe Hegel's theology.

Turning from the *Phenomenology* to the Logic,¹⁶ we find that Hegel came to identify Logic with Metaphysics. "Thus *logic* coincides with *metaphysics*, with the science of *things* grasped in *thoughts* that used to be taken to express the *essentialities* of the *things*" (EL, 56, ¶24).¹⁷ Thus

> Hegel's idealism is not the transcendental variety Kant espouses (idealism about concepts *as opposed* to objects): it is a much more robust, metaphysical position.... Studying that dynamic character of the world which most immediately surfaces, in our experience, within thought determinations is *the same thing as* studying the world, because that's what the world is: an infinitely dynamic structure. Hence "*logic* coincides with *metaphysics*."¹⁸

We can put it this way. Logic is metaphysics because it gives us the Aristotelian forms of things. Hyppolite sees this equation as Hegel's repudiation of theism.

> The transformation of the old metaphysics into Logic implies the negation of a transcendent being that reason could know, but which would be an intelligible world over and against this reason ... there is no second world; there is however a Logos and an absolute speculative life.... In fact, for Hegel, there is no divine thought, then a nature and a created, finite spirit. The word *creation* is a word belonging to representation.... Just like the Logos, nature is really in itself

divine, is in its totality the Absolute.... To replace the old metaphysics with Logic is to sublate the viewpoint of... for example, a transcendent God.[19]

Thus, to say that the Logic is "the exposition of God as he is in his eternal essence before the creation of nature and a finite mind" (SL, 50) is to say that it presents the essence(s) of the world apart from the natural and human worlds whose form(s) they are. It is to deny rather than to affirm the monotheistic maker of heaven and earth.

Given the subordination of history in the Logic of which Harris speaks, we might expect that Hegel's Logic would be developmental only in a structural and not in an historical sense. That is true enough so far as its content is concerned[20]; but surprisingly, Hegel gives a specific historical location, and thus historical preconditions, for his theory of pure thought as a whole. His opening paragraph bemoans the fact that the dramatic philosophical changes that have occurred in Germany during the past twenty-five years "have had but little influence as yet on the structure of logic" and laments living in a time "when a nation loses its metaphysics, when the spirit which contemplates its own pure essence is no longer a present reality in the life of a nation" (SL, 25).[21]

N.B. Logic (= Metaphysics) is not only era-relative but even nation-relative. So logic is out of date, strange as that may sound. A new Logic is not only needed; it is inevitable, since "once the substantial form of the spirit has inwardly reconstituted itself all attempts to preserve the forms of an earlier culture are utterly in vain; like withered leaves they are pushed off by the new buds already growing at their roots" (SL, 26). Deploring the fact that logic "has not undergone any change since Aristotle," he concludes "that it is all the more in need of total reconstruction; for spirit, after its labors over two thousand years, must have attained to a higher consciousness about its thinking and about its own pure, essential nature" (SL, 51).

N.B. Moving from Spinoza's metaphysics of nature to Hegel's own metaphysics of spirit is a move to historical thinking made possible by historical development. It is history itself that gives rise to historical thinking. Thus, Frederick Beiser writes,

> Historicism was an intellectual revolution... because it replaced the older ahistorical ways of thinking, which had prevailed from antiquity throughout the Middle Ages, with a new historical way of thinking, which had begun in the middle of the eighteenth century. The older ahistorical way of thinking saw human nature, morality and reason as absolute, eternal and universal; the new historical way regarded them as relative, changing and particular."[22]

So Hegel presents his Logic as a work "belonging to the modern world" (*SL*, 42). It is not merely a higher level of consciousness; it belongs to and is made possible by a more developed historical world.

There is a second way in which Hegel locates his Logic in a particular historical world. Before presenting the categories of pure thought that make up its content, he poses the question, "With What Must the Science Begin?" (*SL*, 67–78). He gives a complex argument to the effect that the "choice" of Being as the first category is presuppositionless and not arbitrary. More interesting in the present context than the details of the argument is this expression of Hegel's desire to see his philosophy as uncontaminated by particular presuppositions.

But at the same time, he acknowledges that the Logic does have a major presupposition, namely the *Phenomenology of Spirit*. He takes its culminating account of Absolute Knowing as warrant for the very project of a speculative logic. "Logic, then, has for its presupposition the science of manifested [*erscheinenden*] spirit . . . in logic, the presupposition is that which has proved itself to be the result of that phenomenological consideration—the Idea as pure knowledge" (*SL*, 68–69). But as we have seen, the *Phenomenology* reaches its goal not only through a structural hierarchy of forms of consciousness but eventually through an historical sequence of worlds of spirit. This is one way of seeing how the Logic, like the *Phenomenology* on which it depends, must be seen as "belonging to the modern world" (*SL*, 42).

So not even the Logic escapes the historicism of Hegel's Preface to the *Philosophy of Right*, "Whatever happens, every individual is a child of his time; so philosophy too is its own time apprehended in thoughts. It is just as absurd to fancy that a philosophy can transcend its contemporary world as it is to fancy that an individual can overleap his own age, jump over Rhodes" (*PRi*, 11).[23]

Given this commitment to the historical relativity of philosophical thinking, one might expect Hegel to take the hermeneutical turn and abandon the fiction of presuppositionless Reason. In distancing himself from both Spinoza and Kant, he has put himself in a position to see (1) that the versions of reason to which they appeal are not only incompatible with each other but also with the version of reason to which he appeals, and (2) that this is because each rests on historically particular presuppositions. Thinkers sometimes reshape the world in which they live; but they do so on the basis of assumptions they have inherited and not merely created. They shape the world as those who have been shaped by the hermeneutical circle in which they find themselves.

This means that Reason's vaunted autonomy rests not on an ahistorical universality that gives it a privilege over religious diversity. So far as religion within the limits of mere reason is concerned, it reduces to a declaration of independence from a particular presupposition, namely that there is a divine revelation with normative authority for human thought. Such a declaration is itself historically particular and comes in historically different versions as different from one another as the three Abrahamic monotheisms, Judaism, Christianity, and Islam. Perhaps instead of speaking about Reason we should speak of S-reason, K-reason, and H-reason, or perhaps Spinoza's language game, Kant's language game, and Hegel's language game. Wittgenstein reminds us that like other games, different language games have different goals and different rules. We don't become good basketball players by putting the puck in the back of the net. A backcourt violation in basketball is more or less the opposite of an offside penalty in football (American or international) or hockey. If there is some universal truth about all games, it is very abstract and not very informative.

Although his historicism puts him in a position to recognize all this, Hegel resists making the hermeneutical turn. He tries to retain the idea of a presuppositionless philosophical reason in both the *Phenomenology* and in the *Science of Logic*. The "shapes of consciousness" and "shapes of a world" that are expounded and examined in the *Phenomenology* are called "phenomenal knowledge" (*das erscheinende Wissen*). This has a double meaning. Since Hegel calls all of these shapes except the final one, Science or Absolute Knowing, "untrue knowledge" (*unwahres Wissen*) or "cognition that is without truth" (*nicht wahrhaften Erkennen*), we have echoes of the Kantian distinction between the phenomenal and noumenal or between appearances and things in themselves (*PS*, 48–49).[24] Each shape will fall short of the truth it claims for itself along a journey that culminates in Absolute Knowing, the appearing of Science.[25]

This last phrase expresses the second meaning. Even Science "comes on the scene" (*PS*, 48). Insofar as it appears, it too is *das erscheinende Wissen*, but in a different sense.[26] All the forms of consciousness and of a world are phenomena, not in the pejorative, Kantian sense but in the sense that they become objects of thought that we can describe, analyze, and evaluate. But describing, analyzing, and evaluating would seem to be activities and not passivities. As such they raise what Solomon calls "*The Question of the Criterion*."[27] From what perspective do we describe; with what assumptions do we analyze; and by what criteria do we evaluate?

There is an additional way in which this problem arises for the *Phenomenology*. The moments that make up the journey through natural consciousness (untrue knowledge) to Science are not to be strung together in an arbitrary manner. They represent a developmental movement, sometimes structural and sometimes historical, that is meant to have some kind of necessity. Hegel's narrative

> can be regarded as the path of the natural consciousness which presses forward to true knowledge; or as the way of the Soul which journeys through the series of its own configurations as though they were stations appointed for it by its own nature, so that it may purify itself for the life of the Spirit, and achieve finally, through a completed experience of itself, the awareness of what it really is in itself.... The necessary progression and interconnection of the forms of the unreal consciousness will by itself bring to pass the *completion of the series*. (PS, 49–50)[28]

Two things to notice here. First, it is not just the *presentation* of each of the stages or stations but their *ordering* and the promised *completion* that raises questions about perspectives, assumptions, and criteria. Does the whole rise out of the parts because both the goal and the possibility of reaching it have been presupposed from the outset? Is there a hermeneutical circle here in which the question of the possibility of metaphysics is begged?

In the aftermath of Hegel,[29] that sort of hermeneutical critique has been at least implicit and often explicit in the thought of Kierkegaard, Marx, Nietzsche, Dewey, Heidegger, Gadamer, Ricoeur, Derrida, Quine, Kuhn, and Rorty (as different as these are among themselves).

Second, the promise of completion[30] not only raises these questions; it also gives us a hint of how Hegel can overcome the relativity of his historicism. If thought is always a child of its time, it could surpass its relativity in Absolute Knowing only if its time were somehow itself absolute, the time as the telos to which all other times were relative. This could only signify eschatological time, for Hegel is borrowing the form of Jewish or Christian messianism and giving it a non-theistic content.

The form is familiar from the world of sports. Thus, for an (admittedly finite) sequence of a sports season, the stages of good preseason preparation, of winning this game, of winning our division or conference or league, and of winning various playoff series all derive their meaning from the ultimate goal, winning the World Series, the Super Bowl, the Stanley Cup or the World Cup. Only that final victory gives completion to a season; apart from it the season remains in some sense a disappointment, having failed to reach its goal. But with that final victory the earlier wins and losses become essential ingredients in a championship season.

Hegel sees his world as a winner. He has what theologians call a realized eschatology. Like his Enlightenment predecessors, he believes he lives in a time in which human history has come to its fulfillment and fruition, at least in principle. What was always an oak tree is no longer merely an acorn or a sapling or a teenage oak, but a full growth oak tree.[31] What the stages or stations turn out to be relative to is the telos that was their true essence from the start, even if we can only see it at the end. Hegel thus seems to be committed to an "end of history" thesis, not in the sense that nothing happens any more, but in the sense that history is an organically teleological process that has come to full fruition. Only for this reason is Science finally possible.[32] It is Absolute Knowing because the world to which it is relative, whose ideology it is, is somehow the absolute world in its social and political structures, its art, its religion, and its politics. Thus, for example, Christianity is the "consummate" (*vollendete*) religion, although it needs to be, as we shall see, radically reinterpreted by a philosophy whose alleged autonomy we are exploring.

Already in the nineteenth century, but even more so after the horrors of the twentieth, such a realized eschatology seems hopelessly naive to many, and those who wish to draw on Hegel rather than to bash him often refuse to attribute such a view to him.[33] One can cite texts both for an against such an interpretation. What is decisive for me is that the logic of Hegel's argument requires an "end of history" thesis, whether or not he consistently affirms it. Without the realized telos of history, the strong claims he makes for his philosophy as Science, as Reason rather than mere Understanding, as Concept (*Begriff*) rather than mere Representation (*Vorstellung*), and as Speculation rather than Reflection dissolve into a hermeneutical relativism. Instead of being the voice of universal Reason his claims show themselves to rest on a quite particular world and its ideologies. Unsurprisingly, his version of religion within the limits of reason alone differs dramatically from those of both Spinoza and Kant since his reason, like theirs, is contaminated with particularity.

Hegel himself raises "the question of the criterion" in relation to the *Phenomenology*. Regarding the "*method of carrying out the inquiry*" that relates phenomenal (untrue) knowledge (Understanding that has not risen to the level of Reason or Science) as a necessary movement with a successful completion, "it would seem that it cannot take place without some presupposition which can serve as its underlying *criterion*," and at the beginning of the journey, no such criterion has been justified (*PS*, 52–53).³⁴

Not to worry, Hegel assures us. "Consciousness provides its own criterion from within itself, so that the investigation becomes a comparison of consciousness with itself . . . we do not need to import criteria . . . since what consciousness examines is its own self, all that is left for us is to simply look on [*reine Zusehen*]" (*PS*, 53–54). "We" are the neutral observers he needs; we occupy the "view from nowhere." Solomon cuts through the density of Hegel's account of how this works by saying that each form of untrue knowledge will negate itself by virtue of "its inadequacy according to its own criteria."³⁵ In the process new criteria emerge and with them new objects, for "as the knowledge changes, so too does the object, for it essentially belonged to this knowledge" (*PS*, 54). An example, not Hegel's, is that the heavenly bodies are essentially different objects in Copernican-Galilean astronomy from what they were in Ptolemaic-Aristotelian astronomy. In other words, the movement from one hermeneutical circle to another, or from one paradigm to another produces a new world inhabited with new objects.³⁶ Hegel calls this the "experience of itself which consciousness goes through" (*PS*, 56).

The essential *presupposition* here is that while the world may be opaque and evasive, consciousness is transparent to itself. It is not shaped by factors and forces of which it is not fully aware. When in reflection it turns its attention away from external realities and inward toward itself, there is no hindrance to full insight.³⁷ This assumption also shows up in Hegel's immediate predecessors, Kant and Fichte, and represents for each of the three the form in which they ground German idealism as transcendental philosophy in the Cartesian tradition. Thus for Kant, the *Critique of Pure Reason* is not "a critique of books and systems" but of reason itself. It can promise completeness, certainty, and clearness with regard to human knowledge because "I have to deal with nothing save reason itself and its pure thinking; and to obtain complete knowledge of these, there is no need to go far afield, since I come upon them in my own self." The results will not have the form of hypotheses but are "to be regarded as absolutely necessary" (*CPR*, A xii–xv).

Similarly, Fichte writes,

> Everybody, one hopes will be able to think *of himself*. . . . Let us hope, too, that he will be able to distinguish *this* act from the *opposite* one, whereby he thinks of objects outside him, and to find that in the latter the thinker and the thought are opposed so that his activity has to be addressed to something

distinct from himself, whereas in the act required of him, thinker and thought are the same so that his activity has therefore to revert into itself.

From this act of "self-reversion" (*in sich Zurückkehren*) Fichte promises to give a "complete deduction of all experience."[38] In other words, the inward turn of reflection provides the solid foundation of all knowledge. In the formulations of both Kant and Fichte there are strong echoes of Plato's doctrine of knowledge as recollection; the truth is already within us and we just need to "remember" it.

Unfortunately, the assumption that consciousness is transparent to itself, that the problem of knowledge disappears or rather is directly solved when the self turns its intentional gaze inward, away from its external others and toward itself, is just that: an assumption. Giving it axiomatic status does not make it self-evident; it rather makes it a presupposition by which one enters a particular hermeneutical circle, a Platonic-Cartesian one.

Dieter Henrich claims that Fichte (sometimes) rises above the simple view of reflection according to which consciousness is usually directed away from itself toward outer "objects" but occasionally directs itself inward toward itself in reflection and that when it does so it is fully transparent to itself. Rather, there is a pre-reflective self-consciousness that is ingredient in all consciousness. More to the present point, Fichte claims "that mental self-reference is a highly complicated structure that the apparent transparency of the mind to itself hides."[39] Karl Ameriks extends this "defense" of Fichte to Kant.[40]

By "the apparent transparency of the mind to itself" Henrich presumably means the pre-philosophical confidence with which I might say, for example, "I know what I meant when I said. . . ." This common sense semantic and epistemic language game or paradigm has been challenged by psychoanalysis. Freud writes that our "*naïve* self-love" has suffered three major blows. First, Copernicus taught us that we are not the center of the universe but "only a tiny fragment of a cosmic system of scarcely imaginable vastness." Then Darwin "proved [our] descent from the animal kingdom and [our] ineradicable animal nature." Finally, psychoanalysis "seeks to prove to the ego that it is not even master in its own house, but must content itself with scanty information of what is going on unconsciously in its mind."[41]

Freud acknowledges that psychoanalysis is not the only or the first way of making this point. He probably wasn't thinking of the apostle Paul, but he might well have been. For Paul teaches that in "ungodliness and wickedness" we "suppress the truth" (Rom. 1:18). Thus Augustine writes,

> O Lord, you were turning me around to look at myself. For I had placed myself behind my own back, refusing to see myself... in this way brought me face to face with myself once more so that I should see my wickedness and loathe it. I had known it all along, but I had always pretended that it was something different. I had turned a blind eye and forgotten it.[42]

This suppression, like psychoanalytic repression, is a hiding of ourselves from ourselves that makes us opaque to ourselves. We have blind spots of our own making. But just as there are blind spots in our vision and while driving a car that arise from our location rather than from our own making, so there can be blind spots in our thinking that arise from our semantic and epistemic location, the particular traditions and practices, language games and paradigms in which we live and move and have our being.

Deciding to do transcendental philosophy is not likely to magically dissolve such kinds of opacity into transparency. Even if we grant that Kant and Fichte have more sophisticated theories of reflection than the "apparent transparency of the mind to itself" that pervades common sense, the aura of a transparency claim lingers. The need for transcendental arguments makes it clear that any such transparency is not immediate. But their promise of absolute certainty and completeness implies that philosophical reflection is unconditioned and uncontaminated by anything particular and contingent to which it might be relative and thereby the expression of a particular mode of reasoning rather than Universal Reason itself.

If we make the move with Hegel from forms of consciousness to forms of world, from individual consciousness to social practices and institutions,[43] the problem intensifies. Now, a psychologically oriented hermeneutics of suspicion[44] becomes ideology critique, the claim that at the sociological level we do not fully know what we think, what we do, or who we are, that collectively as well as individually our self-knowledge is always partial and often false.

Within existentialism (Kierkegaard and Nietzsche), ideology critique (Marx and the Frankfurt school), and philosophical hermeneutics (Gadamer and Ricoeur) we find a sustained counterclaim to what we might call the Axiom of Transparency. Our misunderstanding of ourselves is sometimes due to mere finitude; but sometimes it is motivated by desires such as the desire to look better than we are, so that it can be said that we manage not to notice who we are.[45]

In his Jena essays, *The Difference between Fichte's and Schelling's System of Philosophy* (1801) and *Faith and Reason* (1802), Hegel develops a critique of *Reflexionsphilosophie*. At first it may not seem relevant here, for Hegel is working with a broader concept of reflection than either a turning from other "objects" to make oneself the object of consciousness or a pre-reflective self-consciousness in which I am always already given to myself. The opposite of Reflection is Speculation, a distinction that maps quite directly onto that between Understanding and Reason; thus it anticipates the *Phenomenology*'s distinction between "untrue" and "true" knowledge.

But this analysis is relevant for understanding the Axiom of Transparency, for while is rises above the "the apparent transparency of the mind to itself" presupposed by common sense, it affirms that although transparency is not immediate, it can be achieved through the philosophical thinking that moves from Reflection (in this broader sense) to Speculation. All the challenges raised by existentialism, ideology critique, philosophical hermeneutics, psychoanalysis, and Pauline theology (including Augustine and Kierkegaard) are as easily raised against mediated transparency and against immediate transparency.

The distinctive mark of reflective philosophy is the positing of unresolved opposition between such moments as finite and infinite, the human subject and God, faith and reason, subject and object, freedom and necessity, causality and teleology, and so forth.[46] To use a language that Hegel himself almost never uses, reflection is the analysis of reality into antitheses that never achieve synthesis. Thus Hegel writes, "Dichotomy [*Entzweiung*, opposition, antithesis, contradiction] is the source of *the need of philosophy*; and as the culture of the era, it is the unfree and given [positive] aspect of the whole configuration. In [our][47] culture, the appearance of the Absolute has become isolated from the Absolute and fixated into independence" (*DFS*, 89). Hegel finds *Entzweiung* in both Protestantism and the Enlightenment,[48] and he takes Kant, Jacobi, and Fichte to be the philosophical expression of this culture, philosophy as "its own time apprehended in thought," *Reflexionsphilosophie* as a child of its time.

> The fixed standpoint which the all-powerful culture of our time has established for philosophy is that of a Reason affected by sensibility. In this situation philosophy cannot aim at the cognition of God but only at what is called the cognition of man.... He does, however have the faculty of faith so that he can touch himself up here and there with a spot of alien supersensuousness. (*FK*, 65)

This faith is not that of Luther but that of Kant, Jacobi and Fichte as Hegel sees them, the combination of an intellect that can only grasp the finite, the feelings, sighs, and prayers of the heart, the longing and yearning [*Sehnsucht* and *Sehnen*] for the Absolute and Eternal that can never attain to clear and certain knowledge. It is this denial of discursive knowledge that makes these three versions of *Reflexionsphilosophie* into philosophies of faith, even if the terms in which Hegel describes it seem more suited to Schleiermacher and other German romantics.[49] This faith is not a form of trusting cognition of what is not immediately present but rather of longing for what is simply absent.

By contrast, Speculation achieves knowledge, and is, if you like, a metaphysics of (mediated) presence. It is "philosophy as it has finally come into its own truth" with an intuition of the organic whole that is "God, nature, and self-consciousness or reason."[50] It *achieves* the intellectual intuition (presence and transparency) that Kant had denied to human knowledge. Kant's denial, and the consequent distinctions between appearances and things in themselves, phenomena and noumena, consistently appeal to the difference between human and divine knowledge.[51] Where Fichte, Schelling, and Hegel claim that philosophy overcomes these dichotomies, they do so by denying a qualitative difference between human and divine knowing, replacing it with a distinction between two modes of human knowing, such as, in Hegel's case, Reflection and Speculation, Understanding and Reason, or "untrue" and "true" knowledge.[52] Their theory of Reason turns out to be a theory of God, one with anticipations of Feuerbach's claim that theology, properly understood, is anthropology. For the "divine" knowledge that is the criterion of the real and the achievement of both presence and transparency is a mode of human knowledge: speculative philosophy

There is a metaphysical as well as an epistemic sense in which Hegel's account of "the pilgrimage of reason" and "the odyssey of spirit"[53] is a pantheistic theology. In the background of Hegel's thinking here is Schelling's Philosophy of Identity, which, in turn, reflects Spinoza's third kind of knowledge, which he calls "intuition"[54] and which grasps natura naturata and natura naturans in their inextricable unity, *Deus sive Natura*. Philosophy must undertake the journey from Reflection to Speculation. In this movement, "reflection nullifies itself" (*DFS*, 94).

What is this nullification? In a lecture from the time of our two essays, Hegel writes that speculation "gets [reflection] out of the way" [*aus dem Wege räumt*].[55] If we took this to mean that reflective philosophy is simply cast aside and left behind we would be mistaken. Hegel twice uses his beloved term, *aufheben*, in this context (*FK*, 9–10).[56] No single term, such as 'suspension,' adequately captures Hegel's double meaning of negating something in its supposed autonomy and self-sufficiency and affirming it as a subordinate part of a larger whole. If athletes thought Hegelese when saying "there is no 'I' in 'team,'" they would mean that the team is the *Aufhebung* of each member, even its star player. But they don't leave the star player on the bench. This is why "consume and consummate" (*FK*, 66) and "abolish and adsorb" (*LP*, 190) are happy translations of *aufheben*. What is consumed and abolished is the separate self-sufficiency of something (the I) that is absorbed and consummated in the larger whole (the team) of which it is a "moment."

Thus, the "*true* infinite of life does not exist simply as a thought or concept to be *reflected* on by the finite consciousness. It is an infinity that contains the finite, a concept that involves existence,[57] an ideal that is the life of the real" (*FK*, 16).[58] Accordingly, the task of philosophy is "to posit dichotomy in the Absolute, as its appearance; to posit the finite in the infinite, as life" (*DFS*, 93–94). We are prepared to learn in the *Phenomenology* that the forms of "untrue knowledge" are *erscheinendes Wissen* in both a negative Kantian sense and a positive Hegelian sense. They give us merely appearances and not the "thing in itself," but at the same time they are the appearings, however incomplete and inadequate, of the Absolute and of Absolute Knowing. This is why Hegel can say that "if the Absolute is supposed merely to be brought nearer to us through this instrument [knowledge, cognition, *Erkennen*] . . . like a bird caught by a lime-twig, it would surely laugh our ruse to scorn, *if it were not with us, in and for itself, all along*, and of its own volition" (*PS*, 47; emphasis added).[59]

Just as for the theist, while God the creator is distinct from the world as created, God is present in and through the world (Rom. 1:19–20), so for Hegel the Absolute, while not adequately presented in the various forms of "untrue" knowledge, it is nevertheless present in those forms of consciousness. The task of philosophy is to take what is merely *an sich* (implicit) in natural consciousness and make it *für sich* (explicit) as Science or Speculation.[60] Hegel sees himself at an historical location where that has become possible. He is the Joshua who will take us into the promised land up to which Moses has led us without quite entering it himself.[61]

Notes

1. The classic statement is Richard Kroner's *Von Kant bis Hegel* (Tübingen: J. C. B. Mohr, 1921/1924). See also Frederick Beiser, *German Idealism: The Struggle against Subjectivism, 1781–1801* (Cambridge, MA: Harvard University Press, 2002); Dieter Henrich, *Between Kant and Hegel:*

Lectures on German Idealism, ed. David S. Pacini (Cambridge, MA: Harvard University Press, 2003); and *The Emergence of German Idealism*, ed. Michael Baur and Daniel O. Dahlstrom (Washington, DC: Catholic University of America Press, 1999).

2. As early as 1795, in thinking about the Absolute Self as it was emerging in the thought of Fichte and Schelling, Hegel objected to using the category of substance in describing it. See *HL*, 42–43.

3. In correspondence with Schelling about Fichte.

4. In this conversation with Spinoza, Hegel speaks of the True and the Absolute. But the argument of the *Phenomenology* is not that the Absolute is Spirit but rather that Spirit becomes absolute in Absolute Knowing. The term 'absolute' ends up as an adjective rather than a noun. This remains the case in Hegel's *Encyclopedia*, where the third part of the *Philosophy of Spirit* is "Absolute Spirit." To speak of the Absolute is to speak abstractly; to speak of Spirit is to speak concretely. That the telos of spirit is to become Absolute Spirit is the justification for using the upper-case S in Spirit. I regularly substitute 'concept' for Miller's 'notion' as a translation of '*Begriff*.'

5. For a critique of those who wish for a Hegel without tears, that is, without metaphysics, see Adriaan T. Peperzak, *Modern Freedom: Hegel's Legal, Moral, and Political Philosophy* (Boston: Kluwer, 2001), pp. 5–18. While there is no law against finding Hegel's social philosophy to be what remains of interest from his work, Peperzak challenges the notion that any part of his thought is metaphysically neutral.

6. Kant himself uses the term 'metaphysics' in a broader sense to cover any a priori knowledge. Thus the "metaphysics of morals" is not metaphysical in the sense just given.

7. No one has developed this theme as fully as Cyril O'Regan in *The Heterodox Hegel* (Albany: State University of New York Press, 1994). Speaking of correspondence with Schelling in 1795, Butler writes, "Hegel's own conscious affiliation with the tradition of Gnostic Christianity becomes apparent here. The mature Hegelian philosophy is in fact the most systematic expression of that tradition" (*HL*, 37). Kevin Hart suggests that what Hegel translates into Philosophy is not Christianity but Gnosticism. *Kingdoms of God* (Bloomington: Indiana University Press, 2014), p. 51.

8. Robert Tucker, *Philosophy and Myth in Karl Marx*, 2nd ed. (New York: Cambridge University Press, 1961), p. 46.

9. Tucker, *Philosophy and Myth*, p. 31.

10. Attributes and modes in Spinoza's parlance.

11. Michael N. Forster, *Hegel's Idea of a Phenomenology of Spirit* (Chicago: University of Chicago Press, 1998), pp. 505–10.

12. H. S. Harris, *Hegel's Ladder I: The Pilgrimage of Reason* (Indianapolis, IN: Hackett, 1997), p. 11.

13. This is the actual title, *The Phenomenology of Spirit* being the subtitle.

14. Harris, *Ladder I*, p. 11.

15. On Hegel as a kind of Aristotelian, see G. R. G. Mure, *An Introduction to Hegel* (Oxford: Clarendon, 1940).

16. Used without italics, the Logic refers indifferently to both mature versions, the first part of the *Encyclopedia of the Philosophical Sciences* and the *Science of Logic*.

17. Cf. ¶24, Z1 and *SL*, 27, 39, 45, 50, 63. On Hegel's Jena lecture courses "Logic and Metaphysics," see H. S. Harris, *Hegel's Development: Night Thoughts, (Jena 1801-1806)* (Oxford: Clarendon, 1983), pp. xlix, 102–4, 201, 203n., and 576–78; and *The Jena System, 1804-5: Logic and Metaphysics*, trans. John W. Burbidge and George di Giovanni (Montreal: McGill-Queens University Press, 1986).

18. Ermanno Bencivenga, *Hegel's Dialectical Logic* (New York: Oxford University Press, 2000), pp. 37 and 41. The interior quotation is from the passage just cited above.

19. Jean Hyppolite, "The Transformation of Metaphysics into Logic," in *Logic and Existence*, trans. Leonard Lawlor and Amit Sen (Albany: State University of New York Press, 1997), pp. 58–59, 64.

20. Hegel does suggest, however, that different levels of the Logic are dominant for different historical figures and eras.

21. Thus "the strange spectacle of a cultured nation without metaphysics—like a temple richly ornamented in other respects but without a holy of holies" (*SL*, 25).

22. Frederick Beiser, *The German Historicist Tradition* (New York: Oxford University Press, 2011), p. 1.

23. Forster's *Hegel's Idea* is the most comprehensive analysis of historicism in the *Phenomenology*. He defines the relevant sense of the term as "the recognition that human thought undergoes fundamental changes during the course of history" (p. 293). We can gloss "fundamental" by suggesting that what changes is not merely the content but especially the axioms, the presuppositions, the criteria of human thought. It is less like adding new theorems to Euclidian geometry and more like changing over to Riemannian geometry. Thomas Kuhn's notion of a "paradigm shift" is helpful here. See *The Structure of Scientific Revolutions*, 2nd ed. (Chicago: University of Chicago Press, 1970).

24. Hegel will reprise this distinction between "untrue" and "true" knowledge in his distinctions between Understanding and Reason and between representations (*Vorstellungen*) and concepts (*Begriffe*).

25. This journey has often been compared to the romantic *Bildungsroman*. In this connection, Jean Hyppolite mentions Rousseau's *Emile*; Goethe, *Wilhelm Meister*; and Novalis's *Heinrich von Ofterdiingen*. "Through a series of experiences, each comes to abandon his first conviction: what had been a truth becomes an illusion.... But according to Hegel such a history of consciousness is not a novel but a work of science." Jean Hyppolite, *Genesis and Structure of Hegel's Phenomenology of Spirit*, trans. Samuel Cherniak and John Heckman (Evanston, IL: Northwestern University Press, 1974), pp. 11–12. Given the theological import of the *Phenomenology*, it has also been compared to Bonaventure's *The Soul's Journey into God* and to the stations of the cross.

26. "Thus we have "two forms of 'appearing knowledge'—the 'true' (or noumenal) knowing of philosophical 'Science,' and the 'untrue' (or empirically phenomenal) knowing of ordinary consciousness." H. S. Harris, *Hegel's Ladder: I*, p. 174. Cf. p.199n25, where Harris suggests that this second meaning is the fundamental one.

27. Robert C. Solomon, *In the Spirit of Hegel: A Study of G. W. F. Hegel's* Phenomenology of Spirit (New York: Oxford University Press, 1983), pp. 307–11.

28. "But the *goal* is as necessarily fixed for knowledge as the serial progression; it is the point where knowledge no longer needs to go beyond itself, but where knowledge finds itself, where Concept corresponds to object and object to Concept. Hence the progress towards this goal is also unhalting, and short of it no satisfaction is to be found at any of the stations on the way" (*PS*, 51).

29. I once had a colleague who gave a course with the wonderful title, Hegel and the Aftermath.

30. See *PS*, 49–51, 56. "The necessary progression and interconnection of the forms of the unreal consciousness will by itself bring to pass the *completion* of the series" (p. 50).

31. Hegel is fond of such imagery. See *PS*, 2, 7, 12.

32. See *PS*, 3–7. I have given an "end of history" reading to the *Phenomenology* in *History and Truth in Hegel's Phenomenology*, 3rd ed. (Bloomington: Indiana University Press, 1998). Such a view of history is not so strange, but is rather quite "American" as the view that democratic capitalism as practiced by the United States and quite a few other countries around the world is the goal of history. The task of everybody else is to catch up with that multinational "us." See, for example, Francis Fukuyama, *The End of History and the Last Man*.

33. See, to give just two examples, Hyppolite, *Logic and Existence*, and Catherine Malabou, *The Future of Hegel*.

34. Maybe, a la Descartes, some method could provide the needed neutral criteria. For Hegel's critique of the idea of method as an instrument for getting through whatever medium stands between us and the object of knowledge, see *PS*, 28, in relation to 46–47.

35. Solomon, *In the Spirit*, p. 307.

36. Another example would be the famous two tables of which Sir Arthur Eddington spoke. The everyday, familiar table is very solid, while the "same" table as seen by the physicist is mostly empty space. Under the rubrics of incommensurability and methodological anarchism, Paul Feyerabend raised the question of just what sense two such tables are the "same." Hegel smiles.

37. This appears to be the assumption Derrida attributes to Husserl in *Speech and Phenomena*.

38. Fichte, *Science of Knowledge* (Wissenschaftslehre) *with the First and Second Introductions*, trans. Peter Heath and John Lachs (New York: Appleton-Century-Crofts, 1970), p. 37.

39. Henrich, *Between Kant and Hegel*, p, 250. See also pp. 241–45 and 249–62. For the full statement of Henrich's interpretation see "Fichte's Original Insight," *Contemporary German Philosophy* 1 (1982): 15–52. For an analysis of the issues involved in an extensive historical and contemporary context, see Manfred Frank, "Subjectivity and Individuality: Survey of a Problem," in *Figuring the Self: Subject, Absolute, and Others in Classical German Philosophy*, ed. David Klemm and Günter Zöller (Albany: State University of New York Press, 1997), pp. 3–30.

40. Karl Ameriks, "From Kant to Frank: The Ineliminable Subject," in *The Modern Subject: Conceptions of the Self in Classical German Philosophy*, ed. Karl Ameriks and Dieter Sturma (Albany: State University of New York Press, 1995), pp. 217–30.

41. Sigmund Freud, *Introductory Lectures on Psychoanalysis*, in *The Standard Edition of the Complete Psychological Works of Sigmund Freud*, ed. and trans. James Strachey (London: Hogarth, 1953–74), vol. 16, pp. 284–85.

42. Augustine, *Confessions*, trans. R. S. Pine-Coffin (Baltimore: Penguin Books, 1961), VIII, 7 (p. 169). I know of no better illustration of what Sartre calls bad faith in *Being and Nothingness*.

43. That is, from Subjective Spirit to Objective Spirit (Family, Civil Society, and the State) and Absolute Spirit (Art, Religion, and Philosophy) in the System as presented in the *Encyclopedia*. See PM, *Hegel's Philosophy of Spirit*.

44. I have defined the hermeneutics of suspicion as "*the deliberate attempt to expose the self-deceptions involved in hiding our actual operative motives from ourselves, individually or collectively, in order not to notice how and how much our behavior and our beliefs are shaped by values we profess to disown.*" *Suspicion and Faith: The Religious Uses of Modern Atheism* (New York: Fordham University Press, 1998), p. 13.

45. I use the idea of managing not to notice as a gloss on Sartre's notion of bad faith in *Being and Nothingness*. He presents it as an alternative to Freud's excessively mechanistic notion of unconscious aspects of thought and action. As in the previous note, I apply it to both the individual and society. We are talking about motivated self-deception. Also see David Pears, *Motivated Irrationality*, where wishes distort reason with respect to both beliefs and actions; Mike W. Martin, *Self-Deception and Morality*; and Mike W. Martin, ed., *Self-Deception and Self-Understanding*.

46. When Hegel speaks of contradiction, he usually means oppositions of this sort rather than formal contradictions such as A and not-A. For a definitive account of speculation see *EL*, 125–33, ¶¶79–82, with Remarks and Additions. Reason, as distinct from Understanding, is divided into a negative (dialectical) and a positive (speculative) moment, but the former is linked to Understanding as Reflection that is not yet Speculation.

47. Hegel uses a definite article here *der*. Harris and Cerf put 'any' in square brackets, but the argument of the two essays suggests that Hegel is speaking of the modern world, hence my 'our.'

48. Anticipating his discussion of faith and pure insight in chapter six of the *Phenomenology*. See the helpful discussion in Solomon, *In the Spirit*, pp. 149–51. For mere Christianity *Entzweiung* is not a product of finitude but rather of sin. Thus, in Bach's *St. Matthew Passion*, we hear

| Buss und Reu | Penitence and remorse |
| Knirscht das Sündenherz entzwei | Grind the sinful heart in two |

49. Through his contacts with the Schlegels, Schleiermacher, Schelling, Novalis, and Tieck during his Berlin years, Fichte was an important factor in the development of German romanticism, in

spite of crucial disagreements. See Manfred Franck, "Philosophical Foundations of Early Romanticism," in Ameriks and Sturma, *Modern Subject*, pp. 65–85; Kenneth Schmitz, "The Idealism of the German Romantics," in Bauer and Dahlstrom, *Emergence of German Idealism*, pp. 176–97; and Frederick C. Beiser, *The Romantic Imperative: The Concept of Early German Romanticism* (Cambridge, MA: Harvard University Press, 2003), chaps. 7 and 10;

50. Walter Cerf, "Speculative Philosophy and Intellectual Intuition: An Introduction to Hegel's *Essays*," p. xvi. This essay appears as pp. xi–xxxvi in both *DFS* and *FK*.

51. See my "In Defense of the Thing in Itself," *Kant-Studien* 59, no. 1 (1968): 118–41.

52. For Hegel's explicit critique of Kant on the unknowability of the thing in itself and noumenal reality, which includes God, see *EL*, 80–108, ¶¶40–60, and *HP/H*, 443–57.

53. These are the subtitles of the two volumes of Harris's *Hegel's Ladder*, corresponding to "shapes of consciousness" and "shapes of a world."

54 Developed in Part II of the *Ethics*. "To Hegel, English empiricism from Locke on as well as continental rationalism (with the exception of Spinoza) were reflective philosophies. The whole philosophy of the Enlightenment was reflective. And so was most of Kant's transcendental idealism." Cerf, "Speculative Philosophy," p. xvii.

55. Preserved in Karl Rosenkranz, *Georg Wilhelm Friedrich Hegels Leben* (Darmstadt: Wissenschaftliche Buchgesellschaft, 1963), p. 10, and cited in H. S. Harris, "Introduction to *Faith and Knowledge*," *FK*, 10.

56. In the citation from Rosenkranz.

57. This phrase indicates how Logic can be Metaphysics and why Hegel gives his own version of the ontological argument. See *EL*, 98–100 and 268–71, ¶¶51 and 193, with Remarks; *SL*, 86–90 and 705–10; *LP*, 347–67; and *LPR*, 181–89, 420–21.

58. This passage nicely summarizes Hyppolite's argument in "Transformation of Metaphysics into Logic."

59. Just as it is misleading for Hegel to use personal pronouns for his impersonal Absolute, so it is misleading to speak here of "volition." If this were poetry, that would be an acceptable metaphor, but this is metaphysics and, at the very least, such a usage calls for commentary. As we shall see in the next chapter, Hegel will offer an account that seeks to justify the "untrue knowledge" that uses personal language for an impersonal Absolute.

60. It is along these lines that Hegel reinterprets the traditional proofs for the existence of God in *Lectures on the Proofs of the Existence of God* (*P*).

61. I think it is fair to say that Moses here stands for the Enlightenment as an autonomy project, but more specifically for the pantheism of Spinoza and the idealism of Kant, Fichte, and Schelling.

9

HEGEL'S HERMENEUTICS

Let us see where we are with regard to Hegel's theology and hermeneutical theory. We have seen him turn away from the theism of a personal God, a Creator, Lawgiver, and Redeemer of a world distinct from God, a world separated and united by creation, separated by the fall, and reunited in redemption. As Luther puts it, commenting on Psalm 51, "That gigantic mountain of divine wrath that so separates God and David, he crosses by trust in mercy and joins himself to God."[1]

Although Hegel claims to be a Lutheran,[2] he finds such a theology to embody an opposition (*Entgegensetzung* and *Entzweiung*) that precludes acceptable unification (*Vereinigung*) or reconciliation (*Versöhnung*).[3] He replaces it with a pantheism that draws on Spinoza and Schelling but distances itself from them by replacing nature with spirit as the primary metaphysical category. In spite of, or perhaps because of its Feuerbachian overtones,[4] Hegel attributes this "Spinozism of freedom" or "pantheism of spirit" to Jesus, whom he portrays as "against the thought of a personal God." In this way, he claims Jesus as his ally over against biblical religion in both its Jewish and Christian forms and against the "mere Christianity" that had become the faith of Christendom right down to his own day.

We have seen this theology develop in the early theological writings, where the divine is conceived as like the life of a clan that indwells and enlivens each member and like "a nation of men related to one another by love." While both that life and that nation have persons as members, neither is itself a person. While the notion of one common life animating all the members of a clan remains biological, the notion of a nation united in reciprocal love completes the movement away from Spinoza, from nature to "spirit" as Hegel will use the term.[5] For him 'life' is not a category of history and freedom, while 'nation' (*Volk* not *Staat*) is.[6] Hegel's theology is a sociopolitical theology. Since this life and this nation or people are wholes of which individuals are parts, without being the Creator of the parts, this theology is a pantheism; and since both the wholes and the parts are human, it is a pantheism of Spirit.[7]

We have also seen this pantheism emerge in Hegel's transformation of logic into an Aristotelian metaphysics of essences and in his account of the overcoming of *Reflexionsphilosophie* in Speculation. We are prepared to see it emerge once again in the movement of the *Phenomenology* from "untrue knowledge" to Science.

So far as hermeneutics is concerned, in Hegel's persuasive redefinition of God as a living and interactive whole made up of human persons, we find an interpretive practice formally like that of Spinoza and Kant while substantively opposed to both Spinoza's pantheistic naturalism and Kant's deistic personalism.

But the situation is dramatically altered by the notion that both Spirit and Reason as its highest power are essentially historical. By locating both the standpoint of Science, which emerges as Absolute Knowing at the conclusion of the *Phenomenology*, and its detailed working out in the *Science of Logic* as possible only at a particular moment of history (Hegel's present), Hegel abandons the notion that Reason is universal by being timeless and ahistorical. He tells us that "it is not difficult to see that ours is a birth-time and a period of transition to a new era. Spirit has broken with the world it has hitherto inhabited and imagined, and is of a mind to submerge it in the past, and in the labour of its own transformation" (*PS*, 6).

This opens the possibility of a hermeneutical turn in which one's historical/cultural location constitutes a particular, finite hermeneutical circle or paradigm to whose presuppositions (for example, Spinoza's axioms, Kant's a priori ethics) thought is relative. Note the hermeneutical significance of the phrase, "the world [Spirit] has hitherto inhabited and imagined," in relation to the phenomenological move from forms of consciousness to forms of world. It is a passing world now giving way to a "new era."[8]

But Hegel remains committed to the Enlightenment ideal of Reason as universal, and we have seen Hegel resist any move to hermeneutical relativity in three ways. First, by the notion that the succession of worlds and the modes of Reason relative to them can be brought to completion. In the new era one is no longer just at once of the stops along the route of the Orient Express but has arrived at the final destination, Istanbul (or Paris, if you prefer to travel in the opposite direction). Otherwise Science would not be possible. It would be only "*love* of knowing" and not "*actual* knowing" (PS, 3).[9]

Second, by the notion that the criteria by which thought moves through all the finite and "untrue" forms of consciousness and forms of world in the *Phenomenology* do not come from "us" in our finite and contingent location but are so immanent in experience itself that the movement is self-directed while we merely look on as observers. We presuppose nothing, bring nothing a priori to the process.

Third, by the notion that the starting point of the Logic is not arbitrarily chosen by us but once again given by the very nature of thought. Our point of departure does not depend in any way on us but on Reason as unfolding itself; once again, as thinkers we are stenographers rather than authors.

It would seem that in spite of his historicism, Hegel shares with his ahistorical predecessors the ideal of a presuppositionless philosophy, relative to nothing merely finite and particular. In spite of its historicity, Reason will somehow have to be, or better, become universal.[10] We have seen that in the aftermath of Hegel's heyday, there is a widely shared critique that finds none of Hegel's strategies to this end to be successful. As the Arab proverb would have it, having let the historical camel get his nose in the tent, Hegel soon finds the whole camel inside and unwilling to leave. To switch metaphors in midstream, we might say that there is an historical hole in Hegel's dike and no little Dutch boy to save the day by putting his finger in it.

But whether we side with Hegel or his critics vis-à-vis his reluctance to adopt what we might call an historicized, hermeneutical Kantianism, a theory of the finitude of human knowledge grounded less on the senses and more on the a priori role of sociocultural location and tradition—the question of Hegel's hermeneutics is not limited to this question: has he taken the hermeneutical turn, and if not, why not? His theology, like Spinoza's, rests on a reinterpretation of the idea of God, and it will come as no surprise that his mature philosophy of religion, like Kant's, rests on a systematic reinterpretation of various themes from "mere Christianity." There is also the question of Hegel's hermeneutical guidelines. What is the hermeneutical theory that guides his reinterpretations of Christian themes? What are the criteria?

A second question about Hegel's actual interpretations arises from the striking change in tone that takes place between the early theological writings and the mature philosophy of religion found in the *Phenomenology* (1807) and subsequent texts. While the former are marked by a strident, even Nietzschean hostility toward everything Jewish and Christian (except for Jesus, whom Hegel seeks to rescue from that milieu),[11] the mature, published writings are (in their own rather condescending way as we shall see), far more respectful of the Christian religion. In both the *Phenomenology* and the *Lectures on the Philosophy of Religion*, it is the highest form of religion. In the former it is the revealed (*offenbare*) religion,[12] or absolute religion, while in the latter it is the consummate (*vollendete*) religion. As it turns out, if we answer the first question about the theory that guides Hegel's hermeneutical practice, we will find the answer to this second question about the remarkable change in tone. Christianity can be praised as the highest form of religion, in spite of the heteronomy it embodies, as long as speculative philosophy retains the right to correct its inadequacies.

The formula for Hegel's strategy is simple enough: reinterpret religious Representations (*Vorstellungen*) as philosophical Concepts (*Begriffe*), though just what this means is not so simple. This precept emerges for the first time in a sketch from 1805–1806 of his Philosophy of Spirit and is utterly basic to the *Phenomenology*. It represents the major turning point in Hegel's philosophy of religion and is the key to the substantive continuity between his early theological writings and his mature theology in spite of the difference of tone.

There are three Jena drafts of (at least part of) the System Hegel wished to develop, anticipating the three parts of his mature system: Logic, Philosophy of Nature, and Philosophy of Spirit. The first of these is a partial Philosophy of Spirit from 1803–1804.[13] The second of these is the Logic and Metaphysics cited above.[14] The third, from 1805–1806, contains a Philosophy of Nature and a Philosophy of Spirit.[15]

The mature Philosophy of Spirit as developed in the *Encyclopedia*[16] divides into Subjective Spirit, Objective Spirit, and Absolute Spirit. Subjective Spirit concerns spirit as individual consciousness and can be called a philosophical psychology. Objective Spirit concerns spirit as the outward objectification of personal inwardness in social and political institutions that make up a world and can be called a social and political philosophy. The movement between these two maps closely onto the distinction between forms of consciousness and forms of world in the *Phenomenology*.[17] They also signify the I and We whose dialectical intertwining constitute Spirit in the *Phenomenology*. Absolute Spirit is the awareness or knowledge that spirit has of itself in varying degrees of adequacy, both as consciousness and self-consciousness, in Art, Religion, and Philosophy.

In the 1805–1806 Philosophy of Spirit this language has not reached its final form and what will become Absolute Spirit is treated as a subdivision of what will become Objective Spirit.[18] But here for the first time we encounter Art, Religion, and Philosophy (actually Science, anticipating the language of the *Phenomenology*) as the culmination of the system. In these the "absolutely free spirit . . . brings forth another [kind of] world . . . where its work is completed and it achieves an intuition of *itself* as *itself*" (*JR*, 263). It is in this world that the acorn becomes the oak tree and it becomes possible to say, It is what it is, or It has become what it always was. The in-itself has become for-itself. Absolute Being as Absolute Spirit is fully revealed in Art, Religion, and above all, Philosophy in their stages of development. In the modern forms of these worlds the historical process reaches its culmination. Being as Absolute Spirit has fully unfolded itself both as "God" and as "God's" self-knowledge.

What is important for our purposes is that modes of cognition of these three worlds are specified, respectively, as Intuition (*Anschauung*), Representation (*Vorstellung*), and Concept (*Begriff*).[19] "And now, for the first time, Hegel distinguishes religion primarily by its theoretical form: it has its object neither in the form of intuition, as in art, nor in that of conceptual knowing, as in science, but in the form of representation."[20] Here Hegel introduces us to the hermeneutical first principle of his philosophy of religion, namely that philosophy has the same content as religion but in the form of the Concept rather than of Representation (*JR*, 272).

Hegel uses this claim as the first thesis of his mature system (*EL*, 24–28, ¶¶1–5). Philosophy presupposes religion because "in the order of time consciousness produces *representations* of objects before it produces *concepts* of them . . . the *thinking* Spirit only advances to thinking cognition and comprehension [*zum denkenden Erkennen und Begreifen*] by going *through* representation and turning attention *to* [*sich wenden auf*] it" (*EL*, 24, ¶1; translation altered).[21]

The double claim is (a) that in the translation of Representations into Concepts the form changes but the content remains the same and is preserved, and (b) that only when thus translated or reinterpreted does the content of consciousness, including religious consciousness, achieve its "proper" form

(*EL*, 23 and 28, ¶¶3, 5, and 5Z). Whether or not one is sympathetic with the second claim and thus with Hegel's hermeneutical practice and theological theory, the first claim strikes me as manifestly false. Like the reinterpretations of Spinoza and Kant, Hegel's replace a fairly well-defined content, whether one likes it or not, with a very different content.

Ironically, in his *Logic* Hegel suggests that a change of form is a change of content, since "content is what it is only in virtue of the fact that it contains developed form within itself." Moreover, the right form "is so far from being indifferent with respect to content, however, that on the contrary, it is the content itself" (*EL* 202–3, ¶133Z). Only in a very external relation, as between a book that is handwritten or printed, can the form change without changing the content. Hegel assumes, without argument that I can find, that the difference between the forms of religious and philosophical discourse is of this external sort.

So what is the difference between these two levels of thought? *Vorstellung* is sometimes translated as "picture thinking." But there are two reasons why this is not a happy rendering. First, it loses touch with the fact that this is the standard Kantian term, regularly translated as 'representation,' for the thinking done by the Understanding (*Verstand*) that gives us the empirical knowledge of common sense and natural science but is inadequate for metaphysical knowledge. Hegel has not forgotten Kant, even if his translators sometimes have. Second, Hegel's analysis of the inadequacy of representations for Philosophy as Science is not reducible to the role of sense perception and imagination in this level of thinking. So let us see how the distinction between the Representations of Religion and the Concepts of Philosophy is developed, first in the 1805–6 Philosophy of Spirit and then in the *Phenomenology*.[22]

In 1805–6 the point of departure is art. It produces a spiritual world. However, this is not the "clear, self-knowing Spirit" but a "limited [*beschränkten*] Spirit" because "in this element [*Anschauung*] it is inadequate [*unangemessen*] to Spirit" (*JR*, 265).

Hegel tells us three things about this inadequacy. First, as Intuition art is the realm of sensation and image (*Empfindung* and *Bild*). We should not be too quick to limit art here to sense perception, for *Empfindung* can mean feeling and sentiment as well as perception. In any case, Hegel includes poetry among the other arts he mentions (pure music, dance, sculpture, and painting), and it is not a matter of simple sense perception. Whatever feelings and images poetry evokes are already mediated by language. Secular music also (leaving aside sacred music as a mixture of art and religion) relies on language and not just sight and hearing in opera, madrigals, *Lieder*, and the rich variety of pop songs.

In the second place, Hegel tells us art is an immediacy that is unmediated (*JR*, 265). As we have just seen, this clearly cannot mean sense perception or affect unmediated by language. In the absence of an account of what it does mean we can surmise that it might mean that interpretations of art do not themselves belong to art. The art critic, the music critic, and the literary critic are not artists, musicians, poets, or dramatists (except accidentally, as in the case of Robert Schumann or George Bernard Shaw). The meaning of a painting or a poem, Hegel may be telling us, is the painting or the poem itself. The reflection that interprets and (sometimes) evaluates a work of art takes us into a world that is not the world of art itself but a world of theory by which the world of art is mediated. By contrast, we might continue to speculate, the immediacies of religious life are mediated by theoretical interpretations in scriptural texts, liturgies, creeds, and theological writings, all of which belong themselves to the world of religion and religious life.

Thirdly, Hegel tells us, "Intuition, this medium of finitude, cannot grasp the infinite; it is only an *intended* infinity." Hegel here seems to be thinking of the gods of Greek sculpture, hymns, and mythology, whose world "is *intended* not *true* representation [*Vorstellung*]. It lacks necessity, the form of thinking (*Denken*)" (*JR*, 265). Perhaps we are being reminded here that religion is inherently metaphysical, thinking in terms of infinity and necessity and already moving in that direction in the transition from art and its *Anschauungen* to religion and its *Vorstellungen*. In this sense, religion is the truth of art (*JR*, 266).

Both art and religion are forms of knowing, and both are the "knowledge that Absolute Spirit has of itself as Absolute Spirit." But while art thinks in terms of individuality, religion raises this content to the level of universality. It sees the individual spirit (one of the gods) as but a "moment in the movement of the whole" (perhaps, in the language of Spinoza, a mode or attribute of the divine). "In religion Spirit becomes object to itself as the absolutely universal, or as the essence of all nature, being, and doing, and in the form of the immediate self" (*JR*, 266).

We expect Hegel to say "but in the form of the immediate self" rather than "and." For there seems to be a dialectical tension between the pantheistic sounding universality that is the essence of all things and the monotheistic sounding individual self or personal God. Over against the pluralism of polytheism, both pantheism and monotheism have a universalism that signifies a universe, a one that unites the many. That sets them off from the fragmentary world of (Greek) polytheism. But the difference between a universal essence of all being and an immediate—that is, individual—self distinguishes them from each other and enables us to understand the essence of the difference between the Representations of religion and the Concepts of philosophy. It is the difference between the impersonal and the personal, even if the Impersonal Ultimate includes human persons as "parts," the locations in which it becomes aware of itself in art, religion, and philosophy, the activities of finite, human persons and cultures.

In the immediately following passage we get a second indication of the difference between representation and concept. It contains the same unresolved tension. It is clear that by "the absolute religion" Hegel means Christianity. His new hermeneutical principle allows him to give it a place of honor. It is, he tells us,

> this knowledge that God is the depth of the spirit that is certain of itself[23] and in this way the self of all.[24] It [this knowledge] is the essence, the pure thought;[25] *but when this abstraction is made concrete* [entäussert] *he* [sic] *is an actual* [wirkliches] *self. He is a human person* [Mensch] *with ordinary spatial and temporal existence. And all individuals are this individual. The divine nature is not other than human nature. All other religions are deficient* [unvollkommen]. (JR, 266)

Here again Hegel says "and" where "but" would be more appropriate. "And all individuals are this individual." The tension here is between "mere Christianity" as the claim that the human and divine natures are thoroughly united[26] uniquely in Jesus of Nazareth and the reinterpretation offered here by Hegel according to which Jesus is everyone. Whereas the churches proclaim the Incarnation as a unique event that occurred at a quite particular time and place, philosophy acknowledges it as a universal, atemporal, ontological truth.[27] That is what the difference between representations and concepts means in this context.

Here we have the basis for Hegel's ongoing claim that Christianity is the absolute religion because it has this universal truth as its content; but it is deficient because it has it in the form of representations and thus it (mis)takes a universal, ontological truth for a particular, historical event. This is what I meant above when I said that Hegel's newfound respect for Christianity as the highest form of religion has a rather condescending tone. His compliment is more than a bit left-handed.

A third account of the difference between religious representations and philosophical concepts begins with a reminder that Hegel has not yet fully distinguished Objective Spirit from Absolute Spirit as the self-consciousness of the former.[28] "But the government stands above all as the Spirit that knows itself as the universal essence and universal actuality—the Absolute Self" (*JR*, 267). Here what will become a moment of Objective Spirit is already, like Absolute Spirit in the later writings, Spirit conscious of itself.[29] We are reminded that in the early theological writings the models for God are the Arab clan and the nation united by love. But Hegel qualifies the relativity of religion to a particular social order. "In religion each one raises himself to this intuition of himself as universal self." The particularities of one's place in the social hierarchy fade away so that "he is equal to the prince." But just for this reason, "the two spheres, the realms of actuality and of heaven come to lie over against each other. Only beyond [*jenseits*][30] this world is Spirit reconciled with itself; not in its *present*" (*JR*, 267).

This allows Jaeschke to say that for Hegel "eschatology is regarded as the prima example of the failure of religion."[31] I would put it differently. In the first place, I would speak of the limitation of Religion rather than its failure. For in Hegel's view it is not the task of Religion to be Philosophy. Like art, it has its own distinctive, if cognitively imperfect task to perform. As he will put it later,

> Religion is for everyone. It is not philosophy, which is not for everyone. Religion is the manner or mode by which all human beings become conscious of truth for themselves.... In religion the truth has been revealed as far as its *content* is concerned; but it is another matter for this content to be present in the *form* of the Concept, of thinking, of the Concept of speculative form (*PR*, 106, 425).[32]

Only by failing to recognize this division of labor can we speak of religion simply as failure. Only by accepting the elitism presupposed here can we consider philosophy inherently superior to religion. While such elitism is no stranger to western philosophical traditions, there is no room for it in mere Christianity.

Second, a future-oriented eschatology is only one example of the kind of *Jenseits* that is the fatal flaw of the "manner or mode" of religious thinking. Thus, in the 1805–1806 Philosophy of Spirit the distinction between *Vorstellungen* and *Begriffe* signifies a threefold replacement of transcendence (whatever is *jenseits*) with an immanence: first, the translation of monotheistic discourse into pantheistic modes of thought; second, the replacement of an incarnation that happened at some *past* time with a present ontological structure; and third, the replacement of a reconciliation that will be fully accomplished at some *future* time with a realized eschatology in which the new era, the present age is all the reason in history we should hope for. It doesn't get any better than this.

It becomes clear that the distinction between Representations and Concepts is not primarily some generic epistemological issue, such as the dependence of thought on sense perception and imagination. Introduced here as the fundamental hermeneutical principle of Hegel's philosophy of religion, it is rather a quite specifically theological gesture that functions to define a particular hermeneutical circle. It is best understood from its specific employment. It is with the help of this hermeneutic that Hegel is able to sound more friendly toward Christianity than in his earliest writings. It can be the highest form of religion because religion as such is a cognitively inadequate form of human life that can and should be surpassed (at least by the intellectually elite) in a speculative pantheism.

Almost immediately Hegel goes into print with this new key to his philosophy of religion in his *Phenomenology of Spirit* (1807). In chapter 7 he tells us that Religion is the self-consciousness of Spirit as Absolute Being, indicating that in Religion the subject and object of thought and experience are the same (*PS*, 410–11). This is his ontological guarantee of epistemic and ethical autonomy. In two previous chapters, he tells us in great detail what he means by Spirit.

In chapter four we make the transition from consciousness to self-consciousness and thus to the concept of Spirit. For this is not an inward, Cartesian I think but a socially mediated self-consciousness.

> A self-consciousness exists *for a self-consciousness*.... What still lies ahead for consciousness is the experience of what Spirit is—this absolute substance[33] which is the *unity* of the different self-consciousnesses which, in their *opposition* enjoy perfect freedom and *independence*:[34] "I" that is "We" and "We" that is "I." (*PS*, 110; emphasis added)

Spirit is here defined as human community in its dialectical tension between the unity and independence of individuals. Athletes are fond of saying "There is no 'I' in 'team.'" Hegel is saying there is no team without a bunch of I's, but, of course, they cannot be the I's they are in isolation from the team in whom they live and move and have their being. To make clear that in addition to making a point about social ontology he is making a theological point, Hegel continues,

> It is in self-consciousness, in the Concept of Spirit, that consciousness first finds its turning-point, where it leaves behind it the colorful show [*Schein*] of the sensuous here-and-now [*Diesseits*] and the nightlike void of the supersensible beyond [*Jenseits*] and steps out into the spiritual daylight of the present. (*PS*, 110–11)

This is Hegel's way of saying, "I'm spiritual but not religious"; that is, "I am not satisfied with the empirical richness of the world in its secular interpretations; but I am equally estranged from the heteronomy involved in theistic transcendence and Christian particularism. I opt for a spiritual humanism that is neither."

There follows the famous section on lordship and bondage, the struggle for recognition. We have seen that in the *Philosophy of Right* Hegel sees love as the basis of the family and law as the basis of the state. One way to think of recognition in the *Phenomenology* is that it splits the difference between the two; it is a somewhat thinner concept than love, but a thicker one than law. In other words, both love and legal standing are forms of recognition. In both cases I am recognized as someone who counts, who matters, who is a valued member of the team, or, in Kantian language, who is an end in myself and not merely a means to the ends of others. In Religion it is Spirit as this entirely human I/We that will become conscious of itself as Absolute Being. In a new language, this is our old friend, the pantheism of freedom.

Chapter 6 also tells us what Hegel means by Spirit. It "is the *ethical life* of a nation [*sittliche Leben eines Volks*] in so far as it is the *immediate truth*" (*PS*, 265).[35] The qualifier "*immediate truth*" signifies that no nation or people as such exhausts the meaning of Spirit, just as no 'I' is the complete embodiment of the 'We.' Spirit is the totality of nations or spiritual worlds in the historical unfolding of the teleological essence that is the truth realizing itself in each. Even the spiritual world in which the process finally reaches its immanent telos is not significant simply as one of humankind's spiritual worlds but rather precisely as that culminating world that is the goal of all the others.

So, at the level of what will become Object Spirit and the content of the *Philosophy of Right*, chapter 6 offers a rather selective narrative of European (*sic*—is this universal? or a complacent eurocentrism?) history. It culminates in a culture of forgiveness in which reciprocal recognition is achieved. If we ask what the historical referent is, the answer isn't immediately clear. Since it does not come in the chapter on Religion or in his discussion of Christianity, it does not seem to be the description of a religious community. It comes closer to being an account of a trans-confessional community of religious tolerance. Those who once saw those different from themselves as evil solely by virtue of that difference, now acknowledge their own evil (particularity) and now recognize, in the strong sense, the right of others to their own place in the sun. Hegel here is not Thomas Jefferson arguing for a "separation of church from state." His point is a moral rather than a legal one. The state is surprisingly out of the picture.[36] He seems to be referring to a new, national and possibly international ethos of religious tolerance. It is a real if fragile force in the world today, thanks to a variety of Enlightenment thinkers.

In any case, the "forgiveness" in question is among human persons and groups, not between God and sinners. Here again we encounter the I/We structure of Spirit, and, perhaps, a restatement of the idea of a nation united by love enlarged to the whole of humanity in a form of Enlightenment cosmopolitanism.[37]

> The word of reconciliation is the *objectively* existent Spirit, which beholds the pure knowledge of itself *qua universal* essence in its opposite, in the pure knowledge of itself *qua* absolutely self-contained and exclusive individuality—a reciprocal recognition which is *absolute* Spirit. (PS, 408)

Where the struggle for recognition does not result in various forms of domination, mastery and slavery, but rather results in human rights, reciprocal respect, and tolerance, that human community is Absolute Spirit. It is the objective reality that in Religion will be (inadequately) understood as a transcendent, personal God.

> The reconciling *Yea*, in which the two 'I's let go their antithetical *existence*, is the *existence* of the "I" which has expanded into a duality, and therein remains identical with itself, and, in its complete externalization [*Entäusserung*] and opposite, possesses the certainty of itself: it is God manifested [*der erscheinende Gott*] in the midst of those who know themselves [self-consciousness] in the form of pure knowledge. (PS 409)

Here again, this human community is at once the object and the subject of religious knowledge. Religiously speaking it is the self-knowing God; philosophically speaking it is Absolute Spirit.

In Titus 2:13, believers are described as waiting "for the blessed hope and the manifestation [*epiphaneia*] of the glory of our great God and Savior, Jesus Christ."[38] The reference is clearly to the second coming of Christ. In the epistles to Timothy, the same Greek word is used four times,[39] translated as 'manifestation' or 'appearing' and referring either to the first or to the second coming of Christ. As one Christian liturgy has it

> Christ has died.
> Christ is risen.
> Christ will come again.

These references clearly presuppose a temporal *Jenseits*, past or future, that Hegel is eager to eliminate, not through outright rejection,[40] but through reinterpretation. I cite these passages because in Hegel's Bible, the Luther translation, all these passages render *epiphaneia* as *Erscheinung* (appearance, manifestation). The appearing of Christ, whether in his first or second coming, is his *Erscheinung*. So when Hegel identifies Absolute Spirit, defined in terms of the social ontology of a human community of reciprocal recognition, as *der erscheinende Gott*, his biblically literate readers, in all probability including himself, will hear overtones of the pastoral epistles and will realize that a bold substitution is being offered. Something present is replacing something past and future. The human race, in its enlightened maturity, is replacing the biblical God.

In chapter 7 of the *Phenomenology*, Christianity appears as the highest form of religion by virtue of the doctrine of the Incarnation. Here "God is sensuously and directly beheld as a Self, as an actual individual man [*als ein wirklicher Mensch da ist*]; only so *is* this God self-conscious." So much for God the Father. Human self-consciousness is the only self-consciousness Apart from the Incarnation there is no personal God who could be an agent and a speaker, a God of covenant. Hegel continues,

> This incarnation of the divine Being ... is the simple content of the absolute religion ... in this religion the divine Being is *revealed* [*geoffenbart*]. Its being revealed [*Offenbarsein*] obviously [*offenbar*] consists in this, that what it is, is known.... The divine nature is the same as the human, and it is this unity that is beheld." (*PS*, 459–60)[41]

But by virtue of its form, as religion, this knowledge is "imperfect" (*PS*, 462), "incomplete" and "defective" (*PS*, 463), and "not yet perfected" (*PS*, 477). Its inadequate form is that of Representations that have not yet been raised to the level of Concepts.[42] Hegel regularly attributes immediacy to this knowledge, which is a standard locution for what needs to be *aufgehoben* in some form of reinterpretation. This immediacy and thus the inadequacy of even the highest form of religious knowledge is spelled out in four contrasts between *Vorstellungen* and *Begriffe*.

The first is the difference between individuality and university. For Christianity "the divine nature is the same as the human" uniquely in Jesus of Nazareth. The Incarnation signifies "an exclusive One or unity which has the still unresolved form of a sensuous 'other.' ... Spirit as an individual Self is not yet equally the universal Self, the Self of everyone. In other words, the shape has not yet the form of the Concept, i.e., of the universal self" (*PS*, 461–62). As Spirit, every 'I' is *homoousious*[43] with the Father precisely by belonging to the 'We' that comes in various sizes but is ultimately universal because it is human nature that is divine.

As Hyppolite puts it, "The Christocentric point of view of the Bible tends to disappear to make place for this universal Christ which is the community."[44] For this reason the death and resurrection of Jesus need reinterpretation. Jesus "*passes over into 'having been,'*" and

> just as formerly [in the language of *Vorstellungen*] He rose up for consciousness as a *sensuous existence*, now [in the language of *Begriffe*] He has arisen *in the Spirit*. For a consciousness that sensuously sees and hears Him is itself a merely immediate consciousness ... it knows this objective individual, but not itself as Spirit.[45] In the vanishing of the immediate existence known to be absolute Being the immediacy receives its negative moment; Spirit remains the immediate Self of actuality, but as the *universal self-consciousness* of the community [*Gemeine*]. (*PS*, 462, cf. 463, 473)[46]

Second, there is the contrast of consciousness and self-consciousness. For Christianity the union of the divine and human natures has the remoteness of an event in time and space (*PS*, 462, 474). Like the heavenly, Creator God, this divinity is an intentional object of consciousness for the faithful, not the object of the believer's own self-consciousness. But for Hegel, religious consciousness "must raise its intuition of absolute Substance into the Concept, and equate its consciousness with its self-consciousness" (*PS*, 463, cf. 477); for it is the nature of Spirit to be "simultaneously *consciousness* of itself as its *objective* substance, and simple *self-consciousness* communing with itself" (*PS*, 454). The reason is as simple as it is bold.

> God is attainable in pure speculative knowledge alone and *is* only in that knowledge and is only that knowledge itself, for He [sic] is Spirit; and this speculative knowledge is the knowledge of the *revealed* religion[47]. ... The hopes and expectations of the world up til now had pressed forward solely to this revelation, to behold what absolute Being is, and in it to find itself. (*PS*, 461)

The world is not the product of a divine creation; it is rather the history in which God comes gradually into being as Art, Religion, and Philosophy develop and, more particularly, Philosophy reaches its own fulfillment in Speculative Science, the System for which the *Phenomenology* is the introduction. The hopes and fears of all the years will be met in the philosophically tutored humanity that knows itself to be the Ultimate Reality and the Meaning of History.[48]

Third there is the contrast between the here and now (immanence) and the beyond (transcendence). Christianly understood, the Incarnation is an event remote in time and space (*PS*, 462, 474). Because this restricts it to the form of Representations rather than Concepts, to a consciousness of something other rather than a consciousness of oneself, there is "an unreconciled split into a Here and a Beyond [*Entzweiung in ein Diesseits und Jenseits*]. . . . Before the true content can also receive its true form for consciousness, a higher formative development of consciousness is necessary" (*PS*, 463), namely the conversion of consciousness into self-consciousness just described.

Here Hegel completes his philosophical reformulation of the doctrine of the Trinity as a double overcoming of the *Jenseits* with which Christianity remains burdened. The Incarnation is the end of God the Father, transcendent in a heavenly realm beyond the here and now of earthly actuality; it is the end of the monotheism of the Jews that is also the fate of Christianity. Then the death of Jesus is the permanent end to the union of the divine and human in a unique, only begotten individual whose presence to us can only be past and future. Finally, in the resurrection the Holy Spirit emerges in and as the human community, the I/We Spirit that realizes that it is the site of that union.[49]

Perhaps these three contrasts are summed up in a fourth. Representational thinking "interprets and expresses as a *happening* [*Geschehen*] what has just been expressed as the *necessity* of the Concept" (*PS* 465). The concept of necessity in the *Phenomenology* is more than a little elusive. But what is clear here is that that historically unique events can be significant for speculative thought only as an expression of a universal ontological structure.

Hegel's mature philosophy of religion is presented in other texts, most especially in his lectures on the philosophy of religion, given in Berlin in 1821, 1824, 1827, and 1831 (see *PR* in *sigla*). They add detail but nothing substantially new to what we find in the early theological writings and the *Phenomenology*.

Spinoza, Kant, and Hegel lived in a world where religious pluralism was, quite literally, a matter of life and death. Religious wars, inquisitions, persecution, and intolerance were all too real. The idea of religion within the limits of reason alone had an obvious appeal—if reason could be the theological touchstone that could replace sectarian particularity with cosmopolitan universality. In *Nathan der Weise* Lessing gave classic expression to this widely shared dream.

But two problems gradually but clearly came to light. First, the elitism ingredient in all three theologies was a kind of self-fulfilling prophecy. The deisms and pantheisms of reason caught on among various groups of intellectuals; but they did not supplant on any large scale the confessional, scripture grounded religions whose diversity continued to proliferate.[50] The hoi polloi, whom the philosophers treated condescendingly at best, went on their merry ways. The different traditions continued to present themselves as the fullest expression of the truth. But thanks in large part to Enlightenment critique and in varying degree, they found resources within their own traditions for greater tolerance and increasingly abandoned attempts to spread or enforce the faith by means of violence. Enlightenment universalism did not succeed in eliminating the "scandal of particularity," only in making it more tolerant.

The other problem was more fundamental. It concerned truth and not just market share. By moving from the abstract idea of religion within the limits of reason alone to working out a comprehensive theology within such a horizon, our three authors (along with many others who shared the general project with them) deconstructed their own claim that reason is universal. They showed and continue to show, to anyone who will merely look, that the religion of reason is not one but many different things, as different from each other as Judaism, Christianity, and Islam; Orthodox, Catholic, and Protestant; or Protestant, Catholic, and Jew. The problem of particular paradigms or hermetic hermeneutical circles (fundamental a priori presuppositions) was not eliminated; it was only relocated. I have presented three versions of the autonomy project in theology in some detail, though far from comprehensively, in order to let that deconstruction show itself.

Our three authors do succeed in maintaining autonomy vis-à-vis biblical revelation. While they borrow language from it, they do not allow it to have any normative significance. Hegel puts the point nicely in a passage already cited. "Consequently, what this self-revealing Spirit is *in and for itself*, is not elicited by, as it were unraveling the rich life of Spirit in the community and tracing it back to its original strands, to the ideas, say, of the primitive imperfect community or even to the utterances of the actual man himself" (*PS*, 463). In other words, neither the scriptural witness of prophets and apostles nor even that of

Jesus himself has authority.[51] What they say has to be reinterpreted and rendered "adequate" with speculative philosophy as the highest criterion.

But once philosophical reason shows itself to speak with many, mutually incompatible voices, the prima facie privilege of speculative philosophy over scriptural theology disappears. The promise of a universal religion cannot be kept. The idea of a neutral, presuppositionless criterion in matters theological gives way to the hermeneutical insight that we are always somewhere specific and never enjoy the view from nowhere (or, as Hegel might want to put it, the view from everywhere). The choice between religion within the limits of reason alone and reason within the limits of religion alone is just that, a choice,[52] and the criteria by which the matter is to be decided are themselves part of what is in question. It is hard to see how the decision to trump scriptural authority (in partnership with some ecclesial traditions) with the authority of some speculative project (itself embedded in a stream of philosophical traditions) is more "objective" or "scientific" or "neutral" than the opposite decision. Of course, one can always effectively define "objective" or "scientific" or "neutral" so as to exclude divine revelation, but that would be to beg the question.

Hegel tells us that religious Representations are "imperfect" (*PS*, 462), "incomplete" and "defective" (*PS*, 463) unless corrected by philosophical Concepts. Luther, as if to reply, carries on a sustained polemic against philosophical speculation and writes, "Indeed, reason is the light in this dwelling [the body] and unless the spirit which is lighted with the brighter light of faith, controls this light of reason, it cannot but be in error. For it is too feeble to deal with things divine."[53] For Luther, of course, faith is the trusting response to the promises of God and an obedient response to the commands of God as revealed in Scripture.

Here Luther's heteronomy vis-à-vis Scripture represents what I have been calling "mere Christianity," and Hegel's hegemony of speculative reason represents what I have been calling the autonomy project. One says that pertaining to God and human identity, we need cognitive help and there is a God who is willing and able to help us. The other says either that there is no God of the kind who could help us in this way or that even if there were, we are better off on our own. Freud will say that the heteronomy of "mere Christianity" is a sign of infantile immaturity; but that invites the response that the Enlightenment's autonomy project is a sign of adolescent rebellion and overconfidence. Of course, both may be true in particular cases. The content of one's belief is no sure sign of the maturity of the believer.

So have I said anything yet in praise of heteronomy? I haven't even tried to argue that the heteronomy alternative is true or a preferable choice. What I have tried to show is (1) that the autonomy project is not able to provide the universality it promises; (2) that there are deep differences between theologies of autonomy and those of heteronomy, that they are not saying the same thing (content) in a different language (form); and (3) that given the evident paradigm particularity of "autonomous" theologies, the debate between them and heteronomous theologies will have to be carried out on a level playing field, that is, without any a priori privilege for reason over revelation. In contexts where the lamp of Enlightenment still burns brightly that is to speak in praise of heteronomy, seeking to secure for it an equal place at the table where theology is debated.

Notes

1. "Psalm 51," in *Luther's Works*, vol. 12, ed. Jaroslav Pelikan (St. Louis, MO: Concordia, 1955), p. 317.

2. "We Lutherans—I am a Lutheran and will remain the same—have only this original faith" (HP/H, 1, 73). See also his 1827 letter to Tholuck in *Hegel: The Letters*, trans. Clark Butler and Christine Seiler (Bloomington: Indiana University Press, 1984), p. 520. On the nature of Hegel's Protestantism, see Walter Jaeschke, *Reason in Religion: The Foundations of Hegel's Philosophy of Religion*, trans. J. Michael Steward and Peter C. Hodgson (Berkeley: University of California Press, 1990), pp. 324–37; and, more generally, my own "Hegel and the Reformation," in *Hegel, Freedom, and Modernity* (Albany, NY: State University of New York Press, 1992), pp. 149–63.

3. Note the *zwei* in *Entzweiung* and the *ein* in *Vereiniung*. Hegel seeks to replace a twoness with a oneness, transcendence with immanence, and heteronomy with autonomy.

4. See the suggestion by Jean Hyppolite that Hegel opens the door to Feuerbach. *Genesis and Structure of Hegel's* Phenomenology of Spirit, trans. Samuel Cherniak and John Heckman (Evanston, IL: Northwestern University Press, 1974), pp. 532, 543. Since Marxian atheism draws directly on Feuerbach, Robert Tucker can write, "Marx's atheism, however, meant only a negation of the transmundane God of traditional Western religion. It did not mean a denial of a supreme being... 'man' should be regarded as the supreme being or object of ultimate concern." *Philosophy and Myth in Karl Marx*, 2nd ed. (New York: Cambridge University Press, 1961), p. 22). So far forth, Marx is a good Hegelian.

5. See chapter 7, notes 39 and 55.

6. See the quotation from *SL* at chapter 8, note 21, where Hegel worries about a nation without an up-to-date logic.

7. Henri de Lubac begins *The Drama of Atheistic Humanism*, trans. Edith M. Riley (Cleveland, OH: World Publishing, 1963) with Feuerbach, but he could just as easily have begun with Hegel. For Feuerbach's atheism simply makes explicit the anti-theistic nature of Hegel's theology.

8. Science is "the crown of a world of Spirit" (*PS*, 7). On this theme of a new age, see p. 54, n. 46 in my *History and Truth in Hegel's Phenomenology*, 3rd ed. (Bloomington: Indiana University Press, 1998).

9. Etymologically, of course, 'philosophy' is 'love of wisdom.' Perhaps that is why, along with the prestige of the new natural sciences, Hegel uses Science as a synonym for the completion of Philosophy's history.

10. Let us not forget that a major motive for wanting Reason to be universal is religious, a felt need to supersede the religious particularity that all too often expressed itself in intolerance, persecution, inquisition, and holy wars. For Spinoza, Kant, and Hegel, among many others, this is always near the surface. Of course, a felt need is no guarantee that a proposed remedy is sound.

11. For Spinoza's praise of Jesus as a prophet surpassing even Moses, see *TPT* 1, 19, and 4, 63–65. Spinoza's Jesus apprehends eternal truth adequately and thus universally because he grasps it intuitively without dependence on words and visions or images. (Has Spinoza read the parables?)

12. In the brief discussion in the *Philosophy of Spirit*, it is the *geoffenbarte* religion. This latter term suggests revelation as something given by God, while *offenbar* suggests what is manifest and evident rather than hidden. See PM 298, ¶564. For Hegel, the latter tends to prevail over the former. Thus in the German text of *PS*, 459, we read that in Christianity the divine being (*Wesen*) is "*geoffenbart. Sein Offenarsein besteht offenbar darin* [N.B. this repeat of *offenbar* is translated in *PS* as "obviously"], *dass gewusst wird, was es ist.*" Thus if we say that his face revealed his anger even though he tried to hide it from both himself and his wife, we can say that it was *geoffenbart* only in the sense that it became *offenbar*, evident. There was no act of revealing. To remind us of this Walter Jaeschke speaks of Christianity as "revelatory" religion for Hegel, rather than revealed. *Reason in Religion*, pp. 204–5. This is a bit awkward, but it signifies the important distinction between 'revealed' in the sense of having become clear and 'revealed' in the sense of having been told to someone by someone. But Kevin Hart argues that from the perspective of mere Christianity, "we have no a priori right to assimilate 'revelation' and 'manifestation.'" *Kingdoms of God* (Bloomington: Indiana University Press, 2014), p. 135.

13. Translated as the second part of Hegel's *First Philosophy of Spirit*, in *System of Ethical Life and First Philosophy of Spirit*, trans. H. S. Harris and T. M. Knox (Albany: State University of New York Press, 1979).

14. See chapter 8, note 17. As we have seen, Hegel will replace this "and" with an "is."

15. Translated by Leo Rausch as *Hegel and the Human Spirit* (Detroit, MI: Wayne State University Press, 1983). I give my own translations from *JR*. While Hegel did not publish these texts (nn. 13–15) himself, they were public in a way the early theological writings were not, for they were manuscripts for lectures he gave in the university.

16. The three editions are from 1817, 1827, and 1830.

17. Thus the promise of the Preface, "To help bring philosophy closer to the form of Science, to the goal where it can lay aside the title '*love* of knowing' and be *actual* knowing—that is what I have set myself to do.... To show that now is the time for philosophy to be raised to the status of a Science would therefore be the only true justification of any effort that has this aim, for to do so would demonstrate the necessity of the aim, would indeed at the same time be the accomplishing of it" (*PS*, 3–4).

18. On this latter point, see the discussion of Jaeschke, *Reason in Religion*, pp. 175–79. Similarly, in the *Phenomenology* art is treated as a moment within religion.

19. This triple distinction becomes permanent. In the final Philosophy of Spirit, the section on Subjective Spirit has a subsection entitled "Theoretical Spirit." It is subdivided into Intuition, Representation, and Thinking (*Denken*). The third moment itself has three moments, the highest of which attains to the Concept. "Only on the third stage of pure thinking [*Denken*] is the Concept as such known. Therefore, this stage represents comprehension in the strict sense of the world [*eigentliche Begreifen*] ... on this stage thinking has no other content than itself ... in the object it seeks and finds only itself. Here, therefore, the object is distinguished from thought only by having the form of being, of subsisting on its own account. Thus thinking stands here in a completely free relation to

the object" (*PM*, 227, ¶468Z). This is what Hegel means by the identity of Thought and Being. The freedom of thought in this identity is perhaps his strongest statement of theoretical autonomy.

20. Jaeschke, *Reason in Religion*, p. 180.

21. Representations are *"metaphors* for thoughts and Concepts" (*EL*, 26–27, ¶3Z), and it is the task and triumph of philosophy to convert their poetry into cognitively superior prose.

22. I find no significant changes in Hegel's later writings on the philosophy of religion.

23. One way to think of self-certain spirit is in terms of epistemic autonomy, the spirit whose knowledge is recollection since it already has the truth within itself. The Platonic soul and the Cartesian subject are two examples. The claim then is that the knowledge produced by them, when properly purified of dependence on sense and tradition, is the divine knowledge that is the measure of all things.

24. This picks up on the idea just above of Spirit as "the essence of all nature, being, and doing," and reminds us of the discussion above (chap. 7) of Fichte's notion of God as the Absolute (but impersonal) Self.

25. In chapter 8 we saw the Logic defined as "the exposition of God as he is in his eternal essence before the creation of nature and a finite mind" (*SL*, 50)

26. The Council of Chalcedon (451) affirmed that when "for us and for our salvation" the Son of God "became man" (Nicene Creed, 325), the human and divine natures were united "without confusion, without change, without division, and without separation." See the discussion of *homoousious* in chapter 7.

27. Though its discovery, like that of Euclidian geometry, occurs at a particular time and place.

28. "Even [this third draft of the System] does not finally release philosophy of religion from the sphere of ethical life." Jaeschke, *Reason in Religion*, p. 178.

29. Thus Peter Ackroyd can describe the governing structures created or extended by King Athelstan (tenth century) and comment, "So from this foundation there would spring a civil service, a judiciary, and a parliament. The nation was becoming conscious of its own identity." Or again, with reference to the oft-execrated King John, "Yet out of his rule emerged a new or at least an intensified sense of the nation. That is the meaning of the Magna Carta." *The Foundations: The History of England from its Earliest Beginnings to the Tudors* (New York: St. Martin's, 2011), pp. 70 and 175. Americans are surely conscious of their identity in terms of the Bill of Rights, even if members of the American Civil Liberties Union focus on the first amendment freedoms of speech, press, assembly, and religion while members of the National Rifle Association focus on the second amendment right to bear arms. The result, of course, is two quite different national identities in spite of significant overlap.

30. The link between the *Jenseits*, that which is beyond, and the religious stage of self-awareness is a constant theme for Hegel from this point on.

31. Jaeschke, *Reason in Religion*, p. 185.

32. Cf. *EL*, 11, Second Edition Preface.

33. Hegel retains Spinoza's language while moving decisively beyond his nature pantheism.

34. This unity in independence that is freedom sounds a lot like Rousseau.

35. This comes after a more abstract social ontology of the I/We that is Spirit. "Spirit is the *actuality* of [ethical] substance. It is the *self* of actual consciousness to which it stands opposed, or rather which it opposes to itself as an objective, actual *world*, but a world which has completely lost the meaning for the self of something alien to it, just as the self has completely lost the meaning of a being-for-self separated from the world. . . . Spirit, being the *substance* and the universal, self-identical, and abiding essence, is the unmoved, solid *ground* and *starting point* for the action of all, and it is their purpose and goal, the in-itself of every self-consciousness expressed in thought. . . . Spirit is thus self-supporting, absolute, real being. All previous shapes of consciousness are abstract forms of it . . . they are only moments. . . ." (*PS*, 264). Forms of consciousness are functions of forms of world, and these worlds are the ethical life (*Sittlichkeit*) of various nations or peoples (*Völker*).

36. See my "Verzeihung und Anarchie," *Hegel Jahrbuch*, 1972, pp. 105–9. For Hegel on church and state, see *JR*, 269–73 and *PRi*, 165–74, ¶270Z.

37. Cf. Kant's essay, "Idea for a Universal History from a Cosmopolitan Point of View," in Kant, *On History*, ed. Lewis White Beck (Indianapolis, IN: Bobbs-Merrill, 1963), pp. 11–26. Hegel's nationalism is *aufgehoben* in world history in the final paragraphs (341–60) of the *Philosophy of Right* and in his lectures on the philosophy of history. See *Lectures on the Philosophy of World History: Introduction*, trans. H. B. Nisbet (New York: Cambridge University Press, 1975).

38. KJV reads "glorious appearing." There is a significant convergence of meaning between *epiphaneia* and *parousia* (coming, presence, arrival), a term often used to refer to the second coming of Christ. See N. T. Wright, *Paul and the Faithfulness of God* (Minneapolis, MN: Fortress, 2013), pp. 1081–85.

39. 1 Timothy 6:14; and 2 Timothy 1:10, 4:1, and 4:8.

40. As in Lessing's "against which my reason rebels." See the reference in chapter 2 at note 15.

41. See note 12 above.

42. Kevin Hart suggests that such a "raising" is a regression. That the message of the Kingdom of God "comes to us by way of the humility of metaphor and narrative, rather than from the grandeur of metaphysics, is a facet of the divine condescension." To insist on translating the personal concreteness of metaphor and narrative into the impersonal abstractions of metaphysics is to say, in effect, that God got it wrong and we can do better. *Kingdoms of God*, p. 157, cf. p. 154, "It is the study of metaphor and narrative that grounds Christian theology, not metaphysics or philosophy."

43. See the discussion of this term in chapter 7.

44. Hyppolite, *Genesis and Structure*, p. 568. He also says, "But if Hegel does seem to lean toward this humanism, he rejects the complete reduction of God to man. He always maintains that to some extent man necessarily had to surpass himself.... Hegel speaks of the *universal divine man* who succeeded that *God-man*" (pp. 543–44). Granted. But I cannot find that this universality signifies anything but the denial that any empirical 'We' is simply identical with God, even the empirical totality of human history (and prehistory). What is divine is that totality metaphysically interpreted as the unfolding of the cosmic acorn that is *in itself* divine into the cosmic oak tree that, in Art, Religion, and Philosophy, that is as Absolute Spirit is *for itself* divine.

45. Here we see the importance of Hegel's claim that Religion is the *self-consciousness* of Spirit as Spirit. See the next contrast.

46. Given the logical primacy of universality over particularity, it is not surprising that Hegel's Christology focuses on the death of Jesus in which his historical particularity is replaced by the community of (the) Spirit. In this context the resurrection of Jesus is downplayed to the point of disappearance. See Kevin Hart's chapter on Hegel in *Kingdoms of God*, pp. 57–74. Cf. Hegel, *Three Essays* (see *LJ* in sigla), p. 86, where the "only effect" of the doctrine of the bodily resurrection of Jesus "was to prevent the concept of the human soul as a spiritual and incorporeal essence from becoming more universal."

47. Given this understanding of revelation, it follows that "what this self-revealing Spirit is *in and for itself*, is not elicited by, as it were, unraveling the rich life of Spirit in the community and tracing it back to its original strands, to the ideas, say, of the primitive imperfect community, or even to the utterances of the actual man himself" (*PS*, 463). This is strong epistemic autonomy.

48. Just as the missionary task of Christianity was (1) to give to Jews a new and different understanding of Israel's covenant relation with God and (2) to invite Gentiles to be part of the new covenant community, so the missionary task implicit in Hegel's theology is (1) to give to Christians a new and different understanding of the Incarnation and (2) to invite the rest of the world to join in this pantheistic humanism.

49. For an early draft, see *JR*, 269. For a detailed analysis of Hegel's discussions of the Trinity, see Dale M. Schlitt, O. M. I., *Hegel's Trinitarian Claim: A Critical Reflection* (Leiden: Brill, 1984) and my

review in *Journal of the American Academy of Religion* (Summer 1990), pp. 312–14. Schlitt brackets the question of the relation of Hegel's thought to Christian tradition in order to focus on its success or failure by his own criteria.

50. The great Yale church historian, Kenneth Scott Latourette, once told me that his research had discovered twenty-seven different Baptist denominations in the United States.

51. The teachings of Jesus are to be reinterpreted or rejected. "Once the community is established, once the Kingdom of God has attained its determinate being and its actuality, these teachings are either interpreted in other ways or else they fall by the wayside" (PR, 459).

52. See Nick Wolterstorff, *Reason within the Bounds of Religion* (Grand Rapids, MI: Eerdmans, 1976). I do not mean to suggest that it is an arbitrary choice, like flipping a coin. Such "decisions" emerge gradually over time as the self is formed by external forces and forms itself by the choices it makes in response to the circumstances in which it finds itself.

53. *Luther's Works*, vol. 21, ed. Jaroslav Pelikan (St. Louis, MO: Concordia, 1956), p. 303.

10

THE INEVITABILITY OF HETERONOMY

In its original, modern mode, religion within the limits of reason alone regularly presents itself as the voice of a single, universally operative reason. The actual, substantial differences among various versions of this project undermine this claim and show human reason to speak with a variety of quite particular voices, each one relative to the paradigm that it presupposes. In the absence of any evidently universal reason, even the criteria for choosing among alternatives appear to be more nearly internal to the different theologies than "neutral" or "objective." Epistemically speaking, we are operating within one of many possible hermeneutical circles. No "view from nowhere" is available. Reason is as sectarian as revelation.

By calling attention to this fact I have spoken an indirect word in praise of heteronomy, and in this chapter I want to make it more explicit. For the autonomy project is closely linked to the universality claim. Where thought is relative to particular worldviews or paradigms that provide axioms or foundational first principles it is heteronomous in relation to them. They may have become interior to a given thinker so that they can be "recollected" in a quasi-Platonic sense; but the key word here is 'become.' If they are "inside" the thinker, giving the appearance of autonomy, it is because they somehow got there from "outside." As a result, "We come to believe we have created what we have only heard."[1]

A genuinely universal reason might be thought of as simply a dimension of human nature, always already "inside"; but sectarian versions of reason would seem to have contingent, historical origins as particular as their content. Thought that is relative to them is dependent on them. Descartes is right to speak of thought in the firstperson singular: cogito, I think. But something other than myself is the condition of the possibility of my thought. Autonomy presupposes a prior heteronomy.

When we speak of tradition, or formation/education (*Bildung*), or socialization, or culture, or language games we are speaking of processes by which something other to me and prior to me gets internalized and becomes part of my identity. But, to repeat, the autonomy that results is only secondary; the heteronomy is more basic.

In *The Ego and the Id*, Freud writes (following Groddeck), "We are 'lived' by unknown and uncontrollable forces."[2] The analogous hermeneutical insight might well be expressed in Heidegger's (in)famous apothegm, *"die Sprache spricht,"*[3] that is, we are spoken by language. This does not need to mean that language is the "voice of being"[4] or the "house of being"[5] in some quasireligious, mystical sense in which Being takes the place of God as the one who speaks to us. It merely needs to mean that only as heirs to language games we did not invent do we have cognitive access to the real.

In other words, we are "thought" by assumptions and points of view (perspectives) we have received from others and of which we are neither fully aware nor firmly in control. They have chosen us before we have chosen them, or modified them, or repudiated them.[6] They are the family in to which we have been born and in which we have been raised. We can be born again into other "families," but there, too, we inherit much before we can create anything. We never create ourselves *ex nihilo*.[7]

This is what I call the hermeneutical situation. It has three elements: (a) the *particularity* of the a priori, (b) the *penultimacy* of judgments governed by the a priori, and (c) the *exteriority* of the a priori.

A) Particularity. When we "think for ourselves," we are guided by "recollections," anticipations that we bring with us to the matter at hand. In crime fiction there are often more than one detectives working on a case. Different ones will "like" different suspects for the crime, that is, they will differ among themselves on who is the most likely suspect.

Each of the investigators is working within a hermeneutical circle in which they are guided by beliefs, habits, hunches, attitudes, etc., that are a priori. They bring them with them to the investigation rather than having them arise out of the investigation. To be sure, a particular piece of evidence arises in the course of the investigation. But what its significance may be, if any, and what weight should be given to it is a matter of interpretation; and interpretation is guided by presuppositions that will vary from one investigator to another.

The hermeneutical turn can be seen as the claim that what is universally true about human reason is that it is not universal but particular, not one but many, not neutral but prejudiced (relying on prejudgments), not the view from nowhere but always the view from somewhere. In other words, the sectarian or denominational character of religion within the limits of reason alone is not an accident, the product of careless oversight, or a failure to maintain an impartial posture. It was inevitable given the nature of human thought. We not only live east of Eden but also after Babel.[8]

In order to be coherent, the hermeneutical turn will have to have to practice the selfdenying ordinance of selfreference. It will have to acknowledge that it is itself an interpretation like the theories it discusses, operating within a particular hermeneutical circle, shaped by linguistic and cultural factors that are the conditions of its possibility. It illustrates the heteronomy its preaches.

B) Penultimacy. Each detective claims, with greater or lesser conviction, that their theory of the crime makes more sense of the available evidence than the alternatives; but usually, right up to the time of the denouement in which Miss Marple or Poirot shows us that it couldn't have been the butler but only the younger nephew, there remain loose ends that none of the theories can account for. *In medias res* we have conflicting theories but no final "fact of the matter."

Thus, in a case of murder, past experience often leads investigators to suspect a family member or at least a known associate before they suspect a perfect stranger. But, of course, there is no guarantee that such prejudices (prejudgments) are correct in any given case. While it is perfectly clear that the victim is dead and that he has been shot or she has been strangled, no such certainty attaches to any of the penultimate theories of the crime. Each sees the evidence from a particular perspective, but it remains to be seen whether that location reveals what they most need to see or serves to hide it from them. To "like" the butler too quickly and too strongly may blind us to indications that it was the younger nephew. For that is just what perspectives do: they enable us to see some things while keeping us from seeing others. As the lenses through which we see, they are like telescopes and microscopes. In detective fiction, the ultimate theory as given by, say, Sam Spade, is always the right one. We surpass what Ricoeur calls "the conflict of interpretations" and attain the one (now) plain truth of the matter.[9]

But real life is lived in the penultimate. The ultimate theory as given, say, by a jury verdict, is not automatically itself beyond reasonable doubt. See the Innocence Project (http://www.innocenceproject.org/). According to the website, "To date, more than 300 people in the United States have been exonerated by DNA testing, including 18 who served time on death row. These people served an average of 14 years in prison before exoneration and release."

The theological analog of the jury verdict would be a state church, or a de facto official religion, or a prevailing orthodoxy within the academy—a particular interpretation given *universal* status.[10] It is the truth for everyone, but only in the eyes of a *particular* community, for whom it is the shared paradigm. Its official status does not erase its particularity nor guarantee its superiority to alternatives. It is this insight that leads to the separation of church and state, or at least to religious liberty and freedom of speech, including freedom of the press in liberal democracies. No particular group, including the state, has a monopoly on truth. It is because of this particularity that our beliefs and practices can only be justified penultimately. The same point can be made in terms of necessity, along with universality the traditional mark of the a priori. Thus C. I. Lewis writes, "What is *a priori* is necessary truth not because it compels the mind's acceptance, but precisely because it does not. . . . The *a priori* represents an attitude in some sense freely taken, a stipulation of the mind itself, and a stipulation which might be made in some other way if it suited our bent or need. . . . What it anticipates is not the given, but our attitude toward it."[11]

To speak here of the hermeneutical situation is simply to recognize that it is the very nature of human understanding to take the form of interpretation, that is, to have this perspectival and penultimate character.[12] Of course, that neither keeps our interpretations from claiming to be the truth of the matter or from actually being that truth, at least in the sense of being superior to the presently available alternatives. It may well be the younger nephew who did it; it may be that God is a personal being, capable of action and speech; and it may be that women and racial minorities have a right to equal standing before the law and in the marketplace.

What I have been calling the hermeneutical turn is the acceptance of this interpretation of human understanding as interpretation and the consequent double loss of the universality and ultimacy promised by modernity. Spinoza, Kant, and Hegel do not make this turn. We have noted the difference between Hegel and his two predecessors on this point insofar as he takes the historical character of human understanding seriously. But we have seen that he, no more than they, presents his theology as a penultimate, perspectivally particular interpretation of the Divine and of human nature. He presents himself as Sherlock Holmes, giving us, not a particular hypothesis in need of further examination and support, but the only possible narrative.[13] The case has been solved. It would fly in the face of reason to entertain any other. No doubt the charm of detective fiction and the original attraction of Hegel relies on this closure, for which we feel a deep need.

Another way to speak of this penultimacy is to say that religion within the limits of reason alone is an act of faith in spite of itself, or rather many such acts. It is the adoption of a particular and therefore penultimate version of reason as the highest norm for our beliefs and practices, but without an "objective" or "neutral" proof of its superiority.[14] By faith here I do not mean adherence to the scriptures and official teachings of some "organized" religion. I mean an epistemic status of what Kierkegaard calls "objective uncertainty," the absence of neutral guarantees for our beliefs. To speak this way is not to deny that there is such a thing as truth; it is only to acknowledge the limits of our apprehension of it.

Thus what Ricoeur says about biblical faith is equally true about the wagers modern philosophers make in betting on various versions of "reason." He describes biblical faith as "a *culturally contingent symbolic network*" that ought to "assume its own *insecurity*." It is "a *chance happening* transformed into a destiny by means of a *choice constantly renewed*, in the scrupulous respect of *different choices*." It needs to protect itself from "the temptation ... of taking over the henceforth vacant role of *ultimate foundation*," for it is "a faith that knows itself to be *without guarantee*." It needs to "protect itself from the hubris that would set it up as the heir to the philosophies of the cogito and as continuing their selffoundational claim."[15] What we see when we make the hermeneutical turn is that these descriptions and these warnings are as appropriate for the "rational" theologies of modernity as for biblical faith, as the italicized phrases suggest. To give some version of reason hegemony over revelation is itself an act of faith. It is "without guarantee" and rests on no "ultimate foundation."

One helpful way of differentiating modern philosophy from its postmodern alternatives is to make the hermeneutical turn one of the essential, defining marks of the postmodern, acknowledging particularity and penultimacy and abjuring claims to universality and ultimacy. I hope it is clear that I am using the terms 'modern' and 'postmodern' as ideal types and not strictly as chronological markers. "Modernity" may be said to begin with Plato and there are postmodern thinkers (in this sense) during the high tide of modernity.[16]

As the term *philosophical hermeneutics* suggests, this move is often and rightly associated with Martin Heidegger, Wilhelm Dilthey, HansGeorg Gadamer, Paul Ricoeur, and Alasdair MacIntyre. But it is by no means limited to them. With various nuances is it found in the pragmatism of John Dewey and C. I. Lewis; in the deconstruction of Jacques Derrida; in the genealogy of Michel Foucault; in the irony of Richard Rorty; in the personal knowledge of Michael Polanyi; in the anti-foundationalist, anti-evidentialist Reformed epistemology of Alvin Plantinga and Nicholas Wolterstorff; in the analytic philosophy of Hilary Putnam, Willard Van Orman Quine, Wilfrid Sellars, and Ludwig Wittgenstein, and in the philosophy of science of Thomas Kuhn, N. R. Hanson, and Paul Feyerabend.[17]

There are strange bedfellows here. Thus Hanson writes, "There is a sense, then, in which seeing is a 'theory-laden' undertaking. Observation of x is shaped by prior knowledge of x."[18] And Heidegger writes, "By showing how all sight is grounded primarily in understanding . . . we have deprived pure intuition of its priority. . . . 'Intuition' and 'thinking' are both derivatives of understanding, and rather remote ones. . . . Interpretation is never a presuppositionless grasping of something previously given. Any interpretation which is to contribute understanding, must already have understood what is to be interpreted."[19]

These critiques of what Hegel calls immediacy and Derrida calls presence are echoed in the critiques of classical foundationalism found in Plantinga and Wolterstorff on the one hand and Rorty on the other. The former seek to undermine the attempt to ground knowledge on propositions that are "self-evident or incorrigible or evident to the senses,"[20] while Rorty opposes the notion that knowledge can be grounded on "frameworks beyond which one must not stray, objects which impose themselves, representations which cannot be gainsaid."[21]

Nor is this only a matter of philosophers' shop talk. People who have never heard of Thomas Kuhn speak of paradigms and paradigm shifts. One finds such references in the sports news and in mystery novels from those who don't realize that they are drawing on a major cultural revolution. For his paradigms in natural science are the hermeneutical circles and particular perspectives to which postmodern philosophers call attention.[22] Spinoza, Kant, and Hegel illustrate this particularity and penultimacy while disclaiming it.

This cultural paradigm shift comes to light in a review of Mark Greif's book, *The Age of the Crisis of Man: Thought and Fiction in America*. With reference to the books Greif discusses, the reviewer writes,

But most of these books, dominated by what Greif calls a "discourse"—a shared rhetoric of concerns and clichés—regarding the universal nature of humanity or the fundamental dignity of man, have not, he maintains, aged well. "One of the striking features of the discourse of man to modern eyes, in a sense the most striking," he writes, "is how unreadable..., how tedious, how unhelpful" such books can seem today. *For a variety of reasons, we are more likely to identify (and, as we like to say, to celebrate) the differences among human beings than to corral them into some hortatory category like "universal man."*[23]

The "we" of this last sentence is itself surely not universal. Modernity may well be wounded but it is not dead.[24] But this "we" surely includes the French postmodern thinkers who adopted "anti-humanism" and "death of man" slogans. Thus, for example, Foucault

> concluded quite early that the strongest wall of the contemporary mind's prison was humanism and the figure of man that was at its core. Foucault's thought is probably best known for its proclamation of man's death, its understanding that our understanding of man is but temporary and contingent.... Humanism represented the incarceration of human beings within a specifically modern system of thought and practice that had become so intimately a part of them that it was no longer experienced as a series of confinements but was embraced as the very substance of being human.... The philosophical confinement consists in an egocentric illusion in which man himself is regarded as an ahistorical nature and as the privileged object of reflection, and in which his ego is taken as the autonomous source of all thought and meaning.[25]

C) Exteriority. Foucault introduces us to an important third dimension of the hermeneutical turn when he writes,

> the Enlightenment [itself] is an event, or a set of events and complex historical processes, that is located at a certain point in the development of European societies. As such, it includes elements of social transformation, types of political institution, forms of knowledge, projects of rationalization of knowledge, and practices, technological mutations that are very difficult to sum up in a word.[26]

As a result its humanism is only one of the various humanisms and antihumanisms that are part of the story of Europe, conditioned by contingent historical factors.

What is new here is not just that there are particular paradigms at work; there are historical processes and events at work in their formation and propagation that are external to any given thinker. It is at this point more than any other that the disintegration of universality is the demise of autonomy. In the remainder of this chapter I want to explore these externalities, these heteronomies, if you will, under three heads: language, tradition, and social practices.

1) *Language.* Foucault introduces us to the first of these when he writes that "in Western culture the being of man and the being of language have never, at any time, been able to coexist and to articulate themselves one upon the other. Their incompatibility has been one of the fundamental features of our thought."[27] By "man" Foucault means the purported universal man of Enlightenment humanism; and by language he means something like the concrete language games of Wittgenstein rather than the abstract capacity for language (that is universal). So we could read him to say something like this: the irreducible plurality of language games, properly understood and taken seriously, undermines every attempt to think of "man" and of human understanding as universal and autonomous, that is, independent of historical particularity and conditioning. If, as they say, all politics is local, so is every philosophy and every theology. As Hegel put it, "Whatever happens, every individual is a child of his time; so philosophy too is its own time apprehended in thoughts."[28]

But it is not just that language games are local; they are also the inherited wealth on which human thought is always dependent. No matter how hard it works nor how creative it is, it is never the product of "self-made man." Precisely in its particularity human understanding is heteronomous.[29]

This is already true to a degree of natural languages in their distinctive grammar, syntax, and vocabulary. Polanyi writes that "speech can be acquired only a-critically, and the practice of speech in one particular language carries with it the acceptance of the particular theory of the universe postulated by that language."[30] To say that language is learned "only a-critically" is to say that we accept the worldview presupposed by a given language without first providing the kind of neutral justification required by foundationalist, evidentialist Enlightenment strategies of universal doubt. Such learning is an act of trust, or, if you will, of faith. The "I" that thinks has first been thought by language.

> Implicit here is Polanyi's critique of the Enlightenment as a critique of Cartesian doubt. It has been taken for granted [N.B.] throughout the critical period of philosophy that the acceptance of unproven beliefs was the broad road to darkness.... Descartes had declared that universal doubt should purge his mind of all opinions held merely on trust and open it to knowledge firmly grounded in reason.... [But] the doubting of any explicit statement merely implies an attempt to deny the belief expressed by the statement, in favor of other beliefs which are not doubted for the time being.... So long as the

reconsideration of any single belief is undertaken against an overwhelming background of unquestioned beliefs, the beliefs forming this background cannot simultaneously be alleged to be doubtful.[31]

Polanyi is already thinking more concretely about language than, say, the differences among English, French, and Swahili. Similarly, I have been speaking of what Wittgenstein calls language games,[32] the rich variety of activities mediated by the rich variety of kinds of speech acts that make them possible. Among the many examples he gives are "[a]sking, thanking, cursing, greeting, praying."[33] The meaning of such practices, their goals, and the rules governing them (mores, meaning both morals and manners) vary among diverse cultures and subcultures.[34] Moreover, and this the present point, they are the inherited wealth or burden passed on to or imposed upon those who develop competence in these "games" and more concretely so than in the case of language as merely a specific grammar, syntax, and vocabulary.

Derrida gives us a comprehensive view of the hermeneutical turn, which he makes simultaneously with the linguistic turn.[35] It begins with the(in)famous claim: *"There is nothing outside the text"* (Il n' y a pas hors-texte).[36] This is not to affirm some kind of linguistic idealism. Derrida writes, "It is totally false to suggest that deconstruction is a suspension of reference. Deconstruction is always deeply concerned with the *other* of language. I never cease to be surprised by critics who see my work as a declaration that there is nothing beyond language, that we are imprisoned in language; it is, in fact, saying the exact opposite."[37]

We might speak here of a qualified realism, qualified in both a Kantian and an Hegelian sense. The Kantian sense simply affirms the hermeneutical circle. Just as every text requires interpretation and every interpretation involves presuppositions, so it is with (apparently) nontextual realities. This is expressed in the claim, "Being must always already be conceptualized . . . 'must always already' precisely signifies the original exile from the kingdom of Being . . . and signifies that Being never is, never shows *itself*, is never *present*."[38] Derrida's sustained polemic against presence, or better, his argument that every presence is mediated by what is absent and thus is never pure presence, is a critique of all Cartesian inspired foundationalisms that seek to ground knowledge on meanings or facts intuitively self-evident, or, in his language, simply present.[39]

In extending the structure of textuality to being, Derrida also gives an Hegelian twist to this Kantian insight. But with a difference. Like so many post-Hegelian thinkers, Derrida is an Hegelian holist without the whole, a dialectical thinker without speculative closure. For him writing is the realm of the penultimate, of the undecidable that is not yet fully determined because its context (semantic or ontic) is incompletely specified, and eschatology is the historically ultimate denouement in which all is decided: the Sherlock Holmes solution with which the case is *closed*. "The horizon of absolute knowledge is the effacement of writing.... Yet all that Hegel thought within the horizon, all, that is except eschatology, may be reread as a meditation on writing. Hegel is *also* the thinker of irreducible difference."[40] We are neither the Alpha Point required by Cartesian foundationalisms nor the Omega Point required by Hegelian eschatology. In other words, we are not God but thoroughly finite knowers, always *in medias res*.

Derrida takes this Hegelian meaning to be more radical than the Kantian point. He doesn't challenge the commonsense notion that texts point to realities outside themselves, for example, Rousseau, Mamma, and Thérèse in relation to Rousseau's *Confessions*. But he insists that "beyond and behind what one believes can be circumscribed as Rousseau's text, there has never been anything but writing." What this means is most succinctly expressed when Derrida says, "*The thing itself is a sign.*"[41] Just as linguistic signs point to "things," those "things" in turn point beyond themselves to other "things." Their being is only determinate and their meaning decidable when the entire context in which they occur is given. This is the eschatology required by absolute knowing. Earlier I have argued that for Hegel knowledge can be absolute only if the world it presupposes is itself ultimate. Here Derrida adds, in effect, "and completely specified."

Both in their meaning and in their factuality "things" refer to something else. In their meaning they refer to the interpretations that precede our encounter with them (a priori anticipations of experience) and that arise subsequently when we set out explicitly to understand them. That is the Kantian point, the semantics of the hermeneutical circle. But there is an ontological correlate. In their factuality they are no atomic, stand-alone, self-contained entities. They refer beyond themselves because they are what they are only by virtue of their relations to what they are not, and, accordingly, can only be understood in their relational context. In other words, the text is a metaphor for the world; the old idea of the book of nature is truer than originally guessed, but in a different way. As writing, it is not a code to be deciphered but a totality to be traversed, always incompletely (penultimately).

Derrida's two glosses on "there is nothing outside of the text, namely "being must always already be conceptualized" and "the thing itself is a sign" are nicely summarized when he writes, "Nothing *exists* outside of context."[42] Together these signify the structure of writing as the denial of immediacy, of presence without absence, of identity without difference, of sameness without otherness. By calling Hegel a philosopher of writing and difference he takes him to be in agreement that we are not the Alpha Point of a foundational immediacy.

But Hegel spoils this with his eschatology, the claim that he can capture the relational context of things in its totality. For that is what is required by Absolute Knowing, the full understanding of "things" (textual or otherwise) that refer beyond themselves to the contexts that are the conditions of their meaning and their being.[43] As a holist without the Whole, Derrida parts with Hegel, insisting that human understanding occurs neither at the Alpha Point (immediacy) nor at the Omega Point (totality). In other words, to repeat, we are not God. Since modernity effectively deifies human reason, we might hear in this critique an echo the ancient Jewish critique of idolatry, treating anything but the Maker of heaven and earth as divine.

Since as a qualified Kantian in his hermeneutical turn, Derrida never presupposes the universality and necessity of the preunderstandings that are always already at work in interpretation, he expresses the *particularity* of the hermeneutical situation. And since as a qualified Hegelian he never presumes to have encompassed the totality of contexts presupposed by every text and every "thing" as a sign, he expresses the *penultimacy* of the hermeneutical situation.[44] But what about the *exteriority*, presumably our current theme?

If, as I believe Derrida's texts suggest, we take his discourse about language to be about language games and not just the grammar, syntax, and vocabulary of natural languages, we can say that exteriority/heteronomy/dependence on something other is both presupposed and implied even when the focus is on particularity or penultimacy. But he makes it quite explicit when he writes, "Language has started without us, in us and before us . . . even before I have been able to say I.[45] . . . There would be no responsibility without this *prior coming (prévenance)* of the trace, or if autonomy were first or absolute. Autonomy itself would not be possible, nor would respect for the law . . . in the strictly Kantian sense of these words."[46]

Unsurprisingly, there are religious as well as moral overtones here. Of religion itself, Derrida writes "that it is always a response and responsibility that is prescribed, not chosen freely in an act of pure and abstractly autonomous will. There is no doubt that it implies freedom, will and responsibility, but let us try to think this: will and freedom *without autonomy*. Whether it is a question of sacredness, sacrificiality or of faith, the other makes the law, the law is other."⁴⁷ Then, in the context of discussing biblical and Kierkegaardian materials, he writes,

> There is no face-to-face exchange of looks between God and myself, between the other and myself. God looks at me and I don't see him and it is on the basis of this gaze that singles me out that my responsibility comes into being.... But not in the sense of a autonomy by means of which I see myself acting in total liberty or according to a law that I make for myself, rather in the heteronomy... where I cannot preempt by my own initiative whatever is commanding me to make decisions, decisions that will nevertheless be mine and which I alone will have to answer for."⁴⁸

There is an autonomy here. My actions (including my beliefs, since my language shapes me theoretically as well as practically) are my own, and I am responsible for them. But this autonomy is subsequent and derivative. Derrida writes, "Language has started without us, in us and before us. This is what theology calls God." But he does not call it God. He calls it language. Although he turns to religion to illustrate its structure—autonomy that presupposes a prior heteronomy—he does not number himself among the Jewish or Christian theists for whom God is rightly and irreplaceably the Other in relation to whom we are heteronomous. Rather, in language he finds a secular analog of the relation between creature and Creator, moral agent and Moral Lawgiver. It is an otherness that relativizes and conditions the autonomy that it not only permits but makes possible.

Derrida's atheism is not integral to his argument. He presupposes it rather than argues for it. He works within that hermeneutical circle. He spends his philosophical energy trying to show that we are not God, relative and not absolute, a point on which theists and atheists might well agree. The analyses that purport to show this are silent on the question whether someone else might be God. Since I can find no conceptual or logical link between Derrida's analysis of the finitude of the human knower and his atheism, I see no reason why theists should not appropriate (recontextualize) these central aspects of deconstruction as helpful ways of expressing the created finitude of human understanding. Those who believe themselves to be in receipt of a divine revelation are in constant need of such a reminder,⁴⁹ just as those who do not believe need to be reminded that belief does not take us from autonomy to heteronomy but from one heteronomy to another.

In other words, there is no epistemic privilege to unbelief. Just as shaking off the authority of religious beliefs and practices grounded in a putative divine revelation does not free one from the particularity and penultimacy of the hermeneutical situation, as Enlightenment thinkers so curiously thought, so keeping God at a safe distance through some kind of atheism does not free one from de facto dependence on language games we did not invent and whose rules we cannot ignore except at our peril, as Derrida so clearly sees. Even for the most creative thinkers and writers among us, who wish to be autonomous, language is more nearly our creator than we its.[50] Heteronomy is inevitable. To neutralize divine revelation in the name of reason is only to jump out of the frying pan into the fire.

Derrida distinguishes the rabbi from the poet as "two interpretations of interpretation." The rabbi, who lives in a world of a *"sacred text surrounded by commentaries,"* is a symbol of heteronomy, while the poet, who presupposes no divine revelation, is a symbol of autonomy. They seem to be stark antitheses. "Poetry is to prophecy what the idol is to truth." So, at least, says the rabbi. But they are not entirely dissimilar. As interpretations of interpretation they recognize that "In the beginning is hermeneutics," knowing that they live in exile from the garden in which God's speech is so direct as to require no interpretation. Both have been born *"elsewhere."*[51]

We might expect Derrida to cast his vote for the poet. But he not only acknowledges that "there will always be rabbis and poets"—he also adds, "I do not believe that today there is any question of *choosing*" between them. Rather we must search for their "common ground."[52]

What is this common ground? Both have made the hermeneutical turn to interpretation. But that is not all. The autonomy aspired to by the poet turns out to be illusory.[53] The poet represents "the poetic revolution of our century, the extraordinary reflection of man finally attempting today—*and always in vain*—to retake possession of his language (as if this were meaningful) by any means . . . and to claim responsibility for it against a Father of Logos."[54] Perhaps we could put it this way: poets have their own "bibles," texts, and traditions that they (re)interpret.[55] Hermeneutics is heteronomy, whether or not one affirms divine revelation.

Like Foucault, Derrida identifies with the Enlightenment conception of philosophy as critique.[56] But together they point to the irony of the

Enlightenment, namely, that what is universal about human understanding is the kind of particularity whose externality undermines every autonomy, religious or secular, with a prior heteronomy; and they do so in terms of language.

2) *Tradition.* Hans-Georg Gadamer speaks much about language. But tradition is a more basic category for him when speaking about the alterity ingredient in the hermeneutic situation.

Sounding a lot like Derrida, we might hear him saying, "Tradition has begun without us . . . even before I have been able to say I." Traditions are the bearers of the prejudices (pre-judgments, presuppositions, paradigms) that are always already at work as we interpret the world (including the texts we find in it).

Sounding a lot like Foucault, we might hear him saying, "The Enlightenment is itself a tradition, or better, a confluence of traditions. It arose under specific historical conditions and has become a significant part of the world we have inherited from our predecessors, shaping us even before we can accept, or resist, or reformulate its claims on us."

In Gadamer's own words, it goes like this: we are

> situated within traditions. . . . In fact history does not belong to us; we belong to it. Long before we understand ourselves through the process of self-examination, we understand ourselves in a self-evident way in the family, society, and state in which we live. . . . *That is why the prejudices* [Vorurteile] *of the individual, far more than his judgments* [Urteile], *constitute the historical reality of his being.*[57]

This is what the Enlightenment did not see. Its irony is that "there is one prejudice of the Enlightenment that defines its essence: the fundamental prejudice against prejudice itself, which denies tradition its power."[58] In other words, the tragic flaw in the Enlightenment is making a tradition out of denying tradition its power.

By presenting the hermeneutic turn in terms of tradition and its power, Gadamer calls our attention to all three of its dimensions. There is the *particularity* of reason, hermeneutically understood. Reason itself is always already interpreted as it is delivered over to us by traditions in the plural, and it is relative to the forms of objective spirit, namely family, society, and the state, in which we find ourselves. Totally missing from this account, and actively resisted in other texts, is the Hegelian move that integrates all this historical diversity into an eschatological unity, a final narrative in which there is a place for everything and everything is in its place.

In other words, in its particularity, rational discourse is always *penultimate*. On the stream of traditions we have been brought to a place in history that has been shaped by its past and open to its future. Unless we are prepared to declare ourselves to be the moral, political, economic, and social equivalent of the Kingdom of God, we have to acknowledge that we remain *in medias res* and have not become the Omega point of history.

> *To be historically means that knowledge of oneself can never be complete.* . . . *Every finite present has its limitations. We define the concept of 'situation' by saying that it represents a standpoint that limits the possibility of vision. Hence essential to the concept of situation is the concept of "horizon."*[59]

Gadamer's fallibilism reinforces this point. Our historical locatedness provides "insight into the limitations of humanity, into the absoluteness of the barrier that separates man from the divine. . . . The truly experienced person is one who has taken this to heart, who knows that he is master neither of time nor the future."[60] The prejudices provided for us by tradition are a mixed bag. Some are "true" and some are "false," which is to say that some help us to understand while others lead to misunderstanding.[61] Whether we are interpreting texts or the world, we never transcend the place where our interpretations are open to and in need of revision or even replacement.[62]

In stressing our openness or, perhaps, our vulnerability to a future that may change our vision in ways we cannot anticipate, Gadamer never lets us lose sight of the way our present is conditioned by our past. This is the *externality* of the human condition: hermeneutics is heteronomy. If we go back to the first citation from Gadamer we are reminded that we are situated within and shaped by traditions we did not invent, that we belong to history rather than the reverse[63]; that what is self-evident to us is not eternal truth but a reflection of the social structures in which we are embedded[64]; and that these self-evidences (prejudices), transported to us and transplanted in us by tradition, are the conditions of the possibility of any critical reflection. Critique itself is historically conditioned. To the surprise of some, Gadamer, Foucault, and Derrida are in agreement on this point.

There is self-evidence, the immediacy of the truth within us that can be recollected, and there is the possibility of epistemic, moral, political, and religious critique with this recollected truth as its criterion. This is what the Enlightenment sees. What it does not see is that by virtue of the role of tradition this self-evidence and the kinds of critique that appeal to it are not the work of a liberated autonomy but of a systemic heteronomy. This is not a call to abandon critique and liberation, only to understand them more humbly or, perhaps, more humanly.

3) *Social Practices.* Where Derrida speaks of language (games) and Gadamer speaks of tradition(s), Foucault speaks of social practices. While these three terms are not synonymous, they overlap considerably and show, both by themselves and together, that heteronomy is ineluctable. The practices Foucault has in mind are the kinds he has studied in some detail: psychiatry, medicine, criminal justice, and sexuality. Such practices carry within themselves norms for both theory and practice; in the process, they produce the truth that in turn justifies the practices. (This is what Marx means by ideology.) They do this by producing "logic, strategy, self-evidence, and 'reason.'"[65]

The task of critique is, in the first instance, to disrupt all foundationalist strategies by "shaking this false self-evidence" and creating a "breach of self-evidence." This is done by showing the "singularity" of the historical conditions embodied in any practice, thereby undermining all claims to universality and necessity. Where self-evidence is relative to singular practices, we have a "plethora of intelligibilities, a deficit of necessities." The historical investigations that show the contingency of alleged necessity and the particularity of assumed universality Foucault calls genealogy, making Nietzsche one of his major mentors.[66]

He situates himself in relation to other major predecessors. He recognizes that his critique of false self-evidence is a critique of Platonic recollection and suggests "counter-memory" as an alternative to memory as a model, since what can be recollected is not eternal truth but only truth "at a certain moment" or "at a given moment."[67]

In addition to shaking the foundations of foundationalist strategies, Foucault repudiates any Hegelian closure that would provide "apocalyptic objectivity." A historical sense "confirms our existence among countless lost events, without a landmark or a point of reference."[68] He locates himself closer to Marxian ideology critique. He calls attention to the fact that the processes by which practices produce the norms that govern action and thought are concealed and disguised, and he asks who is served by any particular discourse.[69] In effect, he paraphrases Marx so as to say, "The ruling ideas of every epoch are the ideas of the prevailing practices." His hermeneutics of suspicion is inspired by both Nietzsche and Marx.

As an historian, Foucault studies various social practices; as a philosopher he draws epistemic lessons from his studies. Human knowledge is historical.

It is always *in medias res* and, moreover, always conditioned by and relative to practices whose singularity is easy enough to see.[70] These practices produce the truth that serves to legitimate them, and their power is "always already there." The effects of this power are "constituted as individuals."[71] The self and its "reason" are produced by practices that precede them, beyond their awareness and their control. Norms for theory and practice are internal to the practices, but the practices themselves are external to the individuals and cultures that are shaped by them. For it is not only individuals but cultures and societies as well that inherit language games, traditions, and social practices. This is the heteronomy that is inescapable by virtue of our historical finitude. To acknowledge this is to speak a word in praise of heteronomy, to defend it against the apostles of autonomy, who think it can be escaped.

The question of justified belief is approached differently by philosophers in the "analytic" and "continental" traditions. But in either case, if they are postmodern by virtue of the hermeneutical turn, they see typically modern accounts as spoiled by self-deception. In her masterful treatise on virtue epistemology, Linda Zagzebski gives the following definition: "A *justified belief* is what a person who is motivated by intellectual virtue, and who has the understanding of his cognitive situation a virtuous person would have, might believe in like circumstances."[72] She regularly treats autonomy as an intellectual virtue, but since honesty and humility are also on the list, we may ask how they fit together.

If one is motivated by autonomy, one will desire to think for oneself and not simply follow what others say. But if one is also motivated by honesty and humility, one's "understanding of his cognitive situation" will have to take into account the evidence that we are cognitively conditioned and significantly constituted by what others have already said and put into institutional practices. This is not to deny epistemic/legislative autonomy; but it is to qualify and relativize it to a considerable degree. My argument is that it will be a Derridean, Gadamerian, Foucauldian autonomy, one subsequent to and derivative from a deeper heteronomy. This is true quite independently of the position one takes on the possibility of divine revelation.

Notes

1. Harold Bloom, *The Anatomy of Influence: Literature as a Way of Life* (New Haven, CT: Yale University Press, 2011), p. 18. Bloom's example is literary rather than religious. "We have, almost all of us, thoroughly internalized the power of Shakespeare's plays, frequently without having attended them or read them . . . we are so influenced by him that we cannot get outside of him." *The Anxiety of*

Influence: A Theory of Poetry, 2nd ed. (New York: Oxford University Press, 1997), pp. xviii and xxvii. To say nothing of what we have internalized from television and the movies.

2. Sigmund Freud, *The Standard Edition of the Complete Psychological Works of Sigmund Freud*, ed. and trans. James Strachey (London: Hogarth, 1953–74), 19:23. He is referring to the id, our inherent, primal desires. Speaking of Shakespeare's *Twelfth Night*, Harold Bloom writes that "there is almost no significant action, perhaps because nearly everyone behaves involuntarily . . . forces somewhat beyond the characters seem to be living their lives for them." *Shakespeare: The Invention of the Human* (New York: Riverhead Books, 1998, p. 228). Like Freud's statement, this one overlooks the derivative autonomy that accompanies this heteronomy in the realm of action. Hermeneutics points to a similar asymmetry in the realm of cognition.

3. "Language speaks." Martin Heidegger, "Language," in *Poetry, Language, Thought*, trans. Albert Hofstadter (New York: Harper & Row, 1971), p. 190. We take up our place "within *its* speaking, not our own," though, of course, we can make it our own. On the difference between Heidegger and Levinas on being possessed by language, see John Llewelyn, "Levinas and Language," in *The Cambridge Companion to Levinas*, ed. Simon Critchley and Robert Bernasconi (New York: Cambridge University Press, 2002), pp. 122–24.

4. Martin Heidegger, *What Is Philosophy?*, trans. Jean T. Wilde and William Kluback (New Haven, CT: College and University Press, n.d.), pp. 89–93.

5. Martin Heidegger, "Letter on Humanism," in *Pathmarks*, ed. William McNeill (New York: Cambridge University Press, 1998), pp. 239, 243, 254, 272, and 274.

6. This insight underlies Richard Rorty's notion that the contingency of language games is not a matter of arbitrary choice but something that happens in us and to us:

> The realization that the world does not tell us what language games to play [what hermeneutical circle to enter or what paradigm to adopt] should not, however, lead us to say that a decision about which to play is arbitrary [subjectivism], nor to say that it is the expression of something deep within us [objectivism]. . . . It is rather that the notions of criteria and choice are no longer in point when it comes to changes from one language game to another. . . . That sort of shift was no more an act of will than it was a result of argument. (Richard Rorty, *Contingency, Irony, and Solidarity*, New York: Cambridge University Press, 1989, p. 6)

When he says that criteria are not "in point" he means that the changes are not made in accord with previously warranted and universally operative criteria but rather give rise to criteria as particular as the new paradigms. Cf. Richard J. Bernstein, *Beyond Objectivism and Relativism: Science, Hermeneutics, and Praxis* (Philadelphia: University of Pennsylvania Press, 1985).

7. On the significance of the concept of inheritance for Derrida, see Samir Haddad, *Derrida and the Inheritance of Democracy* (Bloomington: Indiana University Press, 2013).

8. See George Steiner, *After Babel*; and Jeffrey Stout, *Ethics After Babel*. Alasdair MacIntyre writes that classical political liberals have "been reluctant to recognize that their appeal is not to some tradition-independent rationality. Yet increasingly there have been liberal thinkers who, for one reason or another, have acknowledged that their theory and practice are after all that of one more contingently grounded and founded tradition, in conflict with other rival traditions and like certain other traditions in claiming a right to universal allegiance." He gives Rawls, Rorty, and Stout as examples. *Whose Justice? Which Rationality?* (Notre Dame, IN: University of Notre Dame Press, 1988), pp. 345–46.

9. Paul Ricoeur, *The Conflict of Interpretations: Essays in Hermeneutics*, ed. Don Ihde (Evanston, IL: Northwestern University Press, 1974).

10. See note 8 above.

11. C. I. Lewis, "A Pragmatic Conception of the *a Priori*," in *Readings in Philosophical Analysis*, ed. Herbert Feigl and Wilfrid Sellars (New York: Appleton-Century-Crofts, 1949), p. 286. We

should not take "in some sense freely taken" to suggest an arbitrary choice. See note 6 above. This contingency of necessity is developed famously in Willard Van Orman Quine, "Two Dogmas of Empiricism," in *From a Logical Point of View* [N.B. logic as a point of view!] (New York: Harper & Row, 1963), pp. 20–46.

12. See my "Hermeneutics as Epistemology," in *The Blackwell Guide to Epistemology*, ed. John Greco and Ernest Sosa (Oxford: Blackwell, 1999), pp. 415–35, reprinted in my *Overcoming Onto-theology* (New York: Fordham University Press, 2001), pp. 47–74. We find ourselves in the hermeneutical situation especially, but by no means exclusively, in religion, ethics, and politics.

13. Hence his regular talk about necessity. For example, with respect to the phenomenological journey from "untrue knowledge" to Science, he writes, "But the *goal* is as necessarily fixed for knowledge as the serial progression." Consciousness is its own criterion. "It is this fact that guides the entire series of the patterns of consciousness in their necessary sequence. . . . Because of this necessity, the way to Science is itself already *Science*" (*PS*, 51, 56).

14. Cf. Harold Bloom's adoption of Shakespeare as the Bible of his secular worldview, in *Shakespeare: The Invention of the Human* (New York: Riverhead Books, 1998). This is better described as an act of faith than of reason, and it tells us as much about Bloom as about Shakespeare.

15. Paul Ricoeur, *Oneself as Another*, trans. Kathleen Blamey (Chicago: University of Chicago Press, 1992), p. 25 (emphasis added).

16. On my reading, Augustine has a modern semantics and a postmodern epistemology.

17. See Richard Rorty, *Philosophy and the Mirror of Nature* (Princeton, NJ: Princeton University Press, 1979); and Nancey Murphy, *Anglo-American Postmodernity: Philosophical Perspectives on Science, Religion, and Ethics* (Boulder, CO: Westview Press, 1997). On the issue of whether even the natural sciences have a hermeneutical character, see, in addition to the authors just mentioned, Robert P. Crease, "The Hard Case: Science and Hermeneutics," in *The Very Idea of Radical Hermeneutics*, ed. Roy Martinez (Atlantic Highlands, NJ: Humanities, 1997); and the debate between Gyorgy Markus, "Why Is There No Hermeneutics of Natural Sciences? Some Preliminary Theses," and Patrick Heelan, "Yes! There Is a Hermeneutics of Natural Science: A Rejoinder to Markus," in *Science in Context* 1, no. 1 (1987): 5–51, and 3, no. 2 (1989): 469–80, respectively.

18. N. R. Hanson, *Patterns of Discovery: An Inquiry into the Conceptual Foundations of Science* (Cambridge: Cambridge University Press, 1961), p. 19.

19. Martin Heidegger, *Being and Time*, trans. John Macquarrie and Edward Robinson (New York: Harper & Row, 1962), pp. 187, 191–92, 194 (¶¶31–32).

20. See *Faith and Rationality: Reason and Belief in God*, ed. Alvin Plantinga and Nicholas Wolterstorff (Notre Dame, IN: University of Notre Dame Press, 1983), p. 59. Quine's argument for the contingency of conceptual necessity challenges the first of these, while Sellars's attack on "the myth of the given" takes on the other two. See Quine, "Two Dogmas of Empiricism" and Wilfrid Sellars, *Empiricism and the Philosophy of Mind* (Cambridge, MA: Harvard University Press, 1997).

21. Rorty, *Mirror of Nature*, p. 315.

22. I have been influenced by all of these thinkers, especially through the privilege of having studied under Sellars, Hanson, and Gadamer and having Plantinga and Wolterstorff as good friends over many years. It was my undergraduate mentor, Arthur Holmes, who first taught me that philosophy is always perspectival.

23. Christopher Benfey, "The Case of the Skeptical Pragmatist," *New York Review of Books*, June 25, 2015, p. 53 (emphasis added).

24. Paul Ricoeur speaks of the "wounded cogito," the damage done to the modern, Cartesian project of making thought self-grounding and thus autonomous. In *Freud and Philosophy: An Essay on Interpretation*, trans. Denis Savage (New Haven, CT: Yale University Press, 1970), p. 439, and in *The Conflict of Interpretations*, pp. 172–73 and 243, the dialogue is with Freud. In *Oneself as Another*, trans. Kathleen Blamey (Chicago: University of Chicago Press, 1992), pp. 11–16, where Ricoeur

speaks of the "shattered cogito," the dialogue is with Nietzsche. In an interview, he says, "I advanced the notion of a wounded or split *cogito*, in opposition to the idealist claims for an inviolate absolute subjectivity. It was in fact Karl Barth who first taught me that the subject is not a centralizing master but rather a disciple or auditor of a language larger than itself." *Debates in Continental Philosophy: Conversations with Contemporary Thinkers*, ed. Richard Kearney (New York: Fordham University Press, 2004), p. 109.

25. James Bernauer, *Michel Foucault's Force of Flight: Toward an Ethics for Thought* (Atlantic Highlands, NJ: Humanities, 1990), pp. 8–9. For an exploration of French philosophy of religion in this context, see Stefanos Geroulanos, *An Atheism That Is Not Humanist Emerges in French Thought* (Stanford, CA: Stanford University Press, 210). This book can be read as a kind of postmodern sequel to Henri de Lubac, S.J., *The Drama of Atheist Humanism*.

26. Michel Foucault, "What Is Enlightenment?," in *The Foucault Reader*, ed. Paul Rabinow (New York: Pantheon Books, 1984), pp. 43–44.

27. Michel Foucault, *The Order of Things: An Archaeology of the Human Sciences*, trans. not given (New York: Random House, 1973), p. 339.

28. See chapter 8, note 23.

29. See the quotation from Ricoeur in note 24 above on the priority of language to the subject. Bloom writes that "self-appropriation involves the immense anxieties of indebtedness, for what strong maker desires the realization that he has failed to create himself." Then he adds that "poetic influence need not make poets less original." *Anxiety*, pp. 5 and 7.

30. Michael Polanyi, *Personal Knowledge: Towards a Post-Critical Philosophy* (New York: Harper & Row, 1964), p. 295.

31. Polanyi, *Personal Knowledge*, pp. 269, 272, 294. Cf. *The Collected Papers of Charles Sanders Peirce*, ed. Charles Hartshorne and Paul Weiss (Cambridge, MA: Harvard University Press, 1960), 5:264: "We cannot begin with complete doubt. We must begin with all the prejudices which we actually have."

32. Ludwig Wittgenstein, *Philosophical Investigations*, trans. G. E. M. Anscombe (Oxford: Basil Blackwell, 1958), sec., p. 11, where he writes that "the *speaking* of language is part of an activity, or form of life."

33. Wittgenstein, *Philosophical Investigations*, sec. 23, p. 12.

34. Think of the differences between the way men and women engage in conversing between and among friends, as described by Deborah Tannen. "If women speak and hear a language of connection and intimacy, while men speak and hear a language of status and independence, then communication between men and women can be like cross-cultural communication, prey to a clash of conversational styles," *You Just Don't Understand: Women and Men in Conversation* (New York: Ballantine Books, 1990), p. 42.

35. In analytic philosophy the linguistic turn became the hermeneutical turn only with the move from the early Wittgenstein (*Tractatus*) to the later Wittgenstein (*Philosophical Investigations*). For this history, see Rorty and Murphy as listed in note 17 above, and Scott Soames, *Philosophical Analysis in the Twentieth Century* (Princeton, NJ: Princeton University Press, 2003), vol. 1, pts. 3–5; and vol. 2, pt. 1.

36. Jacques Derrida, *Of Grammatology*, trans Gayatri Chakravorty Spivak (Baltimore, MD: Johns Hopkins University Press, 1976), p. 158. It is also on this page that Derrida gives the decisive refutation of the notion that deconstruction means that we can play with texts and make them mean anything we want. See the discussion of doubling commentary higher up on p. 158; "Edmond Jabès and the Question of the Book," *Writing and Difference*, trans. Alan Bass (Chicago: University of Chicago Press, 1978), pp. 75–76; and "Force and Signification," in *Writing and Difference*, p. 12., where Derrida writes, "Being has always already begun. To create is to reveal."

37. An interview with Richard Kearney in *Debates in Continental Philosophy*, p. 154.

38. Derrida, "Edmond Jabès," p. 74. Derrida is just a good Heideggerian here.

39. 'Intuition' here signifies what does not require interpretation, and 'self-evident' signifies what needs no evidence other than itself to support itself. Hegel uses the term 'immediacy' for both aspects and insists that every immediacy is mediated. Speaking of Husserlian phenomenology, Kevin Hart says that "phenomenology is not the study of presence but of presence and absence." So perhaps Derrida and Husserl are not as far apart as is often thought. *Kingdoms of God* (Bloomington: Indiana University Press, 2014), p. 161.

40. Derrida, *Of Grammatology*, p. 26.

41. Derrida, *Of Grammatology*, pp. 158–59, 49.

42. Jacques Derrida, *Limited Inc*, trans. Samuel Weber (Evanston, IL: Northwestern University Press, 1988), p. 152.

43. For Derrida as for Hegel, semantic holism is simply a mirror of ontological holism. In Hegel's System, this comprehensive understanding occurs conceptually in the Logic, mechanically and organically in the Philosophy of Nature, and historically in the Philosophy of Spirit.

44. We might say that his Kantianism is qualified by his Hegelian holism, and his Hegelianism is qualified by his Kantian finitism.

45. Jürgen Habermas cites Mead as saying that "one has to be a member of a community to be a self" and "[t]he self... is essentially a social structure, and arises in social experiences." *Lifeworld and System: A Critique of Functionalist Reason*, vol. 2 of *The Theory of Communicative Action*, trans. Thomas McCarthy (Boston: Beacon Press, 1987), pp. 24 and 40. Habermas has a chapter entitled "Individuation through Socialization: On George Herbert Mead's Theory of Subjectivity," in *Postmetaphysical Thinking: Philosophical Essays*, trans. William Mark Hohengarten (Cambridge, MA: MIT Press, 1992). The linguistic character of community and social experience in his own work is utterly basic.

46. Jacques Derrida, "How to Avoid Speaking: Denials," in *Derrida and Negative Theology*, trans. Harold Coward and Toby Foshay (Albany: State University New York Press, 1992), p. 99. The notion that moral autonomy presupposes a prior heteronomy is also developed in "Force of Law: The 'Mystical Foundation of Authority,'" in *Deconstruction and the Possibility of Justice*, ed. Drucilla Cornell, Michael Rosenfeld, and David Gray Carlson (New York: Routledge, 1992).

47. Jacques Derrida, "Faith and Knowledge: The Two Sources of 'Religion' at the Limits of Reason Alone," in *Acts of Religion*, ed. Gil Anidjar (New York: Routledge, 2002), p. 71. Although, as the title suggests, Derrida is resuming the Kantian project, he sides here with Levinas against Kant on the question of autonomy.

48. Jacques Derrida, *The Gift of Death*, trans. David Wills (Chicago: University of Chicago Press, 1995; 2nd ed., 2008), p. 91.

49. Once again, see Ricoeur's warning in note 24 above, and my "Appropriating Postmodernism," in *Overcoming Onto-theology*, pp. 75–88.

50. I take it that this is the central point of Harold Bloom in *The Anxiety of Influence*. "Cultural belatedness is never acceptable to a major writer.... Belatedness seems to me not a historical condition at all, but one that belongs to the literary situation as such" (p. xxv). Bloom's "belatedness" is Derrida's "inheritance." See note 7 above.

51. Derrida, "Edmond Jabès," pp. 66–67. Derrida is sometimes quoting Jabès.

52. Derrida, "Edmond Jabès," p. 67; and "Structure, Sign, and Play in the Discourse of the Human Sciences," in *Writing and Difference*, p. 293. On the dialectical relation of the rabbi and the poet, see Keith Putt, "Friends and Stranger/Poets and Rabbis: Negotiating a 'Capuphalian' Philosophy of Religion," in *The Future of Continental Philosophy of Religion*, ed. Clayton Crockett, B. Keith Putt, and Jeffrey W. Robbins (Bloomington: Indiana University Press, 2014), pp. 34–44, along with responses by Jack Caputo and myself.

53. As is the hope of the rabbi to return to the garden by means of interpretation, as if by interpretation, understood as deciphering, one could escape the need for interpretation. This, it seems to

me, is what the objectivist hermeneutic of E. D. Hirsch in *Validity in Interpretation* amounts to. See my discussion in *Whose Community? Which Interpretation?* (Grand Rapids, MI: Baker Academic, 2009), chaps. 4–5.

54. Derrida, "Edmond Jabès," p. 73 (emphasis added).

55. That is the argument of Bloom in the works cited in notes 1 and 50 above.

56. See Foucault, "What Is Enlightenment?" pp. 42–47; and Derrida, "Of an Apocalyptic Tone Newly Adopted in Philosophy," in *Derrida and Negative Theology*, p. 51; and "Force of Law," p. 27, where Derrida writes, "Nothing seems to me less outdated than the classical emancipatory ideal."

57. Hans-Georg Gadamer, *Truth and Method*, 2nd ed. rev., trans. Joel Weinsheimer and Donald G. Marshall (New York: Crossroad, 1991), pp. 276, 277–78. The second page reference refers to the 2004 edition of the same translation that, inexcusably, has different pagination. For a brief but more comprehensive overview of Gadamer's thought, see my discussion in *Whose Community?*, chaps. 6–9. For a fuller treatment that fits nicely with my argument, see James Risser, *Hermeneutics and the Voice of the Other* (Albany: State University of New York Press, 1997).

58. Gadamer, *Truth and Method*, p. 270/pp. 272–73.

59 Gadamer, *Truth and Method*, p. 302/p. 301.

60. Gadamer, *Truth and Method*, p. 357/p. 351.

61. Gadamer, *Truth and Method*, pp. 298–99/pp. 298. Cf. p. 277/p. 278 and p. 295/p. 295.

62. Gadamer, *Truth and Method*, p. 267/p. 269.

63. Belonging is a very important category for Gadamer. See my "The Dialectic of Belonging and Distanciation in Gadamer and Ricoeur," in *Gadamer and Ricoeur: Critical Horizons for Contemporary Hermeneutics*, ed. Francis J. Mootz III and George H. Taylor (New York: Continuum, 2011), pp. 43–62.

64. Here again we have a mediated immediacy, an autonomy (recollection) derivative from a prior heteronomy.

65. Michel Foucault, "Questions of Method: An Interview with Michel Foucault," in *After Philosophy: End of Transformation?*, ed. Kenneth Baynes, James Bohman, and Thomas McCarthy (Cambridge, MA: MIT Press, 1987, pp. 102–3. Cf. p. 108; and *Power/Knowledge: Selected Interviews and Other Writings 1972-1977*, ed. Colin Gordon (New York: Pantheon Books, 1980), p. 93. Also see Alasdair MacIntyre's definition of a practice as "any coherent and complex form of socially established cooperative human activity through which goods internal to that form of activity are realized in the course of trying to achieve those standards of excellence which are appropriate to, and partially definitive of, that form of activity, with the result that human powers to achieve excellence, and human conceptions of the ends and goods involved, are systematically extended." *After Virtue: A Study in Moral Theory* (Notre Dame, IN: University of Notre Dame Press, 1981), p. 175.

66. Foucault, "Questions," pp. 104–7; *Power/Knowledge*, pp. 83–84 and 117; and "Nietzsche, Genealogy, and History," in *Foucault Reader*, pp. 76–100.

67. Foucault, "Nietzsche," p. 93. "Questions," pp. 102–3.

68. Foucault, "Nietzsche," pp. 86–89.

69. Foucault, *Power/Knowledge*, pp. 95, 115.

70. William J. Wainwright argues for the "person-relativity" of philosophical arguments and, by implication, analyses. So far so good. But it is also true that "person-relativity" is to a very significant degree conditioned by and relative to transpersonal language, traditions, and practices. See *Reason, Revelation, and Devotion: Inference and Argument in Religion* (New York: Cambridge University Press, 2016), pp. 40–47.

71. Foucault, *Power/Knowledge*, pp. 141, 98.

72. Linda Trinkaus Zagzebski, *Virtues of the Mind: An Inquiry into the Nature of Virtue and the Ethical Foundations of Knowledge* (New York: Cambridge University Press, 1996), p. 241.

11

HETERONOMY AS FREEDOM

So far, the argument against the autonomy project or, more specifically, the religion-within-the-limits-of-reason-alone project has proceeded in two stages, unequal in length. First, a crucial premise of the enterprise has shown itself to be unsustainable. It is the assumption that human reason is universal, part of the standard equipment of human nature. As such, it is presumed to be objective, neutral, presuppositionless, the only source of reliable knowledge. As such, it is "nonsectarian" by contrast with the plurality of "religions of the book," those that appeal to the authority of some particular divine revelation and are in this way heteronomous. Heteronomy means relying on a particular revelation rather than on universal reason.

I have looked in considerable detail, but by no means comprehensively, at the philosophical theologies of Spinoza, Kant, and Hegel in order to make clear (1) how different they are from one another; (2) how different they are from biblical theism, and especially "mere Christianity," the "religion of the book" that was the prevailing faith in the world in which they worked; (3) how their "method" of biblical interpretation was a combination of outright denial and rather systematic reinterpretation in the name of "reason"; and (4) how this involves an elitism that says in effect, "Traditional understandings of the Bible may be useful for the hoi polloi, but for those of us who are intellectually sophisticated, it is necessary and possible to find new and improved meanings more in tune with who we are as rational beings, whether this involves outright rejection or systematic reinterpretation." Failure to conform to human reason disqualifies any claim to be a divine revelation; nothing counts as revelation that has not been ratified by human reason.

My argument has not been that the claim to a rational universality is false but that it is plainly false, that anyone who looks closely at these three (quite typical) thinkers will see that it is false, that their religions-within-the-limits-of-reason-alone are quite as sectarian as the traditional faiths they seek to transcend. That is why I say that their enterprise "has shown itself to be unsustainable." Like Judaism, Christianity, and Islam, they are particular faiths making claims to universal significance. These claims are justified by the appeal to Reason only for those who have already bought into some version of reason that is mutually incompatible with the other versions. Reading Spinoza, Kant, or Hegel or hearing them clearly explained may result in such a buy-in, but that is like coming to a theistic faith by reading the Bible or Koran, or by hearing them clearly explained. The authority of the norm or criterion comes into being with the faith that seeks to be guided by it. It is not established by some prior, neutral process.

The second stage of my argument builds on the first. If philosophers are as sectarian as prophets and apostles and the various religions of reason are as particular as the religions that appeal to a special divine revelation, we can ask for the source(s) of the norms and criteria by which traditional faiths are either repudiated or radically revised. They can no longer be justified by appeal to universal human nature as if they were "factory-installed" standard equipment, as distinct from dealer-installed options. When only some luxury cars have tinted windows, it is hard to argue that tinted windows belong to the very essence of an automobile.

This leads to what I've been calling the hermeneutical turn, developed, especially in the twentieth century, by a wide variety of philosophers. It is the recognition that in its particularity, human reason is relative to the presuppositions it brings with it to experience, that these vary from one individual or society or culture to another, and most importantly, that they are conditioned by historically particular processes and events external (prior) to the individual thinkers or communities of thought that hold to them. If language games (Wittgenstein, Derrida), traditions (Gadamer), and social practices (Foucault) are the carriers of the presuppositions that are the a priori conditions of the possibility of the rationality in question,[1] they are what is prior (in their particularity) to the operative a priori (in its claims to universality). We are heteronomous in relation to our presuppositions because we are heteronomous in relation to the cultural carriers from whom we have received them. We inherit them, we do not invent or merely discover them.² They come to us from outside and govern what is self-evident;³ they even constitute who we are inside. We recollect what we have heard, what "they say," and in this way become historically situated "Platonists."

Heidegger calls this passivity that makes recollection possible falling, idle talk, inauthenticity, and alienation.⁴ He speaks of language as "the way things have been expressed," and notes that there lies "hidden" in this "already" our understanding of ourselves and our world. To be authentic (*eigentlich*) is to be "one's own self" (*sich zueignen*).⁵ But we are "constantly delivered over to this interpretedness, which controls and distributes the possibilities of average understanding and the state-of-mind belonging to it."⁶ Heidegger denies that the negative language he uses for this heteronomy signifies "any negative evaluation," as if inauthenticity were "a bad and deplorable ontical property of which, perhaps, more advanced stages of human culture might be able to rid themselves."⁷ It is simply the human condition, and to deny this is not to be enlightened but self-deceived. The Enlightenment needs to be enlightened by a postmodern critique that has taken the hermeneutical turn.

So if Heidegger speaks of authenticity, and he surely does, it is not to signify an autonomy which leaves behind inherited interpretations the way a snake shucks off its skin. These are rather the soil in which authenticity grows, by which it is nurtured, and without which it would not be. It is an autonomy that is honest about its derivative and finite character, of which death is an even more ultimate symptom than language.⁸ Death signifies that our life is not self-sustaining, language that our life is not self-initiated. We do not preside over our beginning or our ending. We were not even there at our beginning, for our beginning started without us because it started before us.⁹

With the phrase "particular faiths making claims to universal significance," I have been pointing to an important epistemic equality between the rational theologies of the Enlightenment and the revelational theologies of the Abrahamic monotheisms. All are doubly particular—both in their content and in the norms by which they seek to be guided and to which they appeal for justification. The former give hegemony to some version of reason over the faiths that take certain sacred texts to be their highest standard; the latter do just the reverse and seek to develop, as Wolterstorff's title puts it so succinctly, "reason within the bounds of religion."¹⁰

Certain postmodern theologies are only partly different from the modern theologies from which they seek to distance themselves. These include those of Jacques Derrida, Gianni Vattimo, Mark C. Taylor, John D. (Jack) Caputo, Richard Kearney and others. They have taken the hermeneutical turn and do not profess to speak as the voice of some universal view from nowhere. But if their understanding of reason is postmodern in this sense, they give it the same hegemony as their Enlightenment predecessors over the special revelation on which the "religions of the book" seek to ground themselves. They offer outright rejections and systematic reinterpretations of Abrahamic monotheism and "mere Christianity" that are formally on a par with those of Spinoza, Kant, and Hegel.

In other words, just as some postmodern thinkers have not abandoned the Enlightenment ideal of epistemic and social critique, so some have not abandoned the project of religion within the limits of reason alone. It should be noted that their faith in the resultant religions can be just as strong and (epistemically) intolerant as the faiths that seek to ground themselves on special revelation. But they are faiths, nevertheless—rival faiths.

I have stressed the equal vulnerability of "rational" and "revelational" theologies to their own particularity and historical conditioning because it is so often overlooked. Enlightenment thinkers talked as if by demoting revelation to religion for the intellectually immature and unsophisticated, badly in need of upgrading and updating, they had already become the autonomous voice of pure reason, universal, presuppositionless, and unconditioned. That assumption is often still with us, most frequently in various forms of scientific naturalism. Science is supposed to be the one royal road to truth even when the questions are not scientific but moral and metaphysical.

But there is a real difference between "religions of the book," that try to give hegemony to divine revelation over merely human understanding and those theologies, whether modern or postmodern that do just the reverse.[11] Revelational theologies choose to be subject to the voice of One who is Wholly Other; rational theologies are also heteronomous, as I've been arguing, but not in this way, which we might call biblical heteronomy. Rational theologians will have their "bibles," written by the likes of Plato, or Aristotle, or Wittgenstein, or Heidegger, or Derrida or whomever, but they will not attribute divine origin and authority to their master texts.

So, if all theologies are heteronomous in relation to the language games, traditions, and social practices which are the "parents" from whom they have inherited their a priori assumptions but only some can be said to be biblically heteronomous, a question arises. Is there something about biblical heteronomy, the attempt to give hegemony to divine revelation over human reason, that makes it especially problematic? Should we, like some postmodern rational theologians, flee this deliberate dependence as alienating and dehumanizing even while we acknowledge our de facto dependence on the human theories and practices by which our thinking has been formed?

Some might be inclined to say yes because they are appalled (not to put too fine a point on it) by the jihadist ideology of some Muslims, by the Catholic view of abortion and birth control, or the right-wing politics of some evangelical Protestants. But this would be a non sequitur. There are Muslims and Catholics and evangelical Protestants who repudiate such interpretations of their scriptures and traditions. To reject the idea of God because some people do horrific things in God's name, or to reject the idea of divine revelation because some interpretations of putative revelation are repulsive to one's own (human, all too human) understanding, is to cut oneself off from possible truth in order to avoid a perceived error. As Hegel puts it in another context, "what calls itself fear of error reveals itself rather as the fear of truth."[12] One risks throwing out the baby with the bathwater.

In favor of the possibility that biblical heteronomy is not inherently immature, alienating, and destructive of human dignity, I offer, not an argument, but testimony.[13] The epistemic significance of testimony has received renewed attention of late.[14] I say "renewed" because sometimes it draws on the philosophy of Thomas Reid.[15] Appealing to Reid, Plantinga writes,

> Testimony is the source of an enormously large proportion of our most important beliefs; it is testimony and learning from others that makes possible intellectual achievement and culture; testimony is the very foundation of civilization. The Enlightenment looked down its rationalistic nose at testimony and tradition, comparing them invidiously with science; but without learning by testimony, clearly science would be impossible.[16]

The first testimony I offer is Jewish. It comes from the Psalms. But it is also Christian, since the Psalter has provided prayers and songs for Christians for two millennia. It begins by declaring "happy" or "blessed"[17] those whose

> delight is in the law of the LORD,
> and on his law they meditate day and night. (Ps. 1:2–3)

Or again,

> The law of the LORD is perfect, reviving the soul;
> the decrees of the LORD are sure, making wise the simple...
> More to be desired are they than gold, even much fine gold;
> sweeter also than honey and the drippings of the honeycomb.
> (Ps. 19:7, 10)

Psalm 119 is the longest Psalm and reads like an extended meditation on or, musically speaking, a long development of this theme. Virtually every one of the 176 verses makes reference to the law of God. Different terms are used: law, decrees, ways, commandments, statutes, judgments, word or words.[18] There is both an ontological and an epistemic heteronomy here. The working assumption is that God and not the psalmist is the origin and ground of these norms and that, consequently they have been learned not by Platonic recollection but by divine revelation. The moral teacher is the prophet, not the philosopher.

What is striking about this very un-Kantian psalm is the psalmist's enthusiasm for the commandments that come from a voice not his own.[19] They make him happy, are an occasion for thanks; he wants to keep them with his whole heart; they are sweet and dear and a source of joy to him, objects of longing and desire. But the most frequent responses are that he loves the law of God (seven times) and that he delights in God's commandments (ten times). Perhaps he has been reading Enlightenment thinkers, for on two occasions he takes rather explicit exception to their autonomy project: he finds liberty, not "self-incurred minority" (Kant as a typical modernist) or "slave morality" (Nietzsche as a typical postmodernist), in his love for the law of God (vv. 32 and 45).[20]

We might think that the psalmist lived in the childhood of the human race and had not matured enough to aspire to think for himself. He had not learned from Plato to find true knowledge only in recollection or from Rousseau and Kant to find liberty only in a law that he had prescribed for himself. But, as if he anticipates the condescension that will be directed his way by those who are "enlightened" and "rational," he is eager to tell us why his embrace of God's commandments is so cheerful.

In the first place, the revelation of the law of God fills a felt epistemic need.[21] It provides the psalmist with instruction, counsel, understanding, discernment, knowledge, and wisdom. At the same time, it fills certain felt existential needs. It provides comfort, help, life, light, and peace. He experiences his heteronomy not as an alienation or enslavement but as the help he needs to become his truest and most fulfilled self. One can dismiss this as a symptom of a childhood that is to be outgrown, but that would be simply to beg the question against a poet of faith who has inspired many up to, through, and past the hegemony of the Enlightenment's autonomy project. What he says makes eminent sense if we have such needs and if there is a God who is willing and able to help us in relation to them. It is much easier to join with Freud, say, in calling such faith infantile than to show that it is mistaken about our needs and about God.

If Nietzsche explains "*The background of our cheerfulness*" in terms of the death of God,[22] our psalmist gives the ground and background of his cheerfulness in terms of the most basic structure of ancient Hebrew faith: the covenantal relation with God. It has three basic elements. First, there is belief in a personal God, that is, a God who, among other powers, is capable of speech acts.

Second, at the divine initiative, a relation between God and human beings, both individually and collectively, is established in terms of the two most basic covenantal speech acts: promises and commandments. (While focusing on commandments or instruction, Torah, our psalmist mentions the promises of God fourteen times in Psalm 119.) In the Hebrew scriptures Yahweh enters into covenant relations with and through Abraham, Moses, and David, and through Jeremiah promises a new covenant. The New Testament interprets this new covenant as established through Jesus the Christ.[23] The God of the Bible is not only the Maker of Heaven and Earth but also the Maker of Covenants.

Third, the divine purpose is expressed in what can be called the formula of the covenant: I will be their God, and they will be my people.[24] Both the commandments and the promises come from God, and together they are the conditions of a blessed relation with a God who wants to be the God of a people who reflect God's love, both as the righteousness of divine commands and the mercy of divine promises.

This relationship starts out with Abraham, but it is not just for him. It is also for his descendants. In the first instance, they are the Jews, but it is not just for them either. They are to be a light to the nations.[25] When Paul argues, especially in Romans and Galatians, that Gentiles, too, can become children of Abraham by faith[26] and heirs of the covenant promises, he is only echoing the claim, deeply embedded in the Psalms, that a particular revelation is of universal significance, that the God of the covenants with Israel is the God of all peoples.[27]

If the historical and metaphysical claims of covenantal religion are true, then biblical faith is not a slave religion but the path to relational fulfillment. This does not become less true when human institutions and practices, religious, political, and social, arrogate to themselves divine authority and do enslave their victims (and their perpetrators). It is easy to show that the latter has happened again and again in human history; it is much harder to show that the claims of covenantal religion are false; and it is to beg this latter question to slide surreptitiously from the latter to the former.

The second testimony I offer comes from Orual, daughter of the King of Glome, and, after his death, Queen of Glome. She is the protagonist of what I take to be C. S. Lewis's finest novel, *Till We Have Faces*.[28] This is his retelling of the ancient myth of Cupid and Psyche.[29] It has the form of a memoir by Orual that she presents as her case against the gods.

First we need the basic story; then we can look for its bearing on our theme of autonomy and heteronomy. Unsurprisingly, in Lewis's telling it has obvious Christian overtones that I shall not belabor. Lewis resisted the notion that his fiction belongs to the genre of allegory. I take him to mean that while his stories, such as the Narnia chronicles and this novel, are free to evoke Christian themes with abandon, the stories have their own integrity as such. They have real characters who are not merely "Christ figures" or the personifications of various moral or metaphysical abstractions.[30]

Our protagonist is Orual. She is ugly; in fact, through much of the story she wears a veil so that people won't notice how ugly she is. Then there is the King, who treats her badly. He is a brutish man interested only in his pleasures and power. But she reserves her anger for the gods, as we shall see. After her mother's death, her father remarries and her stepsister is born. Psyche is beautiful and intensely sensitive to beauty around her. Their tutor, the Fox (also "Grandfather") is a Greek slave, taken in war. He is a philosopher with a Stoic superstructure built on a Platonic foundation. The happy times in life are her early years that she and Psyche spend with the Fox. Her other mentor is Bardia, commander of the palace guard, hardworking and loyal, both to the king and then to her when she becomes queen.

Finally there is the priest of Ungit. Ungit is the goddess of Glome. She is a shapeless, black stone who dwells in a "holiness" that consists in equal parts of darkness and the smell of blood from the sacrifices that are the primary temple ritual. There is a rumor that she has a son, the god of the Grey Mountain, who is beautiful; but this son is also referred to as the Brute.[31] (It is worth noticing that

Orual's *J'accuse* is directed not primarily directed against Ungit but against the god of the Gray Mountain, whom Psyche finds to be beautiful.)

The King treats Ungit exclusively in terms of *do ut des*, a commercial transaction in which one pays for favors or, perhaps more precisely, one bribes the goddess to remain friendly to Glome.

Somehow stories begin to circulate about Psyche. A mother thinks her child will be beautiful if Psyche kisses her. Her touch is said to heal the sick, and it seems that some were indeed healed. She is called a goddess by some, Ungit in mortal shape by others.

But even if, as the Fox insists, the gods are not jealous,[32] celebrity is fickle. When plague, drought, and bad harvests weaken Glome and her enemies become more threatening, lots are cast, and the people accept the verdict that Psyche is the accursed source of their misfortune. The priest of Ungit pronounces that she must be offered as an expiatory sacrifice (p. 45) to the god of the Gray Mountain. So in a solemn procession led by the King and the Priest, Psyche is taken to the mountain, tied to a tree, and left for the Brute to take as he will. Psyche calls this a "ransom"; but rather than think of her death as a bribe, she says, "There must be so much that neither the Priest nor the Fox knows" (p. 72).[33]

After a while Orual decides to be Antigone, to return to the mountain, find the remains of Psyche, and give her a decent burial. She makes the difficult journey with help from Bardia, but instead of finding bones she finds—Psyche, alive and radiantly happy.

As a child, Psyche had always dreamed of being the queen of a great king and living in a gold and amber castle on the Gray Mountain. She longed to go there "where all the beauty came from" (p. 75). For that reason, she had willingly gone to her sacrifice. Now she claims that her dream has come true. She is the bride of the god of the West-wind, actually the West-wind himself. "He was in human shape. But you could not mistake him for a man" (p. 111). The house where they now live together has become her home. It "wasn't, you see, just the gold and amber house I used to imagine. If it had been just that, I might indeed have thought I was dreaming." This was the truly real. "It's more likely everything that had happened to me before this was a dream" (p. 112).

This might have been good news for Orual but for two problems. First, when she asks to see the palace, Psyche replies in surprise that they are already in it. She can see it, but Orual cannot. Second, Psyche tells her that though at the beginning she saw the god, he now comes to her at night and insists that she not see him in the darkness.

Needless to say, Orual has no trouble imagining horrible versions of the situation in which some brute (Bardia's view) or a thief and murderer (the Fox's view) is taking cruel advantage of Psyche. She persuades Psyche to test her story by shining a light at night to see whether her husband is a beautiful god, a gruesome beast, or a merely human felon. She does this, and the result is fourfold: there is a violent physical storm; Orual gets a brief glimpse of the overwhelming beauty of the god (in this context more *tremendum* than *fascinans*); Psyche is sent, weeping, into exile; and Orual, no longer in doubt about the reality of the gods, awaits her punishment.

It is after these events that Orual takes the veil, the Priest of Ungit dies, the King dies, the Fox dies, and Orual becomes queen on her own, a very good one in terms of peace and prosperity as criteria. It is also after these events that she writes her memoir, the novel we are reading. She has learned that there is more truth in the supernatural worldview of the Priest of Ungit than she ever suspected, though his view of it was rather one-dimensional. She has also learned that the Fox's naturalistic world view is less comprehensive than she thought. Perhaps Psyche was right when, in her longing to be wed to a god, she suspected early on that "the Fox hasn't the whole truth" (p. 70). Since the philosopher and not the priest had always been her tutor and mentor, Orual addresses her memoir as an accusation against the gods and addresses it to the Greeks, as if to vindicate herself before the tribunal whose criterion is their Reason. Her "theology" is no longer that the gods are priestly fictions but rather that they are all too real, but cruel and unjust.

In the course of her narrative a double decentering takes place, on the one hand ethical and on the other hand epistemic.[34] Orual discovers that by virtue of her autonomy project, placing herself at the center of her universe as the self-sufficient and unquestioned criterion of the good and the true, she had become cruel (the ethical) and blind to important truth (the epistemic).

First the ethical decentering. It is her own narrative that reveals to Orual that she had never really loved her other sister, Redival, her loyal servant Bardia, or her "beloved" tutor, the Fox. They all mattered to her just to the degree that they met her needs and desires, and she was too self-occupied to concern herself with their needs and desires.[35] This was a subtle self-centeredness and thus easy to overlook; but it was just as real as the crude self-centeredness of the King and the Priest (between whom, ironically, Psyche had walked to her sacrificial death).

Far more devastating, of course, was the discovery that she had never truly loved Psyche. The heart of her complaint against the gods was that "Psyche was mine" and the gods stole her. They "shall not have her" (pp. 60, 120–21, 152, 183, 290–91). No prosecuting attorney could have portrayed a more possessive "love" than Orual's own words, words that eventually undermine her increasingly desperate denials, insisting "I had at least loved Psyche truly" (p. 285). She complains that in going willingly to her death, the "parting between [Psyche] and me cost her so little" (p. 71). Because Psyche now loves her divine husband more than her, she accuses Psyche of no longer loving her at all, pleading with her to "come back where we were happy" instead of "leaving me ... turning your back on all our love" (pp. 124–25), only gradually realizing that this "we" and this "our" were unilaterally defined on Orual's terms, permitting no freedom for Psyche's faith and newfound happiness. That faith makes Psyche her "enemy," whom she has come to "hate" and against whom she is willing to use "force" to get her back, even to "kill" her. To which the Fox had responded, "Daughter, daughter. You are transported beyond all reason and nature.... There's one part love in your heart, and five parts anger, and seven parts pride" (pp. 117, 127, 148).

When Orual eventually comes to recognize herself in the story as she has told it, she confesses: "Oh Psyche, oh goddess.... Never again will I call you mine; but all there is of me shall be yours. Alas, you know now what it's worth. I never wished you well, never had one selfless thought of you. I was a craver" (p. 305).[36] It is as if she has understood Levinas without ever reading him. The (human) other makes an unconditional, ethical claim on her that she cannot refute but has never overtly acknowledged, much less satisfied.

Orual's epistemic decentering is also metaphysical, for it relates to the divine Other and not the merely human other. It is epistemic because the self she places at the center as the condition for possible belief is the self formed (contingently and in particular) by the Fox's Platonic/Stoic idea of Reason. He praises philosophy over poetry and speaks disparagingly of the poets as liars.[37] He insists that the gods are not jealous[38] but that priests are schemers in search of power and wealth. He espouses a twofold Stoic universalism, the cosmopolitanism that views all humans as of one blood and the rationalism that makes of nature the one criterion of the good and the true, presumably accessible to all who follow the way of philosophy rather than poetry. This includes a defense of suicide as in accord with "the god within me" (p. 18) when fate turns cruel. As in Hegel, art and religion are downgraded in favor of philosophical reason.

This "god within me" signifies the correlation of nature (being) and reason (knowing). This is what Hegel will call the identity of thought and being: being is intelligible and human reason is the site and actualization of this intelligibility.

In Orual's story the epistemic autonomy of this Greek enlightenment shows itself in several ways. The Fox's Stoic naturalism, ancestor of today's scientific naturalism, grounds the demythologizing according to which Psyche's spouse can be neither the Brute of popular superstition nor the beautiful son of Ungit that some suspect but only some human thief and murderer.

If Orual speaks of the gods at all, it is with scorn. The world is a hostile place, and this is their fault. It is "this god-haunted, plague-breeding, decaying, tyrannous world." She has

> the strongest reason for distrust. The gods never send us this invitation to delight [has she been overlooking the Psalms?] so readily or so strongly as when they are preparing some new agony. We are their bubbles; they blow us big before they prick us ... I ruled myself. Did they think I was nothing but a pipe to be played on as their moment's fancy chose?" (p. 97)

She seeks to discredit Psyche's belief that the gods are real and, in the final analysis, beautiful, by insisting repeatedly that Psyche must be mad, her illusion due to insanity (pp. 117–18, 122, 125, 135, 138, 141, 144).[39]

Though Orual's unbelief is often vociferous, it is not always confident. Confronted with Psyche's testimony, she writes, "If this is all true, I've been wrong all my life. Everything has to be begun over again" (p. 115). She asks herself, "Was I believing in her invisible palace?" (p. 117). "I came almost to a full belief" (p. 120). "Try as I would, I could not quite put out of my head the fear that I had been wrong. A real god ... was it impossible?" (p. 169).

She defends herself against these temptations by reminding herself that the Greeks would laugh at such belief (p. 117) and by noting that in addition to the Fox, neither Bardia nor any of the people of Glome would believe her story about a beautiful god and magnificent palace (p. 161). We, all of us, know better. ("We" have become the embodiment of wisdom and sanity by virtue of not believing that Ungit has a beautiful son. Of course, like Lessing, "we" would put it the other way round. Because we are wise, we do not believe. "Our" wisdom precludes it.)

But her strongest defense is her own will. She does not want to believe. "Anyway, my whole heart leaped to shut the door against something monstrously amiss—not to be endured. And to keep it shut ... [since] the whole world was slipping out of my hands." So when Psyche suggests that she has glimpsed the palace for herself, "I found myself screaming 'Stop it! Stop it at once! There's nothing there!" (pp. 117–18). And when Psyche suggests that she will learn to see, she replies, "I don't want it! . . . I don't want it. I hate it. Hate it, hate it, hate it" (p. 124). As in her violent hatred of Psyche, she is hardly the dispassionate embodiment of reason the Fox had sought to cultivate. Orual's own narrative cries out for a vigorous hermeneutics of suspicion.[40]

Her frantic screaming arises because, in fact, she has had a glimpse for herself. Twice, actually. On her first trip to visit Psyche, she briefly sees the palace (pp. 132–34), and on her second trip she sees the god himself, overwhelmingly beautiful. "He made it to be as if, from the beginning, I had known that Psyche's lover was a god, and as if all my doubtings, fears, guessings, debatings, questionings . . . had been trumped-up foolery, dust blown in my own eyes by myself" (pp. 172–73).

As if she has been channeling Bertrand Russell, she denies that this is genuine evidence. When asked what he would say if God asked him on judgment day why he did not believe, he is reported to have replied that he would say, "Not enough evidence, God. Not enough evidence!" Orual demands "a world in which the gods show themselves clearly and don't torment men with glimpses" (pp. 243–44). After the gods had taken Psyche from her, "They would not tell me whether she was the bride of a god, or mad, or a brute's or villain's spoil. They would give no clear sign, though I begged for it. I had to guess" (p. 149).

In other words, her reason was the criterion of what could count as evidence and the gods must meet that standard if they would be taken seriously. In a courtroom, the judge decides what counts as admissible evidence. Tutored by the Greeks, Orual lives in a world in which philosophical reason is that judge and religion must accept that hegemony. It must be willing to be religion within the limits of "reason" alone if it would receive Philosophy's Seal of Approval.

The peroration of her long prosecutory brief accusing the gods of stealing "those we love" reads like this:

> It would be far better if you were foul and ravening. We'd rather you drank their blood than stole their hearts. We'd rather they were ours and dead than yours and made immortal. But to steal her love from me, to make her see things I couldn't see . . . oh, you'll say (you've been whispering it to me these forty years) that I'd signs enough her palace was real, could have known the truth if I'd wanted. But how could I want to know it? Tell me that. The girl was mine . . . it makes no difference whether you're fair or foul. That there should

be gods at all, there's our misery and bitter wrong. There's no room for you and us in the same world. You're a tree in whose shadow we can't thrive. We want to be our own. I was my own and Psyche was mine and no one else had any right to her.... What should I care for some horrible, new happiness which I hadn't given her and which separated her from me? (pp. 291–92).[41]

At this point it is Nietzsche's Zarathustra that Orual has been channeling: "*if* there were gods, how could I endure not to be a god! *Hence* there are no gods."[42]

As with the first decentering, Orual eventually comes to recognize herself, long hidden from herself but now revealed in her own narrative. Once she had insisted that the gods would punish her for her book "because they have no answer" (p. 250). In the end, she comes to realize, "The complaint was the answer" (p. 294). Her resistance has broken down. "There was no rebel in me now" (p. 280).

Orual's story is by no means that of Psyche, who always wanted to go "where all the beauty came from" (a perfection beyond her power to embody or encompass, p. 75). Nor is it that of the Psalmist who, apparently without pain and struggle, "delights" in a claim on his life that comes from Another (heteronomy).[43] Her wounds are still raw. She has not forgotten "the gods' surgery. They used my own pen to probe my wound" (pp. 253–54). The gods "would not let me die till I had died" (p. 281). She had to be dragged to her faith kicking and screaming.

But her "no rebel in me" confession was not mere resignation before superior power. With help from Psyche and the god himself she has learned that the gods actually are beautiful (pp. 173, 301, 304), even if it takes us a long time to recognize this. What is more, she herself had become beautiful. During that brief glimpse of the beautiful god she was told that she would come to know herself, and "You also shall be Psyche" (pp. 172–74). At the end, when Psyche has returned from her exile and the god comes to judge Orual, two figures appear before him. "Two Psyches, both beautiful (if that mattered now) beyond all imagining, yet not exactly the same,"[44] and she hears a voice saying, "You also are Psyche" (pp. 307–8).

Just as Peter says, "You are the Messiah, the Son of the living God" (Matt. 16:16) and Thomas, on the other side of his doubting, confesses, "My Lord and my God" (John 20:28), Orual writes, "I ended my first book with the words *no answer*. I know now, Lord, why you utter no answer. You are yourself the answer. Before your face questions die away. What other answer would suffice?" (p. 308).

These are her dying words. We might say that hers was a deathbed conversion, but not from fear of

> what dreams may come
> When we have shuffled off this mortal coil...⁴⁵

It is because she has discovered something she could not learn from the Fox's philosophy: who she really is.⁴⁶ Although she acknowledges that she has become beautiful in the way that matters most, she doesn't harp on this. Perhaps this is a sign of a new humility; or perhaps because the poet in her (now that philosophy no longer serves to scorn the images and narratives of the poets) has a better language to express the meaning of her transformation. She asks, "How can [the gods] meet us face to face till we have faces?" (p. 294) She now realizes that what her veil had served to hide was not so much her lack of physical beauty, but the fact that her face, with or without the veil, had served only as a false front to hide her true self not only from others but most importantly from herself. "Till we have faces" signifies that her overblown, possessive self was a false self that needed to be deflated (decentered) if she was ever to become and then to know who she truly was.

Orual's journey of self-discovery from the autonomy of Greek philosophy to the heteronomy of a holiness that was at once indescribably beautiful and beyond the power of that philosophy to discover, to teach, or even to comprehend was long and painful. Her testimony to the value of reversing the project of religion within the limits of reason alone is very different from the Psalmist's. Accordingly, her wish is not that it become the hymnbook of the people of the covenant, joyfully subject to the promises and commands of God; she rather hopes, as the new Priest tells us in an epilogue, that someone will take her book to its intended audience, the Greeks. Perhaps both the pre-philosophical polytheists and the philosophical demythologizers of popular religion will learn from her story. Ironically, she dies like Paul, as an apostle to the Greeks.

I do not pretend to be neutral on the questions I've been discussing. I think that biblical heteronomy is a better home for the human spirit than philosophical autonomy. But I have not tried to prove that. By concluding my "argument" with testimony I have sought to call attention to that fact. If I have sought to be a defender of the faith whose content is first of all Abrahamic monotheism and then mere Christianity, it has been in the mode of a defense attorney. The task of such a lawyer is not to prove the defendant innocent, but to show that the prosecution has not proven the defendant guilty beyond a reasonable doubt.

I have tried to show that modern and postmodern versions of the religion-within-the-limits-of-reason-alone project have not shown biblical heteronomy to be guilty in such a way as to validate the hegemony of philosophical theory over biblical revelation. The "not guilty" verdict I have supported has sought to show that the sophisticated versions of this project developed by Spinoza, Kant, and Hegel are rival alternatives to each other as well as to Abrahamic monotheism and mere Christianity. The three philosophical theologies relate, individually and collectively, to the Abrahamic monotheisms including the Christian version the way in which Republicans relate to Democrats, Michigan relates to Ohio State in football, and Walgreens relates to CVS.

This means that the would-be autonomous theologies do not relate to the self-confessedly heteronomous theologies of the book in the way in which adulthood relates to childhood. To assume that they do is to beg too many important questions. To show that one can reject some aspects of the latter theologies outright and systematically reinterpret other themes is not to provide evidence in support of that assumption. It is only to show an irreconcilable difference between Platonic-recollective autonomy and biblical heteronomy, a difference that has long been insisted on from the side of the latter.

Notes

1. See the discussion in chapter 10.
2. For a helpful analysis of such inheritance, see Samir Haddad, *Derrida and the Inheritance of Democracy* (Bloomington: Indiana University Press, 2013).
3. When Thomas Jefferson says, "We hold these truths to be self-evident . . ." the appropriate question is, who are we? and then, what about the slaves? and the women? Such questions do not mean we should be ungrateful to Jefferson, only honest.
4. Martin Heidegger, *Being and Time*, trans. John Macquarrie and Edward Robinson (New York: Harper and Row, 1962), ¶¶34–35, 38.
5. Heidegger, *Being and Time*, ¶42–43. Translation modified.
6. Heidegger, *Being and Time*, ¶35.
7. Heidegger, *Being and Time*, ¶38. We can hear anticipations here of Gadamer's critique of Enlightenment as the prejudice against prejudice.
8. Hubert Dreyfus assimilates Heidegger's talk about language to Wittgenstein's notion of language games, to Gadamer's notion of tradition, and to Foucault's notion of social practices when he identifies Heidegger as a "practical holist." "Holism and Hermeneutics," *Review of Metaphysics* 34, no. 1 (September 1980): 3–23.

9. When T. S. Eliot says, in the final stanza of *Four Quartets* that
   ... the end of our exploring
   Will be to arrive where we started
   And to know it for the first time[,]
this sounds too Platonic, too Cartesian to me; as if there were one definite place at which we made an absolute beginning and to which we could return in recollective reflection.

10. Nicholas Wolterstorff, *Reason within the Bounds of Religion*, 2nd ed. (Grand Rapids, MI: Eerdmans, 1984).

11. I have used such verbs as 'seek' and 'try' to acknowledge that while revelational theologies affirm the primacy of their scriptures, these have to be interpreted by human, all too human thinkers. The scriptures may be divinely inspired, but the theologies that appeal to them are not. (See Ricoeur's warning in chapter 10, at note 15.) That is why Karl Barth finds it necessary to distinguish "revelation" from "religion." See *Church Dogmatics*, vol. I.2, *The Doctrine of the Word of God*, trans. G. W. Bromiley and T. F. Torrance (Edinburgh: T & T Clark, 1956), sec. 17, "The Revelation of God as the Abolition of Religion." 'Abolition' is a terrible translation of *Aufhebung*. Garrett Green corrects this in *On Religion: The Revelation of God as the Sublimation of Religion* (New York: T & T Clark, 2006). 'Sublimation' seems too psychological to me; I prefer 'relativizing.' If revelation as God's speech to us is absolute, our interpretations of that speech are human, all too human, and thus only relative in their authority.

12. G. W. F. Hegel, *Phenomenology of Spirit*, trans. A. V. Miller (Oxford: Clarendon Press, 1977), p. 47.

13. As noted in the Preface above, my argument is "weak," limited in scope. I do not purport to show that people should be monotheists in the Abrahamic sense, much less than they should adopt "mere Christianity." I have rather sought to show that one widespread argument against these options, namely the argument from (or for) autonomy, fails to be convincing. The testimonies that follow present ways of seeing what I've been calling biblical heteronomy as liberating rather than alienating and demeaning.

14. In addition to texts cited in the next two notes, see, for example, C. A. J. Coady, *Testimony* (Oxford: Clarendon Press, 1992) and the discussion in Richard Bauckham, *Jesus and the Eyewitnesses: The Gospels as Eyewitness Testimony* (Grand Rapids, MI: Eerdmans, 2006), chap. 18; Paul Ricoeur, "The Hermeneutics of Testimony," in *Essays on Biblical Interpretation* (Philadelphia, PA: Fortress, 1980), pp. 119–53; and Anne Cubilié, *Women Witnessing Terror: Testimony and the Cultural Politics of Human Rights* (New York: Fordham University Press, 2005). See also the discussion of the relation between trust, authority, and autonomy in Chris Dragos's review of Linda Trinkaus Zagzebski, *Epistemic Authority: A Theory of Trust, Autonomy, and Authority in Belief*, in *Faith and Philosophy* 32, no. 2 (April 2015): 211–19.

15. See Nicholas Wolterstorff, *Thomas Reid and the Story of Epistemology* (New York: Cambridge University Press, 2001).

16. Alvin Plantinga, *Warrant and Proper Function* (New York: Oxford University Press, 1993), p. 77. On the limitations of testimony as a source of knowledge, see pp. 87–88. "Testimonial evidence is indeed evidence; it is not always the evidence of choice."

17. In Greek philosophy happiness or blessedness is *eudaimonia*. The psalmist and the Greek philosopher can be seen as offering rival theories of *eudaimonia*.

18. I am using my favorite version of the Psalter, the one found in *The Book of Common Prayer*.

19. I use a masculine pronoun here in view of the traditional ascription of the Psalms to King David. I make no assumptions about the identity or the gender of the author of any psalm.

20. This juxtaposition of Kant and Nietzsche shows how this aspect of Enlightenment thought lives on in postmodernity. Cf. the "Nietzschean" aspects of the early Hegel as described in chapter 7 above.

21. The psalmist is surely thinking of the revelation through Moses and possibly also of that by some of the subsequent prophets.

22. Friedrich Nietzsche, *The Gay Science*, trans. Walter Kaufmann (New York: Random House, 1974), sec. 343.

23. Especially in Hebrews. Cf. Matt. 26:26–29; Mark 14:22s; Luke 1:54–55, 72–77 and 22:14–20; 1 Cor. 11:23–26; and Ga. 3:16–18.

24. See chapter 7, note 44.

25. Isa. 41:1 and 6; 49:6; 60:3.

26. Did Paul know of the claim by John the Baptist that God could raise up children to Abraham from stones? (Matt. 3:9; and Luke 3:8).

27. See Psalm 2, 18, 22, 33, 45–48, 57, 66–68, 72, 75–76, 82, 86–87, 96–100, 102, 108, 110, 113, 117, 138, 148. Cf. Isa. 2:2–5; 12:4–5; 27:6; 42:1–6; 45:14–25; 49:3–9; 51:4–5; 55:3–5; 60:1–3. See N. T. Wright's discussion of the universal significance of Zion in *The Case for the Psalms: Why They Are Essential* (New York: HarperColllins, 2013), chap. 4, "Where God Dwells" and in *Paul and the Faithfulness of God* (Minneapolis, MN: Fortress, 2013), pp. 1044–58.

28. C. S. Lewis, *Till We Have Faces* (Grand Rapids, MI: Eerdmans, 1966). Page references in the text are to this edition. For the record, I love the Narnia Chronicles and am fond of the science-fiction trilogy but find this novel to be even better than either.

29. From *Metamorphoses* or *The Golden Ass* by the Latin poet Apuleius. Though there are earlier Greek versions.

30. Like the characters Virtue, Fortune, and Love in Monteverdi's opera, *The Coronation of Poppea*, drawing on the tradition of the morality play.

31. Lewis seems to have Rudolf Otto in mind throughout. Ungit is the *mysterium tremendum et fascinans*. *Mysterium* in the darkness and shapelessness of the goddess, beyond image or concept; *tremendum*, overwhelming in a repelling sense in her ominous, nonnegotiable demands for blood sacrifice; and *fascinans* in the beautiful son who, if ever found, might show an attractive side to an otherwise harsh and demanding deity. The priest expresses the *mysterium* to a degree, but mostly the *tremendum*, without a touch of the *fascinans*. He is a power broker, mirror image and well-suited rival of the King. We are reminded of the conflict between Phillip II and the Grand Inquisitor in Verdi's *Don Carlos*.

32. See Plato, *Phaedrus*, 247a, and *Timaeus*, 29d–e; Aristotle, *Metaphysics* I, 982b28–983a5. Following Aristotle, Hegel makes this an epistemological point. "The conception of divine justice in the ancient Greek poets depicts the gods as hostile to those who rise above mediocrity, or are happy or who excel. This conception was dispelled by the purer thought of the Divine. Plato and Aristotle teach that God is not *envious* and does not withhold from mankind knowledge of himself and of Truth. For what else would it be but *envy* if God denied to man a knowledge of God." Hegel's Foreword to H. Fr. W. Hinrichs' *Die Religion im inneren Verhältnisse zur Wissenschaft*, trans. A. V. Miller, in *Beyond Epistemology: New Studies in the Philosophy of Hegel*, ed. Frederick G. Weiss (The Hague: Martinus Nijhoff, 1977), p. 243. Cf. *Lectures on the History of Philosophy, 1825-26*, trans. Robert F. Brown and J. M. Steward (Oxford: Clarendon Press, 2006), II, 208.

33. Cf. p. 70, "Do you know, Sister, I have come to feel more and more that the Fox hasn't the whole truth. Oh, he has much of it. It'd be dark as a dungeon within me but for his teaching. And yet..." (Ellipsis in Lewis's text).

34. In multicultural theory decentering involves a challenge to making Western (or perhaps Northern) civilization and culture the fixed norm for the rest of the world (the East and the South). In postmodern philosophy, decentering is a challenge to the (de facto and de jure) autonomy of the Platonic/Cartesian "rational" subject or self as the fixed and final authority for knowing, doing, and being. The hermeneutics of Gadamer and Ricoeur, the genealogy of Foucault, and the deconstruction of Derrida are all theories of decentering or relativizing the self. See, for example, Jacques

Derrida, "Structure, Sign, and Play in the Discourse of the Social Sciences," in *Writing and Difference*, trans. Alan Bass (Chicago: University of Chicago Press, 1978), pp. 278–93. He argues that every posited center is relative to, challenged by, and in various contexts replaced by some other center in a process that can be halted only arbitrarily.

35. In *Works of Love*, Kierkegaard argues that erotic love and friendship are forms of self-love, not because they are always selfish but because they are preferential. We choose lovers and friends because of what we hope to get out of the relationship. Those who are not attractive to us in this way remain unchosen. Such love is also spontaneous; it comes naturally to us and does not require conversion and transformation of our natural self-centeredness.

36. See note 35 above.

37. Both Plato and Aristotle speak of the poets as liars in spite of Aristotle's praise of poetry.

38. See note 29 above.

39. In *Fear and Trembling*, Kierkegaard insists that that from the standpoint of Hegelian "Reason," biblical faith in the person of Abraham must look like madness, an absurd paradox.

40. In *Suspicion and Faith: The Religious Uses of Modern Atheism* (New York: Fordham University Press, 1998), I have defined the hermeneutics of suspicion as "*the deliberate attempt to expose the self-deceptions involved in hiding our actual operative motives from ourselves, individually or collectively, in order not to notice how and how much our behavior and our beliefs are shaped by values we profess to disown*" (p. 13).

41. C. B. Macpherson describes liberal capitalism as "the political theory of possessive individualism" in his book by that title. Moving from politics and economics to morality and religion and from theory to practice, Orual's memoir confesses to another kind of possessive individualism.

42. Friedrich Nietzsche, *Thus Spoke Zarathustra*, part II, 2, "Upon the Blessed Isles."

43. Levinas is more nearly Kantian. We find duty but not delight in his account of the other's unconditional claims on us. That is one of the reasons I read him as an atheist.

44. "Not exactly the same." St. John of the Cross is fond of saying that while God is divine by nature, we become "gods through participation." *The Collected Works of St. John of the Cross*, trans. Kieren Kavanaugh and Otilio Rodriguez (Washington, DC: ICS Publications, 1991), pp. 93, 560–61, 671, 677, 706; cf. p. 595. The Pauline way of making a very similar point is to say that we are children of God by adoption. See Rom. 8:15, 23; Gal. 4:5; and Eph. 1:5.

45 Shakespeare, *Hamlet*, III, 1, 67–68.

46. Without having read Calvin's *Institutes*, she has learned that we only come to know who we are as we come to understand who God is (I.1.1).

INDEX

Abrahamic monotheism(s), xvi, xxi, 225–26, 227n13; divine revelation versus human reason in, 71, 82n54, 213–14; Freud and, xiii–xiv; God's covenant with Abraham, xvi, xviii, 135, 145nn46 & 47, 217; Hegel and, 132–33, 139, 141, 154; Islam, xxiv (note 8), 35n11; Kant and, 84, 104; Kierkegaard and, 229n35. *See also* Judaism/Jews
absentee landlord God, 70
Absolute Knowing, 153, 154–56, 162, 163n4, 168, 198–99
Absolute Self, 129, 163n2, 175
Absolute Spirit, 149–51, 163n4, 170–73, 175, 178–79, 187n44
Ackroyd, Peter, 186n29
acosmism, 140
action theory and executive autonomy, 4–5
Adorno, Theodore W., 65
agency: and deism, 68–71, 77–78, 81n43, 84; and executive autonomy, 2, 7, 20n33; as mark of personal God, 84; and personhood, 6, 68; restricted, 81n43; wrong to impede others,' 18n12
Age of the Crisis of Man, The (Greif), 194–95
ahistorical purity claims, 48
Alexandrian tradition, 55n13
Allison, Henry, 18n11, 21n48
Alpha Point (immediacy), 198–99
"always already," 197, 199, 205, 208n36
America as "God's own Country," xiii–xiv
Ameriks, Karl, 158
analogy, 25, 81n42
Anderson, Pamela Sue, 113
Anselm, 21n53, 34n5, 121n39

anthropomorphisms, 25, 28, 47
"antitheological," Hegel as, 124–25
apatheia and *ataraxia*, 46, 50
"apocalyptic objectivity," 204
a priori, the, 113, 190, 192
Aquinas, Thomas, 25, 35n17, 81n41
Arab clan, 138, 167–68, 175
Archimedes, xxii
Aristotle, 28, 74, 82n55, 151–52, 168, 228n32
art: C. S. Lewis and, 221; Hegel on, 149, 171–74, 181, 187n44; Mann on, 22n61
assertoric knowledge or faith, 86
ataraxia and *apatheia*, 46, 50
atheism: Derrida and, 200–201; Feuerbach and, 113, 184nn4 & 7; Fichte and, 129, 131; Hegel and, 131, 140–42; Kant and, 113; Levinas and, 229n43; Marx and, 184n4; methodological, 81n45; no epistemic privilege to unbelief, 201; pantheism as, 140–42; and postmodernism, xx, xxi; Spinoza and, 31–34, 37n41, 67, 142
Athens and Rome, 131
atonement: Hegel on, 126, 128, 134–35, 143n13; versus justification, 82n56, 121n34; Kant on, 108–11, 115, 121nn34 & 35, 128; sacrifice as, 143n13; satisfaction theory of, 121n39; versus victory over death, 121n37
aufgehoben, 140–41, 149, 179
aufheben, 161–62
Augustine, 19n24, 23, 73, 158–59, 207n16
Aulén, Gustaf, 121n37
aus Pflicht, 4, 7
authenticity and autonomy, 213

231

author not claiming neutrality, xxiii, 225
autonomy, 2, 6, 7; automotive metaphor of, 3; demise of, 195; democracy as political form of, 98n38; epistemic, 69, 71, 85, 88, 104, 132; executive, 2–4, 6–8, 18n12, 19n28, 58; as foundation of morality, 20n33; Kant equating legislative and moral, 8, 11–12, 58; as secondary, 190, 199–200
autonomy project, xvi–xviii, xix, 107, 184; argument against, 211; Hegel's hegemony of speculative reason, 183; heteronomy versus, 3, 6–7; Kant's, 119n12; legislative mode of, 23; Luther and Hegel, 183; Orual and, 220; Psalms and, 216; versus "scandal of particularity," xviii; Spinoza and, 53; straying from biblical roots, 18n16; three versions of, 182; and universality claims, xvii, 189
Axiom of Transparency, 159–60

Bach, Johann Sebastian, 121n40
bad faith (Sartre), 165nn42 & 45
Badiou, Alain, xx
Baillie, John, 5–6
Barth, Karl, 34n5, 57n36, 208n24, 227n11
"Battle Hymn of the Republic" (Howe), 35n10
Baumgarten, Alexander, 81n42
beatific vision (Spinoza), 45
Begriffe (Concepts), 156, 163n4, 164n24, 170–71, 175, 180
Being and Nothingness (Sartre), 165nn42 & 45
Beiser, Frederick, 152
"belatedness," 209n50
Bennett, Jonathan, 29, 36nn26, 31, 56n23
biases and prejudices, 16–17, 47, 55n16
Bible: allegorical, "spiritual" interpretation of, 55n13; and biblical heteronomy, 214–15, 225–26, 227n13; and biblical monotheism, 24–25; Book of Amos, xiv; Book of Genesis, 20n43, 121n43, 135, 145n46, 145n48; Book of Isaiah, 40, 121n40; Book of Psalms, 14, 19n31, 62, 167, 215–17; Book of Revelation, 37n34, 135; divine authority of, 40, 49; elitism toward, 211–12; Epistle to Philemon, 111; Epistle to the Romans, xxi, 14, 82n52, 86, 111, 121n39, 158; Epistles to Timothy, 133, 178–79; Epistle to Titus, 178; First Epistle of John, 40; First Epistle of Peter, xiv, 121n40; God as supreme authority, 10; God's election of Israel, 48; Gospel of John, 121n40, 122n49; Gospel of Matthew, 11; as highest norm, 41; Holy Spirit and, 40; Kant and, 64, 96, 107, 109, 116, 118, 120n27; as lacking authority, 49; Luther's translation of, 179; Palmquist on, 122n62; as postmodern legislative heteronomy, 3–4; retributivist views in, 15; Second Epistle to Corinthians, 134; *sola scriptura* doctrine, 41–43, 49; speech acts in, 25, 84; Spinoza on, 49–50, 52, 54n9; theme of divine judgment in, 14; "vengeance" translation in, 14, 21n56; writers of and "religious genius," 97n15
biblical faith: Hegel on, 54n7, 229n39; and hermeneutical turn, xxi; Luther on human reason and, 54n7; Ricoeur on, 193; as "slave religion," 218
Black September group, 21n55
blood, connections of, 140
Bloom, Harold, 55n19, 205n1, 206n2, 208n29, 209n50
Blumenberg, Hans, xxiv (note 6), 17n5
Bonhoeffer, Dietrich, 39, 54n1
book of nature, 198
Burrell, David, 81n41
Butler, Clark, 143n19, 163n7
Butler, E. M., 142n3
Butler, Joseph, 69
Byrne, Peter, 66, 72, 77, 82n56, 85, 96n2, 106–7, 121n34

Calvin, John, 40–41, 54n6
Canner, Abigail, 33
Caputo, John D (Jack), xx, 56n32, 214
Carter, Stephen L., 37n50
Cassirer, Ernst, 120n18
categorical imperative, 6–8, 12, 18n16, 64
censorship, 18n9, 23, 35n14, 38, 65, 103
changes of form, content, 172
Chignell, Andrew, 114
"chosen people," xiii, xvii–xviii
Christianity: and autonomy project, 18n16; Climacus on, 123n70; as consummate (*vollendete*) religion, 156; C. S. Lewis on, xvii–xviii; God's authority within, 10; Hegel and, 124–34, 137, 170, 176, 179, 185n12; as heteronomous, 66, 130–33; and Incarnation, 174, 179–81, 187n48; Jesus "rescued" from Judaism, 130, 133–36, 170, 187n48; Kant and, 57n35, 64, 76, 94–96, 104–5, 116–18; reason for success of, 130–31; as slave religion, 116, 218. *See also* Abrahamic monotheism(s); Bible; mere Christianity
church and state: as babysitters, 21n46; claiming divine authority, 10–11; separation of, 130, 192
clan, Arab concept of, 138, 167–68, 175
classics, meaning of, 44, 55n17
Cleopatra, 32
Climacus, Johannes (pseud.), 17n6, 35n17, 118, 123n70
commandments, 4, 145n37, 216–17

"commands (laws) of morality" (Kant), 12
concentric circles, Kant's experiment, 106–7
"conflict of interpretations" (Ricoeur), 17, 29, 49, 65, 191
consciousness, 157–58, 171–72, 180, 207n13
consequentialism, 21n49, 22n58
consubstantiality, 137
"consume and consummate" (*aufheben*), 161–62
"contradiction" (Hegel), 165n46
conversion (Kant), 72, 74, 75–78, 108–10, 112
Cooper Union speech (Lincoln), 1
Copernicus, 158
"counsels of prudence" (Kant), 12
"counter-memory" (Foucault), 204
"court of pure reason" (Kant), 13
covenant: basic structure of Hebrew faith, 217; making, breaking, renewal, 135–36; monotheism, 25, 35n13
creational monotheism, 25
Cur Deus Homo? (Anselm), 121n39
Curley, Edwin, 37n36

Darwin, Charles, 146n62, 158
Davenport, John, 18n10
David, King, 54n7, 167
Death in Venice (Mann), 22n61
decentering, 20n45, 220–21, 224–25, 228n34
deconstruction, 197, 208n36
deism: and agency, 68, 84; Dryden's, Stillingfleet's, Johnson's, 84; epistemic, 69, 85; Kant's, 66–68; and natural religion, 84–91, 93–96, 128; of restricted agency, 81n43; and revelation, 96n2; versus theism, 68–69; Wood's synthesis, 84
Deissmann, Adolf, 97n15
delusions, religious and philosophical, 108
democracy as political form of autonomy, 98n38
Derrida, Jacques, xxi, xxiii, 35n9, 197–202, 214; on autonomy, 199–200; and Hegel, 197–99; on language, 200; "nothing outside the text," 197, 199; on presence, 194; on rabbis and poets, 201, 209–10n53; on religion, 199–200; "religion without religion" project, xx
Descartes, René, 190, 196
design argument, 69
Despland, Michael, 65
detective fiction, 191
Deus sive natura, 26, 30, 96, 161
dialectical image of God, xiv
Dialectic of the first Critique (Kant), 114, 122n55
Dichotomy (*Entzweiung*), 160
Dickens, Charles, 22n61

Difference between Fichte's and Schelling's System of Philosophy, The (Hegel), 159
di Giovanni, George, 83n64, 91, 103, 116
Diotima, 45
divided line, 45, 46
divine agency/assistance: deists' views of, 68–71, 81n44, 84; Kant's view of, 70–71, 73, 75, 77–78, 83n74, 109, 115; revelation as special case of, 81n43, 94, 108; and watchmaker God, 69
divine revelation, xxiii, 87; Bible as, 40; conflicting traditions on, 49; heteronomy/autonomy and, xv, xvii–xx, xxiii, 18n9, 26, 48; versus human reason, xv, xx, xxiii, 15–17, 71, 82n54, 154, 183, 200–201, 211–12; inner versus outer, 118n2; Kant and, 13, 17, 85, 90, 93–94, 103–5, 115; Luther on, 24; "religions of the book" and, 214–16; Runzo on, 98n24; through speech acts, 84. *See also* heteronomy
divine wrath, justice, love, 15
dogmatic hegemony, 26
Dreyfus, Hubert, 226n8
Dryden, John, 84
Durkheim, Emile, 144n32

Early Theological Writings (Hegel), 124
Eckhart, Meister, 141
"écrasez l'infâme," 95
Eddington, Sir Arthur, 165n36
Eden, serpent in, 20n43
editing God, xiv
education of the human race thesis, 93
Eliot, T. S., 227n9
elitism, 47–48, 110–11; in biblical reinterpretation, 211
"end of history," 156
engine, executive autonomy and, 3
Enlightenment: autonomy, 2, 3–4; autonomy and heteronomy, 201–4; claiming universality, xvii; eliminating mystery from religion, 24; as emergence from childhood, 94, 183; Hegel and, 125, 142n7, 168; people as ethical beings, 54n1; philosophy as critique, 201; postmodern critique of, 213; presuppositions of, 26; project of, 23; as tradition, 202; universal doubt strategies, 196
epistemic autonomy: and deism, 69, 71, 85, 88; and developmental dependence, 104; and Hegel, 132
Erscheinung, 179
eschatology, 155–56, 175–76, 198–99
Ethical Life (*Sittlichkeit*) (Hegel), 145n39
Ethics (Spinoza), 27–28, 36nn23 & 24, 38–39, 45
Eucharist, 136

eudaimonia, 227n17
evidentialist/classical foundationalist model, 65
executive autonomy, 2–4, 6–8, 18n12, 19n28, 58
executive heteronomy, 3
existentialism, 159–60
exteriority, 195–205

factory- versus dealer-installed options, 212
faith: as "objective uncertainty," 193; pure faith unreliable, 101; versus reason, 35n17; in reason or in revelation, xx–xxi, xxiv
Faith and Reason (Hegel), 159
"false self-evidence," 204
fascinans, God as, xiv–xv
fear of error or fear of truth, 215
felix culpa "happy fault," 134
Feuer, Lewis Samuel, 32
Feuerbach, Ludwig, 78, 113, 131–32, 161, 167, 184n4
Feyerabend, Paul, 165n36
Fichte, Johann Gottlieb, 128–29, 157–61, 165–66n49, 186n24
'fideism,' xx
finite in the infinite, 162
Firestone, Chris L., 66, 82n55, 88, 94, 105, 113–16
Fish, Stanley, xix, xxi
folk religion, 125–31
formula(e): of categorical imperative, 7–9; of the covenant, 217; *Deus sive natura*, 26, 30, 96, 161; kingdom of ends, 8–9, 18n12; of Universal Law and of Autonomy, 20n37, 21n50
Forster, Michael N., 150, 164n23
Foucault, Michel, 195–96, 204
Fox (C. S. Lewis character), 218–25
freedom: and autonomy, 2–3, 18n11, 200; deduction of, 71; as defined by Kant, 2; and evil, 82n55; and folk religion, 127; of God, 28, 30, 37nn34 & 35, 67–68; and heteronomy, 211; of the press, 17, 18n9, 23, 38–39, 58, 192; and prisoner analogy, 46; of speech, 38–39, 192; "Spinozism of," 127–28, 132, 139–40, 148, 167–68; of the will, 18n14
Freud, Sigmund: on blows to "self-love," 158; experiencing anti-Semitism, xxiv (note 2); faith as infantile, 217; on Groddeck, 18n14; on heteronomy, 183; "'lived' by unknown . . . forces," 3, 190; on religion as wish fulfillment, xiii–xiv, xxi

Gadamer, Hans-Georg, 16, 22n63, 47, 65, 102, 202–5
genealogy (Foucault), 204, 228n34
genealogy of biblical religion (Nietzsche), 15, 21n57, 127
Genesis, Book of, 20n43, 121n43, 135, 145nn46 & 48

geoffenbarte religion, 185n12
German Idealism, 148
Gesetzgebung, 7
gnosticism, 149, 163n7
God: attaining consciousness, 149; as cause, world as effect, 30; compared to Internal Revenue Service, 95; "desire for glory and dominion," 14; as doting Grandfather, xiv–xv; editing, xiv; as *fascinans*, xiv–xv; as "it" versus "he," 36n26; Kant on promises of, 104; rendered guilty by association, 11; responsibilities of, 68; source of our concept of, 13; as speaker, 35n13; Spinoza's redefinition of, 28–29; as undemocratic, xviii; as vigilante, 14–15
Goethe, Johann Wolfgang von, 36n27
Goldilocks parenting, xiv
grace, four means of, 63
grammatico-historical hermeneutic, 42, 51–53
Grandfather, God as doting, xiv–xv
Greek "folk religion," 125, 127
Green, Garrett, 227n11
Greene, Theodore M., 91
Gregory, Philippa, 20n42
Greif, Mark, 194–95
Groddeck, Georg, 18n14, 190
Groundwork of the Metaphysics of Morals (Kant), 2, 4–9, 11–13, 16, 71–72
guilt before and after conversion, 95, 108–9

Habermas, Jürgen, 18n13, 146n62, 209n45
Hanson, N. R., 194
happy versus good, 12
Hardenberg, Friedrich von (Novalis), 31
Hare, John E., 6, 18n 12, 21n50, 57n35, 78, 79n5, 94, 96, 104
harmony thesis (Kant), 105–8, 118
Harnack, Adolf, 136
Harris, H. S., 150, 152, 164n26, 166n53
Hart, Kevin, 54n1, 163n7, 187n42, 209n39
Hatfield, Henry, 36n27
Haufniensis, Vigilius, 62
Hayden, Franz Josef, 121n43
Hegel, G. W. F., 51; and atheism, 140–42, 151; and Christianity, 124–34, 137, 170, 176, 179, 185n12; claims to universality, xvii; correspondence with Schelling, 128–29; early works of, 124; on Fichte, 128; on folk religion, 125–27; and freedom of speech, 144n25; on Gospel of John (verses 1:12–14), 137; hermeneutical theory of, 169–70; and immediacy, 194; on Jesus, 133, 136; on Jews, 130–33, 136, 137; on Kant, 149, 160–61;

on 'life' versus 'nation,' 168; love more basic than life, 139; and mere Christianity, 133–34, 174; on need of philosophy, 160; pantheism, 30, 125, 140, 161, 168; parts as same as whole, 138; philosophies as children of their times, 196; redefining God, 168; on reflective thinking, 139; reinterpretation strategy, 170; on separation of church and state, 130; on sex, 146n60; sociological pantheism of, 132; and Spinoza, 138–42, 148–51; on Spirit, 149–50

Hegel's Idea (Forster), 164n23

Hegel's Ladder (Harris), 164n26, 166n53

Hegel's theologische Jugendschriften (Nohl), 124

hegemony thesis (Kant), 100, 102, 105–6

Heidegger, Martin, 36n25, 213; on authenticity, 213; "*die Sprache spricht*," 190; phenomenology "corrects" theology, xx; sight grounded in understanding, 194

Heine, Heinrich, 31, 143n21

Henrich, Dieter, 126–27, 139, 145n39, 158

Herberg, Will, xvii

Herbert of Cherbury, 81n44

hermeneutical situation: exteriority, 195–205; particularity, 190–91; penultimacy, 191–95

hermeneutical turn, xix–xxiii, 153–54, 168–69, 191–201, 205, 212–14

hermeneutics: Caputo on, xx; Gadamer on prejudice within, 16; hermeneutical hegemony, 27; Kant's principles, 100–107; of suspicion, xv, xxi, 159, 165n44, 204, 223

Herodotus, 87

Heterodox Hegel, The (O'Regan), 163n7

heteronomy, 1, 2, 7; Allison on, 21n48; biblical, 214–15, 225–26, 227n13; as defined by Kant, 7, 10; and divine revelation, xv, xvii–xx, xxiii, 18n9, 26, 48; and Enlightenment, 201–4; executive, 3; freedom and, 211; Freud and, 183; hermeneutics as, 203; as inevitable, 53, 201; Luther and, 183; mode of severity of God, xv; not based on universal reason, 66; postmodern legislative, 3–4

heteronomy versus autonomy project, 3, 6–7

Hilliman, Jonathan, 33

historical holism, 126

"historical Kant," 79n7

historicism, 152–55, 164n23

Hobbes, Thomas, 146n62

Holy Communion, 136

Holy Spirit, 40, 181

homo economicus, 131

homoousious, 137–38, 146n53, 180

"horizon" (Gadamer), 203

Horkheimer, Max, 65

Howe, Julia Ward, 35n10

Hudson, Hoyt H., 91

human being as divine being (Feuerbach), 131

humanity as end not means, 7

human reason: and biblical heteronomy, 215; both finite and fallen, xxi; divine revelation versus, xv, xx, xxiii, 15–17, 71, 82n54, 154, 183, 200–201, 211–12; faith goes against, 35n17; Hegel on, 222; Luther on, 54n7; modernity's self-deification of, 4, 199; moral law embedded in, 110, 113; Spinoza on, 43, 48–49; universality of, xxi, 8, 191, 211; Wood on, 85

humans "begotten not made," 138

Hume, David, 69

husk and kernel, 111

Husserl, Edmund, xvi, xxv (note 20)

Hyppolite, Jean, 151–52, 164n25, 180, 187n44

Idea (Kant), 112–14, 122n47

ideology, xxv (note 30), 159–60, 204, 215

imagination, Spinoza on, 36n20

immanence versus transcendence, 181

immediacy: Derrida and, 199; Hegel and, 173, 179–80, 194, 209n39; mediated, 210n64

"immediate truth," 177

immortality, God and: Hegel on, 125, 143n15; Kant on, 58–62, 70–72, 77–78, 115–16, 122n55

Impeachment of Abraham Lincoln, The (Carter), 37n50

Incarnation, 174, 179–81, 187n48. See also Christianity

inclination and duty (Kant), 4–6, 8, 60–61, 72

"infinite resignation," 33, 46

"informed consent," 19n19

Innocence Project, 192

"intellectual love of 'God'" (Spinoza), 31–33, 46

Internal Revenue Service, God compared to, 95

intuition, 45–46, 172–73, 194, 209n39

"iron cage," 46

Isaiah, Book of, 9–10, 40, 121n40

Islam, xxiv (note 8), 35n11

Israel, Jonathan, 52–53, 55n16

I/We structure of Spirit, 177–78, 181, 186n35

Jacobi, F. H., 35n16, 129, 160

Jacobs, Nathan, 66, 82n55, 88, 111, 113–16

Jaeschke, Walter, 175, 185n12, 186n28

Jefferson, Thomas, 56n31, 226n3

Jenseits, 175, 177, 179, 181

Jesus: as everyone, 174; as example to follow, 110–11; 'having been,' 180; Hegel on, 130, 133, 136, 167, 187n46; Incarnation, 174, 179–81, 187n48; law in two Commandments, 64; "rescued" from Judaism, 130, 133–36, 170. *See also* Christianity

John, First Epistle of, 40

John, Gospel of, 111, 121n40, 122n49, 137

John of the Cross, 137, 229n44

Johnson, Samuel, 84

John the Baptist, 103–4

Jones, Rufus, 83n67

Judaism/Jews: connection of Christianity to, 104, 130, 133–36, 170, 187n48; God's covenant with Abraham, xvi, xviii, 135, 145nn46 & 47, 217; Hegel on, 130–31, 145n37. *See also* Abrahamic monotheism(s)

jury verdicts, 192

justification, doctrine of, 82n56; versus atonement, 82n56, 121n34; Kant's, 70, 74–75, 108–9; Pauline, 95, 121n39

justified belief, 114, 205

"justifying grace," 121n34

just punishment, retributivist view of, 15

Kant, Immanuel, xvi, 2–9, 11, 16, 20n35, 104; on atonement, 108–11, 115, 121nn34 & 35; belief in God a need not a duty, 98n27; and Christianity, 57n35; "Christology" of, 108, 111, 113; claims to universality, xvii, 65–66; classification of moral principles, 12; as a deist, 66–68, 71, 77–78, 95; delusion of God's promises, 104; delusion of service to God, 63; denying knowledge for faith, 61, 71; dispensability thesis, 103–4; dogma as scaffolding, 98n31; experiments, 106–7; on forced interpretations, 100–101, 106; and freedom of press, 58; God as moral governor, 59; good prejudices of, 17; on grace, 63, 77; harmony thesis, 105–8, 118; Hegel on, 160; hegemony thesis, 100, 102, 105–6; historical particularity of, 107; on Holy Spirit, 112; humans as radically evil, 71–72; immortality, God, and freedom, 58–59, 61–62, 70–72, 77, 115; immortality and happiness, 59, 115; inconsistencies in, 5; on justification, 70, 95, 108; kingdom of ends, 8, 9; legislative and executive autonomy, 58; meaning of "literal," 119n4; means/end thesis, 102–3; on minority, 2; *minority* as defined by, 2; moral feelings as superficial (Kant), 13; morality leading to religion, 58, 62–65; moral versus physical feeling, 12; moving beyond "rational ethics," 62; natural versus revealed religion, 86, 90–93; need to be worthy of grace, 75; New Testament as source, not authority, 104; "ontological" version of morality, 13; own religion incompatible with Christianity, 116–17; and Plato, 121n42, 122n47; "polemical redefinitions," 116; prototype of Son of God, 111–16, 121n44; pure rationalism versus supernaturalism, 92–93; radical evil, 59, 61–62, 71, 77, 115–16, 128; as a rationalist, 87, 91–92; reason and revelation, 13, 85–86, 90, 94, 96; recollection thesis, 104–5; redefining of biblical material, 96; relationship with parents, 120n18; on *Religion*, 120n27; religion within the limits of reason alone, 58; on self-incurred minority, 2; similarities with Feuerbach, 113; similarities with Marcion, 13–14; on Son of God, 110–12; statutory versus moral teachings, 101; summary of general revelation, xxiv (note 7); "theological" version of morality, 13; thinking beyond knowledge, 114; three philosophical questions, 59; "vicious circularity" in, 106–7; "What Is Enlightenment?," 2, 17n8, 23

kattallag 'reconciliation,' 134

Kearney, Richard, xx, 214

kernel versus husk, 106, 111, 117–18

Kierkegaard, Søren, 33, 73, 75, 145n40, 193, 200, 229n35

Kingdom of God, 103, 109, 139, 187n42, 188n51, 203

kingdom of heaven, 11

Kitcher, Philip, 22n61

Knox, T. M., 124

Koran, 84

Korsgaard, Christine, 19n28

Kuhn, Thomas, 57n39, 102, 164n23, 194

Kuhnrath, Heinrich, 38

language games, 197–201, 205, 206n6

Latourette, Kenneth Scott, 188n50

Law of God, xv, 215–17

Lectures on the Philosophy of Religion (Hegel), 170

legislative autonomy: children and, 10–11; confusion with executive autonomy, 8; definition of, 7; justification for, 6; and self-legislation, 8–9

legislative heteronomy, 3

legitimating norm of moral law, 8

Lessing, Gotthold Ephraim, 187n40, 222; and cosmopolitan universality, 182; on Islam, 35n11; *Nathan the Wise* (Lessing), 35n11, 130, 143n10, 182; on orthodoxy, 143n20; "pantheism controversy" and, 35n16; and Spinoza, 128–30; on truths of reason, 25–26

levels of knowing, Spinoza on, 45–46

Levinas, Emmanuel, 206n3, 209n47, 221, 229n43
Lewis, C. I., 192
Lewis, C. S., xvii–xviii, 16, 25, 218–24
Lincoln, Abraham, 1, 35n10
linguistic turn, 197
"literal," meaning of, 119n4
Locke, John, 142n5
Logic (Hegel), 172
Lord's Prayer, 20n45
love, redefining, 33, 139–40
Luther, Martin, xxiv (note 4), 24, 40–41, 73, 34n7, 35n8, 183
Lutheranism, 63–64, 73, 143n8, 167, 184n2

MacIntyre, Alasdair, 28, 206n8, 210n65
Maimonides, 43, 46, 52, 55n13
Mann, Thomas, 22n61
Marcion, xiii–xv, 13–14, 16
Marx, Karl, xxi, 184n4, 204
"masters of suspicion," 19n18
Matthew, Book of, 11
McCammon, Christopher, 83n74
meaning versus truth, 43–44, 120n31
means/end thesis (Kant), 100, 102, 106
medieval consensus of revelation over reason, 23, 34n5
Meno (Socrates), xv, 68, 87, 92, 104, 112
mercy and justice, 108
mere Christianity, xxi, xxiii, 16, 64, 94; Freud on, 183; and Hegel, 133–34, 137–38, 174; incompatible with Kant's, 107, 116–17; Luther and, 183; universality of, 101
Mere Christianity (Lewis), 25
mere monotheism, 48–49, 51–52
mere reason, 85
mere theism, 25, 27–28, 33, 34n3
Metaphysics and Logic (Hegel), 151–55, 166n57, 170
metaphysics of morals, 163n6
"method of tenacity," xxii
Meyer, Ludwig (Lodewijk Meijer), 43, 52
Michalson, Gordon E. Jr., 66, 74, 78, 83n75, 113, 116, 120n21; on Kant, 102–3, 121n38
miracles, Spinoza's rejection of, 26
missionary task, 187n48
Modern Freedom (Peperzak), 163n5
modernity, rise of, 11
"modern" versus "postmodern" philosophies, xxv (note 19)
Monk, William, 139–40
moral heteronomy, xv
moral law, three presentations of, 9

moral maturity, duty and, 6
Moral Philosophy (Kant), 23
moral psychology, 4, 6, 8
moral sense philosophies (Kant), 11–13, 16
Moser, Paul, xv
"motivated irrationality," xxi
motivated self-deception, 165n45
Munich Olympics, 21n66
murder mysteries, 191
"must always already," 197
mysterium tremendum et fascinans, God as, xiv–xv
mystery, elimination from religion, 24
mythos-to-logos story, 102

Nadler, Steven, 36n24
Nancy, Jean-Luc, xx
Nathan the Wise (Lessing), 35n11, 130, 143n10, 182
natural consciousness (untrue knowledge), 155–57
naturalism, 26, 87, 89
natural languages, 196
natural law, 68, 146n62
natural reason, 40
natural religion, 84–91, 93–96, 128
"natura naturans" versus "natura naturata," 30, 37n36
Nazi ideology of blood and soil, 140
necessary truths of reason, 101–2
new covenant, 145nn47 & 48, 217
Nicene Creed, 136–38
Nietzsche, Friedrich: as admirer of Spinoza, 53; cheerfulness over death of God, 217; denying freedom of will, 18n14; *Ecce Homo*, 143n14; on foolishness versus sin, 127; "human, all too human," 4; influencing Kant, 116; "ressentiment," 15; on revenge versus justice, 21–22n57; Zarathustra, 224
Nohl, Herman, 124
no neutral standpoint, xxi–xxii
Novalis (Friedrich von Hardenberg), 31
"nowhere," thought not beginning, xxi

Oatman, Johnson Jr., 134
obedience to law as liberty, 19n32
objective and subjective religion (Hegel), 125
Objective Spirit, 170–71, 175, 177
occasionalism, 105, 120n22
Oedipus, 3
old man and new, 109–10
Omega Point (totality), 199
On the Genealogy of Morals (Nietzsche), 15
onto-theology, 36n25, 78, 81n39

O'Regan, Cyril, 163n7
Orual (Queen of Glome), 218–25
"otherworldliness," 113
Otto, Rudolf, xiii–xiv, 228n31
"ought implies can" principle, 70, 72–78

Paley, William, 69
Palmquist, Stephen R., 96, 99n42, 103, 116, 122n62
pantheism: in Germany, 143n21; and good and evil, 141; Hegel and, 127, 133, 135, 139–41, 173–74; "pantheism controversy," 35n16; of spirit, 139–40, 167; versus theism, 30, 81n41; Tillich on defining, 36n33
paradigm shift, 57n39, 164n23, 194
particularity of the a priori, 190–91
Paul (Apostle): believers as adopted by God, 137; doctrine of justification, 95, 108, 121n39; and duties to God, 86; Gentiles as heirs of covenant, 217; and John the Baptist's claim, 228n26; as philosopher, 34n6; as religious genius, 97n15; and second unification, 134; and spirit of God, 41; on suppression of truth, xxi, 158
Peirce, Charles Sanders, xxii
penultimacy, 191–95, 198
Peperzak, Adriaan T., 163n5
perfect being theology, 13, 21n53
perfection traditions, Kant on, 13
Perry, Anne, 139
personal God concept: biblical monotheism and, 24; Hegel and, 128–29, 138, 167, 173, 178–79; Kant and, 68; requires agency and speech, 24, 84, 217; Schelling, Fichte on, 128–29; Spinoza and, 53
personhood and agency, 6
"person-relativity," 210n70
"persuasive definition," 27
Peter, Apostle, 224
Peter, First Epistle of, xiv, 121n40
phenomenal knowledge (*das erscheinende Wissen*), 154
phenomenology, xvi, xx, 16, 150–51, 209n39
Phenomenology of Spirit (Hegel), 148–56, 160–62, 164n23, 168–72, 176–81
Philemon, Epistle to, 111
philosophical hermeneutics, 159, 194
Philosophy, Interpreter of Scripture (Meyer), 43
Philosophy as Rigorous Science (Husserl), xvi
Philosophy of Identity (Schelling), 161
Philosophy of Religion (Kant), 23
Philosophy of Right (Hegel), 140, 153, 177
Philosophy of Spirit (Hegel), 170, 172, 177
physical versus moral feeling (Kant), 12

Pippin, Robert, 19n32
Plantinga, Alvin, xxvi (note 34), 194, 215
Plato/Platonism: epistemic, 123n70; hoi polloi, 47; Kant's Platonic pietism, 121n42; and revelation of beauty, 45; Socrates and the slave boy, 68, 87, 104; and Son of God prototype, 112–14; truth, knowledge as recollection, xv, xvi, 158
"plausibility structure," xxi, xxv (note 30)
poets, 201
Polanyi, Michael, 196–97
"polemical redefinitions" (Kant), 116
political censorship, 35n14
politically liberal thinkers, 206n8
"Positivity of the Christian Religion, The" (Hegel), 128, 129
postmodernism: atheism and, xx, xxi; Bible and, 3–4; and hermeneutical turn, xix–xx, 193–95, 205, 213–14; no non-circular arguments, 56n32; and the *tremendum*, xv
pou sto, desire for epistemic, xxii
practical unreason, 50
pragmatism, 22n62
presence, 161, 194, 197, 199, 209n39
present conditioned by past, 203
presuppositionless philosophy/reason, 16, 26, 51–53, 100–102, 153–54, 169, 194, 211
presuppositions: and circular reasoning, 158; and heteronomy, 212–13; interpretation guided by, 191; Kant's, 13, 108; unavoidable, xxii
Preuss, J. Samuel, 49
priesthood of the believer, 39–40
Primal Presuppositions, 49
"principle of autonomy of the will" (Kant), 7, 9
"principle of happiness" (Kant), 12
"principle of humanity" (Kant), 7–8
"principle of perfection" (Kant), 12
prisoner analogy, 46
prodigal son, 95
progress and justification, 108–9
promises as covenantal speech acts, 217
Protagoras, 17n6
Protestant Reformation principles, 39–40
"protest of reason," 27
prototype of Son of God (Kant), 111–16, 121n44
providential monotheism, 25
Psalms, Book of, 14, 19n31, 62, 167, 215–17
Psyche (Till We Have Faces), 218–24
psychoanalysis, 158–59
punishment, conversion as, 109–10
pure cognition of the prototype, 113–15
pure rationalism, 87, 89–92

qualified realism, 197
"Question of the Criterion, The" (Solomon), 154, 156

radical evil, 59
rational discourse always penultimate, 203
rationalism on natural versus revealed religion, 87
rational theologies, 86, 214
rational universality, 212
realized eschatology, 156
Reardon, Bernard M. G., 96
Reason: always already interpreted, 202; both finite and fallen, xxi–xxii; in C. S. Lewis, 220–21; as form of faith, xxiv; Hegel on, 26, 153–54, 156, 160–61, 168–69; historical, 150; inherent pluralism of, 69; Kant on, 72, 101, 108, 157; within limits of religion, 183; mutually incompatible versions of, 16, 183; Platonic, 26–27, 156, 168–69; postmodern critiques of, xx, 214; presuppositionless, 153–54; "protest of," 27; as pure and universal, xvi–xvii, 15–16, 65, 100–101; versus revelation, xvii, 6–7, 17, 106; as universal, 101, 125–26, 136, 159, 168–69, 189, 211; versus "wishes," 19n18
Reath, Andrews, 19n32, 20nn33 & 37
recollection(s): anticipations as, 190; versus "counter-memory," 204; Heidegger and, 213; Kant and, 104–5; knowledge as, xvi, 69, 88, 132, 158, 190
Reflexionsphilosophie, Hegel on, 160–61, 168
Reid, Thomas, 215
religion, positive (Hegel), 129
religion of the heart, 126
religions of the book, 211, 214
religion within the limits of reason, xix–xx, xxiii, 35n9, 183, 193
Religion within the Limits of Reason Alone (Kant), xvi, 23, 34n3, 59
"religion without religion," 35n9
religious childhood, 94
religious genius, 88, 97n15
religious pluralism, 181–83
religious tolerance, Hegel and, 178
Representations and Concepts, 171–76, 179, 183
resignation before God, 33, 46
retributivist theories of punishment, 15, 108
revelation, 205; and deism, 85; and divine agency speech acts, xxi–xxii, 94, 97n4; as epistemic heteronomy, xv; general versus special, 85; outer versus inner, 118n2; possible but not necessary, 94; and reason, xvii, 6–7, 49, 85; revealed versus natural religion, 87–88; revelatory versus revealed, 185n12; special revelation, xvi; theologies of, 214

Revelation, Book of, 37n34
revenge versus justice, 21–22n57
Ricoeur, Paul, 17, 19n18, 29, 65, 191, 193, 207–8n24
Rieuwertsz, Jan, 38
Romans, Epistle to the, 14, 82n52, 86, 111, 121n39, 158
Rome and Athens, 131
Rorty, Richard, 194, 206n6
Rousseau, Jean-Jacques, 19n32, 97n17, 98n38, 186n34, 198
"rules of skill" (Kant), 12
Runzo, Joseph, 86, 98n24
Russell, Bertrand, 223

Sartre, Jean-Paul, 165nn42 & 45
satisfaction theory of Atonement, 121n39
Savage, Denis, 61–62, 90, 97n5
"scandal of particularity," xviii
Schelling, F. W. J. von, 128–29, 143nn17 & 19, 159, 161, 163n7
Schiller, J. C. Friedrich von, 5, 98n25
Science as Absolute Knowing, 156
Science of Logic (Hegel), 152–54, 168
scientific naturalism, 29, 49, 52–53
scripture: minds of prophets versus mind of God, 44; seeking only moral meaning in, 107; *sola scriptura*, 41–43. *See also* Bible
Scuff, 140
Second Inaugural Address (Lincoln), 1, 35n10
sectarianism, 101
secularism, rise of, 11
seeing as 'theory-laden' undertaking, 194
"selectiveness" of chosen people notion, xviii
"self-assertion," xv, xxiv (note 6), 1, 17n5, 21n46
self-consciousness: in philosophy, 149; of spirit, 151, 171, 175–81
self-evidence, 56n31, 203–4
self-incurred minority (Kant), 2
self-legislation (Kant), 8–9
"self-subjection" to law, 20n32
separation of church and state, 130, 192
serpent in Eden, 20n43
Severity of God, The (Moser), xv
Shakespeare, William, 205n1, 206n2
Shema, 144–45n37
Silva, Daniel, 21n55
sin as "motivated irrationality," xxi
slave religion, Christianity as, 116, 218
Smith, Kemp, 97n21
social humanism, 139
social practices, 204–5

sociological pantheism, 132
sociopolitical theology, 168
Socrates, xv, 68, 87, 92, 104, 112
sola scriptura, 41–43, 49, 52
Solomon, Robert C., 154, 157
Son of God, 110–13
soul versus spirit, 24
"Sovereignty Thesis," 19n32
special revelation, xvi, 85
Spinoza, Baruch, 26–28, 42–44; and autonomous reason, 51; Bennett on, 29; biblical criticism, 42; on biblical writers, 44–45, 47; as child of his time, 48; claims to objectivity, 51–53; claims to universality, xvii; on "common people's" limitations, 47–48, 51; (re)definition of God, 27–29, 96; denying atheism charges, 31–34, 36n23; on emotions, 48; Feuer on, 32; Fichte and, 128; freedom of speech and press, 38; and good and evil, 141; and grammatico-historical hermeneutic, 42, 51; and Hegel, 138–42, 148–51; Heine on, 31; as hermeneutical textualist, 49; on imagination, 36n20; on intuition, 45–46, 161; on Jesus, 185n11; on levels of knowing, 45–46; MacIntyre on, 28; on Maimonides, 43, 46, 52; as masochist, 32; on meaning of "prophets," 54n9; on meaning of subversion, 39; on meaning versus truth, 43–44, 47, 49, 53; Novalis on, 31; and pantheism, 30; philosophy over theology, 38–39, 50–51; as rationalist and naturalist, 87; Reformation themes of, 40–41; rejecting miracles, 26; *sola scriptura*, 41–43, 49, 54n8; Stevenson on, 28; Velthuysen on, 31; virtues becoming vices for, 57n57n37
Spinoza and the Irrelevance of Biblical Authority (Preuss), 49
"Spinozism of freedom," 127, 132, 139–40, 148, 167
"spiritual but not religious" claims, 37n41
spirit versus soul, 24
sports metaphors, 155–56, 162, 176
stages/stations of soul's journeys (Hegel), 155
statutory versus moral teachings, 101
steering wheel, legislative autonomy and, 3
Stevenson, Charles, 27–28
Stillingfleet, Edward, 84
Storr, Gottlob Christian, 129
Stump, Eleanor, 19n20
subjection to law, 20nn32 & 35
subjective and objective religion (Hegel), 125
Subjective Spirit, 170
subjectivity and objectivity, 129
substitution motif, 109–10, 121n40
sufficiency of reason deism, 85

suicide, avoidance of, 4
supernationalist rationalism, 87, 91–92
supernatural revelation and religious childhood, 94–95
sursum corda, 64
symbolic theology, 111
sympathy, 5, 19n21
Symposium (Plato), 45
System of Science (Hegel), 151

Tannen, Deborah, 208n34
Taylor, Charles, 66
Taylor, Mark C., xx, 214
telescope/microscope metaphor, 22n63
testimony, 215–16, 227n16
The Ego and the Id (Freud), 190
theism versus pantheism, 30, 81n41
"The Life of Jesus" (Hegel), 143n8
Theological-Political Treatise (TPT) (Spinoza), 27, 38
theological version of morality (Kant), 13
theology as the metaphysics of God, 51
"Theoretical Spirit," 185n19
Thérèse, 198
"The Spirit of Christianity and Its Fate" (Hegel), 132
"things" as signs, 198
Thomas (Apostle), 224
Thomism, 81n42
Tillich, Paul, 36n33
Till We Have Faces (Lewis), 218–25
Timothy, Epistles to, 133, 178–79
Titus, Epistle to, 178
Toplady, Augustus, 121n37
Tracy, David, 55n17
tradition, 202, 205
training of inclinations, 6
transforming grace, 77–78
transparency of mind to itself, 157–59
trichotomist analysis, 24
Trinity, 112, 181
Truth and Method (Gadamer), 102
"Tübingen Essay" (Hegel), 125, 127, 129
Tucker, Robert, 149, 184n4
Turow, Scott, 79n6
Twelfth Night (Shakespeare), 206n2
Tyrell, George, 136

ultimacy, 192
undecidable calls for decision, xxiii
Understanding (*Verstand*), Hegel on, 125

Ungit, 218–20
United States and "end of history," 164n32
"universal divine man," 187n44
universal doubt strategies, 196
universal laws: Hare on, 21n50; Kant on, 7, 9, 65–66
universal reason, xvii, 65, 102, 125–26, 189
universal religion, 93, 183, 213
universal truths for particular communities, 192

Valjean, Jean, 59–61
Vattimo, Gianni, xx, 214
Velthuysen, Lambert Van, 31, 33
"vengefulness" of God, 14
Venn diagrams versus concentric circles, 107, 117
"view from nowhere," xvii, xxi, 189
vigilante, God as (Kant), 15
Viorst, Judy, 98n35
virtue as happiness, 32
"volition," 12, 162, 166n59
Voltaire, 95
Vorstellung (Representation), 156, 164n24, 170–73, 175, 180

Wainwright, William J., 210n70
Wake, Peter, 142n3, 145n38
Ward, Keith, 96
watchmaker God, 69
Weber, Max, 46, 56n26
Wesley, Charles, 95–96
What Is Christianity? (Harnack), 136
"What Is Enlightenment?" (Kant), 2, 17n8, 23
White, Ronald Jr., 1
white Christian religion, iii–xiv
will-giving universal law (Kant), 7
Wisdom of Solomon, 34
wish fulfillment, religion about, xiii
witness of the spirit, 40
Wittgenstein, Ludwig, 97n13, 154, 197, 208n35, 226n8
Wolterstorff, Nicholas, 42, 64–66, 73, 121n35, 194, 213
Wood, Allen W., 84–85, 91
Word of God as epistemic heteronomy, xv
worthiness to be happy, 74
"wounded cogito," 207–8n24
Wright, N. T., xviii, 25, 34n4, 68, 134

Yovel, Yirmiyahu, 36n24

Zagzebski, Linda, 205
Zechariah, 104, 119n16
Žižek, Slavoj, xx

MEROLD WESTPHAL is Distinguished Professor of Philosophy Emeritus, Fordham University and Honorary Professor, Australian Catholic University. His most recent works include *Whose Community? Which Interpretation?: Philosophical Hermeneutics for the Church; Kierkegaard's Concept of Faith; Transcendence and Self-Transcendence* (IUP, 2004); and *Levinas and Kierkegaard in Dialogue* (IUP, 2008).